Eisenhower Center Studies on War and Peace

ANDREW JACKSON HIGGINS

AND THE BOATS THAT WON WORLD WAR II

▲

ANDREW JACKSON HIGGINS
AND THE BOATS THAT WON
WORLD WAR II

▼

Jerry E. Strahan

LOUISIANA STATE UNIVERSITY PRESS
BATON ROUGE

Published by Louisiana State University Press
Copyright © 1994 by Jerry E. Strahan

Louisiana Paperback Edition, 1998

Designer: Laura Roubique Gleason
Typeface: Sabon
Typesetter: G & S Typesetters, Inc.

Library of Congress Cataloging-in-Publication Data

Strahan, Jerry E., 1951–
    Andrew Jackson Higgins and the boats that won World War II / Jerry E. Strahan
    p. cm. — (Eisenhower Center studies on war and peace)
    Includes bibliographical references (p.) and index.
    ISBN-13: 978-0-8071-2339-3 (pbk. : alk. paper)
    1. Higgins, Andrew Jackson, 1886–1952. 2. Industrialists—United
States—Biography. 3. Higgins Industries—History. 4. Shipbuilding
industry—Louisiana—New Orleans—History. 5. Torpedo-boats—
Louisiana—New Orleans—Design and construction—History.
6. Landing craft—Louisiana—New Orleans—Design and construction—
History. 7. World War, 1939-1945—Equipment and supplies.
I. Title. II. Series.
VM140.H54S73   1994
338.7'6238256'092—dc20
[B]   93-41552
                                                                            CIP
ISBN-13: 978-0-8071-4143-4 (pdf)

Frontispiece: Andrew Jackson Higgins sits aboard one of his PT boats. Courtesy Higgins Family

For
Jane
Chris
Jeff

CONTENTS

ILLUSTRATIONS

PREFACE

In the spring of 1973 I wrote an undergraduate research paper for Stephen E. Ambrose's Modern Military History course at the University of New Orleans. The paper, entitled "Higgins—the Man, the Boat, the Industry," was later expanded into my master's thesis. After receiving my graduate degree in 1976 I entered the business world.

On several occasions during the next fourteen years, I offered Ambrose my source material and encouraged him to do a biography of Higgins. Each time he declined and encouraged me to continue my research. On New Year's Eve, 1990, during a hectic day at work, I received a call from Ambrose requesting that I give a brief lecture at the University of New Orleans in the spring semester. Believing that he wanted me to speak before one of his classes, I accepted, hung up the phone, and forgot about it. A few weeks later the mail brought a program for the War in the Pacific Conference sponsored by the Eisenhower Center for Leadership Studies at the university. Listed as speakers were Major General David M. Jones, delivering a talk entitled "The Doolittle Raid: A Personal Memoir," and George Gay, whose topic was "Witnessing the Battle of Midway." Also included was a long list of well-known scholars—and me.

I called Ambrose and explained that I had received the program and discovered a misprint. He insisted that the program was correct and that I should prepare a paper for his review. It was like fishing. He had thrown out the bait, and before I realized what was happening I had nibbled, was hooked, and was being reeled in.

I continued trying to convince Ambrose to write Higgins' story. He refused. Everyone has heard of professors who supposedly have taken graduate students' research and used it for their own benefit. I was trying to convince one that he should turn my thesis into a book, but with no success. Instead, Ambrose offered to give me any guidance necessary if I would accept the challenge. Finally, during January, 1992, after fifteen and a half years of procrastinating, I began this book. Had it not been for Ambrose, the boxes of documents and hours of taped interviews would still be sitting on the floor of my closet.

His guidance and suggestions have been of immeasurable help. During a period in which he was teaching at UNO, working on plans and funding for a D-Day museum, lecturing across the country, and writing his own book on D-Day for the fiftieth anniversary of the invasion, he still took time to read my work, pointing out my weaknesses and strengths and encouraging me to continue. For his valuable comments, enthusiasm, and support I will forever be grateful.

There are several other people without whose help I could never have written Higgins' story. First is Andrew Higgins, Jr. During 1973, when I was doing research for my undergraduate paper on his father, Andrew, Jr., spent hours with me explaining such technical terms as *bow* and *stern*. He was always patient, understanding, and generous with his time. We met again on several occasions later, during the research for my thesis. The interviews gave me valuable insight into the company's inner workings and his father's relationship with the Bureau of Ships. Many of the letters in my personal collection were given to me by him. I only regret that he died before I began the research on this book. He had always given me encouragement and was responsible for my uncovering many of the key sources I have used. All he asked was that I tell the story as it happened, as factually and objectively as possible.

One of the sources Andrew, Jr., referred me to was Graham Haddock, who has been of immense help. He was responsible for my being able to tour the old Industrial Canal plant in 1974. As a result, approximately ten thousand of the original Higgins landing boat plans were donated to University of New Orleans Archives. His recall of facts has always proved to be exact. The number of meetings and telephone conversations we have had over the years are too numerous to document in the Bibliography. If I had a question, Haddock was only a phone call away. He was always willing to be helpful, and no matter how ridiculous my question, his answer was always intelligent, honest, and accurate.

Two other invaluable sources were Richard A. McDerby and Ted Sprague. McDerby, like Haddock, lives only a few miles from my home.

If I needed information or to corroborate facts, Mac's door was always open. His friendship and help are deeply appreciated.

Sprague lives in Pennsylvania, and I live on the Gulf of Mexico. I did, however, have the opportunity to spend two days interviewing him on the shores of Lake Erie and listening to him reminisce about his past. The last day I was there we spent eleven hours talking and watching films of the tests of the Higgins airborne lifeboat. It was one of the most enjoyable days that I spent in researching this book.

I am deeply indebted to Higgins' daughters, Dawn Higgins Murphy, and her husband, Bob, and Andrée Higgins Stefferud, and her husband, David. Their memories helped to uncover the human, personal side of their father, and their honesty, openness, and kindness made my research easier. Also of great assistance was Higgins' nephew Jack Higgins. Jack was invaluable in helping me understand the engine company, the retail works, and the postwar years.

The willingness of Lieutenant General Victor H. Krulak (Ret.) and Lieutenant Commander Robert Searles (Ret.), to share their experiences is greatly appreciated and has given me an insight into Higgins from the military perspective. Gayle Higgins Jones, Skip Higgins, Vance Vosbein, Fred Horil, David Levy, Ralph Casselman, Leroy Hall, Bob Flautt, John Poche, Ray Samuels, R. E. Carroll, Bill Bohmfalk, and Steve Lozes have given me documents, films, and information that, I hope, have made this book as close to reality as possible. If the book is lacking in any way it is not the fault of those who have so freely given their time and materials but of the author in translating their stories to the printed page.

I also wish to thank the staff archivists, librarians, and other special-ists who have helped me over the years at the National Archives, the Harry S. Truman Library, the Dwight D. Eisenhower Library, the Tulane University Library, and Clive Hardy at the University of New Orleans Archives and Kathi Jones of the Eisenhower Center.

At Louisiana State University Press I wish to thank especially Mar-garet Dalrymple, Catherine Landry, and Julie Schorfheide for their en-thusiastic support and understanding. And for the immensely helpful contributions she has made as copy editor, I am deeply grateful to Trudie Calvert.

Kenneth Sides of PC Pros in Bridgeport, Texas, introduced me to the world of computers. Without his assistance I would still be typing the first chapter.

Last, but not of least importance, I would like to thank my wife, Jane, who during graduate school typed my thesis and has been very understanding over the years. She often accused me of getting a master's in Higgins, not history. She may be correct.

ANDREW JACKSON HIGGINS

AND THE BOATS THAT WON WORLD WAR II

INTRODUCTION

In September, 1943, when the United States Fifth Army landed at Salerno, Italy, and General Douglas MacArthur's forces captured Salamaua in New Guinea, the American navy totaled 14,072 vessels. Of these boats, 12,964, or 92 percent of the entire U.S. Navy, were designed by Higgins Industries, Incorporated; 8,865 were built at the Higgins plants in New Orleans.

Founder and president of this remarkable company was Andrew Jackson Higgins. Higgins was an outspoken, rough-cut, hot-tempered Irishman with an incredible imagination and the ability to turn wild ideas into reality. He hated bureaucratic red tape, loved bourbon, and was the sort who tended to knock down anything that got in his way. To the navy's Bureau of Ships, which favored the big eastern seaboard shipyards, Higgins was an arrogant small boat builder from the South—a thorn in its side. To the Marine Corps, which desperately needed an effective amphibious assault craft, he was a savior.

Higgins rose to international prominence during World War II for his design and mass production of naval combat motorboats—boats that forever changed the strategy of modern warfare. Thanks to Higgins, the Allies no longer had to batter coastal forts into submission, sweep harbors of mines, and take over enemy-held ports before they could land an assault force. "Higgins boats" gave them the ability to transport thousands of men and hundreds of tons of equipment swiftly through the surf to less-fortified beaches, eliminating the need for established harbors.

Higgins designed and produced two basic classes of military craft. The first class consisted of high-speed PT boats, which carried antiaircraft machine guns, smoke-screen devices, depth charges, and Higgins-designed compressed-air-fired torpedo tubes. Also in this class were the

1

antisubmarine boats, dispatch boats, 170-foot freight supply vessels, and other specialized patrol craft produced for the army, navy, and Maritime Commission.

The second class consisted of various types of Higgins landing craft (LCPs, LCPLs, LCVPs, LCMs) constructed of wood and steel that were used in transporting fully armed troops, light tanks, field artillery, and other mechanized equipment and supplies essential to amphibious operations. It was these boats that made D-Day and the landings at Guadalcanal, Iwo Jima, Tarawa, Okinawa, Leyte, Guam, and thousands of lesser-known assaults possible. Without Higgins' uniquely designed craft there could not have been a mass landing of troops and matériel on European shores or the beaches of the Pacific islands, at least not without a tremendously higher rate of Allied casualties.

As late as 1930 Higgins was involved in the lumber importing and exporting business. By 1940 he was producing workboats and prototype landing craft in a small warehouse located behind his St. Charles Avenue showroom. When the government began ordering his craft for military purposes, Higgins expanded into eight separate plants in the city, employing over twenty thousand workers. At the peak of production, the combined output of his plants exceeded 700 boats a month. His total output for the Allies during World War II was 20,094 boats, a production record for which Higgins Industries several times received the Army-Navy "E," the highest award that the armed forces could bestow upon a company.

Higgins was the ideal person for the needs of the time. In World War II, with its massive contracts, his strengths—design and rapid production—were all-important. His administrative weaknesses were suddenly irrelevant. The war offered him opportunity. Had the Japanese not bombed Pearl Harbor, Higgins probably would have remained a successful, but small, southern boat builder. Because of the war, he rapidly became an internationally known figure.

It was the production of landing craft and PT boats that made Higgins' name a household word. With the war draining the labor pool, he staffed his plants with a diversity of employees: healthy males who had not yet been drafted, women, blacks, elderly, and handicapped. Regardless of race, sex, age, or physical disability, all were paid equal wages according to their job rating. They responded by shattering production records.

During July, 1943, Higgins' plants produced more landing craft than all the other shipyards in the nation combined. Senator Homer Ferguson of Michigan, a member of the Special Committee Investigating the National Defense Program, commonly known as the Truman Committee, recognized the accomplishment and declared that Higgins was the number one boat builder in the nation. *Life* followed in August with a nine-page feature story on Higgins.

Captain Harry Butcher, General Dwight D. Eisenhower's personal aide, wrote in his memoirs that during March, 1943, as the invasions of Sicily and Italy were being planned, the general was confronted with a massive shortage of landing craft. Butcher recalled Eisenhower saying that when he was "buried his coffin should be in the shape of a landing craft, as they are practically killing him with worry." [1]

As Higgins increased production to unbelievable levels, much of Eisenhower's worry was relieved. The contribution did not go unnoticed. In his 1944 Thanksgiving Day address to the nation Eisenhower said, "Let us thank God for Higgins Industries, management, and labor which has given us the landing boats with which to conduct our campaign." [2] After his retirement from the presidency, Eisenhower, during a discussion with Professor Stephen E. Ambrose in his Gettysburg, Pennsylvania, office, described Higgins as "the man who won the war for us." [3] Even Adolf Hitler was aware of Higgins, calling him the "new Noah." [4] His influence on amphibious warfare and his contribution toward the Allied victory cannot be overstressed.

Higgins is best known for his unique shallow-draft craft and his phenomenal ability to produce them. The part he played in Harry Truman's becoming vice-president and Franklin D. Roosevelt's reelection has been overlooked by history. Also forgotten was Higgins' long-running battle with the AFL and CIO, a battle that drew national attention and made him the champion of returning veterans and nonunion workers. His part in the Manhattan Project and his company's 27-foot airborne droppable

1. Dave McGuire to Andrew J. Higgins, January 3, 1946, in David R. McGuire Collection, Collection No. 271, Howard-Tilton Memorial Library, Tulane University.

2. *Ideas for United Nations,* Higgins Industries, Inc., film, *ca.* 1945, in Gayle Higgins Jones Collection, New Orleans.

3. Stephen E. Ambrose, interview, February 4, 1993.

4. "Who's Afraid of the Big Bad Wolf? Who's Afraid of the Men of Higgins? No One Less Than Adolf Hitler Himself!" *Eureka News Bulletin,* II (August, 1943), 2.

lifeboat that rescued downed pilots in the Atlantic and Pacific have also faded with the years.

During the 1940s, Higgins was almost legendary, larger than life. He was a small southern businessman who became head of one of the largest industrial complexes in the United States. He took on the Washington bureaucracy, labor rackets, the large New England shipyards, and organized labor, never retreating from his principles or avoiding a fight. A columnist of the period wrote that "Higgins is just a tough guy, who came up the hard way, and who either hasn't had time to mellow or isn't made of material that will."[5]

Captain R. R. M. Emmett, who commanded landing forces in North Africa and later became commandant of the Great Lakes Training Station, wrote during the war, "When the history of this war is finally written by historians, far enough removed from its present turmoil and clamor to be cool and impartial, I predict that they will place Mr. Higgins very high on the list of those who deserve the commendation and gratitude of all citizens."[6]

In 1942 a reporter for the Miami *News* traveled to New Orleans to investigate the city's tremendous growth in the shipbuilding industry. When the *News* inquired why Miami could not achieve such success, the reply was because New Orleans, not Miami, had Mr. Higgins.

5. *Bill Cunningham Visits Higgins* (New Orleans, n.d.), in Strahan Personal Collection.
6. "Biography of Andrew J. Higgins" (Typescript in McGuire collection), 26.

1

THE FORMATIVE YEARS

A ndrew Jackson Higgins was born August 28, 1886, at Columbus, Nebraska, the youngest of ten children of John Gonegle and Annie Long O'Conor Higgins. John was a promising young attorney who in 1870 left a law firm in Chicago to head west and open his own practice. Traveling via the Union Pacific Railroad, he had to pass through the small midwestern town of Columbus, Nebraska. The Chicago *Times*, for which John had worked as a part-time reporter while attending school, requested that he stop in Columbus and interview retired Indian scout Major Frank North.

Higgins intended to spend only a few days researching and writing his story, but he was so taken by the town and its friendly people that he convinced Annie that they should give up their dream of California and settle in Columbus. John's law background led to his being appointed a judge, and later his newspaper experience was responsible for his becoming editor of the Columbus *Democrat*.

Higgins was a close friend of Grover Cleveland and an enthusiastic Democrat, so enthusiastic that he named his new son after the party's twice successful presidential candidate Andrew Jackson. John's influence on his son was to be short, for he died after falling down a flight of stairs when Andrew was only seven years old. In 1893, after her husband's death, Annie moved the family to Omaha.[1]

Mrs. Higgins has been described as courageous, gifted, and versatile. She was well-read in the arts and sciences and educated her children in

1. Andrew J. Higgins, Jr., interview, March 29, 1975; "Biography of Andrew J. Higgins" (Typescript in David R. McGuire Collection, Collection No. 271, Manuscripts Department, Howard-Tilton Memorial Library, Tulane University), 2–3.

the classics. She is said to have been a descendant of the famous O'Conor of Connaught, who in 1848 led the Irish in rebellion against the British. Captured and sentenced to death, O'Conor escaped and fled to America aboard the schooner the *Three Sullivans*. It was from his mother's side that Andrew claimed to have received his determination, strong will, and mechanical ability.

The boy became an innovative and aggressive worker. By the age of nine, equipped with only a sickle, he sought out grass-cutting jobs. Later he purchased a lawn mower and then expanded his operation until he had seventeen mowers under his direction. He hired older boys to do the physical work while he managed the jobs. At the age of twelve he organized newspaper delivery routes for the Omaha *Daily News*, sold the subscriptions, and collected the payments. Again he hired others to do the physical work while he supervised. This venture netted him over a hundred dollars a month, a considerable sum of money in 1898, especially for a twelve-year-old boy. The following year he sold the business to an adult for $1,700.00.[2]

Also at the age of twelve Andrew became the owner of his first boat, a wrecked sailboat that he had salvaged from a lake near his home. After doing extensive repairs, he christened her *Patience* because he had needed plenty of it to restore the damaged craft. She proved to be slow, and Higgins wanted speed. Attempting to satisfy his craving, he replaced the *Patience* with a bobsled of his own design, but it too proved to be slow. Next, he built a boat for sailing on ice. This he hoped would fulfill the thrill he was seeking.

The iceboat, named the *Annie O'* in honor of his mother, was built in the basement of the family's house. Upon completion he discovered that it was too large to be taken out through the basement door or windows. Determined to remove the craft from the house, Higgins gathered his friends, borrowed jacks and timbers from a nearby wrecking yard, and built supporting structures against the basement's front wall. He removed the section of the wall between the two basement windows, brought the boat out, and somewhat successfully had the bricks relaid and the borrowed equipment returned—all before his mother returned from her trip

2. "A Revisal by A. J. Higgins, Sr., President, Higgins Industries, Inc., of Transcript of Hearing Before the Navy Department Price Adjustment Board," October 7, 1943, p. 6 (Sen 79A-F30, OP5, Box 185, U.S. Senate, Record Group 46, National Archives), hereinafter cited as "Revisal"; "Biographical Sketch," July, 1952, Strahan Personal Collection, 5.

to town. The wind-powered boat gave its creator the excitement that he sought, reaching an estimated speed of sixty miles an hour as it glided across frozen Cutoff Lake (now Lake Carter) near Omaha.[3]

Higgins found joy in sailing at high speeds, but he found no thrill in attending school. Because of his disinterest, he exhibited little desire to excel in his studies. He began his education in Omaha's public school system, first at Farnam School, then later at Central High. He quit Central, and his mother enrolled him in Father Williams' Episcopal school at St. Barnabas Church. During those early years Higgins was often in trouble for fighting and playing hooky. When he did attend class he wanted to reorganize the educational process because his ideas of school often clashed with those of his teachers and the administration.

A neighbor, Miss Marshall, recalled that on several mornings she saw Mrs. Higgins marching Andrew out of the house and down the sidewalk. When asked where they were going, Mrs. Higgins usually replied that she was taking Andrew to school. The day before, his teachers had sent him home, declaring that he "could never come back." Finally, in September, 1900, Higgins was enrolled at Creighton High Prep School.[4] Academics still did not appeal to him, but playing right end on Creighton's varsity football team did. He claimed to have played "rather indifferent football, thanks to a hernia about as big as a plug hat." He insisted that even with his physical problem he played a better right end than his teammate Dick Coad did a left end.[5]

Higgins left Creighton after his junior year to join the 2nd Nebraska Infantry, a National Guard regiment that had been commanded by William Jennings Bryan.[6] Mrs. Higgins, a native of Illinois, had always been a southern sympathizer and an admirer of Bryan. It was because of her influence that, after leaving Creighton, Andrew joined the Nebraska militia.

3. Andrew J. Higgins, Jr., interview, March 29, 1975; "Andy Higgins Dies: Built Boats in War," New York *Times*, August 2, 1952, p. 15; "Men of Higgins Build a Navy," *Eureka News Bulletin*, I (August–September, 1942), 16; "Saturday Evening Post Features Higgins," *Eureka News Bulletin*, I (July, 1942), 9.
4. "Those Higginses There Was a Family," Omaha, Nebraska, *World-Herald*, n.d., Sec. 3, p. 4 (Clipping in University Relations Central Files—Andrew Jackson Higgins, Creighton University, Omaha, Nebraska); Souvenir Program, Public Affairs Luncheon, 65th Anniversary of Creighton University, February 9, 1943, *ibid.*
5. Andrew Higgins to Hugh Fogarty, April 15, 1942, *ibid.*
6. Hugh Fogarty to Reverend J. Fred Kriebs, May 12, 1942, *ibid.*

During militia maneuvers in Nebraska, Higgins had his first introduction to amphibious training. The troops had to cross the Platte River by pontoon. This experience, coupled with a strong desire to read instilled in him by his mother, led Higgins to become a student of military history. He claimed to have read dozens of books on battlefield strategy and listed John Paul Jones as one of his early heroes.

As a sergeant-major, Higgins in 1904 led his battalion's drill team through the competition at the St. Louis Fair, winning the $800 national prize. A photograph of him in his uniform shows a slender, well-groomed, confident young man.[7] It was also in 1904 that Higgins gave up his summer work in the Wyoming logging camps to accept a full-time job closer to home. He had spent the last two summers branding logs, and it was then that he developed a love for the woods and learned the fundamentals of the timber industry.

His new occupation was as a truck driver for an Omaha wholesale dry goods concern. Within seven months he had risen to the position of house superintendent. In less than two years his new employer, M. E. Smith and Company, had doubled its business and attributed much of the success to Higgins.[8]

In 1906, at the age of twenty, Higgins decided that his future was in the South. When asked later in life why he left Nebraska, he responded, "I came South because I loved boats and forestry."[9] Using his savings, he purchased a farm and adjacent timber acreage in Mobile County, Alabama. Next, he enrolled in a three-month modern farming course at Auburn University. Afterward, he claimed to have amazed county farm officials with his high yield per acre. To reap the benefits of the timber tract he opened his own sawmill.

Living close to Mobile, Higgins frequently went to town to sell lumber and purchase supplies. On one such trip he accompanied a friend to a band concert in Bienville Square. Here his companion introduced him to a beautiful young brunette, Angele Leona Colsson, the daughter of a successful rancher and furniture store owner. Not long after the concert, Higgins was spending several nights a week riding horseback to visit Angele. After a short but persistent courtship, on October 16, 1908, Angele

7. "Biography of Andrew J. Higgins," 4–5.
8. "Revisal," 7.
9. "Biography of Andrew J. Higgins," 6.

and Andrew were married. The young couple moved to Higgins' farm and together began a new life.

In hopes of expanding his lumber business, Higgins purchased an old schooner. He intended to use it for importing unfinished tropical woods and for transporting his processed lumber to various markets. After making all the necessary repairs to the ship, he christened her the *Angele*, in honor of his bride. At twenty-two years of age Andrew was the owner and operator of his own profitable lumber business and farm, but his success was not to last. The lumber company was forced to dissolve after a hurricane destroyed much of its equipment. The depression of 1908 struck the finishing blow. Needing an increased income because of the impending birth of their first child, Andrew and Angele moved to Mobile, arriving in town with only sixteen cents and a mandolin.

Higgins decided to learn all he could in this port city about ship loading, ship handling, and foreign commerce. First, however, he needed money. He pawned his mandolin to take care of Angele's and his needs temporarily. Then he sought out the most dangerous job he could find, that of hooker-on for timber loading, for the greater the risk, the higher the wages. He worked at this job for only a short time, but during that period he claimed to have developed a revolutionary cargo hook, "the use of which thereafter saved lives and the crippling of men."[10]

It was in Mobile that on October 30, 1909, the couple's first child, Edmond C. Higgins, was born. It was also in this Gulf Coast city that Higgins further prepared himself for his future. Continuing to learn, he got a job as a bill-of-lading clerk for a steamship company. Next, he took a job in the foreign exchange department of a bank. After learning the "rudiment of arbitrage" he quit the bank, continuing to select jobs that would equip him for his objective of being a lumber exporter and manufacturer. He felt this occupation would be profitable and allow him to incorporate his hobby of building small boats into his business operation. He held jobs as a timber cruiser, timber estimator, timber buyer, and timber inspector, frequently changing positions as he learned more about the industry. His background was responsible for his being hired as the chief technical inspector for the Gulf Coast Exporters' Association.

After only a few months with the Exporters' Association, Higgins gave up his position. Early in 1910, at twenty-six years of age, he moved from

10. "Revisal," 8.

Alabama to New Orleans to accept an offer from Phil I. Adam, a lumber export house. Quickly he rose to the position of general manager. While representing the export house, he traveled widely and made many overseas contacts. His association with the firm ended on May 7, 1915, the day the Germans sank the *Lusitania*. Evidently, his views on America's position toward World War I were in contrast to those held by his employer, a company that earlier had gone under the name of Adam & Steinbrugge Lumber and Log Exporters.[11]

It was not simply the philosophical differences between Higgins and his employer that caused him to leave the firm. He realized that the world crisis would be a most opportune time for him to reenter business for himself. Before resigning, he had been assured by a local businessman, William Cady, of a $5,000 investment to help him establish a new lumber importing and exporting company. The terms of the agreement were that Cady would back the venture financially, Higgins would operate it, and they would divide all profits equally. Within the first ninety days the new company showed a profit of $15,000, far more than either man had imagined. Because of the extraordinary growth the business experienced, Cady decided that it would be advisable to incorporate. Each man invested $5,000, and a third investor, J. S. McNary, was included as an equal partner. The new business, incorporated in 1916, operated under the name A. J. Higgins Lumber and Export Company. Higgins opened his office in the Hibernia Building on Carondelet Street, the same building occupied by his former employer, Phil I. Adam.[12]

Cady, as the main investor, was president of the company, and Higgins held the position of manager and vice-president. But it was Higgins who was the driving force. Now thirty years old, he was a strikingly handsome man standing 5 feet 11 inches with blue eyes and wavy, light brown hair. He was strong and rugged, but his face projected a boyish appearance. The appearance was deceiving, for beneath the youthful face was an impatient, never-accept-"no" individual with an explosive Irish temper. Also beneath the innocent face was a talented salesman, a great storyteller, and a man with remarkable charisma.

11. *Ibid.*, 7, 8; "Biography of Andrew J. Higgins," 6–8; "Biographical Sketch," 2; "Andy Higgins Dies: Built Boats in War," New York *Times*, August 2, 1952, p. 15; *Soard's New Orleans City Directory*, Vol. XXXV (1908), 65.

12. United States Eastern District Court of Louisiana, New Orleans Division, Debtor's Petition, Civil Case No. 3174, Andrew Higgins Bankruptcy, 1926, 4; *Soard's New Orleans City Directory*, Vol. XXXV (1908), 65.

Higgins' personality brought out the best in those who worked for him and allowed him to blend in comfortably with the laborers who cut and hauled his lumber. He, like them, worked hard, drank hard, and, when angry, could swear hard. Yet unlike them he possessed the ability and poise to negotiate lumber transactions with heads of companies in a highly articulate manner.

As Higgins' business grew, so did his family. Angele and he now had three sons, Ed, seven, Andrew, Jr., five, and Frank, three. With a growing family and an increased income, Angele, Andrew, and the children moved to a larger house at 917 Eleonore Street. Life for Higgins was moving in a positive direction.[13]

It was also during this period that Higgins purchased timberland in the St. Catherine Creek area near Natchez, Mississippi. The land was bought at a minimum price because it was considered too difficult to log. Boats with enough power to pull out rafts of logs drew too much water to travel the shallow streams. Boats of shallow enough draft lacked the necessary power to perform the task. To overcome this problem, Higgins decided to build a tunnel boat, a type of craft commonly used in the shallow waterways of Holland. The design recessed the propeller in a tunnel that rises upward into the hull, similar to the hump in the floor-board of a car. The propeller is protected even in shallow water, and the boat's draft is considerably reduced.

Higgins' craft succeeded in fulfilling its mission, but it had one negative feature. The reduction in the boat's draft caused up to a 40 percent reduction in power because aerated water was captured in the tunnel and the propeller was turning in froth instead of solid water. This problem so irritated Higgins that he enrolled in a correspondence course in naval architecture hoping to find the answer. He was unsuccessful in solving the problem, but upon completion of the program he received a bachelor's degree.[14]

A. J. Higgins Lumber and Export's main objective was to process southern pine and cypress and to import hardwoods from Central America, Africa, and the Philippines. The imported logs were wholesaled to lumber

13. Dawn Higgins Murphy, interview, November 14, 1992; *Soard's New Orleans City Directory*, vol. XLIII (1916), 594; "Biographical Sketch," 1–2.

14. David S. Oakes, "Boat Builder to the United Nations," *Central Manufacturing District Magazine*, XXVII (March, 1944), 11.

distributors across the South. Business increased rapidly, and through the sale of stock, within a year the firm capitalized at $400,000.[15] Higgins, Cady, and McNary reinvested the company's profits in new ventures such as the Edith and D. V. Johnston companies.

The Edith Company was a shipping firm formed by the three partners to operate a single schooner, the *Edith*. Funds to finance the enterprise were borrowed from the lumber company. The business was organized to import logs for A. J. Higgins Lumber and Export and to transport finished goods to foreign markets. The men saw it as an opportunity to expand their operation, reduce shipping costs, and increase profits.[16]

The *Edith* was captained by an "old sea dog," who during World War I had been involved in the sinking of two German submarines and in turn had his ship sunk by another enemy sub. While he clung to the floating wreckage, the captain's leg had been bitten off by a shark. Looking like the sea pirates of old, the captain also adopted their disreputable ways. He devised a racket wherein he could make enormous profits at the expense of his employers.

The captain purposely flooded his ship's cargo hold and then put into port for repairs. There he would strike up a deal with a local ship chandler to reoutfit the vessel for a substantial kickback. Although his past employers had discovered his scam, it was difficult for them to take action. Maritime law was clear that if a captain was fired after a disaster, it was considered an admission by the owner that his skipper was incompetent. Such an admission limited the underwriter's liability to the worth of the ship, excluding cargo, thus preventing unscrupulous owners from sinking vessels and falsely claiming millions of dollars of lost cargo.

An informant warned Higgins that the skipper of the *Edith* was planning to pull the scam on an East Coast voyage. In an attempt to prevent its occurrence, Higgins wired the Charleston newspapers that he would not accept responsibility for any debts contracted by the ship while it was in port. He then immediately left for South Carolina. By the time he arrived, the ship had already departed and was heading out to sea, unaware that it was sailing into the path of a deadly hurricane.

The 1920 storm devastated the East Coast and was assumed to have

---

15. "Andy Higgins Dies: Built Boats in War," New York *Times*, August 2, 1952, p. 15; Gilbert Burck, "Mr. Higgins and His Wonderful Boats," *Life*, August 16, 1943, p. 100.

16. United States Eastern District Court of Louisiana, Case 3174, 1–3.

been responsible for the disappearance of the *Edith*. Higgins' statement in the paper gave the insurance company grounds to deny all claims against the *Edith*'s lost cargo. The insurer honored the $14,000 policy covering the ship itself, but that was not nearly enough to pay all the claims resulting from lost goods. A. J. Higgins Lumber and Export Company, as the main creditor of the shipping company, had to absorb the loss.[17]

A. J. Higgins Lumber and Export Company was organized as an importer and exporter and was licensed only as a wholesaler. Therefore, Cady and Higgins organized the D. V. Johnston Company to sell directly to contractors. Johnston was included as a front man so retailers would not object when Higgins and Cady broke with trade customs and became involved in both wholesaling and retailing. The three men were to each invest $10,000 to finance the new company. Higgins and Johnston put up their money, but when Higgins asked Cady for his portion he was told to overdraw the Lumber and Export account when additional funds were necessary. The venture was successful because it also invested in gravel pits and sold its product for use in making roads. Its success enabled Higgins to recoup his initial investment plus additional dividends.

Cady, seeing how prosperous their joint venture was, asked Higgins to help him save the failing Cady Gravel Company. The problem was that his gravel could not meet the specifications required by railroad and road contractors. The solution, Higgins thought, was to install a hydraulic plant. Cady claimed that he lacked the $64,000 necessary to purchase and install the equipment.

Higgins and Johnston, through the D. V. Johnston Company, loaned Cady Gravel the money. In return, Cady promised to use his personal influence with the president of the Missouri-Pacific Railroad to secure a contract for both companies to provide gravel for the road's track beds. Cady claimed that he had never before approached his friend because the output of only one pit would not have been sufficient to fulfill the quantity required by even the smallest of the railroad's contracts. Now, with the combined production of both companies, he believed it was possible to competitively supply the gravel required.

17. "Sunken 'Jinx Ship' Recalls Last Launching," New Orleans *Item-Tribune*, n.d., n.p. (Clipping in Skip Higgins Collection, Port Allen, Louisiana).

The plant was installed, and Cady kept his promise, but now that Cady Gravel was a profitable business, its owner decided to sell out to a minority partner. Cady refused to repay the D. V. Johnston Company the $64,000 for the equipment. He claimed that he had sold only the land, not the hydraulic plant. The new property owner refused to allow the plant to be removed from the site and rejected the idea of paying rent for its use. Eventually, he sent Higgins $1,500 for the purchase of the plant.

Cady's refusal to repay the loan, combined with other losses similarly suffered, forced the D. V. Johnston Company to liquidate. It was unable to repay A. J. Higgins Lumber and Export the $100,000 that it had borrowed for equipment and operating expenses. The Lumber and Export Company, unable to meet its obligations, was forced into liquidation in October, 1923.[18]

Higgins realized that the failure of the lumber company was not the result of bad management in daily operations. It was because of poor judgment in extending loans to Cady without proper collateral. He used what resources he had remaining to start a new company under the name of Higgins Lumber and Export Company.[19] By dropping the initials from the previous company's name, he hoped to profit from his earlier advertising and from the reputation he had established both in the South and in foreign countries as a dependable and knowledgeable lumber dealer.

Higgins' lumber was carried in a small fleet of Higgins-owned schooners and brigantines.[20] To service his ships Higgins set up a repair yard on the Industrial Canal, a lock-controlled strip of water that connects Lake Pontchartrain and the Mississippi River. At approximately the same time, he moved his main office to the Audubon Building on Canal Street. It was during this period, 1923 to 1929, that Higgins built barges and push boats and began experimenting with "small water craft, air boats, and flying boats."[21]

Higgins had been importing mahogany logs; when the market declined, he had a large supply but no outlet. He decided that they would

18. United States Eastern District Court of Louisiana, Case 3174, 4–6.
19. *Soard's New Orleans City Directory*, Vol. LI (1924), 776.
20. "Andy Higgins Dies: Built Boats in War," New York *Times*, August 2, 1952, p. 15; Burck, "Mr. Higgins and His Wonderful Boats," 106.
21. Robert A. Flautt, interview, June 25, 1975; "The Boss," *Fortune*, July, 1943, p. 210; 1920 telephone directory, Cumberland Telephone and Telegraph Company, South Central Bell, New Orleans, 92; "Revisal," 9.

be more marketable and bring a greater profit if they were cut up and made into barges. The barges sold, but not nearly as well as expected. He then foresaw a huge profit if the logs were sawed into smaller planks and then used to build boats. To bring the idea to reality, Higgins hired local naval architect and pleasure-boat designer George Huet. Huet's task was to create a pleasure boat that was suited to the materials on hand and attractive to the local market. The result was a narrow, 15-foot model called the *Sea Bird*. Arthur Derbins, Higgins' chief carpenter, had his crew reproduce the boat for retail sales.[22]

Higgins realized that he needed to change his company's direction. Timber supplies in the South were being depleted, and his sailing ships were finding it hard to compete because of constantly dropping freight rates, a result of the Depression. In the late 1920s owners of steamers began soliciting the lumber transport business, a field that for years had been left to sailing vessels. Higgins turned his attention from lumber to small boat design and construction, a move that he had calculated as early as 1923, when he formed Higgins Lumber and Export Company. On his October 6, 1923, Louisiana charter, he had listed the company's primary purpose as the manufacturing of various types of motorboats. The dwindling lumber market forced him closer to his original objective.[23]

By 1926, the lumber business had become secondary to the manufacturing of boats. Higgins began working closely with the U.S. Army Corps of Engineers to try to design a boat to fulfill its needs. He did a great deal of experimentation with heavy-duty transmissions, reverse gears, and clutches. He also took other standard boat equipment and redesigned it to handle the more strenuous requirements of a workboat.[24]

During the great flood of 1927, Higgins' shallow-draft boats were put to the test in extracting valuable marooned equipment up and down the Ohio and Mississippi rivers. This experience of transporting tractors and large farm equipment on a ramped platform resting between two boats

22. Robert A. Flautt, interview, June 25, 1975.

23. H. L. Rosenthal, "Higgins Industries, Inc., New Orleans, Louisiana," August 8, 1942, p. 1 (National Defense Committee Files, OP4, Minor Investigations — Companies and Other Organizations: Higgins Industries to W. R. Holt & Associates, Box 96, Records of the Special Committee of the Senate to Investigate the National Defense Program, Record Group 46, National Archives).

24. "Revisal," 9, 12.

later proved invaluable in Higgins' development of landing craft. It also further showcased his craft to the Army Corps of Engineers, U.S. Coast Guard, and the population along the waterways.[25]

In 1928 Higgins was contacted by representatives of a Dutch syndicate who had seen his rugged tunnel boats being used by a nut growers' association in the tropics and felt that the boats were what they had been looking for. When they awarded him a contract for twenty craft, Higgins was launched into the boat-building business.

Constructing twenty boats of the same design generally warrants using mass-production techniques. By assembling jigs and standardizing parts, costs can be lowered and profits increased. Higgins, however, chose to build each boat individually so he could experiment and improve his design with each new craft. The experiment proved successful. He produced a boat that reached 12.8 miles per hour, a speed that up until then was believed to be impossible for a tunnel boat. Higgins felt that with further experimentation, greater speed could be achieved.

Not long after completing the last of the boats for the Dutch, Higgins received a contract to build several craft for the U.S. Army Corps of Engineers. The small fleet had to be delivered up the Arkansas River. River levels were high, and the water was filled with floating debris. Objects constantly rammed into the bows of the boats. Edmond, the oldest of Higgins' six children (Andrée, Roland, and Dawn were the more recent births in the family) accompanied the boats on the delivery voyage. The nineteen-year-old reported to his father that a new type of bow needed to be developed, one that would ride over the logs and other partially submerged obstacles.

Higgins had earlier seen a film in which blue whales, the largest mammals in the world, had displayed great maneuverability and speed. Along with George Huet, who was now his chief engineer, Higgins and his workers began experimenting with bow designs that would incorporate the lines of the whale's jaw and forward belly. The first experiment led to an increase in the boat's speed of almost 10 percent.[26]

Higgins decided to put his new designs to the test. He built a 16-foot boat called the *And How III* that was powered by an Evinrude outboard motor. With this small boat he thought he could challenge the long-

25. *Ibid.*, 10.
26. Oakes, "Boat Builder to the United Nations," 12–13.

standing record of ninety hours from New Orleans to St. Louis. The old record had been set by the *Robert E. Lee* in her famous race with the *Natchez* and had stood for over fifty years. The *And How III* established a new record in 1930 by making the journey upriver in eighty-seven hours. The following year a 23-foot Higgins motorboat, the *Dixie Greyhound,* powered by a 120-horsepower Gray marine engine and steered by Edmond Higgins, lowered the record to seventy-two hours and four minutes, despite several hours' delay caused by bent propellers and shafts.[27]

Higgins swore that he would eventually design a boat that would make the run without a moment's trouble. To accomplish this, he knew he would have to develop a craft that could pass over floating logs and sandbars without damage to the hull or the propeller.

As increased attention went to boat construction, Higgins moved the offices of Higgins Lumber and Export from the Audubon Building to 539 Carondelet Street. There he opened a small retail outlet to sell the *Sea Bird* and other pleasure boats that the company was now building. He operated at this location until 1929.

On September 26, 1930, he formally incorporated Higgins Industries. The new company was to focus its attention on the manufacturing and sale of various types of boats. The craft were mainly designed to fill the needs of local trappers, oilmen, and lumbermen.[28] Some pleasure boats were produced, such as Higgins' 22-foot model, the *Neptune,* but in the depressed economy only the wealthy could afford such luxuries. With the formation of the new company, Higgins again changed locations. In 1930, Higgins Industries opened at 1755 St. Charles Avenue. Here the company had a showroom in front for displaying boats, motors, and marine supplies and a warehouse and construction yard in the back.[29] In early 1931 Higgins put his lumber and export business into voluntary bankruptcy to eliminate his long-term leases.

A few months later, on July 11, the new company was also placed in receivership. The Depression was taking its toll. Higgins did, however, get a break when a "friendly judge" named him his own receiver.[30] He

27. "Boat Racing on the Mississippi," *Eureka News Bulletin,* II (April, 1943), 62.
28. Rosenthal, "Higgins Industries, Inc.," 1.
29. "The Boss," 210; Robert A. Flautt, interview, June 25, 1975.
30. Rosenthal, "Higgins Industries, Inc.," 1; "Revisal," 10.

was unable to borrow money from the bank, yet he needed further capital. His customers often had a similar dilemma—they needed boats but
lacked the funds to purchase them. To solve both problems, Higgins
formed a new company into which he took investors.

The new business, the Boat Services Company (BSC), purchased boats
from Higgins Industries and rented or leased them to local clients. The
market proved to be exceptionally good. The decision to create a new
company allowed Higgins to maintain complete control of Higgins Industries yet raise the capital necessary to continue operating in depressed
times.

On paper, the new company was managed by Frank O. Higgins, Higgins' son, but in reality it was the senior Higgins who was in charge. The
agreement between the two businesses was that Higgins Industries would
manufacture boats and sell them directly to the Boat Services Company,
which would rent or lease the craft. After all expenses and normal operating costs had been subtracted, the stockholders would share the dividends according to their holdings in the company. This arrangement allowed Higgins Industries to continue to manufacture boats even though
there was not a solid commercial or pleasure boat market at the time. It
also protected him in case one of his buyers was unable to pay for a boat
when it was completed. If this occurred, Higgins simply arranged to sell
the craft to the BSC.

Another advantage derived from the establishment of a separate leasing firm was that when Higgins sold it a boat, he made the total profit on
the sale without having to divide it among stockholders. Also, Higgins,
as a stockholder in the BSC, received dividends from the profits of the
leasing company. Although the BSC was established as a totally separate
and independent business, Higgins helped minimize its expenses by operating the company out of his St. Charles Avenue office but listing as its
address the side entrance of the building that faced Felicity Street. Therefore, Higgins Industries was listed in the telephone directory under a
St. Charles Avenue address. The BSC, which was under the same roof,
was shown as being on Felicity Street.[31]

This arrangement of selling boats to the leasing company allowed Higgins Industries to survive the Depression when many other companies

31. Graham Haddock, interview, July 23, 1975; Robert A. Flautt, interview, June 25,
1975.

did not. It also allowed Higgins to accomplish three other significant feats. First, he kept approximately fifty skilled craftsmen working. These men developed a deep and lasting loyalty to Higgins.[32] Second, it allowed him to go to court on August 28, 1935, with every debt paid, without any current liabilities, and without any receiver's liabilities.[33] Last, it gave him the opportunity to continue his experimentation with designs for shallow-draft boats.[34]

It was because of the BSC that in 1934 Higgins hired a young boat captain named Richard McDerby. Captain McDerby, or Mac as he was known, one day accompanied his cousin Dave Young to the riverfront. Young worked for Higgins and was preparing to take one of the three boats that the BSC had leased to the Corps of Engineers upriver to Natchez, Mississippi. At the last minute, it was discovered that one of the other men hired as a boat operator had failed his qualifying test and therefore had not received a Coast Guard–approved captain's license.

The corps' contract called for boats and operators. They were now short a skipper. Young mentioned that Mac was a licensed captain. Higgins hired him on the spot, and in a matter of minutes the new employee was on his way upriver. McDerby continued to work with the boats leased to the corps until mid-1941, when Higgins reassigned him to an important new undertaking.[35]

Also because of the success of the BSC and the business it helped to create, on April 1, 1937, Higgins hired a young draftsman named Graham Haddock. Haddock joined chief engineer George Huet and Joe Dovie in the company's engineering department. In addition, Higgins began hiring qualified craftsmen. He had earlier made a standing offer to the graduating classes of Delgado Trades School in New Orleans, saying that "the Delgado graduates are excellently qualified craftsmen. They know tools and what to do with them. We can't use ordinary hammer-and-saw carpenters, but we can use Delgado men."[36]

As the business grew, Higgins' sons became increasingly active in the

32. Rosenthal, "Higgins Industries, Inc.," 1.
33. "Revisal," 11.
34. Al Hansen to Engineer-in-Chief, June 8, 1937, in Strahan Personal Collection.
35. Richard A. McDerby, interview, April 11, 1992.
36. "Higgins Staff Is Made Up of Craftsmen," n.d. (Clipping in Skip Higgins Collection). The approximate date of April, 1937, was determined by the two tugs being built in accompanying picture.

company. Ed, the oldest at twenty-eight, was the mechanical genius of the family and served as the company's chief mechanic. Andrew, Jr., now twenty-six, was the office manager and handled most of the administrative duties. His father often referred to him as "his understudy." Frank, twenty-four, was listed as the head of the BSC and served as its field superintendent. The youngest son, Roland, was only sixteen and still in school. His daughters Andrée and Dawn were not involved in the company.[37]

In November, 1938, when businesses began to purchase boats and the need for the leasing company began to fade, Higgins hired a young man named Teddy Sprague. Sprague, like Huet, Arthur Derbins, McDerby, and Haddock, would play a prominent part in the company during the war years.

Sprague had graduated from Carnegie Institute of Technology in June, 1938, and had built a 14-foot sailboat. Being adventuresome, he started down the Allegheny River from up above Pittsburgh, heading for the Gulf of Mexico. He arrived in New Orleans on August 18, with three months' growth of hair and two months' growth of beard. After traveling for a few days on the Gulf Coast, he returned to New Orleans to search for work. Lacking a place to stay, he went to the city jail and asked for a berth, a common request during the Depression years. By doing this a person had a place to sleep and avoided being arrested for vagrancy. Each morning at six o'clock overnight boarders were released.

The jailer, seeing Sprague's ragged appearance, offered to cut his hair and then convinced him that, if he was going to find work, he needed better clothes. Following the officer's advice, Sprague hocked his Rolls Razor that he had bought during a stint in the Naval Reserve. In exchange for the razor, he received a suit, shoes, and socks. His new appearance helped him get a job with a landscape company. Occasionally his duties took him by Higgins' St. Charles Avenue plant, where he saw men performing the type of work that truly appealed to him. Finally, he wrote to Higgins about employment.

Higgins sent word for him to report for an interview. Sprague recalled: "So I went down. He and I had a good conversation. After a while we went back to his office and had a drink. He said, 'I'll pay you thirty cents an hour and just remember that people are standing outside that gate

37. *Ibid.*

that would be happy to have that job.' And there were too." Sprague's first assignment was to grind welds on the bottom of a steel hull. When others broke for lunch, he kept on grinding. Finally, his co-workers could not stand it any longer and pulled him out from under the boat. At the end of the day, when others clocked out, he kept grinding until he was told to leave. This routine lasted for a week to ten days. Higgins, impressed by his new employee's drive, called Sprague to his office and presented him with a problem that needed to be solved. The Corps of Engineers wanted the company to build a boat that had been designed by another firm, and Higgins was not impressed with the design. Aware of Sprague's engineering background, he asked him to figure out how much the boat was going to weigh, where its center of gravity was located, and answers to several other questions. Six weeks later, Sprague completed his calculations. He recalled: "When I took it to him he said, 'That's about what I thought.' So I was happy that he was happy." The corps then sent its engineer to the plant to rework the calculations. After another six weeks, he came out with the same answer. Higgins, impressed with Sprague's work, assigned him to the engineering department with Huet, Joe Dovie, and Graham Haddock.[38]

During the 1930s, Higgins concentrated mainly on building dependable, sturdy workboats. He did build yachts, including one that sold for over $72,000, but there were few people in the South who could afford such luxuries. His market was much different from that on the eastern seaboard, where large pleasure craft and seagoing vessels were produced.

In the swamps and marshes of Louisiana, fur-bearing animals were abundant but were accessible to trappers only by boat. To satisfy the trappers' needs, an exceptionally rugged, shallow-bottomed craft was required. It had to be capable of being run aground so traps could be checked and retract itself from the bank, both without damaging the hull. Also located in the Louisiana marshes were rich oil deposits, often found miles from the nearest road and reachable only by traveling along shallow streams filled with fallen trees, vegetation, and sandbars. The oil companies, like the trappers, needed a special type of craft. It had to be safe and durable and capable of carrying equipment and personnel through rugged terrain to the site of drilling operations.[39] Responding to

38. Ted Sprague, interview, August 2, 1992.
39. "How It All Started," *Eureka News Bulletin,* I (January, 1942), 1.

these needs by trial and error, over a period of years Higgins developed a satisfactory boat, the spoonbill-bow Eureka, the direct ancestor of the famous Higgins boats of World War II.

The predecessor of the Eureka had been a full-tunnel stern craft named the Wonderboat. Higgins advertised it as the homeliest but most efficient boat ever built. With the propeller and shaft housed in a tunnel, the craft was capable of operating in both open water and very shallow areas. But as a tunnel boat, it still suffered from loss of power because of cavitation (the propeller turning in aerated water). Higgins felt that he had made progress, but he continued to experiment. His later Wonderboat models incorporated the idea of the tunnel stern, but, instead of a full tunnel, only a semitunnel was used.[40]

The other innovative structural design was the evolution of a novel type of bow. Higgins' earlier boats had the conventional pointed bow. His new design featured a rounded bow formed from a solid block of pine that was shaped by hand and had the effect of serving as a bumper for the boat. This curved piece of pine, known as a head-log, was strengthened by drilling holes in it, which were plugged with wooden pegs that had been dipped in marine glue. The head-log made the bow the strongest part of the boat, a necessity in a craft designed to run full speed onto riverbanks and sandbars and over floating obstacles.[41]

Another important point about the new model's structural design was that aerated water was trapped under the forefoot of the craft, thus lessening the friction when the boat was moving and allowing for an increased running speed. Aerated water under the bow also had a roller-bearing effect and allowed the craft to turn with exceptional quickness. This quality would be very important in future amphibious operations. Once the craft had retracted itself from the beach and reached deep water, its engines could be reversed so it could turn swiftly enough to face the next wave. Other craft unable to retract from shore and have their bow pointed toward the sea before the next wave arrived often capsized, endangering both the boat and the lives of the men aboard.

Although the aerated water under the forefoot of the boat provided a great advantage, it had to be kept from entering the path of the propeller

40. "The Wonderboat," Higgins Industries, Inc., n.d., Advertisement broadside, in Strahan Personal Collection.
41. "How It All Started," 2.

and causing cavitation. Higgins and his craftsmen had been working on new designs to combat this problem, but it took a fabricating mistake while building a Wonderboat to uncover the solution.

Through a foreman's oversight, two metal plates pulled out of the molding floor, distorting the shape of the Wonderboat's hull so it had a vee section amidship and a reverse curve aft. In the middle of a tirade, Higgins ordered that the boat be completed. This accident solved the long-puzzling problem of cavitation. In trial runs the boat attained an unbelievable speed of more than twenty miles per hour. It was uglier than the Wonderboat, but because of its ability to overcome the 40 percent loss in power and its unusual abilities, it was named the Eureka.[42]

The unique feature that made the Higgins boat successful was that water was forced out from under the forequarters and at the aft. Any object thrown in the water close to the front of a Eureka while it was moving would be pushed away from the boat at a point between the bow and the midship. Any object placed anywhere in the back of midship would be pulled under the craft and into the direct path of the propellers.

The importance of this feature is that the aerated water was forced from under the boat at midship and only solid water reached the propeller. This design allowed a Higgins boat to travel through dense vegetation without having to reduce its speed. Water hyacinths and other floating objects were pushed out of the path of the propeller. This allowed for continuous high-speed running and cut down on the damage to the propeller because floating obstacles very seldom reached it.[43]

Also, because the bottom contour molded from a vee deadrise in the spoonbill-bow, to reverse curved sections amidship, then into two flat planing sections, the boat could achieve a catamaran effect on either side of the cylindrical longitudinal tunnel. This bottom gave the boat remarkable seaworthiness and maneuverability.[44] The Eureka's design also incorporated a strong frame, thick planking, and a heavy keel and skeg to protect the propeller. When operating, the boat drew only ten inches in the hull.[45]

Higgins was proud of his boat. It had speed, durability, and maneu-

42. Oakes, "Boat Builder to the United Nations," 13.
43. "How It All Started," 2–3.
44. "23-foot 'Eureka' model," Higgins Industries, n.d., Advertising letter, in Strahan Personal Collection.
45. C. W. Leveau to W. R. Dillion, February 28, 1940, *ibid.*

verability, though some skeptics questioned the existence of these qualities from time to time. Higgins occasionally had Andrew, Jr., take such
doubters out on Lake Pontchartrain and through a test course in which
a Eureka would jump floating logs, turn in its own length while at full
speed, and then finish by running up the step-type concrete sea wall of
the lake.[46]

The market for Eurekas increased toward the end of the 1930s. Lago
Petroleum purchased approximately twenty-five Eurekas. Standard Oil of
Venezuela bought twenty craft, and about the same number were sold to
subsidiaries of Shell Union Oil and the Texas Corporation. During 1939
several shallow-draft tugs, exploration boats, and workboats were bought
by the Republic of Colombia. Peru also purchased a number of shallow-
draft steel gunboats to be used on the upper Amazon River. Mexico, the
Netherlands East Indies, and several South American countries imported
Eurekas and Higgins workboats to fulfill their needs.[47]

Because many of these boats were shipped to Central and South
America, Higgins found it necessary to develop a craft that could lie in
the tropical sun for months, be placed in the water, and yet not leak. To
waterproof his Eureka, he constructed a double-bottom boat with a piece
of canvas between the layers. The idea of using canvas to prevent leakage
was not new, but the concept of interlocking the corners of the chine and
the keel was developed by Higgins Industries. This alteration in the boat's
construction allowed the craft to be placed in the water after months of
storage and immediately perform without leaking. The conventional
wooden boat, when placed in the water after a lengthy period ashore,
usually leaked heavily, and someone would have to bail water until the
planks swelled, or the boat would sink.[48]

Higgins' reputation had spread throughout the United States and
South America. His shallow-draft boats were coming into demand. The
Army Corps of Engineers and the Biological Survey Agency (BSA) were
using his boats. The Corps of Engineers needed a dependable craft that

46. "Higgins Industries Five Years Ago," *Eureka News Bulletin,* II (April, 1943),
45–46.
47. Higgins Industries, Inc., Drawing Number Book No. 1, pp. 1–15, in Strahan Personal Collection.
48. "How It All Started," 8.

could be used to inspect the levees along the Mississippi River and the low-banked bayous. The BSA ordered a craft capable of traveling twenty miles per hour while not riding over ten inches deep in the water.[49]

In the official report on the craft designed and built by Higgins for the BSA, the agency's naval architect, C. W. Leveau, informed his superiors that the "test results were almost unbelievable." Leveau was particularly impressed that the boat went over the spot not more than ten inches deep at full speed, without touching bottom. There were three men in the boat and sixty gallons of fuel, in addition to full equipment. The contract specifications had called only for the craft to be capable of traveling in water ten inches deep with two men and forty gallons of gasoline aboard.[50] Higgins enjoyed showing potential customers the test film of the craft speeding between two men standing in water less than a foot deep.[51]

The New Orleans boat builder realized that his market was not merely the southern United States and the U.S. oil companies that operated outside the nation's boundaries but also a great part of South America, Central America, and even Asia. Because of his earlier acquaintance with these regions as a lumber importer and exporter, he understood their needs and believed he was capable of fulfilling them. He approached various governments with the idea of introducing his craft as a personnel and freight transporter, a new amphibious transportation system that could save them millions of dollars in road construction, bridge building, and laying railroad tracks. Instead of trying to travel overland across swampy ground, one could simply load trucks carrying freight onto a Higgins amphibious transporter and bypass the marshy terrain.[52]

The outbreak of war in Europe in 1939, however, prevented Higgins from devoting himself fully to developing interconnecting amphibious freight lines in underdeveloped nations. Although he continued working on the project throughout the war, he concentrated most of his resources on solving the enormous needs of his new customers, the United States and British militaries.[53]

49. Burck, "Mr. Higgins and His Wonderful Boats," 108.
50. Leveau to Dillion, February 28, 1940, in Strahan Personal Collection.
51. Burck, "Mr. Higgins And His Wonderful Boats," 110.
52. *Ibid.*; "Business Will Not Fade When War Ends," *Eureka News Bulletin*, I (February, 1942), 3, 24.
53. Burck, "Mr. Higgins And His Wonderful Boats," 110.

2

THE COMPETITION BEGINS

B efore World War II Higgins boats were marketed as sturdy, dependable workboats that could perform the impossible in the shallowest
of waters. They had been purchased by the Corps of Engineers and the
Biological Survey Agency. In the early 1930s Higgins approached the
Coast Guard about using his Wonderboats as patrol craft in the Gulf of
Mexico. After testing the craft, it agreed that the Higgins boat would give
it a decisive advantage over the increasing number of rumrunners operating in the coastal waters.

With the Coast Guard as a customer, Higgins approached the smug-
glers. He suggested that now that the Coast Guard had new, faster patrol
boats they too needed a better craft. He assured them that he could design and produce a boat capable of keeping the rum flowing. Later, Higgins returned to the Coast Guard, recommending that it replace the Wonderboats with a newer, faster model.[1]

By 1935 Higgins was trying to market the Eureka design almost ex-
clusively as his shallow-draft boat, but because of limited budgets few
potential users could afford the craft. Over the next two years his company failed to achieve any real growth. During 1937, determined to increase his sales, he again contacted the Coast Guard. The timing was
perfect. The Coast Guard was preparing to enlarge the number of semitunnel boats it had in service to assure that it would be adequately prepared in case of flooding of the low coastal areas along the Gulf Coast.

Captain William J. Wheeler, commander of the New Orleans district
of the Coast Guard, whose headquarters was located in Mobile, decided
to visit Higgins Industries and inspect the craft. Wheeler was so im-

1. Burck, "Mr. Higgins and His Wonderful Boats," 108; "The Boss," 210.

pressed with the Eureka's capability to operate in shallow water and on the open Gulf that he advised his headquarters to purchase eight boats, six for use in patrolling the Texas coast and two for use on the Mississippi River. Hoping to receive the contract, Higgins wrote to Coast Guard headquarters in Washington and requested that a representative be sent to New Orleans to test the Eureka on a rugged trial course designed by his company. In response, the Washington office sent its small-boat designer and naval architect, Al Hansen, to inspect both the craft and the construction facilities.[2]

In his report to headquarters dated June 6, 1937, Hansen described Higgins' St. Charles Avenue plant as having an "atmosphere of efficiency and cooperation." He was extremely impressed with "the class of materials and workmanship." As was customary, Higgins insisted that the inspector be aboard during the test instead of simply observing from shore. Hansen stated in his report, "The boat was run through shallow water, over sand bars and run full speed up on the seaplane ramp of the Shushan Airport near Pontchartrain Beach." The naval architect was overwhelmed by the Eureka's ability to run over logs as much as three feet in diameter, over a five-gallon floating container, and through clusters of water hyacinths. He stated, "While the general appearance of the boat has no particular 'eyeappeal' as compared to the conventional design of displacement boats its so-called lack of beauty is more than compensated for by its practical usefulness." His general assessment of the company was that it was entirely capable and qualified to undertake and complete any type or size of small boat.[3]

By 1937 the Army Corps of Engineers, the Biological Survey Agency, and the Coast Guard were all purchasing Higgins' boats. But the U.S. Navy, which was trying to develop a landing craft, showed no interest in his unique shallow-draft Eureka. As early as 1928, Higgins had made his first call on the officers of the navy's Bureau of Construction and Repair (BCR). He had gone to the bureau with a congressman and called on several admirals and captains. The builder described them as "nice" but definitely not interested in his boats.

Higgins continued to persist and, in his words, to be "possibly obnox-

2. William J. Wheeler to Andrew J. Higgins, April 12, 1937, in Strahan Personal Collection.

3. Hansen to Engineer-in-Chief, June 8, 1937, *ibid.*

ious" to those he called on. Describing the officers as "gentlemen," he declared that they did not "lend an attentive ear."[4] He realized that as a small southern boat builder with no hired lobbyist, he would have a hard time breaking through the navy's bureaucracy. But all he wanted was a chance to prove his boats' capabilities.

Higgins initially failed to realize that he was not only competing against the large, powerful northeastern yards but also against the navy's own Bureau of Construction and Repair. The BCR was in the process of designing its own landing boat and was not interested in what some small-time boat builder from the South might have developed.

In 1934 Higgins visited Quantico, Virginia, hoping to interest the navy's Equipment Board in the Eureka. Again the navy showed no interest, declaring that it lacked funds to purchase new boats.[5] There was one positive result of the trip, however; Higgins found an organization that was very interested in his shallow-draft craft—the U.S. Marine Corps. The marines were suffering from severe budget constraints, had no funds available for experimental landing boats, but were very impressed with the Eureka's capabilities. Their encouragement led to a strong friendship between the builder and the corps.

Higgins was frustrated in his attempt to break through the navy's bureaucracy, but he was determined to succeed. The marines, meanwhile, were tired of being treated by the navy like a younger brother. According to General Holland Smith, the marines were "a small unit attached to a large force like the Navy which, crippled by its own meager appropriations, tossed us the crumbs." This set of circumstances made it easy for Higgins and the corps to be attracted to each other.[6]

In 1935, the Bureau of Construction and Repair finally advertised bids for shallow-draft boats, hoping to find an already designed craft that could serve in amphibious landing operations as the navy's link between the fleet and the shore.[7] Until this time, the Marine Corps, the only service agency practicing landing operations, was using the standard navy

---

4. "Revisal," 19.

5. Lieutenant Colonel Kenneth J. Clifford, *Progress and Purpose: A Developmental History of the U.S. Marine Corps, 1900–1970* (Washington, D.C., 1973), 48–50.

6. General Holland M. Smith, *Coral and Brass* (New York, 1949), 65.

7. Clifford, *Progress and Purpose,* 48.

launch. It was too heavy, too slow, heeled over when beached, and tended to broach. Additionally, the rudder and propeller were unprotected and often were damaged when beaching. Finally, the launch was considered underpowered for amphibious operations. The marines, tired of the unsuitable boat, wanted a craft that was specifically designed for assaulting beaches.[8]

It is not known why Higgins failed to enter the Eureka in this competition, but it is likely that he was never notified of it. The BCR, however, did receive entries from nine New England companies from which five were chosen to be tested in the summer of 1936. Most of the craft were Atlantic fishing boats with few modifications in their design. Their names reflected the cities from which they came: Red Bank, from the Red Bank Yacht Works of Red Bank, New Jersey; Bayhead, from the Hubert S. Johnson Boat and Engine Works, Bayhead, New Jersey; Greenport, from the Greenport Basin and Construction Company of Greenport, Long Island; and Freeport, of the Freeport Point Shipyard of Freeport, Long Island.[9] The fifth entry was an unsuccessful steel commercial craft.

At the direction of the commandant of the Marine Corps, the four wooden skiff fishing boats participated in the competitive trials at Cape May, New Jersey, from August 5 through October 6, 1936.[10] Higgins found out about the competition. On October 1, 1936, he wrote to BCR officials informing them that he was aware that they were testing sea skiffs for use as possible landing boats. He brashly told them, "We *know* that we have designed, perfected, and are building the very type of boat best fitted for this purpose." Higgins insisted that it would be well worthwhile for the Navy Department to send a representative to see his boat demonstrated.[11] The BCR was not interested. Higgins was discouraged but not beaten.

The board that had been established to conduct the test on the Atlantic fishing boats at Cape May reported that all of the boats had disadvan-

---

8. Senate Documents, Record Group 46, Senate 79A-F30, "Report on Landing Boat Program of the Navy Department," n.d., 3, hereinafter cited as "Report"; Smith, *Coral and Brass,* 89.

9. "Report," 4.

10. *Ibid.,* 6.

11. Andrew Higgins to Bureau of Construction and Repair, October 1, 1936, in National Defense Committee Files, OP-5, Navy Department Matters Ships, Shipbuilding and Related Matters, Box 182, Record Group 46, National Archives.

tages. Their problems were inherent in their designs and could not be eliminated even with alterations. The board also considered the conflicting requirements for a successful landing boat. It must be light enough to be lifted by the smaller booms of merchant vessels and to be handled in beaching operations. Yet it had to be strong enough to take considerable punishment. The craft needed high engine power for speed and retraction from the shore, but the greater the engine and the sturdier the boat, the heavier the craft became. The board realized what the marines had known for years: it was impracticable to try to design a utility boat that could serve as both a general services launch and a landing boat.

In response to the Cape May trials, on January 29, 1937, the BCR and the navy's Bureau of Engineering jointly issued a directive to the Philadelphia Navy Yard authorizing the design and construction of a prototype landing boat. The BCR wanted the navy yard to incorporate all the desirable features of the wooden fishing boats tested at Cape May in an experimental craft that the navy could claim as its own design.[12]

On January 12, the navy had taken a dramatic step forward and officially recognized the need for a landing-craft program. The secretary of the navy, acting on the recommendation of the chief of naval operations, created the "Navy Department's Continuing Board for the Development of Landing Boats for Training in Landing Operations," generally called the Landing Boat Development Board (LBB).[13] This board consisted of members from the navy's Bureau of Engineering, the BCR, the Office of the Chief of Naval Operations, and the Marine Corps. Acting as senior member of the board was the assistant director of the Fleet Maintenance Division in Naval Operations, Captain W. S. Farber.

Simultaneously, the commander in chief of the United States Fleet was directed to organize a board that would report on the actual testing of these craft by the fleet and make recommendations to the BCR. In response, the Fleet Development Board (FDB) was created. The Landing Boat Development Board and the Fleet Development Board were to work jointly, the first coordinating departmental activities toward the development of landing boats and the second testing the craft. A five-year plan with a projected budget of $1,264,000 for landing boat development was drawn up by the naval operations office.[14]

12. "Report," 8.
13. Ibid., 10.
14. Vice Admiral George Carroll Dyer, USN (Ret.), *The Amphibians Came to Conquer: The Story of Admiral Richmond Kelly Turner* (Washington, D.C., 1969), 205.

During February, 1937, the navy held its Flex 3 military exercises off the coast of southern California. The sea skiffs, even after having been modified, performed poorly. They did not prove themselves capable of fulfilling the requirements of a landing boat.

On March 8, 1937, the LBB tentatively approved the design of the BCR's experimental 30-foot boat to be built by the Philadelphia Navy Yard, subject to recommendations from the FDB. The FDB objected to the project because the lower hull design was essentially the same as that of the Red Bank skiff tested earlier. Little would be accomplished by duplicating the design of an inferior boat. The BCR ignored the FDB's objections and proceeded as planned. The only explanation seems to be that the project would allow the BCR to take credit for designing a landing boat.

On March 26, 1937, the senior member of the LBB stated his objections to the Atlantic fishing boats. Noting that the fisherman's method of beaching a boat in rough water was a long process of playing the seas, the board observed one beaching that took over twenty-seven minutes. Under enemy gunfire such an attempt would prove disastrous.[15]

The FDB recommended construction of a new 36-foot boat. The board forwarded a design to the BCR showing such a boat with modifications to remedy the defects that were inherent in the sea skiffs. The LBB, in agreement with the FDB, also recommended that the BCR should attempt to develop a 36-foot landing boat. The new craft would be capable of carrying more men, would be more seaworthy, would have additional space to allow the mounting of machine guns, and would have other characteristics not possible in a 30-foot boat. The LBB suggested that after the design had been completed and approved by both navy landing boat boards, such a craft should be built and placed in competitive tests against the 30-foot models. The BCR disregarded the boards' requests. It continued to develop its own experimental 30-foot Philadelphia boat.[16]

At a meeting of the LBB on April 14, 1937, the various boats were discussed, including the design of a 33-foot Eureka model submitted by Andrew Higgins. Higgins' design was rejected because the weight given

15. Senior Member, Landing Boat Development Board to the Chief of the Bureau of Construction and Repair, March 26, 1937, in National Defense Committee Files, OP-5, Navy Department Matters Ships, Shipbuilding and Related Matters, Box 182, Record Group 46, National Archives.

16. "Report," 11–13.

for the craft was considered excessive. A month later, Al Hansen, the naval architect with the U.S. Coast Guard, who had visited Higgins and tested a Eureka, forwarded to the chief engineer of the BCR an official communication giving the results of the tests that he had performed on Higgins' 31-foot boat.

Hansen reported that the Eureka had fulfilled all claims made by the builder and that its performance was "satisfactory and successful under all operating conditions noted."[17] Incredibly, instead of investigating the Eureka, on July 22, 1937, the LBB met and decided that nothing should interfere with the completion and tests of the BCR's landing boat being built in Philadelphia. It was as though the board members feared that a more promising civilian design would be discovered before the navy's BCR had a chance to complete its experimental craft.[18]

The Philadelphia boat was tested at Cape May, New Jersey, during August, 1937, and later in the West Indies Fleet exercises with the Atlantic fishing boats. The BCR's boat had several notable defects, including poor visibility by the coxswain and a distinct problem in steering. The FDB considered the Philadelphia boat to be the least suitable of all those tested.[19]

As a result of the Cape May trials, the FDB submitted drawings and recommended building a new metal landing boat incorporating the positive features of the individual skiffs. Following this suggestion, the BCR designed a 30-foot metal landing craft and on December 8, 1937, awarded a construction contract to Welin Davit and Boat Corporation of Newark, New Jersey.[20] It appeared that the BCR was finally going to accept the failure of its Philadelphia model. In an unexpected move on February 2, 1938, however, the BCR authorized the construction of five additional Philadelphia-style landing craft. It seems incomprehensible that the BCR would continue to push for production of a landing boat that had been proven unable to fulfill the assault forces' needs. But the BCR was not the only bureau to continue to push its own project even though it was a proven failure. The Bureau of Ordnance designed a torpedo and failed to test it properly. For the first eighteen months of the war it proved to be almost useless, yet the Bureau of Ordnance denied that there was anything seriously wrong with it.

17. Hansen to Engineer-in-Chief, May 28, 1937, in Strahan Personal Collection.
18. "Report," 15.
19. Ibid., 18–19.
20. Ibid., 20.

The following month, as production began on the five Philadelphia boats, Lieutenant Henry T. Koonce, a representative of the BCR, witnessed several demonstrations of Higgins Eurekas while he was in New Orleans. Koonce was able to observe a 33-foot steel Eureka and a 31-foot wooden model. He tested the metal boat for over three hours on Lake Pontchartrain and found it to be rugged and strong. It had good maneuvering qualities and was capable of running over logs and sandbars and at slow speeds up a concrete step sea wall without damaging the hull.

Realizing that he had limited experience in small boat design, Koonce visited Captain Wheeler of the Coast Guard in Mobile. He thought Wheeler's long experience with shallow-draft boats and his familiarity with Higgins Industries would be of great value. Wheeler agreed that the Higgins boat had great possibilities as a landing craft and strongly recommended that it be given a test. Koonce also spoke with S. Dodd, the local Lloyd's surveyor. Dodd was familiar with a 31-foot and a 33-foot Eureka that Higgins had sold to the Eagle Oil Company of Tampico, Mexico. He recalled that the boats were well suited for both shallow water and open seas and had been delivered to Mexico under their own power.

Koonce recommended that if funds were available the navy should purchase a 31-foot wooden Eureka and test it as a landing boat. If it proved successful, the bureau should pursue the purchase of a metal Higgins boat. He felt that the navy should at least make arrangements with Higgins to have a Eureka shipped to Norfolk and demonstrated before the BCR and the LBB.[21]

On March 28, 1938, the senior member of the FDB strongly objected to the building of the five Philadelphia boats. He urged the BCR not to go forward with their construction. The chief of naval operations explained that the contract had been given because of the employment situation at two navy yards. Philadelphia's yard was to build three of the boats, and the Norfolk Navy Yard was to construct the remaining two. The chief thought it was possible to recover approximately $80,000 in lost funds by building the boats and at the same time keep skilled workers employed. He also argued that the boats would serve as useful training tools until a more suitable landing craft was developed.

If recovering the funds and keeping the skilled laborers working were his only intentions, that could have been achieved by building boats other

21. *Ibid.*, 26–29.

than the BCR's inadequate Philadelphia landing boat. If a proper training tool was needed, the chief of naval operations had positive reports from Koonce about the Eurekas, and he could have used the funds to procure them. Instead, he made an indefensible bureaucratic decision to purchase five boats simply because they were designed by the BCR. The bureau's obvious bias toward its own designs was clear to others in the navy.

The assistant to the senior member of the FDB believed that reports coming from the forces afloat were being disregarded. He thought that instead of building a boat similar to the ones that had received unfavorable reports from the fleet, new, radically different boats should be constructed. The senior member of the FDB requested that the chief of naval operations change policy to ensure that in the future the FDB be consulted before the BCR built landing boats. This request disappeared into the bowels of the bureaucracy and was never acted upon.[22]

About the same time, the bureau's metal boat built by Welin Davit was completed and delivered to the Norfolk Navy Yard. During late April and May of 1938 the boat was tested at the Naval Operating Base in Norfolk. In the trials the craft was found to be light enough and fast enough for landing operations. In addition, at 30 feet in length it was small enough to be stored easily below deck in merchant vessels. Even the FDB felt that the metal surf boat represented the greatest advancement yet in the now ten-year-old attempt to develop a suitable landing boat.[23]

The FDB recommended that after additional model tank trials had been performed, two more experimental metal boats should be built as soon as possible. The LBB concurred with the recommendations, except that instead of two boats it suggested that three BCR-designed metal boats be constructed. The LBB strongly believed that it had found the landing craft for which it had been searching. Most satisfying to the bureaucrats, it was designed by the navy's BCR.

During 1937 Higgins met several times with officers of the LBB to try to interest them in his Eureka. Finally, after Higgins had experienced four frustrating years of rejections, Lieutenant Commander R. S. McDowell, who was responsible for landing-craft development in the Bureau of Con-

22. *Ibid.*, 19–21.
23. *Ibid.*, 24.

struction and Repair, contacted Higgins and informed him that $5,200 was available to purchase an experimental 30-foot landing boat. On May 5, 1938, Higgins officially received his first contract from the U.S. Navy.[24] He accepted the offer, though he was vehemently opposed to the 30-foot boat, arguing that the beam was too wide for its length. He also realized that his costs for building the Eureka would be considerably more than the funds allotted by the bureau. But Higgins loved a challenge, and he had long awaited an opportunity to show the navy what he could do.

In late May, the 30-foot Eureka landing boat, powered by a Hall Scott Invader engine, was completed and shipped to Norfolk. Higgins paid all shipping fees and sent along at his expense a retired captain, Bert Oakley, to demonstrate the boat's capabilities. The landing boat ultimately cost Higgins over $12,500 to construct, but what infuriated him the most was that he had to pay "an exorbitant charge to the Navy Yard at Norfolk to use their crane to unload it."[25]

Higgins was taking a big risk. The cost of building and shipping the craft was a tremendous expense his company could hardly afford in 1938. The previous year his business's total net earnings were only $241.42.[26] But he realized that if he did not take the gamble he might never get another opportunity to prove the merits of his boat. In effect, he built the boat on speculation.

On May 27, 1938, Captain Oakley sent a Western Union telegram to Higgins, informing his boss that the Eureka had arrived in Portsmouth, Virginia, well secured on the railroad car and in perfect condition. The Eureka was launched, and an inspection was made of the internal construction. Oakley reported that the entire staff was greatly impressed with the workmanship, strength of the boat, and the details concerning machinery installation. He described the preliminary trials at the navy yard as "very spectacular and a sensation." At landing trials held later that day at Willoughby Spit, in three-foot surf and with a stiff onshore breeze blowing, Oakley landed men on shore with ease and completely dry-footed. According to the captain, the Norfolk Navy Yard's chief boat builder remarked that "the boat was doing the impossible and [he] could

---

24. "Revisal," 20; "Report," 29.
25. "Revisal," 20.
26. Rosenthal, "Higgins Industries, Inc.," 4.

hardly believe what he had actually seen."[27] The test thus far had been easy, and because it was getting late the Virginia Beach trials were postponed until the following day.

The second day, Oakley took on a complete navy crew and members of a special board headed by Lieutenant Commander George H. Bahm.[28] He proceeded toward Virginia Beach, followed by a picket boat escort of Coast Guard officials who were interested in watching the Eureka's performance. When approaching the beach for a landing, the crew prepared to drop a stern anchor, as they had with other landing boats, to assist the boat when retracting from the beach. Oakley persuaded the crew that this was unnecessary. The Eureka passed through the breakers and onto the beach without difficulty. The trial board, consisting of Lieutenant Commander Bahm, Lieutenant (j.g.) R. R. Sampson, and Ensign Farrell, disembarked dry-footed and amazed at the boat's quick retracting ability.[29]

The boat withdrew from shore, turned in the surf, and headed out to sea bow first. For the benefit of the board, this maneuver was repeated several times. On his last landing approach Oakley purposely allowed the boat to broach on the beach. Even this did not hinder the Eureka's performance, it turned and easily retracted. A final inspection of the craft by the board found everything to be in perfect condition. On the return trip to Willoughby Spit the captain exhibited the ruggedness of the boat when he hurtled over a log raft at least thirty feet long. Members of the board, the crew, and the Coast Guard observers were "astonished and pleased with the trials." Oakley concluded his report to Higgins: "Thanks for a pleasant assignment. I think you have something."[30]

On June 1, 1938, Lieutenant Commander McDowell wrote Higgins concerning the previous week's trials. He explained that he had spent two days riding in the Eureka and admitted that his "own opinion based on comparatively smooth water work was quite favorable." Unable to re-

27. Captain Bert Oakley to Andrew Higgins, May 27, 1938, in Strahan Personal Collection.

28. "Report," 29.

29. Oakley to Higgins, May 27, 1938, in Strahan Personal Collection; "Higgins Experimental Landing Boat: Report of Tests," *USS Arkansas,* June 7, 1938, in National Defense Committee Files, OP-5, Navy Department Matters Ships, Shipbuilding and Related Matters, Box 182, Record Group 46, National Archives.

30. Oakley to Higgins, May 27, 1938, in Strahan Personal Collection.

main until rougher conditions occurred, McDowell left the boat with the forces afloat. Further tests were to be made when more severe weather conditions presented the opportunity. The Eureka impressed McDowell sufficiently that he recommended that Higgins contact the Peruvian government, which was preparing to purchase several shallow-draft boats. If interested, he could communicate with Commander M. W. Powers, U.S. Navy, U.S. Mission, Lima, Peru.[31]

A few days later, further tests were held in rougher seas with waves of four to five feet. Lieutenant Commander Bahm, head of the special board conducting the trials, reported that "the Higgins boat is considered generally the best of the Experimental Landing Boats thus far tested for the purpose intended." The performance of the Eureka in the four- and five-foot surf was very impressive. It handled well when landing, even on a very shallow beach, and it could advance faster than the waves. The boat retracted readily and was able to turn and face the incoming sea without broaching. It was light enough and small enough to be handled by merchant ships' booms and davits and could be quickly and cheaply reproduced by ordinary manufacturers. It had exceptional strength, and the bow was low enough that troops could disembark easily and quickly. Finally, the boat was capable of running high enough onto the beach so that the troops were landed practically dry-footed.[32]

Bahm considered the Eureka the best landing boat thus far tested, but he did not find it flawless. It had four objectionable features. First, the boat took a heavy spray over the stern sheets when running in rough seas, which impaired the coxswain's vision. The second undesirable feature was that the controls were in the aft section of the boat. The board thought that if the controls were located forward, the coxswain would have a better view of the water ahead. Third, the square stern should be redesigned so that it would part the waves when the craft was beached or retracting, and, finally, the boat should be of metal instead of wood. Wood required more skilled personnel for construction and therefore was costlier, it deteriorated quicker, and it was more vulnerable to enemy gunfire.[33]

Acting on the information received from Bahm, the LBB recom-

31. Lieutenant Commander R. S. McDowell to Andrew J. Higgins, June 1, 1938, *ibid.*
32. "Higgins Experimental Landing Boat: Report of Tests," 1, 4.
33. *Ibid.*, 5.

mended to the chief of naval operations on June 21, 1938, that Higgins be given a contract to construct four experimental 30-foot boats. Two should be fabricated from wood and two from metal. All were to be provided with armor plating that would protect the coxswain, machine gunner, gasoline tanks, and engine.[34]

Higgins was encouraged by the navy's order, but he was not enthusiastic about the required length of the boat. He later recalled: "I got some experimental orders, again for the goddamned 30' length boat. I built these more or less under protest." In a conference with the Navy Department he brought up the question of length and demanded that the boats be 39 or 40 feet long. The navy's response was that since some transport vessels were already equipped with davits capable of handling a 30-foot boat it had decided to standardize on this length. "To hell with designing a boat to fit the davits," Higgins exclaimed. "They should design their davits to fit a proper size boat." Higgins insisted that from then on the BCR treated him as a "bad boy."[35]

The BCR might not have liked the brashness of this southern boat builder, but the builder was not thrilled with the stubbornness of the BCR. He was irritated that it kept insisting on a 30-foot boat. He was also furious because shortly after the navy began testing his Eureka the BCR came out with "some tubs of their own design, which strangely, incorporated several features" of his Eureka. But he insisted that "they missed the point and the features they tried to copy were defeated by malformed under-water sections."[36]

Two months later, in November, 1938, the BCR, acting on the earlier recommendations of the FDB and the LBB, awarded a contract to build three experimental landing boats. These were to be based on the bureau's metal boat that had been built by Welin Davit and proclaimed after the May test as the biggest breakthrough in ten years. The new models were to incorporate the design changes suggested by the FDB. Three northeastern companies were chosen, each to build one boat. They were Luders Marine Construction Company, Stamford, Connecticut; Welin

34. "Report," 31–32.
35. Andrew Higgins to General Holland M. Smith, February 3, 1948, in History and Museums Divisions, United States Marine Corps, Envelope 22, PC 382: General Holland M. Smith, Washington, D.C.
36. *Ibid.*

Davit and Boat Corporation; and Jakobson and Peterson, Inc., of Brook-
lyn, New York.

Finally, as the LBB had recommended in June, and following approval
of the chief of naval operations, two wooden and two metal Eurekas were
purchased from Higgins on December 1, 1938. Except for two modifications, these four boats were similar to the experimental Eureka purchased earlier by the navy.

During January, 1939, eighteen landing boats were loaded aboard
transports and taken to the Caribbean for the winter fleet exercises. The
amphibious force consisted of a Bayhead, a Freeport, one Red Bank, the
original Philadelphia boat, the five newer, modified Philadelphia boats
that the FDB urged not be built, the original metal bureau landing boat
built by Welin Davit, the three new metal bureau boats incorporating the
FDB's recommended design changes, the original wooden Higgins Eureka, and the two modified wooden Eurekas and two modified metal
Eurekas that were constructed in response to Lieutenant Commander
Bahm's report. By this time, the BCR had allocated funds to build a total
of nineteen landing boats. Only one boat, called the Hickman boat, was
not taken on the exercise.[37]

In 1936 the Marine Corps had requested that a five-year plan be established culminating in the building of 120 landing boats. In 1939 the
navy, with only nineteen boats, was far behind that schedule. The failure
occurred because no serious effort had been made to place landing craft
in a priority position on the list of naval construction.[38] Most military
planners during the interwar period never gave serious consideration to
any future need for large-scale amphibious operations. They assumed
that if war occurred in Europe, the French could hold back the invaders
and their ports would remain open to the U.S. Navy as they had during
World War I.[39]

Except for the Marine Corps, few saw the need for landing craft. During the first phase of World War II, most United States naval leaders
outside the BCR considered the building of landing craft a "foolhardy
gamble with an untried weapon and a waste of resources badly needed

37. "Report," 32–33.
38. Ibid.
39. Vice Admiral Daniel E. Barbey, USN (Ret.), MacArthur's Amphibious Navy: Seventh Amphibious Force Operations, 1943–1945 (Annapolis, 1969), 12.

for Naval Construction."[40] The transports, heading toward the Caribbean in 1939 with only eighteen landing boats, reflected the lack of importance the navy placed on amphibious operations.

The most important result from Fleet Exercise 5 in 1939 was the elimination of the Atlantic sea skiffs from further consideration as landing boats. They had proved to be heavy, clumsy, slow, and difficult to operate in a rough surf. In addition, the original metal BCR landing craft built by Welin Davit and hailed as the biggest advancement in ten years lacked acceptable speed to warrant further production. The bureau-designed boat built by Luders Marine was unacceptable because of faulty construction, and the modified bureau boat constructed by Jakobson and Peterson was considered a "wet boat" because of excessive spray. The original Eureka was deemed unsuitable because of its square stern. This left two types of craft for further consideration, the modified bureau landing boat built by Welin Davit and Higgins' four landing boats redesigned to incorporate the changes suggested by the FDB.

On February 13, 1939, during Flex 5, a BCR representative who witnessed the trials notified his superiors that "of all the boats which I have witnessed tested, this boat [the bureau's Welin Davit boat] impressed me most favorably." On February 19, the boats were subjected to additional tests at Flamingo Beach, Culebra. As a result of these tests, the senior member of the LBB showed a strong preference for the Higgins boats, which he thought were superior to the BCR's. He saw them as more stable, having greater maneuverability, much drier, and retracting with greater ease and certainty. Concerning the bureau's design he stated, "The Welin, altho lighter and faster and consuming less gas, is not so stable nor as dry, nor does it handle as easily on the beach and along side the ship."[41] The board suggested several changes in both designs and recommended that one Higgins and one bureau boat be built, each incorporating the suggested modifications.

On April 5, 1939, the BCR agreed that two new landing craft should be built. Incredibly, instead of following the recommendations of the LBB, the BCR decided to eliminate all competition. It awarded the Philadelphia Navy Yard a contract to construct two new 30-foot BCR-

40. Gordon A. Harrison, *Cross-Channel Attack* (Washington, D.C., 1951), 60–61, Vol. I of *The European Theater of Operations*.
41. "Report," 37–38.

designed landing boats. Except for their wood construction, these boats were very similar to the BCR's boat built by Welin Davit.

The same bureaucratic patronage that Higgins had been fighting since 1934 had operated again. Finally, in June, 1939, three months after the LBB made the recommendation, the BCR effected contracts with Higgins and Welin Davit. Each company was to build one boat incorporating the suggestions made as a result of Flex 5.[42]

In the spring of 1939 the BCR also entertained bids to build patrol torpedo boats (commonly called PTs). A design competition had been held in 1938, and the designs chosen by the navy were put out for bid the following year. Higgins had not entered the competition but did wish to submit a proposal for constructing the 81-foot Sparkman and Stephens–designed motor torpedo boat. The builder thought his earlier experience in building fast boats during Prohibition would be of great benefit.

Higgins Industries had done a considerable amount of business with a British-owned oil company in Mexico, El Aguila Petroleum. The general manager, R. E. Dodds, had once served as a captain in the British navy assigned to the development and use of small, fast boats. In World War I he had commanded a squadron of these craft that were the forerunner of the PT boats. During Prohibition his job with El Aguila often brought him to New Orleans. On these trips he frequently visited Higgins and was of great assistance in furnishing him with information on the craft that he had earlier commanded.

Higgins was open to the new ideas and suggestions presented by Dodds. Perhaps Higgins' greatest attribute was that he always listened to the opinions of persons such as Dodds or to the recommendations of those who worked for him. He might not always agree or accept the idea, but he was never too proud not to listen.

With the knowledge gained from Dodds, input from his naval architect George Huet, and through trial and error, Higgins built boats that were fast, strong, light, and had a long cruising radius. He claimed that they could carry a great deal of weight and at the same time had a shallow enough draft to "make entrances into estuaries infrequently navigated."[43] The only thing he failed to mention was that they were capable of this performance at night with the Coast Guard in hot pursuit.

42. *Ibid.*, 39.
43. "Revisal," 46.

Higgins had considerable difficulty in 1939 securing from the navy the specifications for the 81-foot PT boats. He found it even harder to get an invitation to bid. But once this was accomplished, he submitted his offer. Willing to take a risk, he bid below cost so the BCR would have no alternative but to award him the contract. Higgins was determined to be a factor in designing and building PT boats, and he saw the chance to build the 81-foot Sparkman and Stephens model as the opportunity that he needed. His low bid of $58,000 per boat won him the contracts for PT 5 and PT 6.[44]

Early in 1940, the navy held Fleet Exercise 6 in the Caribbean. U.S. Marine Corps general Holland Smith, who at the time was in command of the 1st Marine Brigade, Fleet Marine Force, considered this exercise the most advanced and realistic operation to date. With the outbreak of war in Europe, maneuvers assumed a new significance, but Smith was looking beyond Europe. He saw Japan as the ultimate enemy and could visualize the difficulties the marines would confront on the islands of the Pacific. To Smith there were two major problems. First, the military did not have enough landing craft. Second, the ones they had were not the right kind.

As part of its amphibious force, the navy included in Flex 6 the original sea skiffs. Smith agreed that these might be excellent for New England fishermen, but they were unsuitable as landing craft. He assessed the BCR's boats as not much of an improvement. But he was encouraged by the performance of the Higgins Eurekas. According to Smith, these boats marked a definite advance and "proved their superiority on the Culebra beaches that spring."[45] The marines were pushing harder than ever for the acceptance of the Higgins boats.

The successful performance of the Eurekas was also noticed by the FDB during Flex 6. The board considered the Higgins craft "the best all around boat for the purpose intended."[46] The only advantage the FDB could find in the BCR's metal boat was the cheapness and speed with which it could be manufactured. On the negative side, the BCR's boats were considered difficult to maneuver and almost impossible to keep from leaking. The BCR's new wooden boat had minor problems but was considered almost the equal of the Eureka.

44. *Ibid.*, 47–48.
45. Smith, *Coral and Brass,* 68–72.
46. "Report," 41.

During February and March, while Flex 6 was taking place in the Caribbean, Higgins was preparing PT 6 for its preliminary acceptance trials. Before bidding on the two PT prototypes, Higgins had studied the design, the construction details, the types of woods, and the grades of lumber that were specified. He believed that with his extensive knowledge of lumber and his past experience designing fast boats he could help the navy develop a successful prototype. He was "dumbfounded and appalled" when he offered design corrections that he felt would improve the boats and found that not only did the BCR not want his suggestions but it "denounced" him for making them. He claimed that even during construction he continuously urged the navy to make modifications in the design but always found the Navy Department very resistant to recommendations he considered sensible.[47]

PT 6, powered by Packard engines, was completed and tested on Lake Pontchartrain in April, 1940.[48] Higgins stated, "The objectionable characteristics and performance we had prophesied were proven in the test."[49] The Sparkman and Stephens design, approved by the navy and built by Higgins, could not pass the U.S. military's acceptance trials.[50]

A month earlier Higgins had executed a contract with Finland for one Scott-Paine-designed 81-foot PT boat and five 70-foot boats of his own design. Finland made advance payments totaling $553,187.24. According to Higgins, the "Administration" desired that the boats be sold to Finland, and he had agreed to lend the services of his company "to effect this transfer in a manner that would not set up an international case or constitute an act of belligerency."[51]

Realizing that PT 6 was unstable in its present state, Higgins absorbed the $26,000 repair cost and virtually rebuilt the boat. He agreed to sell it to the Finnish government, then immediately began designing a replacement for the U.S. Navy. The new boat was designated PT 6 *Prime*. Higgins intended to build it to his own specifications and without interference from the navy. But again navy inspectors forced him to put in additions, modify the hull, and add weight in outfitting the craft.[52] Hig-

---

47. "Revisal," 48.

48. New Orleans *Item-Tribune*, April 14, 1940, n.p. (Untitled clipping in Dawn Higgins Murphy Collection, Jackson, Mississippi).

49. "Revisal," 49.

50. Graham Haddock, interview, July 23, 1975.

51. "Revisal," 49.

52. *Ibid.*, 50–51.

gins felt that the BCR might not know how to build its own boat, but it certainly had definite ideas on how to redesign his.

During May, while Higgins was rebuilding PT 6, the LBB and the FDB recommended continued development of both the Higgins and the BCR's personnel landing craft. The LBB believed that the major objection to the BCR's metal boat, a leaky hull, was caused by faulty welding and not by improper design. The BCR was finding it difficult to admit that its Small Boat Desk was incapable of designing the craft the navy needed. It hoped that given enough time its designers would come up with their own successful landing boat.

In June, 1940, while the BCR worked on its landing boat design, Higgins, in an involved transaction, sold the Scott-Paine-designed 81-foot PT boat and the five 70-foot PT boats that were originally built for Finland to Britain for $750,000.[53] To effect the transfer of the boats from Finland to Britain, Higgins had to agree to build the Finns seven new 70-foot PT boats.[54]

In the meantime, the BCR had revised its designs and on June 28, 1940, awarded a contract to Welin Davit to build a new 30-foot metal personnel landing boat.[55] Higgins did not receive an order from the bureau even though the LBB had recommended continued development of both designs. While awaiting a contract from the BCR, he was desperately trying to interest the British in his Eureka as a landing boat. But he wanted the British to consider using a 36-foot or 40-foot model. In a letter to Whitt and Chambers, Ltd., of London, dated July 8, 1940, Higgins wrote: "We would like to have you lose interest, and do not recommend the U.S. Navy 30-footer, even though it is our own design and our own development. *We do not like this boat* for the reason that the length is too short for the beam."[56]

Higgins explained that because of his improved hull design the 36-foot craft was actually nine miles per hour faster than a 30-foot boat equipped with the same engine. He suggested that his 36-foot landing boat with twenty-four men aboard be used by the British for reconnaissance missions and even raiding parties. The builder felt that his craft's

53. Rosenthal, "Higgins Industries, Inc.," 6.

54. Andrew J. Higgins, Sr. to Whitt and Chambers, Ltd., July 8, 1940, in Strahan Personal Collection.

55. "Report," 44.

56. Higgins to Whitt and Chambers, Ltd., July 8, 1940, in Strahan Personal Collection.

ability to strike anywhere along the enemy-held coast would tie down large numbers of Axis troops and have a considerable demoralizing effect on the enemy. Higgins also recommended that his 36-foot boat be used as patrol boats to protect the British coast. But perhaps his most unusual suggestion was that the Eureka be designed as a self-propelled torpedo, which could discharge as much as 2,500 to 3,000 pounds of explosives. "This boat could be manned by two men, and with special suits to protect them, they could bail out before the boat would hit its objective."[57]

Higgins also informed the British that the 81-foot PT boat and the first of the five 70-foot PT boats would be ready for delivery July 22. The remaining four 70-foot boats would be completed in fifty to sixty days. Then there would be approximately a forty-day delay before the completion of the first of the seven replacement boats for Finland. But he thought the U.S. government would never allow these boats to be delivered for fear that they might fall into German hands. He offered them to Whitt and Chambers at the price of $110,000 per boat.

Of added importance, Higgins told Whitt and Chambers that he would soon begin building a new, larger facility. This new plant would give him greater production capability because his St. Charles Avenue plant was not large enough to handle both his civilian and military orders. What he did not mention was this new City Park plant was financed by using the $553,187.24 that he had received from Finland. The Finns' boats had been resold to Britain for $750,000. They had been sold twice, leaving a huge pool of money. Higgins was now offering to sell the British the seven replacement boats that he was building for Finland. As long as the U.S. government did not allow the boats to be delivered to Finland, he had over a half million dollars at his disposal to use as he deemed necessary.

He explained in his letter that he could not help but think what "a marvelous service a large number of this 36-ft., or this proposed 40-ft. boat would have done with benefit to England and her previous allies, not alone at Dunkerque, but elsewhere as well." And he could not help but take the opportunity to reflect on the British navy's destruction of part of the French fleet. He realized it was a horribly tough decision to make but "was the only thing to do, gruesome as it was." He commented, "It is too sad that there were not in the beginning men directing your

57. *Ibid.*

Government that could make such Titanic decisions." In closing, for the benefit of his Irish colleagues or associates who might have occasion to read the letter, he related that "equally heroic decisions must be reached for them." He considered it sad that "the damn fools, with one golden occasion in history giving them the opportunity, did not grasp it and spring to their own in the defense of their neighbors and the world. . . . It is also sad that the damn fool English did not have enough sense to give Ireland complete freedom a long time ago, for if they had they would have a lot of fighting fools now on their side." [58]

On July 30, 1940, Finland, to show its appreciation, bestowed upon Higgins the title of Finnish consul to New Orleans. At this time the Finnish government assumed it was going to receive the seven replacement boats that Higgins Industries was presently building. The boats eventually were sold to Britain, just as the previous six PTs had been. [59]

On June 28 the BCR had awarded a contract to Welin Davit to build the one metal 30-foot boat it had designed. Finally, eight weeks later, on August 20, a contract was let to Higgins to build sixty-two 30-foot Eureka landing craft. [60]

Higgins was enthusiastic about the order but not about the size of the boats. He recalled, "I got so exasperated that on my own, and without an order, and at my own expense, I built a boat 36-foot of length, and bore all the expenses of shipping it to Norfolk, demanding that it be tested." According to General Smith, when the marines heard what Higgins had done they "whooped." Higgins later wrote the general, "I am quite sure that had it not been for the championing of, and the interest of the Marines, that boat would not have been tested." [61]

On September 11, the chief of naval operations ordered competitive trials to test a landing craft built by Chris Craft Corporation, the Higgins boat, and a metal BCR boat. These tests were conducted by the FDB on September 17, and a full report was given to the secretary of the navy on September 21. The report indicated that the Chris Craft entry, which was

58. *Ibid.*

59. Official Finnish Document (Certificate in Dawn Higgins Murphy Collection).

60. "Report," 44.

61. Higgins to Smith, February 3, 1948, in History and Museums Division, USMC, Washington, D.C.; Smith, *Coral and Brass*, 91.

similar in appearance to the Higgins boat but was powered by twin engines, "performed excellent" but had problems retracting. The FDB recommended against further development of this boat. Higgins' boat was considered, "by far the most superior" and "exceeded in performance any other landing boat that the members of the Board had ever seen."[62] The board found the BCR's metal landing boat the least satisfactory of those tested. Incredibly, on September 23, six days after the test, the Bureau of Ships, which had taken over the combined functions of the BCR and the Bureau of Engineering, awarded a contract for the construction of sixteen metal BCR boats to Gibbs Gas Engine Company of Jacksonville, Florida. This was two days after the chief of naval operations reported to the secretary of the navy that the BCR's boat was the least successful of the boats tested. The bureau was staunchly refusing to admit defeat.

As a result of the trials, the LBB recommended that 335 Higgins 36-foot personnel landing boats be procured. Competitive trials had been held, and the secretary of the navy and the chief of naval operations were both well aware of the superiority of the Higgins boat. The bureau could no longer stall for time while its Design Division's Small Boat Desk tried to produce a suitable personnel landing boat.

According to General Smith, "Through the unfathomable process whereby the official mind finally emerges from darkness into light, the Navy eventually decided to standardize on the 36-foot Higgins boat."[63] To ensure that the best possible boat would be mass produced, Higgins built two new 36-foot landing craft at his own expense. Each featured a different hull design; one had a pronounced vee hull like the Eurekas he was building for the British, and the other had a flatter forward section.

Tests held at Virginia Beach on October 22, 1940, established that the vee bottom had greater speed, but the flatter-bottomed Eureka could retract easier. A further test on November 5 also indicated that the flatter hull had better retracting capabilities and exceeded the navy's speed requirements.[64] As a result of these tests, on November 18, 1940, Higgins was officially awarded the contract for 335 36-foot Eurekas of the flatter hull design.

62. "Report," 46.
63. Smith, Coral and Brass, 91.
64. "Report," 51.

The competition between Higgins and the bureau over the design of the personnel landing boat had come to an end. The New Orleans shipbuilder had shown invincible determination and had forced the navy to accept his 36-six foot Eureka over its own 30-foot boats as its standardized LCP (landing craft personnel). According to General Smith, "Andrew Higgins, a fighting Irishman, won the opening phase of the boat battle singlehanded, with loud Marine applause."[65]

Higgins had won the first battle, but the bureau had not yet surrendered the war.

65. Smith, *Coral and Brass*, 90.

3

ROUND TWO

A s 1940 drew to a close, Higgins Industries was a much different
company than it had been only three years earlier. In 1936 the company had shown a net earnings of $241.42. By 1940 it had a net of over
$250,000. In 1937 its fixed net assets, representing plant and equipment,
had been $13,639. By the close of 1940 this figure had risen to $524,643.
In 1937 Higgins did not have a single navy contract. At the end of 1940
he had over $3,099,366 of hard-fought navy business. Additionally, sales
of $2,278,018 were done with other nations and private companies. Hig-
gins Industries had outgrown its small St. Charles Avenue facility and
was expanding into a new, larger plant on City Park Avenue.[1]

Construction of the City Park plant began in July, 1940, at approximately the same time Higgins was trying to convince the British to purchase his landing boats. He was sure that the United States would enter
the war, and he could foresee increasing demands for his Eureka landing
craft and motor torpedo boats. His plant on St. Charles Avenue was already too small to handle the present volume of commercial and military
business. To solve the problem, he purchased the Albert Weiblen Marble
and Granite Works on City Park Avenue and began transforming it into
a $1.5 million boat-building facility. This new shipyard had the distinc-
tion of being the world's largest boat manufacturing plant housed under
one roof. It was also the first boat-building plant to use mass-production
techniques to build landing craft. And it was the only manufacturing
facility in which boats were built on the second floor and then lowered
by a huge elevator to waiting railroad cars below. It had one other dis-
tinction: it was a boat yard that was not located on water.

---

1. Rosenthal, "Higgins Industries, Inc.," 4–9.

Even while the plant was still in the early stages of renovation, Higgins realized that as presently designed it would not be capable of handling his future landing craft and PT boat production. He had to expand. The problem was where. On one side was the Southern Railway System tracks, which were essential for bringing supplies in and boats out. On the other side was the Delgado Trades School. In front was City Park Avenue. The back of the shipyard was adjacent to Holt Cemetery. Higgins decided to enlarge the plant "knowingly and willingly" by preempting an unused portion of the cemetery grounds. The plant was increased until 40 percent of the new facility was constructed on property to which Higgins held no title, a problem that was unresolved as late as 1947.[2] Construction of Eureka landing boats and PTs was moved into the plant before it was completed, and the new manufacturing site was in mass production before its official dedication ceremonies on August 24, 1941.[3]

Also in 1940, the core of the company's war years management team was in place. Higgins was president and the main driving force behind the company. His brother Frank, who had worked with him since the early days of Higgins Lumber and Export, served as vice-president in charge of retail sales. In addition, Higgins' three older sons, Ed, Andrew, Jr., and Frank, were associated with the business during the war, holding a variety of offices from department head, to plant superintendent, to vice-president. Higgins' youngest son, Roland, served as a superintendent of construction of landing boats until he enlisted in the military on December 10, 1942.

Morris Gottesman was secretary-treasurer of the company; he had first become involved with Higgins in the 1930s, when Higgins had advertised in the paper for investors. Gottesman, who was in New Orleans to help revive a floundering retail store, answered the ad, and thus began a working relationship that lasted until 1946. It is to Gottesman that much of the credit for keeping Higgins financially sound must be attributed. Higgins was an inventor, an organizer, a man with an infinitely wild imagination, and a creative genius. When an idea struck, he moved forward at lightning speed. The expense of turning the idea into reality was inconsequential. Gottesman was the "bottom-line" man who tried to hold the reins without being dragged to death.

2. Statement dictated by Andrew Higgins, January 10, 1947, Statler Hotel, Washington, D.C. (Typescript in Papers of Harry S. Truman, File 633, Harry S. Truman Library, Independence, Missouri), 7, hereinafter cited as Statler Hotel Statement.
    3. Higgins City Park Plant Dedication Booklet, in Strahan Personal Collection.

Another key figure was Higgins' longtime friend and employee George Huet. Huet was a formally trained naval architect with a logical scientific mind. As head of the company's engineering department, he often had to tell Higgins that an idea was great but impossible. Higgins could frequently be heard shouting from his office, "Goddamit George I can't live with you, but I can't live without you."[4]

Arthur Derbins, who had been with Higgins since the 1920s, had risen from a carpenter to supervisor and would soon head the company's new City Park plant. Graham Haddock, Joe Dovie, Ted Sprague, and Art Fleitas were working in the engineering department under Huet. Richard McDerby was still working for Higgins' Boat Services Company. George Rappleyea was an assistant to Higgins, serving as advertising director, assistant in charge of patent procurement, and publicity agent and later would become editor of the company magazine and director of Higgins' school for landing boat operators.

Rappleyea, as a young attorney and mining engineer in Dayton, Tennessee, in 1925, had convinced local biology teacher John T. Scopes to teach evolution in school.[5] The intent was simply to create a bit of excitement. When it got out of control and William Jennings Bryan and Clarence Darrow became involved, George felt it best to leave town. Rappleyea initially served as Higgins' East Coast representative, but in 1939, as business increased, he was brought to New Orleans as a full-time member of the company's staff.

By November, 1940, the number of workers employed at Higgins Industries had grown considerably. In 1937 there were approximately 50 employees. By the fall of 1940, the number had risen to over 400. The Depression was coming to an end, and commercial sales had increased. Also, sales to foreign governments and the order from the U.S. Navy for sixty-two Eureka landing boats required a much larger work force. By the end of December the payroll had grown to 691.[6] The original pocket of loyal employees that Higgins had supported during the Depression was now in the minority.

The addition of workers brought increased attention from labor unions. When his was a small company of family and loyal workers, the unions had had no interest in Higgins. When it became a larger corpo-

4. Graham Haddock, interview, June 26, 1975.

5. Ray Ginger, *Six Days or Forever? Tennessee v. John Thomas Scopes* (Boston, 1958), 19–20.

6. Rosenthal, "Higgins Industries, Inc," 16.

ration with a majority of new faces, Higgins became a plum that attracted the American Federation of Labor.

By the fall of 1940 the new employees wanted to have an election to bring in the AFL. Their main complaint against management was that there was no consistent wage scale. When a man was hired, he was paid according to his individual agreement with the company. Therefore, workers doing identical jobs might not be receiving the same wages. A union, they felt, would solve this problem.

Higgins did not like anyone telling him how to run his business. He was especially opposed to the idea of a union and fought it hard. When he saw that the workers were going to persist in their demands, he decided to have his loyal employees form a company union. The new workers rejected this idea and insisted on the AFL. The stalemate was broken by a vote sanctioned by the Department of Labor.

In November, 1940, all the workers met in an old bar at the corner of Carondelet and Polymnia streets near the St. Charles Avenue plant. Before the ballots were cast, there was an argument over who was eligible to vote. Under a company union all employees, including office personnel and supervisors, would be allowed to participate. Under the AFL rules, only actual laborers could vote. The Department of Labor representative ruled in favor of franchising everyone. Since it was Higgins' policy to promote from within, many of his loyal longtime employees and staunch supporters, now in supervisory positions, were eligible to vote. Higgins hoped that with their backing the company union would be chosen.

But when the ballots were counted, the AFL had won. When the results were reported to Higgins in his office, the Irishman turned red in the face. He thought for a second and then went into the plant and called all his employees together. He told them a story about something that had occurred in a cowboy camp out in west Texas. This camp was located on the open ranges miles from the nearest town. The biggest problem confronting the foreman was keeping a cook. The cowboys made the cook's life miserable. They complained about the menu, the way he prepared the food, and the portions they received. To make matters worse, they constantly made him the target of their practical jokes. Finally, the cook had had all he could take and saddled his horse and took off for the hills.

The foreman, upon hearing that he had just lost his fifth cook, decided to have all of the cowboys draw straws. The one with the shortest straw would become the cook. Then the first one to complain about his cooking would take over the position. The unlucky wrangler who drew the shortest straw hated cooking. He intentionally burned the beans and overcooked the beef. He did everything he could think of to get someone to criticize his meals. Finally, another cowboy complained and became the cook. But no matter what this new cook did, no one would make a derogatory remark. He burned the bacon, served half-cooked food, fixed chicken with the feathers still on it, but no one dared to complain. Desperately, the disgruntled cook decided he was going to force someone to make a disparaging statement about his meals. He made a big, flaky crust. Then he went out to the herd and selected a nice fresh cow pie and put it in the crust and baked it. That night after chow he brought the pie out for dessert.

The cook cut out a large slice and handed it to one of the wranglers. The cowboy took a bite, spit it out, and shouted, "This tastes like shit." But quickly remembering the consequences, he proclaimed, "But I love it." Higgins, ending his story, told his workers, "And you s.o.b.'s that's how I love you."[7]

On November 25, 1940, Higgins entered into an agreement with various unions affiliated with the AFL.[8] He immediately began cultivating good relations with the union. He cooperated in every way he could and became a model employer. Then, when he needed help in Washington to lobby for navy contracts, he called on his newfound AFL friends to exert pressure. The industrialist did not like having the union in his plants, but if it had to be there, he was going to make it work for him.[9]

Also in the fall of 1940, Higgins informed the assistant chief of the Bureau of Ships, Rear Admiral A. H. Van Keuren, that the new City Park plant was ready to begin in-line production of any type of wood or steel boats under 120 feet. He suggested that the best use for the plant would be for producing submarine chasers, PT boats, or Eureka personnel landing boats.[10]

At the end of November, a sub-board of the navy's Inspection and Survey Department conducted preliminary trials of the Higgins-designed

7. Graham Haddock, interview, March 25, 1992.
8. Rosenthal, "Higgins Industries, Inc," 16.
9. Graham Haddock, interview, March 25, 1992.
10. Andrew J. Higgins, Sr., to Rear Admiral A. H. Van Keuren, October 17, 1940, in Secretary of the Navy, 1940–42, QM/P15 (401017) G, Record Group 80, National Archives.

PT 6 *Prime* on Lake Pontchartrain. Engine problems related to a manufacturing defect ended the scheduled tests, but the board did witness the
acceptance trials of one of the 70-foot PT boats being built for England.
The boat, fully loaded and powered by three nine-hundred-horsepower
Hall Scott engines, greatly impressed the inspectors with its forty-knot
speed. Even more impressive was the price of $110,000. The board sent
a memorandum to the secretary of the navy informing him of the PT 6
trials and included information on the Higgins 70-footers. The board
related that the PTs Higgins designed and built for British have "military
characteristics comparable to those of our own 70-foot boats which cost
about twice as much. Its maneuverability is superior and its access and
arrangement are excellent."[11]

The navy asked Higgins why these boats were superior yet less expensive than those it was purchasing. He responded that in his negotiations
with the British he had agreed to build the boats at a limit of 10 percent
profit if they would allow him to design and construct the craft without
interference. When questioned as to why he would not build boats for
the U.S. Navy for the same profit, Higgins replied that he would love to
do so. But because of the navy's insistence on certain specifications and
its constant design changes during construction, he had lost a considerable amount of money on U.S. contracts.[12]

In December preliminary acceptance trials were finally held for PT 5.
According to Higgins, the hull for the boat had been completed for 446
days and sat at his plant waiting for the Vimalert Engine Company to
furnish the engines for installation. The trials proved that PT 5 was not
as maneuverable as PT 6 *Prime* and its speed was inferior. It was recommended that no more boats of this design be built. Interestingly, both PT
5 and 6, which were not Higgins designs, did not meet the navy's standards. PT 6 *Prime* was a Higgins boat, but the navy constantly added
and deleted features. Despite the navy's involvement, the boat proved
superior to both of the earlier PTs. But the boat that impressed the inspectors the most was the British PT designed by Higgins Industries and
built with the stipulation that the company would have total control in
its design and production. Higgins was determined to build the best boat
possible, even if it had to be for the British instead of the U.S. Navy.

11. "Memorandum for the Secretary of the Navy, PT6—Preliminary Acceptance
Trials," November 26, 1940, in Office of the Secretary, General Correspondence, 1940–42,
Box 1003, Folder "PT 6," Record Group 80, National Archives.
12. "Revisal," 56–57.

As 1940 drew to a close, the marines and the navy were preparing for Flex 7. This maneuver, which took place from February 4 through February 16, 1941, was the final exercise held in the Caribbean before U.S. entry into the war. The joint operation involved elements of the 1st Marine Division and the army's 1st Infantry Division. Naval forces included Battleship Division Five with three ships, Cruiser Division Seven with four, Destroyer Squadron Two, and an aircraft group consisting of two aircraft carriers and the 1st Marine Air Group. In command of the combined forces was Rear Admiral Ernest J. King, commander of the Atlantic Fleet.

The planners of the exercise hoped to accomplish three things: first, to train officers in joint command and staff procedure; second, to employ and test existing doctrine designed to govern landing operations; and third, to gain experience in these operations using divisional units. What Flex 7 did accomplish was to bring to the surface the problems inherent when a small unit like the marines is attached to a larger force such as the navy. It was an older brother–younger brother relationship.

When Marine Corps general Smith used the term *beachhead* in reference to landing operations, Admiral King retorted: "I'm getting sick and tired of hearing the word 'beachhead.' It's beach, I tell you, not beachhead. Why don't you Marines get it straight?" On another occasion, when ten thousand gallons of fresh water disappeared from the USS *McCawley*, the ship's captain accused his marine passengers of being responsible. Smith had marine captain Victor H. Krulak investigate the shortage. It was found that the ship's petty officers had been diverting fresh water to flush their toilets.

Differences surfaced even during actual landing operations. Smith was preparing to land a large force on a beach to simulate invading a hostile shore. King had aerial photographs of the beach, which he could have given to Smith for reconnaissance. Instead, he kept them to himself. The marine general later recalled: "I never was able to figure out why he kept them. After all, the Navy and the Marines were fighting on the same side or so I thought." [13]

Another problem haunted the marines during Flex 7: lack of an adequate tank lighter. As early as 1913 the navy had begun trying to develop a craft capable of transporting artillery from ships at sea to the shores of undeveloped beaches. These early craft had to be towed, and they proved

13. Smith, *Coral and Brass*, 74–77.

awkward and useless. In 1923 a new experimental artillery lighter called Troop Barge A, Beetle Boat, or Kelly Cole after Marine Corps colonel Eli K. Cole, who convinced the navy to build it, made its first appearance. The boat was a 55-five foot, twin-engine wooden craft with a steel canopy. It proved unsuitable for the purpose intended.

Little was done in the following ten years to develop lighters because of severe budget constraints. In the 1936–37 winter exercises at San Clemente Island off southern California, the marines were still without a self-propelled landing boat that could put men and artillery ashore over an open beach. They intended to use the Beetle Boat for the maneuvers, but it capsized and sank while being towed from San Diego to San Clemente.[14]

The marines realized that an amphibious force would not be capable of capturing strongly defended enemy-held positions without the use of close-range artillery fire or tanks. The early landing barges were clumsy to navigate in landing operations and proved unsuitable for combat use. By 1938 the BCR had developed a self-propelled lighter that it considered capable of fulfilling the necessary requirements, but further testing was still needed. During Flex 6 in 1940, the BCR's lighter was used in landing operations. According to General Smith, the navy tank lighters "proved mechanical handicaps, almost denying us the use of our five precious tanks. They would have got us nowhere in combat, except killed."[15] Their performance showed no improvement during Flex 7. A tank being transported ashore on a lighter under tow was almost lost when the lighter careened and the tank plunged into the sea. The tank settled in an upright position and was salvaged.

Flex 7 showed the marines they still had far to go to get a craft capable of landing a well-equipped fighting force on a hostile beach. The Higgins Eureka performed successfully in the maneuvers, but the trials exposed minor defects that needed to be corrected. Smith believed that with improvement and modifications the Higgins boats could be "an answer to the Marine prayer." They might be the shallow-draft ramp boat that the corps needed to carry troops to their future island objectives.[16]

In March, 1941, it seemed possible that the United States might have

14. Lieutenant General Victor H. Krulak, USMC (Ret.), *First to Fight: An Inside View of the U.S. Marine Corps* (Annapolis, 1984), 88–90.

15. Smith, *Coral and Brass,* 72.

16. *Ibid.*

to seize the island of Martinique from the French to halt its use as an
Axis base. This operation would require an amphibious assault. Smith
had no faith in the ability of the Bureau of Ships to design and produce
the landing boats the marines would need so he looked to the one person he thought could do it, Andrew Higgins. The general sent Captain
Victor H. Krulak and Major Ernest E. Linsert, secretary of the Marine
Equipment Board, to New Orleans to meet with the industrialist and
discuss the corps' needs.

Higgins was shown a photograph taken by Krulak in September,
1937. With the permission of the marines, the navy, and the Japanese,
Krulak had observed a Japanese amphibious assault against Chinese
forces at the mouth of the Yangtze River. He photographed a wooden
Japanese ramped landing boat that was capable of transporting vehicles
and depositing them on the beach. This was exactly the type of craft the
marines had been pushing to have developed. Krulak forwarded a report
and the photograph to the Bureau of Ships. Upon returning to the United
States in July, 1939, he searched for the material he had sent. He discovered it in the Bureau of Ships files with a note written in the margin
stating it was the work of "some nut out in China." [17]

Krulak and Linsert informally suggested to Higgins that he develop a
Eureka with a ramp to replace the rounded bow.[18] The industrialist accepted the challenge and at his own expense had his men begin working
on a variety of ideas. In late April, 1941, while on a trip to Washington,
Higgins examined a bureau plan for a tank lighter. Across the blueprint
he wrote something to the effect of "This is lousy" or "This boat stinks—
AJH."[19] One can imagine the animosity of the naval architects toward
this southern boat builder, who just a year earlier had succeeded in having his Eureka accepted over their Philadelphia boat as the navy's standardized personnel landing craft (LCP).

Immediately after returning from Washington with a contract for an
additional 188 Eureka landing boats, Higgins had his engineering department begin designing a tank lighter. On May 8, 1941, Higgins Industries' first tank lighter designs and specifications were completed by
Art Fleitas, a Higgins draftsman. This first lighter was a makeshift craft

17. Krulak, First to Fight, 90–91.
18. Ibid., 94.
19. Burck, "Mr. Higgins And His Wonderful Boats," 111; "The Boss," 210.

in which a metal platform resembling a raft was suspended between two 36-foot Eureka landing boats.[20] On May 17, the plan was refined, but the concept still proved unsuitable. The following day Fleitas designed another model.[21] This time the tank lighter was a single-bodied, shallow-draft vessel that resembled a barge or stripped-down towboat. It was powered by two engines and operated from a steering house located on one side of the boat. The craft had a ramp front, and the design showed promise. Fleitas continued refining it.

On May 26, 1941, Commander Ross B. Daggett, USN, representing the Bureau of Ships, and Major Ernest E. Linsert, of the Marine Equipment Board, visited New Orleans to witness the test of three ramped Eurekas. Higgins had built the boats at his own expense in response to the Marine Corps' suggestion.[22] Linsert tested the new ramped Eureka, or LCVP (landing craft vehicle, personnel) as it was later called, on Lake Pontchartrain with a truck loaded on board. He then tested the craft with thirty-six Higgins employees embarking and disembarking to simulate the loading and landing of troops. Linsert reported to Brigadier General Charles Barrett, director of plans and policies at marine headquarters, that the boats were acceptable.[23]

On May 27 at 10:30 A.M., the LBB met to consider the reports from Daggett and Linsert on the previous day's test. As a result of the meeting, R. M. Hinckley, acting senior member of the LBB, recommended to the chief of naval operations that a special board be appointed. This board, composed of Marine Corps and Bureau of Ships representatives, should proceed immediately to New Orleans and officially test the Higgins ramped boats. If the test proved successful, the remaining 87 boats of the 188-boat contract awarded to Higgins on April 30 should be modified to include ramps.

It was further suggested that because not more than eight or ten bureau tank lighters and not more than three or four artillery lighters would be available on the date specified by the marines, Higgins be asked to

20. Higgins Industries, Inc., draftsman's drawing no. 2576, May 8, 1941, in Strahan Personal Collection.

21. Higgins Industries, Inc., draftsman's drawing no. 2580–1, May 18, 1941, *ibid.*

22. Chief of the Bureau of Ships to Under Secretary of the Navy, September 15, 1942, in National Defense Committee Files, OP-5, Navy Department Matters Ships, Shipbuilding and Related Matters, Box 182, Record Group 46, National Archives; Clifford, *Progress and Purpose*, 51.

23. Clifford, *Progress and Purpose*, 51.

develop a 45-foot tank landing craft. It was urgently recommended that if it proved successful a contract be awarded to the builder for fifty tank lighters and that every practicable means be taken to expedite delivery.[24] The bureau was desperate. It could not fulfill its obligation to design and supply the navy with the boats needed. It temporarily swallowed its pride and hoped Higgins could succeed.

After the meeting, the LBB telephoned Higgins to inform him that a group of military representatives would be sent to New Orleans to test the ramped Eureka. The LBB also asked that he begin designing an experimental 45-foot tank lighter. Higgins informed the board that when it arrived, instead of plans he would have a workable craft.

"It can't be done," the navy replied.

"The hell it can't," Higgins shouted back, "you just be here in three days."[25]

Higgins decided that this time he would place stipulations on the agreement. He would accept the challenge but would not work with the navy's representatives. He informed the bureau that he would build a tank lighter but only if it was under the regulation of the Marine Corps. He had dealt with naval bureaucracies too many times. This time he wanted to be associated with someone who appreciated the contribution of a private concern. He realized that the marines favored his craft; they were the principal users, they understood the benefits of a well-designed boat, and they had played a major part in the navy's adoption of the 36-foot Eureka as its standardized personnel landing craft. The navy, in urgent need of a dependable tank lighter, agreed to Higgins' request.[26]

The previous year Higgins had been so certain that he would receive a contract to build a combination towboat and dredge tender for the Mobile Corps of Engineers that he had begun to construct such a craft. When the contract failed to materialize, he was left with a partially completed vessel.[27] The navy had asked for a 45-foot tank lighter. The tow-

24. Senior Member, Development Continuing Board for Development of Landing Boats, to Chief of Naval Operations, May 27, 1941, in Office of the Secretary, General Correspondence, 1940–42, S82–3(1) L4–3 (410527), S82-3/ and plain to V-all, Record Group 80, National Archives.

25. Andrew J. Higgins, Jr., interview, April 20, 1973; "A. J. Higgins Dies of Brief Illness," New Orleans Times-Picayune, August 2, 1952, p. 25.

26. Smith, Coral and Brass, 93.

27. Higgins Industries, Inc., draftsman's drawing no. 2583, May 28, 1941, and draftsman's drawing no. 2511-A, May 31, 1940, in Strahan Personal Collection; Graham Had-

boat was approximately 47 feet long; with alterations it would be the correct length. The width was almost the desired size, and the height could be modified. Higgins and his engineers decided that this craft would be the easiest to convert into a lighter.[28]

On May 27, the same day the navy called, Higgins had the towboat brought from an empty lot, where it had been stored, to his St. Charles Avenue plant. That night his men began to cut out the deckhouse and strip the boat until all that remained was the hull and the engines. They worked constantly, stopping only long enough to hear a radio broadcast by President Roosevelt.[29]

On the morning of May 28, Fleitas refined the tank lighter design that he had originally drawn on May 18. But at the same time, Graham Haddock, another company draftsman, made a quick drawing that altered the towboat so that it could serve as a tank transporter.[30] Workmen had been cutting out the unnecessary structures and were awaiting instructions on how to proceed. It was decided to follow Haddock's design, though his was simply a rough sketch. In reality, the lighter was designed as work on the craft progressed. The draftsmen and Higgins remained only a step ahead of the welders, explaining what was to be done next.[31]

Massive alterations made the lighter a masterpiece of patchwork welding, and the hull was almost complete before a suitable ramp control mechanism had been designed. The controls that had been devised for the LCVP were not adaptable to this craft. The LCVP's ramp tilted outward. The lighter's ramp tilted inward. The lighter had to be large enough to carry modern tanks yet not over 45 feet long so it could be lowered through the cargo hold of merchant vessels. To meet the navy's specifications, the lighter's ramp had to tilt inward, which required a complete new pulley system.

Higgins gathered Huet, his draftsmen, his son Ed, and a few key employees in his office and asked the half dozen or so men to sit down at

---

dock, interview, June 26, 1975; J. A. Dovie's "Drawing Number Book," 66, in Strahan Personal Collection.

28. Graham Haddock, interview, November 9, 1975.

29. *Ibid.*

30. Higgins Industries, Inc., draftsman's drawing no. 2583, May 28, 1941, and draftsman's drawing no. 2580-1-A, May 28, 1941, in Strahan Personal Collection.

31. Graham Haddock, interview, November 10, 1975.

the conference table. The industrialist then informed them that no one would leave until a satisfactory ramp and operating mechanism had been developed. Higgins sat at his desk dictating letters and carrying on his daily business while the men at the table tried to agree on an effective solution. At lunchtime Ed rose from his chair and started walking toward the door. His father bellowed that no one was leaving. Sandwiches were brought to the office.

Earlier, Haddock had made a prototype ramp for the proposed tank lighter using a cigar box as a model. But the controls required two or three operations to lift the lid, which represented the ramp. The other draftsmen and workers in the office had rejected the idea as being too cumbersome and time-consuming so Haddock had placed the model in his desk drawer and forgotten about it. During the discussion at the table, someone mentioned the device.

Higgins quickly looked up from his desk and asked why he had never been shown the "gadget." Then he ordered Haddock to bring the model to the meeting immediately. Once the cigar box was placed before the group, Higgins asked each man his objections to the mechanism. As arguments against the makeshift ramp were raised, the industrialist reminded his men that no one could leave until each problem had been solved. By late afternoon the deficiencies of the ramp had been overcome, and the solution proposed was similar to the actual design used throughout the war.[32]

When the special board of Marine Corps and U.S. Navy officials arrived from Washington to test the 36-foot ramped Eureka, they also found a completed 45-foot tank lighter. The boat had been designed, built, and put in the water in sixty-one hours.[33] The head of the Marine Equipment Board, Brigadier General Emile P. Moses, who was at the St. Charles Avenue facility during the planning and fabricating of the boat, served as the senior member during the trials. Both boats passed with flying colors. Moses later wrote admiringly to Higgins, "I know of no other plant in the country which could have done the same."[34]

After the tests had been completed, either on the night of May 29,

32. Graham Haddock, interview, June 26, 1975.
33. Higgins to Smith, February 3, 1948, in History and Museums Division, USMC, Washington, D.C.
34. General E. P. Moses to Andrew Higgins, April 6, 1944, in Strahan Personal Collection.

1941, or the morning of May 30, Higgins, some high-ranking United States Marine Corps officers who witnessed the tests, members of the bureau in New Orleans, and members of the bureau in Washington were all connected via a conference telephone hookup. It was agreed that Higgins was to proceed as quickly as possible, even before a written order had been officially received, with the development of fifty 45-foot tank lighters of the builder's design. The only stipulation besides the length was that ten of the lighters be delivered to the Naval Operating Base in Norfolk, Virginia, no later than June 15, 1941.[35]

Higgins had some of the engines needed for the lighters because he served as an outlet for Gray-Marine motors, but he did not have the full one hundred required to complete the fifty craft. It would be too time-consuming to order the equipment from the factory so he contacted other Gray-Marine dealers across the nation and purchased engines from their stock.[36] His main problem, however, was that he needed steel with which to construct the craft and additional space for fabrication. When he was building the prototype tank lighter from the towboat, he had the welders save the pieces cut out of the deck housing so they could be used to modify other sections of the craft. It was not a matter of saving material; he simply did not have the steel in stock. As a result of the alterations, the lighter received the nickname Patches.

Higgins discovered that a barge load of the type of steel needed for the remaining forty-nine lighters was anchored near Baton Rouge. He sent a chartered fleet of trucks and armed plant guards to persuade the consignee to release the metal to Higgins Industries. Still more steel was required. The industrialist had a Birmingham steel maker called off the golf course on a Sunday afternoon to persuade him to allocate the needed material. Then he asked President E. E. Norris of the Southern Railway to attach flatcars carrying the steel to the back of one of his passenger trains. Norris insisted that it was against regulations, but after Higgins contacted the navy, the rules were suspended and the train rolled. Never before or since has a Southern Railway passenger train pulled freight cars.

The St. Charles Avenue plant lacked the space in its buildings to fab-

35. "A Statement by A. J. Higgins, of Higgins Industries, Inc., New Orleans," September 24, 1942, pp. 1–3, in Strahan Personal Collection, hereinafter referred to as Higgins' "Statement."

36. Graham Haddock, interview, November 10, 1975.

ricate the boats. Higgins' problem of limited building space was compounded because the City Park plant, even though not completed, was already filled to capacity building the spoonbill-bow Eureka landing boats and motor torpedo boats. The complete production of the newly designed LCVP had also been moved into this plant.

The bureau had requested "that every practicable means be taken to expedite completion and delivery."[37] Those instructions were all the feisty industrialist needed. To solve the problem, he closed off an entire block of Polymnia Street, which bordered one side of his St. Charles Avenue plant, covered it with canvas to protect the workers from extreme weather conditions, and transformed it into a temporary warehouse and fabrication yard. The actual assembling of the craft took place in an old stable, which the boat builder had purchased, only a few hundred feet from his plant.

The ceiling of this building was too low for cranes to be used. Therefore, all of the metal plating that went into the tank lighters had to be carried by hand into the shop and physically put in place. To accomplish this task, "bull gangs" were used—a varying number of men needed to lift a certain piece of steel and transport it on their shoulders into the building. At times they might be carrying over a ton of metal.[38]

The residents of Polymnia Street could not drive their automobiles to their homes, trucks could not make deliveries to the houses or businesses on the closed-off block, and garbage vehicles could not pass through for their collections, all because of the emergency measures taken by Higgins. Few people complained. This was the least sacrifice they could make for the war effort, though a brothel owner whose business was located on the closed-off block argued that the "racket destroyed romance" and threatened to take the matter up with the proper officials.[39]

When Higgins discovered that he could not find a mill to supply the bronze shafting needed for the boats, he began looking to the oil field companies. Shafting was located in Texas, but the owner refused to sell the metal. There was no time to go through the bureaucracy and have the

37. "The Boss," 214; *Ideas for United Nations*, film, n.d., in Gayle Higgins Jones Collection, New Orleans, Louisiana; Andrew J. Higgins, Jr., interview, April 20, 1973; Senior Member to Chief of Naval Operations, May 27, 1941, in National Archives.

38. Graham Haddock, interview, June 26, 1975.

39. "The Boss," 214.

navy expropriate the metal. The need was desperate and called for drastic measures. Higgins had some of his workers illegally remove the metal from the oil well storage depot. With the Texas police in pursuit, they crossed the state line back into the friendly jurisdiction of the Louisiana State Troopers. The workers then apologized for their "mistake" and returned a portion of what had been stolen. The rest was transported under trooper escort to New Orleans to be used on the tank lighters.[40] Nine lighters were completed and ready for shipment by June 12, less than two weeks after the verbal order was given.

To build the LCVPs as fast as possible no time could be wasted producing new jigs or patterns. The workers built a complete LCP, then cut off the bow and installed a hinged ramp. It was an expensive way to construct the boat, but there were no quick alternatives.[41] Twenty-six of the new LCVPs were completed and shipped with the tank landing craft so they would arrive in Norfolk on or before June 15.

The reason for the urgent delivery of LCVPs and tank landing craft (LCMs—landing craft, mechanized) was that the navy had been informed by President Roosevelt that it might have to take Martinique or the Azores.[42] But the Germans failed to make a hostile move toward either objective, and the operations proved unnecessary.

Higgins had already started preparing for what he considered the inevitable. In September, 1939, when Hitler invaded Poland, Higgins speculated and ordered two shiploads of Philippine mahogany, the wood best suited for building boats. He had expanded from his small St. Charles Avenue plant into the City Park plant. His work force had grown from 691 in December, 1940, to over 1,600 in June, 1941. He was building PT boats for the United States, Britain, and the Netherlands. He had proven with his LCP, LCVP, and now his LCM, that his company could design and produce the type of boats that the amphibious forces required. His LCM had been designed and ready for testing in sixty-one hours. This was a man who could quickly grasp an idea, translate it into a practical design, and have his workers construct a prototype while others were still pondering the problem.

40. General Robert E. Hogaboom to Benis M. Frank, November 3, 1975, copy in Strahan Personal Collection.

41. "Notes for Mr. Hugh Fulton," October 15, 1943, pp. 2–3, *ibid.*

42. Krulak, *First to Fight*, 94.

Higgins was especially knowledgeable about small boats, had extremely strong ties with the Marines Corps, and refused to let anything stand in his way. In Washington he was an outsider and perceived by many, including officers in the Small Boat Division of the Bureau of Ships, as a threat. If they could not outdesign him, they had to find a way to control him.

4

THE STATEMENT

In early June, 1941, when the order for fifty tank lighters was awarded to Higgins Industries, it appeared that the adversary relationship between Higgins and the Bureau of Ships was coming to an end. The bureau seemed to accept the fact that Higgins, instead of its own Small Boat Desk in the Design Division, had succeeded in developing the LCP, LCVP, and LCM. In reality, it was simply the calm before the storm. Higgins' war with the bureau was soon to escalate.

As Higgins' workers feverishly fabricated parts for tank landing craft on a New Orleans street, bureau representatives frequently mentioned to the industrialist the possibility of extending the contract to include an additional 131 lighters. The manner in which this contract was finally handled clearly revealed the bureau's true intent toward the New Orleans shipbuilder.

As Higgins was making important advances in tank lighter designs during the spring of 1941, a future key player was emerging on the scene in Washington, D.C., one who would have a direct effect on the contractor, the bureau, and amphibious warfare. He was Senator Harry S. Truman. Truman saw defense spending rising to enormous sums even before the United States entered the war. With increased spending came great opportunities for corruption and inefficiency. He recalled that after World War I several investigations had been held, but by then the investigators were powerless to recover funds from inflated billing and unnecessary waste. He reasoned that the time to do it was while the money was being appropriated.[1] The Senate concurred, and on March 1, 1941, the Special Committee to Investigate the National Defense Program was cre-

1. David McCullough, *Truman* (New York, 1992), 256–59.

ated. It soon became known as the Truman Committee after its originator and chairman.

In 1942 the Truman Committee became involved in the controversy
between Higgins and the Bureau of Ships. On June 8 and 9, the committee held hearings concerning the designing and awarding of contracts for
tank landing craft. On August 5, 1942, it sent a report concerning the
navy's tank lighter program to Secretary of the Navy Frank Knox.

After reading the document, the secretary appointed Professor H. S.
Seward of Yale University to do an internal investigation for the navy. As
a part of Seward's investigation Higgins dictated a twenty-two-page statement on September 24, 1942, giving a personal account of the early hectic days in June, 1941; the controversy over the contract concerning the
additional 131 tank lighters; and his relationship with and assessment of
several key bureau officials.

Higgins' statement is not a polished document prepared by his legal
staff. It is a statement from the heart in which he pulls no punches. It
reveals much of the man, his personality, and the difficulties American
industry encountered as it geared up for total war. It offers us a rare
opportunity to know what he thought and felt, and it gave Higgins the
chance to tell his story and to defend his actions. It is because of the
importance and uniqueness of the statement that it is reprinted here
in full.

A Statement by A. J. Higgins, of Higgins Industries Inc., New Orleans:

This statement is made without any reference to notes, and strictly
from memory.

Following the successful demonstration of steel, twin-Diesel engine
powered Tank Carrying Lighter to a composite board of U.S. Marine
Corps officers, and representatives of the Bureau of Ships, Navy Department, further and numerous telephone conversations were held by a considerable number of people in the Bureau of Ships, and Commander R. B.
Daggett being in New Orleans, or back and forth between New Orleans
and Washington during the very hectic days between May 26th and
May 30th, 1941; the participants of the Bureau of Ships in these conversations being Commander N. L. Rawlings, Commander M. M. Dana (a

very excellent and efficient officer), Commander Jack Huse (a very efficient officer), and other officers assigned from the Bureau of Supplies and Accounts, Navy Department, the traffic department of the Navy, etc. At least 10 or 12 officers of different divisions of the Bureau of Ships being in intermittent telephone conversation with us.

The night of May 29, 1941, which was a Thursday, or the morning of Friday, May 30, 1941, some U.S. Marine Officers in New Orleans, and Bureau of Ships officers here in New Orleans, and numerous officers in the Bureau of Ships at Washington, on a wide conference hook-up by telephone, with A. J. Higgins, instructed that we go ahead without any formal order and proceed with the construction of 50 tank carrying lighters of our own design, these boats to be powered with engines that we, the contractor, would procure. Construction started immediately.

During these days of intense effort, many telephone conversations were held back and forth with Washington, and on several occasions, different officers in the Bureau of Ships discussed an extension of the contract by 131 additional tank carrying lighters, which the writer was advised that the Bureau had the authority and appropriation to procure.

Doubt was expressed on several occasions by officers of the Bureau of Ships as to whether or not our selection of the Gray (General Motors) Marine Diesel Engines was a wise one, as the Bureau of Ships, up to that time, had been greatly prejudiced against the use of this engine.

During these hectic 10 days that the boats were under construction officers present discussed what the cost, or the price would be for these additional tank carrying lighters, with or without engines.

The statement was made repeatedly, either verbally to those present, or by long distance telephone conversations, that based on the performance of the first, experimental tank carrying lighter of our own design and construction, and in view of the great and urgent need for tank carriers, and the successful tests performed by the one we built so hurriedly, it would justify the Bureau of Ships placing an order with us for an additional 131 tank carrying lighters.

During these hectic 10 days, on many occasions, there were conversations held when there were 2, 3, and as high as 4 Navy officers present, they being from the Bureau of Ships, or the Bureau of S&A, discussing our progress in construction, and the manner in which we could prepare ourselves for uninterrupted construction of such lighters,—after our completion of the first verbal or telephoned order for 50, and our ability to complete the total of 181 lighters.

During these negotiations, I repeatedly made the statement that I knew we were going to lose a considerable amount of money on the first 50 tank lighters which we were building, but that I felt that normal construction, if we were permitted to continue without interruption, and not under such terrific pressure, would permit our naming approximately the same price for the additional 131 lighters, and that we felt that we would be safe in the Navy's hands to adjust the price on the additional 131, based on production cost under normal construction conditions.

Based on assurances that we were to receive an additional order for 131 tank carrying lighters, we purchased additional materials, such as steel, and even notified the Gray Marine Motor Co., of Detroit, to adjust their production schedule to produce a minimum of 300 engines, for twin engine installations.

I had promised the U.S. Marines and the Navy that I would deliver 10 tank carrying lighters to the Naval Operating Base, Norfolk, Va. by June 15th, 1941. In addition to the unusual efforts we made to produce these boats and to carry out the wish of the Administration to sub-contract or distribute work as far as possible, we contracted with two other outfits—The Canulette Shipbuilding Co., and the Gulf Coast Towing Co., of Slidell, Louisiana. On the night of May 30th, 1941, we had these people in our office. We made a deal hurriedly with them, that one of them would build 10, and the other concern would build 15 of these lighters. To these concerns (sub-contractors) we sent approximately $50,000 worth of equipment, consisting of Diesel engine driven generators to furnish power and lights; electric welding machines; and various and sundry equipment, cutting torches, etc. We also furnished to these concerns technical men to assist them in starting construction. We furnished them with all the material and equipment, and steel, etc.

Their attempts to build these lighters were abortive, and their cost for attempting to build them, particularly in the case of the Gulf Coast Towing Co., were far beyond the price we received from the Navy.

Our cost for the adventure—in trying to expedite it—was in excess of $82,000 over what we received for the contract, and we received from them only one boat which we had to rebuild and salvage before we could even think of tendering it to the Navy against the contract. The loose equipment we provided for the rest of the boats under sub-contract to them was salvaged after this (mis) adventure.

On or about June 9th or June 10th, 1941, some officers connected with either the traffic or transportation department of the Navy (Bureau of

Ships) telephoned us regarding how we were going to fulfill our contract, or promise, and our guarantee of delivery of these boats to the N.O.B., Norfolk, Va.; that they desired to discuss with us how it would be possible for us to load these boats (tank lighters), which they knew we had very nearly finished, on board an aeroplane carrier; such problems as the availability to us of any derrick equipment with long enough boom to lift 20 tons up to the flight deck of the aeroplane carrier. Discussions were engaged in as to the chartering or commandeering of some vessels in coast-wise trade, particularly a vessel due in port on June 11th, this boat operating under charter to the Waterman S/S Co., this officer pointing out that such method of delivery to Norfolk would be terrifically expensive and that the time for loading and the voyage to Norfolk would cause us to exceed the guaranteed delivery date of June 15th. At this time, we advised this officer, and other officers that the problems of delivery had been solved by us; sufficient to say that 9 of these steel tank carrying lighters, and 26 of another type of boat—our 36-ft. Eureka Ramp Type Landing Boat—a new type of boat which we had also developed simultaneously with the tank lighter—were delivered to the Naval Operating Base, at Norfolk, Va. on or prior to June 15th, 1941, BY RAIL. (Note: All this equipment, if and when unloaded, lay around the N.O.B. and many of these boats were not unloaded off the railway car for quite some time thereafter, in spite of the Navy's urgent request for delivery).

On, and after, JUNE 12 1941, this principal, and others of our organization, attending the execution of this task, were physically exhausted. The writer had a total of intermittent naps of 21 hours over a 11 day period, and thereafter slept 31 hours consecutively. There was a great demoralizing effect on the whole organization due to the fact that the order for the 131 additional tank lighters had not been confirmed, and, further, production was stopped when the 50 tank carrying lighters were completed, or were in line for completion. During the remainder of the month of June, 1941, and the month of July, many conversations were held by the principals of this company, by telephone, with officers in the Bureau of Ships—the very same officers who had at the time of the perturbation, excitement, or need, discussed an extension of the previous order for 50 lighters by an additional 131.

A most peculiar reaction occurred at an inquiry regarding an order for the additional 131 lighters. Mr. S. W. Eaton, Washington representative of Higgins Industries, daily visiting the Bureau of Ships, and with many friends therein, discovered a most peculiar, crab-like reaction on the part of anyone in the Bureau upon questioning or interrogation regarding the order.

On August 19, 1941, or August 20, 1941, Mr. S. W. Eaton telephoned the writer and told me that he had met Colonel Gilly Lockwood at the Army & Navy Club, and that there was with the Colonel a man from the American Car & Foundry Co. The Colonel started off the conversation by saying, "Well, I guess that Higgins will get the 131 tank lighter order." Now, Sam Eaton knew about this will-o-the-wisp 131 boat order, but was surprised to have Col. Gilly Lockwood, Washington representative for American Car & Foundry, refer to it (Note: S. W. Eaton, before he went to work for Higgins Industries, was also in the employ of ACF, under Col. Lockwood, and Eaton therefore knew all of the various negotiations, contracts, etc. that the ACF had with the Navy on the previous and provenly defective or faulty design and construction of tank carrying lighters. Sam Eaton, our representative, then, and now, also knew the circumstances of how the A.C.F. got the orders; the price they got for them; the extras and prices therefor; and the circumstances of the delayed deliveries and of the poor performance). Col. Lockwood is a splendid gentleman and ex-officer, and nothing is here to be inferred as any reflection on him, other than Eaton, unfortunately, by his own admission, registered some surprise, and especially when the other representatives or officer of the ACF remarked that "Well, Higgins could show anybody up on performance, but unquestionably lost his a—— on the order for the 50 lighters. Maybe he will get good sense and bid high enough to where the ACF might have a chance."

Now, the point of this is that the representatives of American Car & Foundry took it for granted that Eaton, Washington representative of Higgins Industries, knew that the Bureau of Ships had prepared specifications and invitations to bid on an order for 131 tank carrying lighters—which unquestionably the ACF knew all about, but which Eaton didn't know a damned thing about.

Now S. W. Eaton is a graduate of Annapolis and is a retired naval officer. Naturally, he has friends in the Navy Department, and he found out that the Bureau of Ships was very much concerned in that Higgins Industries, the company he represented, had within 2 1/2 days time designed and submitted to successful tests a boat that had given an unusual performance; that it was a design that Higgins had previously been trying to get the Bureau of Ships to accept, for years—Eaton found out from gossip and infiltration in the Bureau that the Hull Design Section of the Bureau, and the officers and personnel in the Bureau of Ships had determined that Higgins was going to be "frozen out" and that they were going to rush this thing through and that Higgins was not going to have a chance to bid, or negotiate, or a chance to construct any of the 131 tank carrying lighters. Now, this was not later than August 19th, 20th, or 21st, 1941. During the afternoon of August 23rd, 1941, Eaton found means to see the design and construction drawings of the Bureau's design and telephoned me the night of August 23rd. On August 24th there was held a very elaborate dedication ceremony of the Higgins two million dollar City Park Plant, to which dedication the U.S. Navy sent very estimable officers, to give us "lip service" for our accomplishments, to wit: that this plant and other plants had been built without one cent of subsidy, or by any loan from the Government, and that during the time this plant was started, from nothing, on September 11, 1940, until August 24th, 1941, we had not only built this vast plant, but while building same, had constructed therein 1,668 steel and wooden boats.

Now, it may be worthy of note in passing that 10 days prior to the dedication ceremonies, i.e., on August 14th, 1941, officers of Higgins Industries requested through the proper channels, to the Bureau of Ships, that shipments of boats that would be constructed from that date, August 14th, up until the date of the ceremonies, Aug. 24th, be withheld from shipment so that such boats built during that interim could be used in a great stimulating, morale building, spectacular demonstration. This request was cold-bloodedly refused,—In spite of the fact that construction and shipment and deliveries of boats was way ahead of schedule of contractual requirements. Accordingly, the management of Higgins Industries appealed to its workmen, and absorbing the overtime expense, constructed over and above the advanced rate of deliveries, an additional 52 boats, being the number of boats constructed in a matter of 5 days, starting from August 19th through August 24th, so that on the date of August 24th there were 52 boats of various categories ready for participation in the magnificent marine spectacle.

On the night of August 24th, 1941, while the management was entertaining 1,400 guests at a big reception at the Southern Yacht Club, the writer received a long distance telephone call from our representative, Mr. S. W. Eaton, with further reference about the Bureau of Ships' methods to see to it that Higgins Industries knew nothing about, or had no opportunity to bid on the 131 additional tank lighters. In spite of this information, and this poisonous attitude of the Navy Department, full and due courtesies were continued to the considerable, if not great number, of Navy guests present. A. J. Higgins left for Washington by plane at 10:55 PM the night of August 25th but before catching the plane that night telephoned Commander Ross B. Daggett, at his home, as A. J. Higgins speaking to another individual named R. B. Daggett, making him aware of the writer's knowledge of these peculiar circumstances and of the writer's knowledge that the design of the Bureau type tank lighter was poor.

I will go to another person in this revelation of incidents.

I appealed to Commander Daggett in this telephone conversation, telling him that I thought he was a serious officer. I told him that I had heard he was a leader and the No. 1 man of his department. (I gave him attributes that I knew he didn't have). I told him that I didn't blame him for it. I told him that I believed there was a civilian hierarchy in his department that was undermining him. I told him I thought this was awful. I talked to him of the approaching war. I told him of my experience and recollection of the mismanagement of World War I, and I told him that naturally I felt that we were coming into another one that would be as bad, or worse than the first in mismanagement.

Commander Daggett did not respond to this appeal, but very curtly told me that he was well satisfied and that he thought the Bureau had a very good design of boat (tank carrying lighter). He would not commit himself that there was anything pending, or any prospect for any placement of an order for additional tank lighters. He asked me where I got my information, with the inference that there was something wrong, or surreptitious about my being aware of the thing. I told him that I fought fairly; that I did not have to place this call to him; but that I was telling him and warning him that I had given him the opportunity of reviewing this thing; that I would continue to do this; and that when I arrived in Washington the next day, I would call to see him.

I got to Washington the morning of August 26th. I saw Daggett. His attitude was so cold that I did not pursue the subject. In a way that I will not explain here, I had an opportunity to see the design and construction drawings of this 47-ft. Bureau design tank carrying lighter. It was god-awful.

Up to this time, I had not had much contact with Capt. Ned L. Cochrane. My representative, an ex-Navy officer, Mr. S. W. Eaton, said that he was a wonderful fellow; a hard working man; serious; and above reproach. Other dear friends in the Navy said the same thing. I called Capt. Cochrane over the phone and asked for an appointment. My usual good memory fails me as to the exact hour. I think it was 2 P.M. sharp, August 27th, 1941. I have failed in this narrative to mention that I took to Washington with me Mr. George O. Huet, a most competent man having a B.S. in Naval Architecture; a man with 36 years experience, concentrated and specialized in the design of small boats; a man who has been in my employ, and a friend of mine for 20 years; a man whose experience is outstanding and who has been given the signal honors for his ability and his accomplishments.

At the appointed hour, I went into Capt. Cochrane's office, accompanied by George Huet and Sam Eaton, but, to my astonishment, I found that in addition to Capt. Cochrane, with whom I had the appointment, there was also present Commander Daggett and a number of other officers and civilian employees of the Hull Design Section, and as my memory is very vivid on the subject, a certain Mr. Ed Monroe, being the same party who during the course of a dinner with me had told me that he had not been on a boat for some 15 years, but who had taken over an active part in the work of the Navy's Hull Design Section (Bureau of Ships). I shook hands only with Capt. Cochrane, who asked me to have a chair. After this slight incivility of mine, Capt. Cochrane throwing himself back in his chair, proceeded to give me a lecture on the competency of the Navy; the regulations of the Navy; the routine of the Navy; the judgments of the Navy, etc. Mr. S. W. Eaton and Mr. Geo. O. Huet never said a word and neither did I, but I kept looking at my wrist-watch and at the end of 22 minutes of this diatribe, I stood up and interrupted the captain and said, "Captain, thank you very much indeed. Good day, Sir." Turning to George Huet and Sam Eaton, I said, "Come on, let's go," and the three of us started leaving the office. This movement caused consternation, and Capt. Cochrane and the other officers in the foreground, and the civilian employees trailing, followed us down the corridor, asking, "Didn't you have something to see us about?", and I replied, "Yes, I did, but you have all the answers." Capt. Cochrane said, "Well, there is always two sides to a question." My reply was, "But you have the answers to all sides. Good Day, Sir.".

I then proceeded to the office of Admiral S. M. "Mike" Robinson, and saw his secretary, a Miss, or a Mrs. Hinkle, and asked for an appointment with the Admiral. This was arranged for 3 P.M. the following day, August 28th.

On August 28th, 1941, at 2:30 P.M., I went into the office of Admiral Bryson Bruce, his office being nearby and convenient to the office of Admiral Robinson. I have the highest of regard and respect for Admiral Bryson Bruce. At 5 minutes until 3 P.M., when I was preparing to leave, Capt. Ned Cochrane burst into the office of Admiral Bruce, and started to say something, before he recognized myself and Sam Eaton. Capt. Cochrane was a very embarrassed gentleman.

Admiral Bryson Bruce (who at that time was a captain, but I, a civilian, through the grape-vine had been advised was soon to be an admiral) affectionately put his hand on my shoulder and told me to be calm and to take it easy.

Sam Eaton and I went to Admiral Robinson's office at 30 seconds to 3 P.M. Mrs. Hinkle, his secretary, said the Admiral was waiting for me. I had not informed the Admiral's secretary that I was taking Sam Eaton with me, so in this respect I had presumed on the arrangements of the appointment. I went into Admiral Robinson's office, and was actually shocked and surprised to see that notwithstanding that the appointment which was arranged as a personal one, and promised as a personal one, that there, attendant, in a semi-circle, was quite a group of officers, seated across the room, facing the Admiral, whose back was to the window, facing Constitution Avenue. There was one empty chair in the middle of these officers, apparently placed there for me. There was an officer on the left of the Admiral. I asked this officer if he would let me have his seat, alleging that I was suffering with my eyes. This bumfuzzled or otherwise perturbed the assemblage, but which put me on a parity with the Admiral, both of us being with our backs to the glare of the light from the windows, and gave me, with the Admiral, the advantage over the circle of officers facing us. In the assemblage were Admiral Howard, head of the Hull Design Section of the Bureau of Ships; Captain (and later Admiral) Claude A. Jones, of the Bureau of Ships, Ship Construction Division; Capt. N. L. Cochrane; Commander Ross B. Daggett; Commander E. E. Roth; and many other officers of equal or lesser rank. I was well composed, but inwardly angry. The Admiral, whom I admire, and whom I believe really likes me, as he had previously demonstrated by little gestures such as patting me on the shoulder, etc., turned to me with an ingratiating smile and asked in these exact words, "Well, Mr. Higgins, what do you want to see me about?". I replied, "Well, Admiral, I am surprised that you should ask me that. If you don't know what I want to see you about, then why the hell have you this congregation of officers here? But, I want to ask you one question; is this a Summary, or Drum Head Court Martial? I see I am 'it'." The Admiral smiled, but nobody else did. I continued, "Well, you know what I want to see you about, and inasmuch as I see you have this assemblage here and I occupy an odd seat, I might as well be frank, and blunt. Therefore, I will come to the point rapidly. However, before being frank and blunt, I want to pay due tribute to the Navy; to its parent educational organization, Annapolis; you give a very short 4-year course of training there. The cream of the country, in competition, goes there, and in four short years they acquire certain arts and graces, with some education. They learn a lot of things, for instance, fancy dancing, football, fencing, boxing,—things like that, and better, and thereafter, those who are anointed are selected to become the upper classmen and I am sure that most of these gentleman and officers whom the magic wand has touched and who are so gifted, have an additional opportunity for training and education, usually at one particularly estimable institution of learning, Massachusetts Institute of Technology. And, now, as I said I would, I am going to be frank and blunt. These six years of training are not comparable to what I have had. The things I have to say may hurt, but I hope my remarks will be well taken, because they are meant constructively; but to shock you and to bring it home to you, I want to say that there are no officers, whether present in this room or otherwise in the Navy who know a goddam thing about small boat design, construction, or operation—but, by god, I do."

It is worth all the trouble and torment I have gone through then and have gone through since to have been able to study the facial reactions of the assemblage, but the Admiral did chuckle.

I will pass over a lot of things that transpired at this meeting, but I did tell the Admiral and I told the assemblage of officers in his office a few things, which should they have been well received would have been good for their mortal souls, and should have been a concentration of additional education to such as they had received previously. I pointed out to them, among other things, that it should have been a well known fact to anybody in the Navy, and that if they didn't know it, then they were negligent or incompetent—that I, myself, and my companies had devoted ourselves over the years, and had specialized in the design, successful development, and the building of boats that performed remarkably under various conditions; particularly shallow draft boats. I pointed out to them that if they had any interest in our country, and in the Navy, at that, that they should be aware of the fact,—and it certainly was not any fault of our company that they didn't know it,—that we specialized in such craft; that we were people who knew what it meant to meet a payroll; that we are a commercial firm that had to be efficient because we weren't subsidized by the Government, or otherwise suckled by the tax-payers; that we have customers all over the world who have dealt with us and that whenever the words "shallow draft boats" is mentioned anywhere in the world, anyone concerned with such a problem of navigation thought of Higgins Industries. I referred to letters and tenders to the government, offering everything that we had to our Government and to the Navy in general; our full cooperation, and I pointed out to them and asked them to deny if they had at any one time ever asked our assistance in design, which had many times been previously proffered to them, without any request for remuneration. I told the Admiral and officers assembled there, and reminded them of something they should not have to be reminded of; that I was a fighter—above all, an American—that I was no honor-seeker—that I was no "profit hound"; that all I and my organization wanted was to serve our country—that my record was behind me—but that the Navy had consistently refused to give me the opportunity to cooperate or serve.

On that date, August 28, 1941, I very forcefully brought out the fact that there were specifications outstanding in the Navy Department for additional tank lighters and that bids were to be received and contract awarded on September 3rd, 1941—a few days thereafter—and that by god the Bureau of Ships' monstrosity (and I used that very word, because it came from me originally and spontaneously at the time) of a 47-ft. tank lighter was an 'abortion of a hermaphrodite'—and much to my disappointment, there was not one of those gentlemen in the assemblage—in their perturbation—who had one bit of humor to appreciate this incongruous insult. This was a Kilkenny cat affair—everybody talking at once. I pointed out to the Admiral that there were men in that very room who were responsible for the fact that my company had not received the specifications; the drawings; or the opportunity of giving a competitive bid;

that I did not want to receive it now; that it would be criminal to go ahead with the Bureau design and purchase 131 of these damned poorly designed 47' Bureau type tank lighters. I proposed then and there that we would build one, expeditiously, and without cost to the Navy, to show them how terrible it would be; how unstable, and how unseaworthy it was.

The result was that Admiral Robinson called the pandemonium to order and instructed them that no more than 4 of these should be purchased, and that by reason of the fact that many of our patriotic workmen had been laid off, an order should be negotiated with us, that we should submit a specification, and that an order should be given us to build 20 of the Higgins' design tank lighters. These were the Admiral's instructions, but they were not carried out. The people under him who run the Bureau of Ships saw to it that the order for the Bureau type lighters was increased to 10.

The upshot of it was that we were the low bidders on both types of boats, the Bureau type and our own.

At that hearing, I pointed out that the machinery of the Bureau of Supplies and Accounts functioned peculiarly, by reason of the fact that we had never had the opportunity of receiving the specifications, drawings and invitation to bid on the 131 Bureau design tank lighters, in spite of the fact that we were not only known to be specialists in craft of this type; that we were the foremost and best qualified builders, as was well proven by our previous performance, but that we were properly registered with the Bureau of S&A, and that specifications and invitations to bid on anything in that line should automatically be sent to us, as taxpayers, and as Americans, with an opportunity to bid.

Thereafter, a lot of funny things happened. S. W. Eaton heard—I heard—and various people went out of their road to tell us how terrible we were; that we were going to be punished—and were we punished? Adroitly and cleverly! Our experience before this—and after this—has been goddam awful. It stinks and I have had to be good to live to go through with it.

In the above, I overlooked to set forth the most essential pieces of information, as follows: The specifications called for 131 tank lighters; the bids were to be opened on September 3, 1941. In the Truman Committee Report, there is a note to the effect that the Admirals of the Navy said I was in error as to the date of the opening of the bids. They were confused as to the opening date of the bids, for it was on August 28, 1941, in the confusion in Admiral Robinson's office that he requested that these specifications be recalled and the invitation to bid be canceled. Later, they came out with specifications for, not 4 boats, but 10 of the Bureau type lighters, and 20 of our design, at that time in a length of 47 feet. I think these specifications called for bids to be in not later than the later part of September, 1941. We bid low on the 10 Bureau type lighters and were awarded the contract, and there were no other bids but ours for the 20 lighters of our design. (Note: In the conference of August 28th, in Admiral Robinson's office, I agreed to dedicate my design rights and the use of such patents that we possessed thereon to the Navy without charge for the duration of the war period, giving them the opportunity of requesting competitive bids from others.)

We were the low bidders on both types of tank lighter.

A study should be made of the table of orders as placed by the Bureau of Ships, as shown on the last page of the Truman report, which will reveal that the total quantity of 131 lighters were placed with piece-meal procedure with us and many other firms. I want to bring out that this order for 131 tank lighters was alive in May, 1941 and was not disposed of in that year. The fact that we were not invited to bid until after the hectic meeting in Admiral Robinson's office August 28, 1941 evidences bias and prejudice with wilful intent to disregard our talents.

A study should be made of certain telegrams that Higgins Industries sent to Admiral S. M. Robinson and others in the Bureau of Ships following December 7th, during which time we were in peril of running out of orders. On December 23rd, 1941, the Bureau of Ships gave verbal orders for some 400 of our boats, of which 200 went to Chris Craft Corp., Algonac, Michigan. This order was confirmed to them officially on January 13, 1942. We have proof, and the record of shipments of engines from Gray Marine Motor Co, of Detroit, will reveal that at that time they had shipped to Chris-Craft Corp. 167 engines. (Note: At that time, Chris Craft had not even started construction, or had not progressed very far, whereas we had then only recently been awarded new orders, but had hundreds of boats built for which there were no engines; in other words,—we had the boats and no engines, and Chris-Craft had the engines but no boats built to install them in.)

Whereas the investigations more or less are confined to steel tank carrying lighters, the evidence of prejudice towards us on the part of the

Navy is greater and more forcefully revealed when the Navy's dealings with us on tank carrying lighters and landing boats are combined. Accordingly, it is our opinion that no proper revelation can be made to anyone in the Navy who is really interested in making a correction, unless the affair is viewed and a study is made, as a whole, of the tank lighter program and the landing boat transactions.

Mr. Gottesman, our secretary and treasurer, should furnish copies of letters, to Capt. N. L. Rawlings, containing an analysis of our labor cost and the cost of our higher grade of materials in comparison with the materials as used by others; for instance, the Chris-Craft Corporation, of Algonac, Michigan.

There is another thing which might be too tedious for investigation or study and that is, the possible willful mismanagement on the part of the Navy in delaying the confirmation of orders that had been negotiated; their delay in furnishing contract numbers and priorities; the disturbance this caused, and the delay they caused in our getting steel and other materials when they elected in January and February of 1942 to take the procurement out of our hands on the theory that they could get the materials for us more rapidly than we could,—but which they did not do successfully,—resulting that we, ourselves, had to turn around again and procure our own materials, where the Navy had been unable to accomplish this successfully.

Senator Truman's committee has already compiled and taken a lot of evidence and testimony, and has investigated and obtained reports from the "Forces Afloat" revealing their opinions of the characteristics of the different types of landing boats and tank carrying lighters and it is understood that a great deal of this testimony evidences that the Bureau of Ships paid no attention whatsoever to the requests, or the directives sent in to the Navy Department by the people in the field, using the boats. Whether this was wilful, or just another evidence of their prejudice to keep us from getting orders for our design or craft, I do not know.

Without attempting to make verifications, but resulting from all the contacts with the people in the Bureau of Ships, I would say that the following people, whom I will herein name, are the most responsible, towit:

There is a civilian employee in the Bureau of Ships named ED MONROE. He is employed in the Hull Design Section. This man is of a peculiar character. Outside of the Bureau, he is a lovable character; an American; a Virginian; a scholar; a gentleman; and a very competent man on marine design in the larger type of vessels. He has been for a great number of years in the Bureau of Ships, and he has many successful designs and much hard work to his credit, at a low salary, his successes confined to larger types of vessels. He has never been given the opportunity to go out into the field, or to go out on or to be on and to study the performance of vessels, and certainly knows very little, if anything, about small boats. He is very prideful, and will not take any suggestions from anyone. He won't even communicate with, or cooperate with very competent people in small boat design in the service of the U.S. Coast Guard. Ed Monroe would like to like us, but, unfortunately, without any intent on our part, our designs were so different from his and where our designs performed successfully, his did not; and he has built up a hatred for us which he, himself, doubtless does not realize he holds.

Working under Ed Monroe there is a young chap named FYFFE. Fyffe comes from a family of good boat builders. He has a very competent brother who is operating a yacht and small boat repair yard in the New York City district. Young Fyffe went to some technical school, and thereafter went into the Navy. It is too bad that he didn't go to work with and stay some years with his brother, to become broadened in his knowledge; to gain more experience, and to become wholesome. Working under Ed Monroe, in the Bureau, he has become "bureaucratic" and nasty. He is as smart as a whip, but he has built up for himself an ego that apparently checks his mental growth, and he is very vicious and bitter.

Over these two men is a very estimable naval officer, Commander Ross B. Daggett, who has never ceased to forget that he was No. 1 in his class at Annapolis. He is greatly over-worked and is really over-burdened with duties, and has to rely on Monroe and Fyffe, and, due to his training, backs them up regardless. Commander Daggett is a well intentioned, honorable man, but has a very poor memory. He frequently agrees to things, approves them, and orders them, and later on forgets and denies vehemently having done so, failing to recall his agreements. If there is any officer to blame for the bureaucratic non-constructive and obsolete methods of design and routine in the Hull Design Section of the Bureau of Ships it is Commander Ross B. Daggett,—unless you want to blame it on his immediate superior, who is Captain Ned Cochrane; another finer officer and gentleman you could not meet, outside of his maintaining that he is competent to design small boats, as he most certainly is in the *re-*

pairing of large ships. Capt. Ned Cochrane is a bureaucrat, as all construction officers were, and are, in their place.

There is a very competent officer engaged in engineering for the Bureau of Ships, on a parity with the social attributes of Capt. Cochrane. This is Captain EARL MILLS. This man is a 'go getter'; is very competent and worth while; but he is hamstrung by a lot of incompetent naval assistants who are under him, such as Commander GEORGE PRIFOLD, who has absolutely no competency for the duties he is attempting to perform. The only way he can serve is to do nothing, or to place his faith in the hope that the contractor will give him proper information.

There is another naval officer, COMDR. HEISER. In another place with other duties, he might make a most excellent officer. At the present time, he is a candidate for a Psychopathic Ward, or else he is bordering on a nervous breakdown. He is emotionally and mentally overbalanced. He is very self-opinionated, argumentative, and will not reverse himself, even when he knows that he is wrong.

Again, in this group of young officers, there is a chap named Commander J. W. (Bill) Kern. He was recalled from civilian life and it is surprising that his experience derived from his trade pursuits in civilian life did not benefit him more, for he is not of much service to the Navy in the duties he is attempting to perform. He is rather peculiar in that he always agrees with anyone on a matter for immediate discussion, but takes an opposite position when he has gotten out of sight. He, himself, thinks he is conscientious, but he has made some very bad decisions that were destructive and costly. He will make no decision that he thinks would not meet with the pleasure of his immediate superiors.

ADMIRAL HOWARD, by reason of his age, or otherwise, is completely unsuited for his duties.

ADMIRAL CLAUDE A. JONES was a hero; made a marvelous and heroic sacrifice to save his men in a boiler explosion aboard the *U.S.S. Memphis*. He is very cold-blooded and has strictly carried out a policy laid down by his predecessors, that of concentrating ship construction on the Atlantic Seaboard, which, peculiarly, always seems to be of particular benefit to Bethlehem Steel Co. as well as subsidiaries of the U.S. Steel Co. It has been thought by many that his close friendship and association with Mr. Joseph Powell, a $1.00 per Year man in the Navy, and ex-Vice President of Bethlehem Steel Co., and a class-mate of Admiral Jerry Land

and one Mr. Otterson, may have strong bearing on Admiral Jones' activities and administration.

Of a sinister influence in the Navy is Joe Powell, who brazenly continued his duties in the Navy Department after February 6th, when there was a majority and a minority report from the Supreme Court of the United States which made it plain that Joe Powell can be likened unto the Scotch robber, Rob Roy, who denied being a thief but admitted being a robber. This is reference to the three million dollar suit brought by the Navy against the Bethlehem Steel Co.

Another outside, sinister influence is the Electric Boat Co., and their subsidiary, the Elco Boat Works. Messrs. Sutphen and Chase, and a Mr. Spear, whom Zorinoff (spelling doubtful, here) referred to during World War No. 1 as "My dear Lieut. Spear," compose the nucleus of this organization. The Navy Department, and our Administration has been very cagy and secretive about their subsidization of the Elco Boat Works for the construction of their plant and the construction of Motor Torpedo Boats; sufficed to say that it has not been denied that the U.S. Navy was paying Elco in excess of $250,000 each for a 70' motor torpedo boat at a time when Higgins Industries was building a sturdier 70-ft. Motor Torpedo Boat for the English at a price of $110,000.00 each, which was later found to be too high on some twelve boats, and we refunded the English $38,000.00 on the contract. Note: At the present time, Higgins Industries are building a big, powerful, and sturdy Motor Torpedo Boat, in a length of 78 feet, at a price of approximately $120,000 each, and it is whispered that the contract price to the Elco Boat Works, of Bayonne, N.J., for a more lightly built boat, was in excess of $170,000.00 each; whereas Higgins Industries took their contract with the spirit and intent that the boats were to be complete, with no extra charges, it is common discussion that the Elco Boat Works, on each boat, run up a lengthy bill of extras for items not specifically, (and probably intentionally) not mentioned in the contract.

Higgins Industries, with the single exception of here recently, has not had a sizeable order for motor torpedo boats, and each order has been compromised and held in an uncertain state of querulousness and the Navy has raised questions as to the speed of the boats; such questions being raised in the face of the fact that the Navy has defaulted in furnishing us with the proper government furnished propellers with which to obtain the proper speed. We overcame this by designing and constructing our own propellers to obtain the desired speed. In the month of September, 1942 (this month), we were actually notified to cease construction, at that time, the notification being that there was a possibility that the order would be canceled.

In connection with Landing Boats, even though we were the developers, the patentees, and made great sacrifices to give good performance, and having had great difficulties in even forcing the Navy to even consider the design, we have been badly handled. We have never been given any worth while back log of orders. On each order, regardless of its size, its completion has been hampered by frequent changes desired by the Navy,—many of them silly. The records in the Truman Committee report, and other records available, will show that we were in a continuous state of rush on small, special orders, rushing them to completion only to work ourselves out of a job; then only to have a stop-gap. This has been continuous,—yet, in December, and probably on the 13th of January, 1942, a concern, notorious in that they didn't care for government business, was awarded a contract for 200 boats of our design, the order given them without the Navy so much as saying thank you for the confiscation of our patents, and, immediately following that, the Navy made awards for 1,925 boats of our design to the Chris-Craft Corporation, making this award actually at a time when we were completing the last of the only order we had.

If all of this doesn't show willful prejudice, then I am the Pope of Rome.

Extraneous Comments: Ask the officials of the Navy Department what was the size of the personnel in the whole of the Navy Department during World War No. I. Have them break this down between Operations, Navigation, and what is now the Bureau of Ships. This question will please President Roosevelt, because when he was Assistant Secretary of the Navy, he did have a most efficient organization. He whipped the Navy into line from a dead personnel with rusty boats into an efficient striking force when we went to war. The present Bureau of Ships is an outgrowth of the previous Bureau of Construction & Repair. In the years of 1939, 1940, and early 1941, the Bureau of Ships was a small organization. They, of course, were not doing anything anywhere near comparable to what they are doing now. Many of the excellent officers then with them have been sent to sea. Those who were kept were of the "swivel chair" type. The Bureau of Ships has grown like a mushroom. No industrial concern with the proper management would ever have such a cumbersome, outlandish, and inoperative octopus as has the present Bureau of Ships. They have erected new buildings covering acre after acre; the corridors and offices are a mystic maze. The workings of the personnel are just as mystic and as much of a maze as are the endless corridors, halls and offices. It is too bad that they didn't design the whole Navy Department so that it could be spun. If the "red tape" and the outmoded and outlandish Civil War methods of doing business were eliminated, the work could be done in the Bureau of Ships very efficiently with about one-sixth the present personnel.

Captain N. L. Rawlings attends to the negotiations of contracts and the purchasing; that is, he is the principal one. An accomplished civilian employee, taken from industrial life, and well experienced and qualified could possibly do this much better and certainly free from Navy bias; at least an individual would not be circumscribed by the desire to retain all the Navy prerogatives.

The training of Navy men at Annapolis, and particularly the training of upper classmen, after leaving Annapolis, all tends to make them negative individuals and the Navy organization becomes imbued with their own omnipotence. They do not admit it, but within themselves and amongst themselves, they despise civilians. They even despise lower classmen, and class themselves as superior human beings after becoming a line officer. The construction officer despises the engineering officer, and the engineer looks down on the line officer. Their training is such that they cannot reverse themselves, even when they know they are wrong. They will not take constructive suggestions from an outsider, unless the suggestion comes in a form that they can claim it as an original idea of their own. Whereas the Army Academy is quite similar and the graduates therefrom are imbued with their own importance, the same as the graduates from the naval academy, the Army officer more quickly and generally comes in contact with the public, and with industrial business, and his horizon being broader, he becomes more of a positive type; the result being that the Army is a positive organization, whereas the Navy is a negative one.

Nothing could be healthier for the Navy as a whole, and the country that they really desire to serve, than that there be a 'house cleaning' in the Bureau of Ships. It would be preferable that quite a number of officers and civilians therein go to other duties.

Maybe the dismissal or transfer of only one officer would accomplish the desired results, if it were known throughout the Bureau that it was a punitive measure taken because of actions or attitudes detrimental to the country's welfare. My personal opinion is that the removal of Captain C. A. Jones would be a salutary measure. Certainly Commander Daggett should have another assignment, and the commanders, Kern, Heiser, and Prifold should be placed where they can either do something or nothing, but to prevent them from being obstructive, as they now are in the Bureau of Ships. Commander Roth evidenced his prejudice in the telephone conversation, and he was only sounding the sentiments and the feelings of every officer in the Bureau.

Note:—The table of the placement of contracts, as shown on Page 91, of the Truman report should be studied. It will be noted therefrom that at one time the Navy paid as high as $40,000 each for tank carrying lighters of this size. The deliveries of the total of the first 96 boats took approximately one year.[2]

Higgins' statement shows his anger and frustration with the Bureau of Ships' policies and personnel. He was certain in the summer of 1941 that officers of the bureau had conspired to keep him from building the additional 131 lighters that the navy required. The reason—jealousy.

Officers in the bureau favored their tank landing craft and felt that, given time, the boat's faults could have been eliminated. The Marine Corps and Forces Afloat felt differently. Had Higgins not entered the picture, circumstances might have forced the acceptance of the bureau's lighter. The officers in the bureau were well aware of this. They saw the success of the Higgins boat as a temporary setback, not a total defeat. After all, they held the trump card, the awarding of navy contracts.

Officers inside the bureau, especially those assigned to the Small Boat Desk, tried their best to undermine Higgins' chances of success. They hoped to gain enough time to correct the problems with the navy's lighter. In the summer of 1941 the bureau was losing its second battle

2. Higgins' "Statement," 1–22.

but still was not ready to concede the war. According to General Smith, "In the Navy, tradition never dies while there is a shot left in the locker."[3] In the spring of 1942 the bureau would use one of its last shots in an attempt to gain a decisive victory.

3. Smith, *Coral and Brass*, 93.

5

VICTORY AND DEFEAT

In the summer of 1941 Higgins Industries was a company on the verge of massive changes. It employed approximately sixteen hundred workers in its two plants and was supplying PT boats and landing craft to the British for use in the war against the Axis powers. At the same time, it was building PT boats, LCPLs, LCVPs, and LCMs for the U.S. Navy for use in training maneuvers. By the end of the following summer, Higgins employed over six thousand workers, operated from three plants, challenged the Bureau of Ships' tank lighter in a head-to-head competition, received the largest shipbuilding contract in history, and was an industrial leader in a nation at war. The company was changing at an incredibly rapid pace.

The U.S. Navy's chief of naval operations on June 5, 1941, directed the Bureau of Ships to procure 629 36-foot Higgins LCPLs (landing craft personnel, large). On July 21, 1941, the navy concluded an option for an additional hundred of the newly designed LCVPs (landing craft vehicle, personnel). The Eureka had been tested since 1938 by the navy and the marines. It had evolved into the LCP (landing craft, personnel) and then the LCPL. It was a proven boat with a long history of success. The LCVP, however, had been quickly designed and put into immediate production at the request of the navy. A few days after the order was placed for the one hundred LCVPs, the bureau received a communication from the Forces Afloat reporting deficiencies in the boats delivered in June. The engine needed to be moved slightly forward, provisions needed to be included for mounting machine guns, the coxswain's position left him exposed to hostile gunfire, and there were minor problems with the bilge pumps and the rudder.

On July 28, 1941, a second report was received, which suggested that the ramp structure was faulty and questioned the stability of the boat. Production was halted pending discovery of satisfactory solutions to these problems. Admiral Ernest J. King, commander in chief of the Atlantic Fleet, appointed a special board to study the deficiencies and to present possible solutions to correct the defects.[1]

Another major test of the LCVP occurred during late summer. On August 4, 1941, a massive amphibious training exercise took place at the marines' recently acquired New River, North Carolina, base. The base, with its 110,000 acres and ocean frontage, was an excellent site for practicing landing operations. During this exercise 16,500 men of the 1st Army Division and the 1st Marine Division, along with 300 vehicles and 2,200 tons of supplies, were put ashore over a 1,500-yard stretch of open beach. Participating in the maneuvers were 4 aircraft carriers and 42 various navy vessels.

General Holland Smith noted that the exercise brought out weaknesses an enemy could have exploited, but he considered that the "debut of the Higgins boat, complete with ramp, more than compensated for these deficiencies."[2] Even with its initial problems, the marines considered the Higgins boats far more advanced than any other landing craft thus far produced.

During this critical time of design and development, Higgins was in constant touch with General Smith either by telephone or through personal visits to the marine base.[3] He valued Smith's ideas and suggestions and incorporated them in his boats whenever possible.

As a result of his interaction with the military, Higgins realized that a proper design and high-quality construction were not enough to guarantee his boats' success. He had to be certain the military knew how to use them. The natural tendency of a boat operator is to reduce speed when a boat runs aground on a sandbar. A landing craft operates full throttle and continues to do so until it clears the bar. Even when troops are debarking on the beach, the engines continue running wide open. This procedure is extremely difficult to teach a coxswain to accept if in civilian life he has been trained to do the reverse. Therefore, Higgins knew that if his boats were to be successful his personnel would have to

1. "Report," 55–61.
2. Smith, *Coral and Brass*, 81.
3. *Ibid.*, 91.

teach the enlisted men and officers the proper techniques. The military agreed fully.

In July, 1941, Higgins established the Higgins Boat Operators and Marine Engine Maintenance School at the request of Admiral Randall Jacobs, Captain Robert Emmett, Commander Red Jamieson, and General Holland Smith. The shipbuilder fully funded the school. His only complaint was that he had to pay the heavy Louisiana state and city of New Orleans tax on gas because the Bureau of Ships "refused to take any cognizance or give any appreciation for what we were doing for the Navy." [4]

George Rappleyea was appointed as the school's director. He held his first class in the loft of the St. Charles Avenue plant with two marine officers and eight marine noncommissioned officers attending a ten-day course. The school was later moved to the lobby of the City Park facility, where more space was available for showing films, students had easy access to machine shops to study the boats' engines, and larger classes could be held. As classes continued to grow, the lectures were transferred to the Higgins West End Service Station on the bank of the New Basin Canal opposite the Southern Yacht Club. The building was converted into a school that was equipped with Hall-Scott marine engines, Superior diesel motors, and Gray diesel motors, as well as blackboards, motion picture projectors, models of the various boats, and cutaway models of a variety of key components of the craft. [5]

When the classes moved from City Park to the new West End location, the form of instruction changed from the lecture courses that Rappleyea conducted to the more practical hands-on approach of operating a landing craft. To serve as chief instructor Higgins brought in Richard McDerby. McDerby had started with Higgins in 1934 and had served as a boat operator and boat test pilot for the company since that time. McDerby was given the responsibility for teaching the men the proper techniques for operating and landing the Higgins boats. [6]

The ten-day course was designed to train men of the armed forces in the operation of the craft and in the care and maintenance of various types of gasoline and diesel marine engines. Classes were divided into two

4. "Two Years Ago—When the School Was Young," *Eureka News Bulletin,* II (July, 1943), 41; "Revisal," 39.
5. "Higgins Boat Operators School," *Eureka News Bulletin,* I (January, 1942), 15.
6. Richard A. McDerby, interview, April 11, 1992.

groups. While one group of students was afloat receiving instruction on handling and beaching landing craft, the other group was in class studying the craft's design and care. Practical experience was also offered in such areas as loading and unloading tanks and trucks from the ramped landing craft.

Instruction followed an eight-to-five schedule every day except Sunday. That day was set aside for men to attend church in the morning and then to be taken on a tour of New Orleans and the Vieux Carré in the afternoon. At the end of the ten-day period, each student was given a stiff examination, and grades were immediately forwarded to their commanding officers. Those who graduated were given a farewell party by Higgins at one of New Orleans' most exclusive night spots, the Roosevelt Hotel's Blue Room.[7]

In July, 1941, while Higgins' school was training marines in the proper operating techniques of landing craft, Sprague was taking PT 6, PT 70, and one of the 70-foot PT boats built by Higgins for the British to comparative trials being held by the navy at New London, Connecticut. In addition to the Higgins boats, the navy had four Elco boats, one Huckins Yacht Company PT, and an aluminum hull PT built by the Philadelphia Navy Yard participate in the tests. The objective was to choose a single design for future contracts. Nicknamed the Plywood Derby, the 190-mile full-throttle sea trial was designed to answer questions concerning durability and maneuverability.

The winner of the derby appeared to be Elco, but Higgins contested the results, declaring that his competitor had an unfair advantage. Elco had been issued the required ordnance by the navy and it had been properly installed on its boats, whereas Higgins' PTs had to use pig iron to simulate the ordnance weight. The iron, simply placed on the deck by the navy, moved and pounded the boats, resulting in considerable damage to the hulls during the trials. As a result of the protest, a second derby was scheduled for August 11 and 12.

Higgins' 76-foot PT 70 and one of his 70-foot boats built for Britain were entered in the new trials. His 81-foot PT 6 had already been transferred to Britain under the Lend-Lease agreement. This time, instead of a

7. "Higgins Boat Operators School," 15.

calm ocean as during the first tests, there were swells of six to eight feet and waves of ten to twelve feet. Elco's boat completed the tests with an average speed of 27.5 knots, while Higgins' PT 70 was close behind, averaging 27.2 knots.

As a result of the tests, the navy announced a new set of standards. The boats were to be powered by three Packard engines equipped with silencing mufflers. Their length was not to be less than seventy-five feet or over eighty-two feet. Additional specifications were set with the hope of ensuring that all future PTs would be durable, easy to maneuver, and designed for properly firing torpedoes and guns.

As a result of the derbies and a subsequent conference held by the Bureau of Ships, Higgins, Elco, and Huckins were invited to bid on producing PT boats. Higgins received a contract for twenty-four boats, Huckins for eight, and Elco for thirty-six.[8]

According to Sprague, once Higgins had a contract, the company changed its mind about how the boat should be designed. He recalled, "We went to a boat that wasn't quite so beamy, was stronger, was steeper, and heavier. Elco went to a boat that was more like that 76-footer [of Higgins] than their previous boat. You'd swear somebody must have gone in there and taken the lines off the [Higgins] boat which isn't that hard to do when you know how and used that for their design. Of course who would ever admit it. Though I think Mr. Higgins suspected it. I went to Elco's yard when we took PT 71 and 72 up to Melville. We stopped at Bayonne and I went through Elco's yard there. It sure looked to me like our 76-foot hull. At any rate that's all fair. We went one way [with the design] and they went the other."[9]

In July and August, while Higgins' school was training marines in the proper operating techniques of his landing craft and his PT boats were participating in the plywood derbies, his engineers were working on correcting the problems with the newly designed LCVP. The board appointed by Admiral King recommended to the bureau that Higgins build an experimental craft incorporating its suggested modifications. Instead of building the one experimental boat ordered by the bureau, Higgins

8. Captain Robert J. Bulkley, Jr., USNR (Ret.), *At Close Quarters: PT Boats in the United States Navy* (Washington, D.C., 1962), 52–58.

9. Ted Sprague, interview, August 2, 1992.

designed and built two additional LCVPs at his own expense. The three LCVPs were tested at Fort Story, Virginia, on November 16, 1941. Present at the tests were the chief of naval operations and representatives from the Bureau of Ships and the Marine Corps. On the basis of competitive trials, the most successful of the three boats was chosen and production of the one hundred LCVPs resumed.[10]

The LCVPs were built following the same procedure that was used for the earlier eighty-eight ramp landing craft. A 36-foot Eureka was built, the bow was cut off, and the ramp was installed. It was a costly procedure but necessary because there was no time to retool, and for a hundred-boat order retooling would have been more expensive.

In late October or early November, 1941, the British War Mission opened discussions with Higgins about purchasing a large number of 50-foot tank lighters. When negotiations were finalized at 150 LCMs, the industrialist began seriously considering building a new plant.[11] He mentioned possible expansion to the Bureau of Ships' procurement officer, Captain B. L. Rawlings, and to the head of the bureau's Shipbuilding Division, Captain Claude A. Jones. Captain Jones "shook his finger" at Higgins and advised against such an action.[12]

Not everyone was unappreciative of what Higgins was doing. On December 6, 1941, General Holland Smith wrote to the industrialist, "Often I ponder the question 'Where the Hell would the Amphibious Force have been without you and your boats?'"[13]

The City Park facility was filled to capacity building LCVPs and PT boats, and Higgins ignored the navy's warning and moved forward with plans for a new plant. He was willing to take the risk because he felt the 150 tank lighters for the British were only the beginning. A site was selected on the Industrial Canal not far from where the old Higgins Lumber and Export Company once operated.

A meeting was held on Sunday morning, December 7, 1941, between the owners of the property (the New Orleans Dock Board, of which Higgins was a member) and Higgins. While Higgins and his fellow board members stood on the roadside near the swampy property and discussed

10. "Report," 55–61.

11. Higgins Industries Production Ledger, in Strahan Personal Collection.

12. "Revisal," 36.

13. Lieutenant General Holland Smith to Andrew Higgins, December 6, 1941, in Strahan Personal Collection.

terms, a radio in a nearby car announced the attack on Pearl Harbor. Negotiations were concluded quickly. That same day work began on clearing the site.[14] By January 16, 1942, the marshy ground had been cleared and filled with river sand, pilings had been driven, and concrete foundations had been poured onto which the necessary structures were to be built.[15]

Higgins gave George Huet, his chief naval architect, the task of designing the plant. Graham Haddock, initially a draftsman and later superintendent of the Industrial Canal facility, assisted Huet. Haddock has been described by his fellow workers as an engineer's engineer. He would go on a site and direct the work and when an unforeseen problem arose go to the drawing board and figure out a solution.

Higgins had originally planned to finance this expansion by selling 75,000 shares of preferred stock for $1,295,850. But when only 8,416 shares were sold for $132,768 he resorted to using working capital and $380,800 of personal loans. Higgins put up $240,800, Morris Gottesman contributed $20,000, Frank P. Higgins $10,000, and Sylvester Labrot, a stockholder and director, the final $60,000. The loans were repaid in full within five months.

At the close of 1941, Higgins Industries showed a net profit after taxes of $785,643. Yet there was a deficit of working capital of $706,000. During 1941 the company had paid $600,300 in dividends on its common stock. The major stockholders were Higgins with 65.13 percent, Gottesman with 10.4 percent, and Labrot with 19.97 percent. The company still owed Finland a refund for the never delivered PT boats. With interest, the debt was now $599,718.75.[16]

On November 29, 1941, Higgins made public a lengthy letter he had written to H. J. Procope, Finland's minister to the United States, in which Higgins stressed his long and warm feelings toward the Finnish people but said he was put in a position of producing goods to help defeat Germany, with which Finland now had a military alliance. Higgins wrote: "To hope our side will win, I am forced to hope that hers will lose. Have I any other choice than to resign?"

It was an especially difficult task for Higgins. A young Finnish naval

14. Statler Hotel Statement, 12.
15. "New Higgins Plant on the Industrial Canal," *Eureka News Bulletin,* I (January, 1942), 5.
16. Rosenthal, "Higgins Industries, Inc.," 3, 6, 25.

architect, Jarl Lindblom, had come to New Orleans as Finland's representative to oversee the building of the PT boats. Lindblom, or "Jolly" as he was known, had become a favorite of Higgins. He had also been of valuable assistance to Ted Sprague and Frank O. Higgins in designing the 70-foot Higgins PT boat. When Finland recalled its representative, Higgins allowed Sprague to drive Jolly to New York so the architect could visit the Finnish delegation in Washington, D.C., and then friends in New York before returning to his homeland.[17]

Higgins had sadly relinquished his position as Finnish consul to New Orleans, but he was not yet ready to relinquish the over half a million dollars of Finland's money that he still held.

As Higgins Industries expanded during the latter part of 1941 it also increased its duties and activities. A "house organ," or company magazine, was one of the first innovations. The idea for the publication was submitted by Leroy Hall, a Higgins employee, and accepted by the company's president. As a reward for the suggestion, Hall was presented a twenty-five-dollar United States savings bond.[18]

Rappleyea was named editor of the new company publication, which made its initial appearance in January, 1942.[19] It was quickly labeled the *Eureka*. The magazine was written by and for Higgins employees, including those servicemen the world over who had worked for Higgins before entering the military.

The journal's entire staff consisted of Rappleyea and a few part-time assistants. Even with such limited manpower, the publication often ran from thirty to seventy pages, offering the reader photographs and information on company activities, stories about Higgins, letters of interest from servicemen, exploits of various Higgins craft, world news, editorials, humorous stories, and accounts of games played by the numerous baseball, basketball, and bowling teams sponsored by Higgins Industries. It also included articles written about the company or amphibious warfare that were published in other journals or newspapers.[20] On the more

17. "Higgins Resigns as Finn Consul Here; Tells Why," New Orleans *Times-Picayune,* November 29, 1941, Sec. 1, p. 4; Ted Sprague, interview, August 2, 1992.

18. Leroy Hall, interview, June 23, 1975.

19. "A Newspaper Is Born," *Eureka News Bulletin,* I (January, 1942), 4.

20. "News from Industrial Canal Plant," *Eureka News Bulletin,* I (October, 1942), 47.

serious side, it offered such services as a detailed course in welding, which the army requested because this knowledge was necessary for the repair and maintenance of welded steel craft such as tank lighters. Also appearing in later issues were a home study course in the essentials of celestial navigation and a lengthy article describing how to avoid night blindness.[21]

Like other Higgins-produced materials, the *Eureka* was of superior quality. Despite a part-time staff, Rappleyea published a paper that could meet professional standards. Its cover, photography, printing, and layouts were comparable to those of many commercially printed magazines of the period.

Another addition to the company also appeared in January, 1942, the Higgins Hospital and Clinic. The clinic, which was located on a site opposite the City Park facility, had on duty at all times one or two physicians, a dentist, and several nurses and attendants. The free service was a benefit to both employees and management. Workers were readily able to get the medical attention they might not normally be able to afford, and the company, in a time of tremendous manpower shortages, was better able to maintain a healthy labor force. The clinic also gave new workers their physicals and administered medical assistance to any employees injured on the job.[22]

Higgins saw the need for thousands of landing craft, but not everyone agreed. In November, 1941, the British Admiralty sent a delegation under the leadership of Captain T. A. Hussey of the Royal Navy to Washington to meet with the chief of naval operations and other high-ranking navy officials.[23] At the meeting the British requested production of additional landing craft. Navy officials, reverting to World War I strategy, declared that they could foresee no need for landing craft in a war with Germany. They informed the British representatives that U.S. shipyards were working at capacity building escort ships and transport vessels, and funds appropriated for use for Lend-Lease were already dedicated. It was impos-

21. "First Time in History That a Complete Welding Course Has Been Published in an Industrial House Organ," *Eureka News Bulletin*, II (February, 1943), 61–80.

22. Graham Haddock, interview, March 12, 1976.

23. Barbey, *MacArthur's Amphibious Navy*, 17.

sible, according to the navy, to include additional landing craft in the program.[24]

The British were frustrated. They realized that such archaic thinking was responsible for the low priority the U.S. Navy had given landing craft.[25] Another serious problem that plagued the landing craft program but that the British did not openly discuss was the lack of coordination between the U.S. chief of naval operations and the Bureau of Ships. The awarding of contracts to Higgins serves as an excellent example.

On June 5, 1941, the chief of naval operations directed the Bureau of Ships to procure 629 36-foot LCPLs. On July 21, the bureau ordered 162 of the 629 boats it had been directed to purchase. Earlier, in April, it had ordered 188, but 88 of these were converted to LCVPs. Contracts for 367 boats remained to be awarded. On September 19, 1941, the bureau was directed to withhold another 196 Higgins LCPLs from the contract to be converted to LCVPs. This left 171 boats not awarded by the bureau as per the June 5 directive. It was not until January, 1942, six months after the directive had been given, that Higgins received a contract for these boats.

Contracts for LCVPs fared no better. Orders were constantly delayed and received in piecemeal fashion. This led to an unstable employment situation at Higgins and resulted in higher cost to the navy because of loss of quantity discounts in purchasing material. Higgins actually employed 207 fewer men in December, 1941, than he had in June. When contracts ran out, he was forced to lay off workers until a new contract was awarded.[26]

On December 11, 1941, the Amphibian Force of the Atlantic Fleet, the service that would require most of the landing boats, requested that all future Eurekas be of the LCVP design. On January 19, 1942, the bureau, ignoring this request, awarded Chris Craft a contract to build two hundred Higgins-designed LCPLs.

The bureau then held discussions with two representatives of the Navy Department who had witnessed combat in Europe during 1941. On the

24. Captain S. W. Roskill, *The Offensive* (London, 1960), 13, Vol. III of *The War at Sea, 1939–1945.*

25. H. Duncan Hall, *North American Services* (London, 1955), 356–57, part of *History of the Second World War: United Kingdom Civil Series,* ed. Sir Keith Hancock.

26. "Report," 61–62; Rosenthal, "Higgins Industries, Inc.," 16.

basis of their observations, it was decided that the Eureka should have a smaller personnel ramp. A sketch of the boat along with plans was presented at a meeting of the navy's Landing Boat Board on February 3, 1942. With the approval of the LBB, the Bureau of Ships, and the chief of naval operations, Chris Craft was directed to convert 162 LCPLs into this new personnel ramp boat. The boat had the same features as a Eureka, but instead of the Higgins-designed 6′2″ ramp the bureau had Chris Craft install a smaller 3′6″ ramp.

The boat went into immediate production. No pilot model was ever produced, nor was the Amphibian Force of the Atlantic Fleet consulted. Apparently the Bureau of Ships felt that redesigning the ramp would not affect the stability and seaworthiness of the boat.[27]

Higgins saw this as an attempt by the bureau to steal his design. He complained that he had received contracts for only 384 LCVPs in early 1942, whereas Chris Craft had been awarded contracts for over 2,100 of the bureau's narrower-ramped Eurekas, now known as LCPRs (landing craft, personnel, ramp).

On March 9, 1942, Higgins got his first real quantity order from the bureau. This contract called for the building of 508 LCVPs.[28] Six days after the contract was let, all machinery and production from the St. Charles Avenue plant was moved to the new Industrial Canal yard. The roof of the main building had been completed, but the sides had not been built. Electricity was connected, and tank lighter production began immediately. One crew was building LCMs while another was working around them completing the building. In late March or early April, 1942, the administrative offices were moved from City Park to the new plant. Increased orders resulted in increased hiring. By the end of March, Higgins Industries employed over three thousand workers.

After tank lighter production moved to the Industrial Canal plant, the St. Charles Avenue facility reverted to a retail sales division, as it had been before the war. Under the direction of Frank P. Higgins, Higgins' brother, the downtown location grew to be the largest marine supply distributor in the South.

Higgins Industries had been known throughout the South for years because of its retail sales and shallow-draft boats. Its reputation had now

27. "Report," 60–69.
28. "Notes for Mr. Hugh Fulton," 4–5.

grown to international proportions because of its production of landing craft and torpedo boats. But it still was not as well-known as the old East Coast yards such as the Philadelphia Navy Yard and the one at Newport News. Then in March, 1942, Higgins put the name of his company on the front page of almost every newspaper in the nation. He had just negotiated with the Maritime Commission the largest single shipbuilding contract in the history of the world—a contract for two hundred Liberty ships.

Higgins had first been contacted in February, 1942, by a representative of the Maritime Commission about the possibility of building Liberty ships. At that time, the industrialist was not overly interested in such a proposal and declined the offer. He was then in the midst of the controversy over the design of the LCVP and the LCM. He also believed his present contribution to the war effort was as much as his company could successfully handle, both financially and with the labor available.[29] In March, maritime commissioner Admiral Howard L. Vickery, along with several members of his staff, visited New Orleans and for three days discussed with Higgins the possibility of his entering the Liberty ship program.[30] Higgins was hesitant. Vickery later recalled, "At first Mr. Higgins was not very much interested in it, but at the end of the talks why I think I got a little under his hide because I questioned his ability as to whether he thought he could do it or not, whereupon he took the bit in his teeth and found he could do it."[31]

Higgins agreed to accept the challenge but only with certain stipulations. First, his present shipyards were not large enough to handle a 10,500-ton Liberty ship. Construction of a new plant was required, which he could not finance. The government would have to furnish the necessary capital.[32] Second, because his plan was to construct a movable assembly line similar to the ones used by the automobile industry, he had to be certain that sufficient vessels would be built to make such a method practical. Third, he had to be assured that all of his materials would be delivered on the exact date specified. A shipyard designed according to

29. *House Documents,* 77th Cong., 2nd sess., No. 281, p. 20, hereinafter cited as *Higgins Contracts.*

30. Statler Hotel Statement, 7.

31. Fredrick C. Lane, *Ships for Victory: A History of Shipbuilding Under the U.S. Maritime Commission in World War II* (Baltimore, 1951), 185–86.

32. Statler Hotel Statement, 13.

such a theory could be highly productive, or it could be a complete disaster. If for any reason work on one ship was delayed, then work on all other ships on the line behind it had to be halted.

Once the yard was fully operational, Higgins estimated that it would be able to launch a 10,500-ton Liberty ship per day, as long as production was uninterrupted. He demanded a guarantee that even if every other yard in the nation had to stop production and sacrifice materials, he would still be supplied. He considered that the government's awarding him the contract indicated its acceptance of such an agreement.[33]

Higgins had been using an assembly line in constructing his LCPLs, LCVPs, LCMs, and PT boats, but converting such a plan to build Liberty ships would revolutionize the shipbuilding industry. The idea of movable ways was not the only unconventional aspect of the proposed shipyard. To assure that utmost speed was achieved in building the vessels, Higgins decided that there must be strong competition in the plant.

The shipyard was designed to have two major assembly lines, separated by a huge machine and fabricating shop. The industrialist suggested that one assembly line be manned by an all-white labor force and the other by an all-black force. He informed the public that he planned to establish two separate trade schools to train his laborers, one for each race. Then he assured the unions that the foremen and supervisors in charge of both assembly lines would be white. The idea was accepted by local labor leaders, and they agreed to relax some of the restrictions on the ratio of beginning workers to journeymen. Higgins also felt his plan would appeal to the president and Mrs. Roosevelt because of the implications for the advancement of the Negro.[34]

After Vickery had convinced him to build ships for the Maritime Commission, Higgins traveled to Washington to finalize the contract. He returned home on Saturday, March 14, 1942, at approximately midnight. His train pulled in at the Louisville and Nashville Railroad Station over three hours late, but there were still between two and three thousand people and a brass band on hand to give him an official New Orleans welcome home. Employees strolled along the platform carrying signs that proclaimed: "All-out production for Mr. Higgins. No strikes, no lockouts. This is our pledge." Another jubilant New Orleanian carried a ban-

33. *Higgins Contracts,* 21.
34. Lane, *Ships for Victory,* 186, 188.

ner that read: "Higgins Industries and the American Federation of Labor
will do the impossible. Guard your Liberty." Higgins and officials of the
AFL were placed atop a baggage car to address the cheering crowd. After
the speeches, the industrialist headed home under a police escort for a
well-deserved rest.[35]

Labor leaders were enthusiastic about the new opportunities. William L. Donnels, organizer of the AFL, had pledged to Higgins that if he
brought the Liberty ship contract to New Orleans "there would be no
work stoppages for any reason." This pledge was reprinted on the back
cover of the March issue of the *Eureka*. Inside the magazine appeared a
poem written by local AFL leader Holt Ross titled "Higgins Shipyard."
The last lines were

> So let's build the ways and turn out the ships,
> With no time lost and without slips,
> Then Uncle Sam and our allies afar,
> Will know Higgins men helped win this war.

Later issues included poems by Ross titled "Keep Us Free" and "We'll
Do the Job." In "We'll Do the Job" Ross wrote, "If every man works as
hard as the boss / This production battle will never be lost."

On Sunday evening, March 15, a local radio station, WNOE, broadcast a program featuring Higgins and leading labor officials as its guests.
This was followed on Thursday with a nationwide broadcast presented
by the Mutual Broadcasting System. Concurrently, feature reporters from
all the nation's major newspapers and magazines were arriving in New
Orleans to cover the excitement. Paramount cameramen filmed Higgins
in conferences and captured images of his plants rapidly producing combat craft.

A site had been chosen on the eastern edge of New Orleans for the
new shipyard. Trade schools were being readied to train the thousands of
anticipated new workers. Classes were scheduled around the clock to
prepare the projected forty thousand employees.[36]

New Orleans was alive; opportunities for employment were every-
where. Contractors needed laborers of all types to help build the plant.
Companies were expanding to supply the millions of dollars worth of

35. "Higgins Industries Now Firm of the Hour," *Eureka News Bulletin*, I (March,
1942), 1.
36. *Ibid.*

materials needed for the facility, and a shipyard of such magnitude lifted the economy of the city and directly or indirectly affected everyone. Transportation companies, grocers, gas stations, home builders, board-inghouses, shoe stores, plumbers, welders, truck drivers, and every imaginable type of service or store would be touched by the business generated because Higgins had proved he could do the impossible—take the largest plum in the history of shipbuilding away from the major yards and bring it to New Orleans.

A few days later, on March 21, another important announcement was made. Higgins had acquired the Tucker Aviation Company of Detroit, a company that held government contracts worth $250 million. Preston Tucker announced that the deal had been closed some time earlier in a meeting between himself and Higgins in New Orleans. He said the ne-gotiations began at 6:00 and concluded minutes later at 6:10. They wrote their agreement in longhand, and then both men signed it. Higgins and Tucker had known each other for over two and a half years before entering into this business arrangement.

According to the agreement, Tucker would move his entire operation and personnel to New Orleans and serve as a vice-president of Higgins Industries overseeing the new Higgins-Tucker division. A large plant was to be constructed on Chef Menteur highway on the eastern edge of town. Production was to focus on gun turrets and armament for landing craft and airplanes.[37]

As Higgins was preparing to meet his new challenges, the tank lighter controversy resurfaced. On April 4, 1942, President Roosevelt called for the construction of six hundred additional LCMs to be delivered by September 1 for the North African operation.[38] The Bureau of Ships chose to use this emergency as a chance to increase the number of lighters of its design that were being produced. Instead of constructing six hundred craft, as called for by the president, they decided to build eleven hundred bureau-designed lighters.[39] This would give the bureau a substantial lead over the number of Higgins LCMs in use. Officers at the Small Boat Desk in the bureau hoped a decisive victory might be at hand.

37. "Aviation Armament Plant Brought to Our City by Higgins," *Eureka News Bulletin*, I (March, 1942), 1–2; "Another Great War Plant," *Eureka News Bulletin*, I (March, 1942), 30.
38. Clifford, *Progress and Purpose*, 53.
39. Smith, *Coral and Brass*, 94.

The U.S. Army and Marine Corps, which were the major users of the amphibious craft, preferred the Higgins-built tank landing craft. On hearing that the bureau was going to mass produce its lighter instead of the Higgins LCM, the army decided to take action. In early May, army representatives contacted Higgins and asked permission to borrow his most qualified landing craft designers as expert consultants. The boat builder willingly sent his naval architect George Huet and Industrial Canal plant supervisor Graham Haddock to Washington.

Conferences were held between army and navy officials in which the army pushed the Higgins design and the navy insisted that its lighter was more than adequate for all military needs. The debates were held in the navy building on Constitution Avenue so the army stationed its two borrowed experts in its headquarters nearby. If a question arose that the army representatives were unable to answer satisfactorily, they would quickly send a messenger to obtain the full details or the needed drawings from the Higgins employees.[40]

While Huet and Haddock were in Washington helping the army in its battle with the navy, Higgins was in New Orleans being honored by the city at a testimonial banquet as part of its May 22 Maritime Day celebrations. At an evening affair at the Roosevelt Hotel, Governor Sam Jones praised Higgins as "a man who would shake us out of the lethargy we have been subject to for many years . . . as a man who has started a new era for Louisiana." R. J. Weinmann, chairman of the members' council of the Association of Commerce, described Higgins as a "builder of a great bridge of ships, who has placed at the command of the nation his resourcefulness, his ability, his will to do or die, so that it can be accomplished. He is a refutation of the charge that a democracy cannot fight a successful war." And John M. Carmody, commissioner of the United States Maritime Commission and keynote speaker for the evening, praised Higgins as "a two-fisted builder of ships who has taken his place beside the great production geniuses of modern times." He continued: "What you do here may well mean the difference between success or failure on far-flung fronts where the edge is with the side that has the supplies, enough and on time. What you do here will have a bearing on the civilian morale throughout our land."[41]

40. Graham Haddock, interview, June 26, 1975.
41. "Orleans Pays Real Tribute to Heroes of Ships," *Eureka News Bulletin*, I (May, 1942), 1–3.

William Zetzmann, general chairman of the banquet, then presented
Higgins with a plaque from the citizens of New Orleans in appreciation
for all he had done for the city and the war effort. Higgins rose to accept
the award. As he stood there quietly gazing at the plaque in his right hand
and resting his left hand on his hip, the room remained silent. Slowly he
began to speak in his rich bass voice:

> We are fortunate who remain behind to work in comfort. But we must think
> of those other Americans who haven't those comforts we enjoy. . . . Those
> boys who are about to give their lives for their country, those men who go out
> in their ships, some unarmed, to serve their country, to die, sometimes in
> agony, unsung, unheralded, for their country.
>
> Ships may win this war. I think that we'll build a ship a day. Yes, maybe
> we'll even do better.
>
> They're bringing the war right into our own back yard now . . . and we at
> Higgins have the means to destroy them.
>
> America is coming along, losing her complacency. Bad news won't frighten
> us. It will make us mad. Mad to win the war. We want your help. If we get
> rough, it's only because we're in a hurry. We want to build ships, ships . . .
> and boats too.
>
> But what about the "ships a day" that are being lost? What profit us if we
> build two ships a day, if they are sunk? God grant those in charge of our war
> effort that they will rise above trivialities and do everything possible not to
> defend, but to attack and destroy.

The audience of nearly a thousand political and business leaders had sat
spellbound listening attentively to Higgins' every word. As he returned to
his seat, they broke forth with thunderous applause and a standing ovation. The banquet closed with a musical presentation of Higgins' life. An
actor dressed as King Neptune with full beard, crown, and trident served
as the play's narrator. The various sketches and dances followed the life
of the industrialist from his boyhood in Nebraska to his present-day
achievements.[42]

Once the Maritime Day ceremonies were behind him, Higgins headed
for Washington to join Huet and Haddock. When he realized that the
Bureau of Ships still insisted on producing its inferior tank lighter, Higgins visited Senator Truman, chairman of the Senate Committee on Pre-

---

42. "The Saga of Higgins—A Musical, Dramatized Tableau," *Eureka News Bulletin,* I
(May, 1942), 1; "Orleans Pays Real Tribute to Heroes of Ships," *Eureka News Bulletin,* I
(May, 1942), 1, 3.

paredness. After two additional meetings with the outspoken industrialist, Truman issued a demand to the navy: "Produce one of your boats. Put it in a head-to-head operational test in competition with Higgins's product, and see what happens."[43]

On May 25, 1942, the competition was held near Norfolk, Virginia. In attendance were senior representatives from the Navy Department, the Bureau of Ships, and Higgins' allies the Marine Corps and the U.S. Army. In addition, Higgins brought along as a special guest an administrative assistant from Senator Truman's office. The gathering boarded a large navy boat and headed out to watch the long-awaited competition.

It was a cool, overcast day with winds blowing eighteen to twenty-three miles per hour and whitecaps covering the moderately rough sea. Everyone waited anxiously for the boats to round Cape Henry light. When they first appeared, they were running side by side and all looked fine. But as they turned south and headed into the open ocean, trouble began. The bureau's lighter carrying its 30-ton tank appeared to dive bow down and take on water as it headed into the waves. Several times she stopped and crew members were seen using hand pumps to bail water while other crewmen were attempting to secure the tank. At one point, the lighter began to roll and sway. Everyone watching feared she was going to capsize. The sailors with their life preservers on straddled one side of the craft in anticipation of the boat's going under. The coxswain, realizing that the boat would never make the beach, had left his position and was steering from the rail. He reduced his power and after a few moments slowly turned the lighter and headed back toward safe harbor.

While this near tragedy was taking place, two 36-foot Higgins Eurekas and the picket boat carrying the observers were standing ready in case they were needed for a rescue operation. None of these boats experienced any difficulty in the moderately rough seas.

The Higgins LCM, unaffected by the conditions, throttled its engines up to 1,900 revolutions per minute and proceeded past Little Creek to Fort Story. The only water the lighter took in was a little spray. It successfully landed its 30-ton tank on the beach in spite of poor handling by the coxswain. The lighter broached, but it had enough power to retract itself and return to deep water.

Major Howard W. Quinn of the Operations Division, Transportation

43. Krulak, *First to Fight*, 97–98.

Service of the Quartermaster Corps of the army, was on the Higgins lighter during the trials. The following day, May 26, 1942, he sent a memorandum to the Commanding General of the Services of Supply. Quinn related: "As far as comparisons of characteristics of the types of tank lighters are concerned, it may be stated that on May 25 tests there was no comparison. It was clearly demonstrated even to our enlisted men accompanying the tests that the Higgins lighter could get them there in a choppy sea and the other lighter just couldn't make the trip." [44]

Another interesting perspective may be found in transcripts of a telephone conversation that took place on May 26 between Captain John D. Crecca of the Boston Navy Yard and Commander E. E. Roth of the Bureau of Ships:

> *Captain Crecca.* We just got some disconcerting information regarding a possible change in the design of the tank lighters.
> *Commander Roth.* Possible—it's a sure thing. Yes. Isn't that a blow?
> *Captain Crecca.* It's terrible.
> *Commander Roth.* We can't afford it. We had a test down at Norfolk yesterday. Captain Cochrane went down, Commander Daggett went down, the Army went down (interrupted).
> *Commander Roth.* Well, they had a shakedown at Norfolk but a little breeze blew up. They got up to about 13 knots. The Bureau lighter almost capsized. They couldn't steer it. They just drifted around. They had to pack with the thing. Almost lost everybody on board, almost lost the tank. Higgin's tank lighter came through fine, upside in and made the beach and the poor old Bureau tank lighter was out there wallowing around. Captain Cochrane came back this morning and he saw the Chief and everybody else concerned and they sent out—did you get a copy of the dispatch?
> *Commander Roth.* Commander Daggett is coming in late tonight. I guess he's pretty well tired out. It's a pretty hard blow to him, you know. He sponsored this all along. [45]

As a result of the tests, on May 26, 1942, the Bureau of Ships notified all yards presently building the eleven hundred bureau tank landing craft to convert to the Higgins design. It was discovered that one hundred lighters were too far into production to change designs so they were com-

---

44. Senate Documents, 78th Congress, 2nd sess., No. 71, Report 10, Part 15, *Investigation of the National Defense Program*, 162–63.
45. *Ibid.*, 163–64.

pleted as bureau lighters and the remaining thousand were being built according to Higgins' plans.

To the bureau it was a tough defeat to accept, but it was over. To Senator Truman it was just the beginning. This was the sort of situation that his committee had been formed to investigate. On June 8, 1942, the Truman Committee opened hearings concerning the Bureau of Ships. The bureau was under the impression that the committee was interested in the small boat engine program. Representatives from the navy associated with this program were on hand to answer questions. Once the hearings formally opened, however, it became clear that the committee's chief counsel, Hugh Fulton, was not interested in small boat engines but in tank landing craft.[46]

On June 8 and 9 the committee questioned several key persons in the bureau. Rear Admiral Claude A. Jones, assistant chief of the bureau and formerly head of the shipbuilding program, testified along with Captain B. L. Rawlings, head of the Shipbuilding Division, and Captain Edward L. Cochrane, hull assistant in the Design Division and chief of the Preliminary Design Section. Commander Ross B. Daggett, chief of the Contract Design Section in the Design Division, was questioned, as were Lieutenant Commander R. D. deKay of the Small Boats Branch of the Shipbuilding Division and Lieutenant F. C. Nash, chief of the Special Matters Section. Also offering testimony were Major Howard Quinn of the army, who had been on the Higgins boat during the May 25 competition, and Higgins.[47] After two days of questioning, the committee decided that further investigation was warranted. It would not be until the end of the summer before a report was issued.

In June, while the Truman Committee continued its investigation, newspapers carried stories about a new Higgins Industries business venture. For several months Dudley P. South, a Higgins research engineer, had been traveling the waterways of South America far into the interior of the Amazon Basin. The purpose of the expedition was to see if there was a practical way to retrieve and export crude rubber to the United States. Supplies from the Far East were shut off by the war in the Pacific

46. "Memorandum for the Under Secretary of the Navy," November 6, 1942, p. 4, in Frank Knox Correspondence Files, 1940–44, 8–1 to 12–1, Box 15, Record Group 80, National Archives.

47. *Senate Documents*, 78th Congress, 2nd sess., No. 71, Report 10, Part 15, *Investigation of the National Defense Program*, 140.

and a new source was desperately needed. At the time of the expedition, it took up to ten days by canoe to transport rubber from the interior to Ciudad Bolívar. It was projected that a specially designed Eureka could carry one hundred tons of cargo and make the trip in twenty-four hours. The New Orleans company began producing boats for the U.S. Rubber Reserve Corporation, which was responsible for importing the rubber.

According to Dudley South, it would be possible over a period of a few years to establish regular routes between Brazil, Venezuela, and Colombia using Higgins boats and overland trucks. This could be accomplished without having to build expensive highway systems and bridges. But for now there was a war to win.[48]

In early July, as the committee's investigation continued, Higgins visited Washington. He had gone to the capital, he claimed, to renegotiate the agreement with the Maritime Commission so that his margin of profit would be less. It was not that he was opposed to the idea of profit, he insisted, but "the Government was making all the expenditures, taking all the risk," and it was not fair that he should "make $28,000,000 when many other Americans had their sons getting shot at."[49] He also strongly suggested that not only should his contract be renegotiated because it was unfair to the taxpayers, but so should all other contracts that were designed to allow such tremendous profits.

During the same period, July 9 to 11, while Higgins was discussing the revising of his contract with individual members of the Maritime Commission, the commissioners were meeting in private to consider canceling the contract because of an alleged shortage of steel. The contractor was not informed of the proposed cancellation, but Commissioner Vickery did discuss with him the feasibility of reducing the size of his shipyard. No satisfactory solution for redesigning the yard was reached, and Higgins returned to New Orleans unaware that on July 10 the commission had voted unanimously in favor of closing his new Michaud Shipyard and had notified the president of its proposed action. The commissioners wanted to be positive that Roosevelt would not reverse their decision.[50]

On the morning of July 17, 1942, New Orleans was alive with busi-

48. "Amphibian Carrier Boats Are Planned for Jungles of South America," *Eureka News Bulletin*, I (June, 1942), 1, 6.
49. Statler Hotel Statement, 13.
50. Lane, *Ships for Victory*, 193–94.

ness. Trucks were moving through the city to the site of the huge new shipyard on the eastern edge of town, delivering pilings, gravel, and tons of sand needed to fill the swampy ground. Work on Michaud was moving rapidly, the physical plant was approximately 35 percent complete, job opportunities were increasing daily, and the local press continued to carry stories of the soon-to-be built Liberty ships.

On the morning of July 18, the project came to a halt. White House secretary Marvin McIntyre telephoned informing the commissioners that they had the president's approval to cancel the project. Later the same day, L. R. Sanford, regional director of construction for the Maritime Commission, telephoned the industrialist and instructed him to halt all work on the Michaud facility—his contract had been canceled because of lack of steel.[51]

Immediate protest arose all over the nation. Only four months earlier, the largest single shipbuilding contract in the history of the world had been awarded to Higgins Industries, and now it was canceled. People wanted to know why. The Maritime Commission had previously explained to the public, through the press and radio, that the Liberty ship program was a vital part of the war effort. Higgins' contract, it claimed, had been let only because of the growing need for freight carriers.

In the Maritime Day speeches of 1942, members of the commission had spoken of the Higgins facility and explained its importance in detail. Commissioner Edward Macauley, speaking in San Francisco, had praised the West Coast shipbuilders, but he also spoke of the new yard in New Orleans, where "four shipways are being laid down, each a mile, from which would come 200 ships."[52]

The contract was canceled, allegedly, because of lack of steel. People began to question how the richest nation on earth could be short of such a vital material. Were other facts being withheld from the American public? Editorialists promptly commented on the cancellation. The Utica, New York, *Press* stated: "The contract was cancelled, not because Higgins' system had failed or been disapproved, but because officials sud-

51. *Higgins Contracts*, 23–27. *Michaud* is the spelling most often used for the name of the New Orleans shipyard before 1947 in Higgins' correspondence and in the *Eureka News Bulletin*. Today, *Michoud* is the predominant spelling. It is most likely that the federal government changed the spelling when it took over the site. The spelling used for the original French plantation there was *Micheaud*.

52. Lane, *Ships for Victory*, 189.

denly discovered they did not have enough steel to meet the country's requirements. The experience is both regrettable and humiliating. Furthermore it indicates that our resources have limits, despite all our talk about bigness." Peter Edson, a Newspaper Enterprise Association Service Washington correspondent, referring to the official reason given for the cancellation stated: "If that is the case, it is almost axiomatic that the contract should never have been let. Somewhere along the halls of government, somebody pulled the most colossal, $20 million blunder of this whole cockeyed war." [53]

Higgins had much more to say. He screamed "bias" and "foul play" from the swamps of Louisiana to the halls of Congress. He demanded an investigation into the contract's cancellation. While the Maritime Commission continued to insist that the sole reason for the cancellation was lack of steel, Higgins contended that it was not a lack of steel at all but the rate at which he would produce ships. In his opinion, the eastern seaboard shipyards knew that if he could produce a ship a day as he promised, their yards would be obsolete after the war. He insisted that several sources had informed him that his facility would never be allowed to produce ships. The heads of the large eastern shipyards would let him build his yard so long as it looked liked a "crackpot idea," but once the plan seemed to be the least bit feasible, they would use their influence to have his contract canceled. [54]

The AFL tried to use its influence in Washington to get the cancellation order rescinded. A delegation of twenty-nine labor leaders headed by J. P. McCollough, president of the International Boilermakers Union, informed Higgins that the AFL would be willing to finance completion of the plant if the contract was restored. [55] Louisiana's congressional representatives Hale Boggs and F. Edward Hebert publicly spoke out against the closing of the facility, but the contract remained canceled.

Black leaders were upset at the yard's closing and voiced their opinion. The Michaud facility was designed to have four assembly lines, two of which were to be operated entirely with black labor. The black leaders planned to send an appeal to President Roosevelt on the grounds that the

53. "America's Editorial Opinions on the Higgins Cancellation," *Eureka News Bulletin*, I (August–September, 1942), 23.

54. *Higgins Contracts*, 25–26.

55. "Pledge Higgins AF of L Cash Aid," New York *Mirror*, July 24, 1942, p. 42 (Clipping in Dawn Higgins Murphy Collection, Jackson, Mississippi).

cancellation destroyed "one of the biggest opportunities ever given to the Negro race."[56]

Over $9 million had already been spent on Michaud for the purchase of the site, landfill, pile driving, and construction of some of the smaller buildings. Hundreds of people had moved to New Orleans hoping to find employment in a shipyard that would never be built.[57]

What apparently angered Higgins the most was the manner in which he had been persuaded to accept the contract and then the way he was notified of the yard's closing. The cancellation by telephone particularly upset him. The week before he had been in Washington and the possibility of such an action had not been mentioned. Now he was ordered to stop all work on the yard immediately, which meant that he would have to release those employed at the Michaud plant, retract all orders for materials and equipment that were to be sent to the facility, and cancel all subcontracts relating to the new yard.

Higgins felt that had the Maritime Commission confronted him in person and explained the problem, some part of the project might have been salvaged. He suggested that the commission and Higgins Industries together could have continued the two trade schools until the present twenty-five hundred students had completed their course work. Then, as skilled laborers, they might have found employment in other yards. Also, measures could have been taken to protect what had already been completed at the site, and the remaining ten thousand pilings could have been driven so they would not rot on the roadside.[58]

Higgins left for Washington immediately to protest the closing of the shipyard. Both the Senate and the House investigated the cancellation, but the order remained firm. The Maritime Commission chairman, Vice-Admiral Emory Land, testified before a House investigating committee that the Higgins yard was the last shipyard to go into construction and, because it was not complete, it was considered the easiest to close. He also explained that by halting construction on the huge facility the commission would be able to reallocate tons of steel that would have gone into building Michaud to other already operational yards to be used in the immediate production of ships.[59]

56. "Shipyard Closing Protested in South," New York *Times*, July 19, 1942, p. 1.
57. *Higgins Contracts*, 12.
58. *Ibid.*, 34.
59. *Ibid.*, 76, 84, 90.

Higgins believed that the cancellation was brought about by the American Shipbuilding Association. When questioned during the House investigation, Representative Francis D. Culkin of New York asked Higgins, "Did I understand you to say . . . they were more or less a dominating or controlling influence in the cancellation of your contract, in your opinion?" Higgins replied, "I would be a damn fool if I did not believe so." [60]

Higgins left Washington on July 28, 1942, realizing there was nothing else he could do. He had testified before several congressional committees and met with various maritime commissioners, White House secretary Marvin McIntyre, and scores of other officials. President Roosevelt never saw him personally, he said, adding, "The President was pretty anxious to see me several other times before elections." [61] He denounced the District of Columbia as the "District of Confusion" and the New Orleans Association of Commerce, which unlike the AFL did not protest the yard's closing, as the "Assassination of Commerce." He was quoted as saying, "The most critical shortage in Washington was in common sense." [62] As he left the capital he remarked to a reporter, "I'm a little older, a little wiser, a lot more disgusted than I was when I came up here on March 11. I'm certainly no dumber." [63]

Although Higgins may have been correct when he claimed that the shortage of steel was not the actual reason for the closing of Michaud, he may have been incorrect in assuming that it was only pressure from the large eastern seaboard yards that influenced the decision. The shortage of steel may have been used as the reason because there was a problem, at least in the proper allocation of the metal, though the situation did not seem serious enough to be the sole reason behind the cancellation. In a letter to Mrs. Higgins, Congressman Frank Boykin, a longtime friend of the family and congressional representative from Alabama, wrote, "I want you to know this, as chairman of the sub-committee of the House Merchant Marine and Fisheries Committee, to investigate the so-called shortage of steel, the reason they gave for canceling A.J.'s contract has been gone into very thoroughly by me, and of course, I know as A.J. did

60. *Ibid.*, 46.
61. "Higgins Praises Congress," New York *Times*, July 29, 1942, p. 11.
62. Burck, "Mr. Higgins and His Wonderful Boats," 111.
63. Peter Edson, "Contract Row Makes Higgins Older, Wiser, More Disgusted," *Eureka News Bulletin*, I (August–September, 1942), 22.

that there was no real shortage of steel." The congressman did believe that the large established yards had some influence. He explained, "Well don't you see the old line yards have millions and millions of dollars invested and furthermore don't you see that A.J.'s plans would have put them out of business."[64]

The problems concerning the steel industry and the pressure exerted by the old established yards certainly entered into the decision to cancel the contract, but they were not the only influencing factors. There were several other reasons the commission favored closing the yard. First, the facility had been estimated to cost $29 million when the plans were announced in March. By the end of June, the cost was projected to be over $59 million. This was one of the major reasons Higgins visited Washington in early July and contributed to his offer to reduce the amount of profit his company anticipated making. The industrialist was not overly concerned about a large profit and suggested the reduction to help offset the increased cost of the yard.

The additional $30 million was necessary for several reasons, none of which seemed to have been purposely excluded from the original construction estimates by either Higgins or the Maritime Commission. Almost every shipyard designed and constructed during the war had to revise its contract constantly to cover rising prices, wage increases, transportation costs, or other unexpected expenses. In the case of the Higgins yard, the major portion of the increase was needed to construct a separate power plant and sewage disposal system.[65] Higgins had always predicted that the yard would run in excess of the projected $29 million, and even Vice-Admiral Land had estimated the final price at approximately $44 million. Why the $29 million figure was publicly announced by the Maritime Commission is unclear.

Another unrealistic reason given for cancellation of the contract was the discovery that New Orleans did not have housing available to handle the large influx of new laborers that would move to the city.[66] But the most important factor in the cancellation appears to have been that the Maritime Commission had underestimated the number of ships the existing yards were capable of producing.

64. Congressman Frank Boykin to Angele Higgins, July 29, 1942, in Strahan Personal Collection.
65. *Higgins Contracts*, 30, 92–94.
66. *Ibid.*, 95.

The president had ordered that 9 million tons of merchant ships be the production goal for 1942 and a combined total of 24 million tons for 1942–1943.[67] When the Higgins contract was entered into on March 13, only forty-two ships totaling 448,000 deadweight tons had been completed. It was estimated that the year's tonnage would fall short of the president's directive.

In March an average of 138.6 days was needed to build a Liberty ship from the time the keel was laid until the vessel's launching. The Maritime Commission projected that the construction time would decrease to an average of 105 days once the contractors became familiar with building the ships. By June, as laborers gained more experience and the yards entered into continuous production, the number of days required was lowered to 77.9. One yard actually had lowered production time to 40.9 days. The commission now thought it possible to produce 1,341 Liberty ships in its existing yards during 1943, thereby exceeding the president's directive by 286 ships.[68] The Higgins facility was no longer necessary. Before the House investigation committee Land testified, "We definitely . . . will meet the President's program irrespective of this cancellation."[69]

The maritime commissioners had to decide whether to complete the New Orleans yard, which they no longer deemed vital to the merchant program, or to cancel it. They chose the latter. The commissioners had originally induced Higgins to accept a contract because they believed he would revolutionize the Liberty ship program with his organizational skills and unconventional production techniques. But the already existing yards became more efficient and surpassed the Maritime Commission's projected production schedule before the Higgins yard was completed. Ironically, the very objectives that the commission had hoped to achieve by convincing the industrialist to accept the contract—increased production and more efficient shipbuilding management—were attained without Higgins' aid and were primarily responsible for the cancellation of his contract.[70]

Higgins was shocked at the cancellation but not stunned. He was still

67. Lane, *Ships for Victory*, 173–76.
68. *House Documents*, 77th Cong., 2nd sess., No. 2652, Interim Report, *Investigation of Cancellation of Higgins Contract*, 5.
69. *Higgins Contracts*, 75.
70. Lane, *Ships for Victory*, 201.

one of the largest small boat manufacturers in the nation, and orders were increasing daily for his LCVPs, LCMs, PT boats, and numerous other products. The industrialist remained one of New Orleans' favorite adopted sons, and his small boat production records continued to be unbeatable. New challenges and another record-setting contract would soon place him back on the front pages of the nation's newspapers and lure reporters from such magazines as *Life* and *Time* to visit the marshes on the eastern edge of New Orleans.

Andrew Jackson Higgins, a lieutenant in the 2nd Nebraska Infantry, was later transferred to an engineer regiment.

Courtesy Higgins Family

Higgins' first amphibious crossing experience. He was responsible for the pontoons under the bridge that allowed the troops to cross the Platte River.

Courtesy Higgins Family

Higgins Wonderboats head upriver to be delivered to the Corps of Engineers in St. Louis. The fleet of World War I transport ships, seen in the background, was sold by the U.S. government to the Japanese for scrap metal just before World War II.

Courtesy Graham Haddock

Higgins in 1920 as the head of the A. J. Higgins Lumber and Export Company.

Courtesy Higgins Family

The forerunner of the LCP, the Eureka work boat was able to take trappers and oil-field workers deep into shallow swamps where conventional boats could not go. This is an early model of the Eureka.

Courtesy Eisenhower Center, University of New Orleans

Morris Gottesman, Harry Perbes, Andrew Higgins, Clarence Bocage, Joe Labruzza, and Arthur Derbins (left to right) in a photograph taken in 1937, when the Boat Services Company was helping Higgins Industries stay solvent.

Courtesy Eisenhower Center, University of New Orleans

Andrew Higgins and his sons: Ed; Andrew, Jr.; Higgins, Sr.; Frank; and Roland.

Courtesy Higgins Family

Richard A. McDerby (at helm, wearing short-sleeved shirt) lands his first class of U.S. Marines on the shore of Lake Pontchartrain in December, 1941.

Courtesy Higgins Family

Richard A. McDerby demonstrates the ruggedness of the Eureka as he jumps the boat over a protruding piece of shoreline.

Courtesy Higgins Family

One of Higgins' favorite tests was to run the Eureka up Lake Pontchartrain's steep concrete seawall, then back it off and continue the trials.

Courtesy Higgins Family

Higgins walks with trainees of his Boat Operators School. The group, at West End on Lake Pontchartrain, was likely en route to graduation ceremonies and the large party given by Higgins afterward. Arthur Derbins, superintendent of the City Park plant during World War II, follows behind his boss.

Courtesy Eisenhower Center, University of New Orleans

LCVPs, produced at the City Park plant on a movable assembly line, slowly make their way toward the back of the plant. Once completed, they were loaded on freight cars and carried to the Bayou St. John facility, where they were launched and tested.

Courtesy Graham Haddock

PT boats were also constructed in the City Park plant, in the production bay next to the LCVPs. Once completed, they were loaded onto flatcars and transported to Bayou St. John for launching and testing in Lake Pontchartrain.

Courtesy Graham Haddock

A PT boat is cradled aboard a flatcar as it leaves the City Park plant and heads for Bayou St. John.

Courtesy Eisenhower Center, University of New Orleans

Joe Dovie, George Huet, and Graham Haddock (left to right) were key members of Higgins' engineering department.

Courtesy Graham Haddock

PT boats 6, 7, and 8 in Bayou St. John, ready for testing before being delivered to the Dutch.

Courtesy Eisenhower Center, University of New Orleans

British troops disembark from early model Eurekas along the Scottish shore during a training exercise. The boats were built for the British government at the City Park plant.

Courtesy Higgins Family

The U.S. Bureau of Ships' crew prepares to abandon ship during a competition between the Bureau's model and Higgins' LCM on May 25, 1942. Higgins' LCM was unaffected by the rough seas and successfully completed the test.

Courtesy Graham Haddock

George Rappleyea, Albert Bayley, and Higgins admire the scale model of a Liberty ship built at the City Park plant. The model was to be used for instructional purposes at the Higgins Shipyard Trade School. Master boat builder Bayley and his staff constructed the model.

Courtesy Eisenhower Center, University of New Orleans

6

COMPLEX TIMES

In late July, 1942, Captain Richard A. McDerby, chief instructor at the Higgins Boat Operators School, continued to teach U.S. Navy, Coast Guard, and Marine Corps personnel the proper techniques for handling landing craft. The Truman Committee was in the midst of its investigation into the tank lighter controversy, and Higgins was relentlessly attacking the Maritime Commission for canceling his Liberty ship contract. While Higgins fought Washington over the loss of Michaud, he simultaneously enlarged his company, expanding to a fourth location. The new plant, located fifty miles south of New Orleans in Houma, Louisiana, employed a predominantly local Cajun labor force and concentrated on producing landing craft and rocket-launching landing craft support boats. It was a hectic summer for Higgins. He constantly confronted problems related to his company's rapid growth, continued his confrontational relationship with the Bureau of Ships, and appeared before a variety of Senate and House committees investigating the production of tank lighters and Liberty ships.

The summer of 1942 was also a hectic time for Captain McDerby. The structure of the landing boat school was changing. The school had been established in 1941 to assist the navy by training landing craft coxswains and motor mechanics. From the start, the navy realized it had a manpower shortage and could never supply all the crews required for future amphibious operations. The Marine Corps and Coast Guard assisted by sending trainees to the school as guests of the navy. In less than a year, McDerby had trained more than two thousand servicemen in the operation of landing craft, but thousands more coxswains and "motor macs" were needed to prepare for future assaults on enemy-held beaches.

Early in 1942, General Brehon Burke Somervell offered to help the navy by having the army provide landing boat crews. He assembled the men, but when he tried to transfer the organization from the army to the navy he discovered that the navy did not accept draftees.[1] With the consent of the navy, the New Orleans landing boat operations were transferred to the Amphibian Command of the United States Engineers. At first, the army sent detachments of from twenty-five to fifty men to the Higgins school from the Amphibian Command at Camp Edwards, Massachusetts. The numbers soon increased, and larger quarters were required to train and house the expanded army program. To accommodate these needs, Higgins moved his school from its small West End location to the larger Camp Lincoln Recreation Area on the Industrial Canal, a mile south of his plant. Here, a permanent army detachment under the command of Major Harvey Zorn was established. The Coast Guard continued to participate, but as guests of the army rather than the navy. McDerby remained chief instructor and chose his assistants from the brightest students under Zorn's command.

By June, the navy was acquiring men in such numbers that the base at Norfolk, Virginia, was receiving a thousand new trainees every two weeks. With this large infusion of personnel, the navy realized that it needed to establish its own amphibious training bases. With the help of representatives from Higgins' organization, Navy-operated schools were established at Solomons Island, Maryland; San Diego, California; Little Creek, Virginia; and Carrabelle, Florida. Higgins also assisted the marines in establishing a landing boat school at New River, North Carolina. The new locations were closer to the main military bases and allowed for thousands of additional recruits to be taught the proper techniques for beaching a boat. Most of the instructors for the new training centers had gone through Higgins' school in New Orleans and been taught by McDerby.

As Higgins' school increased its enrollment, it also expanded its curriculum. Instead of the two-week lecture course offered by Rappleyea in 1941, students now received an in-depth six-week course covering every phase of boat handling and maintenance. During 1942 and up to the final preparations for D-Day, the curriculum was modified to address the latest situations being confronted in combat. Higgins wanted those attending the school to be thoroughly trained. When he first approached the navy

1. Dwight D. Eisenhower, *Crusade in Europe* (New York, 1948), 39.

in the late 1930s, he had bragged that his boats would "run on a heavy dew." Now that he was producing the craft for the war effort he wanted to be certain that each coxswain knew the proper techniques and had the necessary skills for landing troops dry on the beach. In addition, he wanted to be positive that each "motor mac" had successfully mastered the requirements associated with engine repair.

Classes began immediately after registration, with the new arrivals receiving an introductory lecture on what to expect during the next six weeks. Their training was broken into three two-week sessions: basic, intermediate, and advanced classes.

During basic training, the men learned the essentials of boat handling and docking, boat nomenclature, small boat navigation, engine room instruction, and plotting courses. Classes were held every day from 8:00 A.M. until 5:00 P.M. except Sunday. Evening classes were scheduled every other night from 7:30 to 9:30 P.M. The nights without instruction were reserved for study. Liberty was allowed on Saturday nights; the French Quarter, Bourbon Street, and sexy peep shows were only a few miles away.

After completing the basic class and passing a written examination, the students advanced to the intermediate level. This instruction began with a tour of the Higgins plants. Future coxswains saw firsthand the care and skill that went into producing the boats they would soon be beaching on enemy-held shores. The remainder of the classes at this level concentrated on the Scripps six-cylinder gasoline engine, the Hall Scott six-cylinder Invader engine, the Buda four-cylinder, the Packard V-12 gas engine, and the Gray and Superior diesels. Additional instruction covered emergency repair to underwater gear, using the compass and compass aids, tides and current sailing, position finding, charts, essentials of celestial navigation, lectures on signaling and personal combat, and preparing charts for patrol.

By the end of the fourth week students were given an opportunity to put their newly learned skills to use. McDerby took his sixteen boats and had the trainees plot a course across twenty-four-mile-wide Lake Pontchartrain to the Tchefuncte River on its north shore. On the return voyage the students chose coordinates on the south shore to represent enemy-held beaches. New Orleans served as an ideal target because the city was blacked out as a wartime precaution. To make the scenario more challenging, Higgins' PT boat instructor Captain Dave Young and his students patrolled the waters in six of the lightning-fast torpedo boats. All craft ran without lights. A landing boat was considered sunk when hit by the beam from a PT's searchlight. Once designated "a kill," the LCPL or LCVP turned on its running lights. Competition was fierce, especially because McDerby and Young were first cousins.

The final two weeks of instruction were spent in the advanced class. On Monday lectures focused on celestial navigation and preparing boats for patrol. On Tuesday the students boarded landing boats and practiced their skills during a run from New Orleans to Gulfport, Mississippi, on the Gulf Coast. The next day they continued their exercise until they neared Mobile, Alabama. Here, offshore in the Gulf, they waited for darkness, then attempted a practice invasion of Fort Morgan. As the boats approached the fort from the open sea, soldiers on shore fired tracer bullets high over the craft. No resistance was put forth once the boats neared the beach. By Saturday night the crews had completed their exercise and were back in New Orleans. Sunday was a day off and Monday was spent discussing problems encountered on the trip. Tuesday and Wednesday were general review days before the final examination given on Thursday. On Friday there was a discussion of the exam, and on Saturday the certificates were presented.

The soldiers looked forward to the liberty passes distributed for their final Thursday, Friday, and Saturday evenings in New Orleans. On Saturday night Higgins entertained the graduates at the Blue Room in the Roosevelt Hotel. The new coxswains and motor macs were treated to music, food, and drink at Higgins' expense. Later, when classes grew too large for the Blue Room, Higgins moved the festivities to West End Park on the shore of Lake Pontchartrain. Here, across from the Southern Yacht Club, every two weeks he hosted a massive outdoor event. Students were given a combination graduation and going-away party complete with beer, food, and music. Many students from small rural settings had never before seen the likes of such a celebration.

Higgins, despite his busy schedule, made every effort to attend the gatherings. He spent the evening drinking with the boys and telling tall tales and humorous stories. He loved the personal contact with the soldiers, and they appreciated his easy manner and down-to-earth style. Higgins worked hard and put in long, grueling hours, but on those Saturday nights he was not a major industrialist but an appreciative American doing what he could for the boys before they were shipped overseas.

He was well aware that many of those with whom he was sitting and laughing would never return from some distant shore.[2]

The presentation of the certificates and the West End party ended six weeks of hard, intensive training. If McDerby ever questioned whether the students appreciated the care and effort put forth by the instructors, all he had to do was read the letters that constantly arrived from servicemen who had been to the school and then gone into combat. One such letter was written to McDerby by navy coxswain Edward A. Weathers, who had received his diploma from the Higgins-sponsored school in January, 1942.

After graduating, Weathers was assigned to the USS *George F. Elliott* and participated in the landings at Guadalcanal. He had made five or six runs to the beach unloading troops and was back aboard the *Elliott* awaiting further orders when suddenly forty Japanese torpedo bombers appeared on the horizon. One of the planes broke formation and headed straight for the ship. Instead of dropping its load, the pilot made a suicide dive directly into the *Elliott*. Both of the sailors Weathers had been talking with were killed, and Weathers was blown thirty feet from where he had been standing. His shipmates quickly carried him to the sick bay, where he was given first aid and then ordered to evacuate the ship. The *Elliott* had taken a fatal hit. All hands abandoned ship and were rescued by a U.S. destroyer.

From a hospital bed in San Diego recovering from shrapnel wounds and third-degree burns, Weathers dictated a letter to Captain McDerby. He wished to thank his chief instructor for the training and guidance he had provided during the six-week course. The letter stressed that the landings made in the Solomons went exactly as planned and just the way they were taught in New Orleans. As a result of the training, all was accomplished with a minimum of casualties. He admitted that during training he often wanted to cut class and resented the fact that McDerby was so strict and demanding. After having been in combat, Weathers understood. He wrote, "Since coming back from real action, we certainly found out and appreciate what you taught us and which we were able to put to good use." The wounded coxswain offered his letter to McDerby

2. Richard A. McDerby, interview, April 11, 1992; *Operators Manual Higgins 36' 'Eureka' Landing Motor Boats*, (New Orleans, 1943), 7–10; "Higgins Boat School Under New Set Up," *Eureka News Bulletin*, I (August–September, 1942), 2–7.

as an aid in helping other students who might feel as he once did. But he stated, "I wish you would put it across in your own words as only you can do it, for their own sake as well as for the good of the service." He now understood why the coxswain and crew had to be prepared when the order "hit the beach" was given. When the bullets and shells started popping, it was too late to learn how to beach a boat.[3]

After Weathers was released from the hospital, he spent part of his sick leave in New Orleans visiting his former instructor. McDerby kept the letter and placed it in his scrapbook. If he ever doubted that he was being too tough or too exacting, he had only to refer to the letter to realize that Weathers and countless others were alive because of the well-built Higgins boats and the rigorous training that he and his instructors had put the men through.

While McDerby was restructuring the school in New Orleans, Higgins was preparing to reorganize the plant in Houma. Shortly after it opened, it was apparent that both production and morale were low. To correct the situation, Higgins sent one of his supervisors, Fred Horil, to take charge. Horil had been responsible for PT boat production on the third floor of the City Park plant and had run an efficient shop. Not long after assuming his new duties, he found that the root of the problem was an unequal pay scale. Two people with the same skills doing the same job often received different wages. Higgins had faced a similar dilemma in the late 1930s, and it was the underlying reason his workers had unionized.

Horil decided the only solution was to fire every employee at the plant and rehire them the next morning. All personnel were rerated according to their ability, and their salaries were adjusted in relation to their skills. The procedure was completed without major incident and resulted in increased production. Fifty years later, Horil recalled the daily trips down the dark, lonely road to the plant and was thankful that he was never met by an angry group of Cajuns whose wages had been reduced.

Horil did find in Houma that almost everyone seemed proficient at building boats. The Cajuns had fished and trapped all their lives and out of necessity were familiar with boat construction. His 175 employees

3. Edward A. Weathers to Richard A. McDerby, December 8, 1942, in Richard A. McDerby Collection, Metairie, Louisiana; "Eurekas and Crocodiles Tops, Says Wounded Gob," *Eureka News Bulletin*, II (January, 1943), 18.

were hard workers, and in a short time the plant was producing seven boats in six days. Many of the parts used were rough cut in New Orleans and then shipped to Houma for assembly and finishing. After completion, the craft were placed in the water and delivered to New Orleans under their own power. The Houma plant helped to increase Higgins' production, and its location enabled the workers to live at home. This saved the employees from having to find work and housing in New Orleans, which was fast reaching capacity.[4]

While McDerby completed the revamping of his school and Horil finished reorganizing the Houma plant, the Truman Committee finalized its report. On August 5, the committee forwarded its findings to Secretary of the navy Frank Knox. The report concluded, "It is clear that the Bureau of Ships has, for reasons known only to itself, stubbornly persisted for over five years in clinging to an unseaworthy tank lighter design of its own. . . . Higgins Industries did actually design and build a superior lighter," but there was "an inherent reluctance" on the part of the bureau "to accept any design but its own, even though this involves a flagrant disregard for the facts, if not the safety and success of American troops." In closing, the report stated, "It is evident from the testimony taken at the hearings that some officers of the Bureau either deliberately attempted to misinform the committee or were not fully cognizant of the facts surrounding the subject under consideration."[5]

Truman was appalled at what his investigation had uncovered and expressed as much in a letter to Knox. He stressed that he could not "condemn too strongly the negligence or wilful misconduct on the part of the officers of the Bureau of Ships" in the planning and production of a vehicle of such importance to any Allied invasion attempt. He wrote that Higgins Industries had been subjected to "bias and prejudiced treatment" and that the "Bureau of Ships should have accepted with gratitude the proved accomplishments of a private concern, instead of insisting as it did upon using models of its own design despite the repeated failures thereof." He ended his letter: "That the war effort has not suffered an irreparable injury is due largely to the ability and energy of Higgins Industries, Inc., and to its repeated criticisms of the shortcomings of the

4. Fred Horil, interview, November 12, 1992.

5. *Senate Documents*, 78th Congress, 2nd sess., No. 71, Report 10, Part 15, *Investigation of the National Defense Program*, 167–68.

designs prepared by the Bureau of Ships. Higgins Industries, Inc., should be commended for doing this without fear of the results which such criticisms might incur with the agency on which it was dependent for war contracts." [6]

On August 6, the day after he received the report, Knox sent a message to the committee stating, "I have gone over the details of the report, and it is my judgement that it would not be in the public service at the present time to publish this report and I hope that it will be withheld." To help pacify the committee, he said that he was immediately initiating an internal investigation of the tank lighter program. The person chosen to look into the matter was Professor H. S. Seward of Yale University. [7]

As Seward began his probe, the House continued to investigate the cancellation of the Liberty ship contract. Higgins had appeared before the House committee in July and realized then that despite the continuing investigation there was no hope of restoring his contract. The committee's only objectives seemed to be finding an acceptable answer as to why the contract was originally awarded and then deciding who to blame for its cancellation. Higgins left Washington frustrated and without hope.

The Maritime Commission continued its investigation into the closing of the Michaud facility, but at the same time it tried to recruit crews to begin removing as much useful material as possible from the site. Unfortunately for the commission, the unions were loyal to Higgins and refused to allow their members to assist in the project. L. R. Sanford, regional director of construction for the commission, angrily stated: "There is a crying need for that equipment elsewhere and the refusal of the unions to permit their members to move the equipment so that it could be utilized on other very important defense jobs is not far short of sabotage. This situation is very serious." [8] The unions realized the seriousness of the matter and also realized that thousands of jobs had been lost because of the cancellation. They were stalling and hoping for a miracle to restore the contract.

Higgins' earlier testimony before the House committee had created a

6. Harry Truman to Secretary Frank Knox, August 5, 1942, (copy in Strahan Personal Collection).

7. *Senate Documents*, 78th Congress, 2nd sess., No. 71, Report 10, Part 15, *Investigation of the National Defense Program*, 133.

8. New York *Tribune Herald*, August 3, 1942, n.p. (Untitled clipping in Dawn Higgins Murphy Collection).

national uproar. He had proclaimed that there was an abundance of steel available and that, when necessary to keep production in his plants uninterrupted, his son Frank purchased the metal on the "Black Market." He added that it was necessary to pay a premium, but steel was available. On hearing the accusations, Roosevelt quickly responded with a statement that persons who sold steel in such a manner should be jailed.[9]

The War Production Board (WPB) investigated and proclaimed, "No evidence was developed to show directly that steel products had been shipped to the Higgins Company in violation of WPB orders." Then, in typical Washington bureaucratic double-talk, the WPB said, "However, there is evidence to indicate that some steel warehouses may have violated WPB regulations."[10]

As the House investigation into the cancellation of the Liberty ship contract proceeded, congressmen began looking for a scapegoat. On August 19, 1942, during the House's hearings into the matter, Congressman Herbert C. Bonner of North Carolina attempted to place the blame on Higgins. In questioning maritime commissioner Carmody the congressman stated: "Now the Higgins are splendid people and I have been greatly impressed with them, myself. Mr. Higgins is a dynamic character and his sons are fine gentlemen, but do you think now that there is anyone in the Higgins family who could have supervised the engineering and have done the construction engineering on this mammoth plant?"

Commissioner Carmody responded: "Yes, I know it is a mammoth plant. It has not occurred to me that he would not get, if he didn't already have them in his organization, people competent to do the job."

Bonner replied: "Well it turned out that he did not do it."

Commissioner Carmody: "But he didn't get the plant into operation."

Bonner closed by commenting: "Did not that have something to do with the delay in construction there?"[11]

When Higgins heard about Bonner's line of questioning he dictated the following blistering response to the congressman:

> My Washington representative employed a court reporter to take memorandums of the proceedings in the open hearings held after Mr. Peterson's committee left New Orleans.

9. "Ship Steel Sales on 'Black Market' Bared at Inquiry," New York *Times*, August 5, 1942, p. 1.

10. "WPB Double-Talk On Steel Violations," *PM*, August 18, 1942, p. 11.

11. *Higgins Contracts,* 229.

At the committee meeting held on Wednesday, August 19, at which Commissioner Carmody gave testimony there were a lot of questions coupled with answers and statements that you made which would make it appear as if the purpose of the committee was twisted around to find a "goat" and that I was to be that "goat." I cannot express too deeply the shock with which I received and read the recordations of the questions and answers.

Every damned thing that I told your committee, even to the "Black Market" and the bootlegging of steel has been verified. I don't have to lie and I don't have to misrepresent things. I don't give a tinker's god dam, accept to do something to help win this war. I am no politician. I don't have to make any more money. I don't have to do a goddam thing except to live decently and die.

I am awfully busy. I am now administering my own business, the Higgins Industries; companies and plants that I built at my own risk and expense with such money that I had or could borrow and go in debt for. I hope this war ends tomorrow, and if it does I will be broke by about six million dollars, for I will pay eight millions of dollars in taxes for this years operations, but I won't worry about it, because I could go back tomorrow and make it back.

I have voluntarily—after looking over some contracts we have with the Government—agreed to refund to the Navy approximately $480,000.00 on one contract alone. Now I am doing this on two contracts for the construction of boats of my own design. Poor imitations of these boats, on which the Navy lost over seven million dollars, cost them over $40,000 per boat. I have reduced the price on ours to $25,000 each.

I am paying the highest schedule of wages in the United States. I am proud of it. Every time I raise wages, the cost of the finished article goes down, because I have a bunch of men working for me who are Americans; this in spite of paying premium prices on steel which I have to get in the "black market" or through steel bootleggers, or where ever I can get it, and our contracts are not cost-plus. When I pay premium for material, it is out of my own pocket.

Now, I told you we were going to pay eight million dollars in taxes for this year. That isn't because we are robbing the Government either. The Government has never put a dime into any of our plants. In spite of increased wages, materials, and the war, I have constantly reduced the price on our finished article, because goddam it I know how to produce and I know how to make men like me—and like to work—and love their country—and I could have done the same goddam thing with the Liberty Ships for the Maritime Commission.

You know how these "bureaucrats,"—the WPB, or the Navy, or the Army, or the Maritime Commission would like to find just one little peg to hang their hats. Do you know that they would like to blame me? But have they, and can they find grounds for such? Hell no, they can't. But there you come, Congressman Bonner, in questioning Commissioner Carmody, and put words in his mouth, as much as if he agreed with you that I was a damned dumbbell, and your questions with your statements to him, that are to become record, as evidence, to the American people that you knew I was a damned fool and that everybody else knew it, too; that neither I, nor anybody employed by me, up to a fee of $1,000,000 or more—which don't think the Maritime Commission would not have approved, if they were friends of the Maritime Commission—didn't have enough sense to pick a proper plant site.

Now, Congressman Bonner, I wasn't born in the state of Louisiana. I picked this place out to live in, but I know as much about the environs of New Orleans as you know about the environs of your birth-place,—yet you came down here and within 2 days, ipso facto, take the position that I don't know how to pick a shipyard site. I guess you have been reading a lot of "poison pen" stuff. I know there have been a lot of people around New Orleans who do not like the idea of our paying a decent schedule of wages. They don't like it that I get along with Labor. They cannot understand why my production costs go down while I pay over the Zone standards. All these kinds of people never will know anything and I am not going to worry about them.

What I do care about is that when people who are not bureaucrats—my kind of people, or what I think are my kind of people—ask and answer their own questions like you did with the questions put to Carmody.

So, my dear Congressman, you may have asked, and answered, these questions with the best intentions in the world, but they are like an indictment of me and I don't "take it" lying down, for you are as wrong as hell.[12]

As Higgins prepared to send the letter, cooler heads interceded and convinced him to compose a new draft. This response in a more diplomatic manner informed the congressman that extensive study had been done on the site by the U.S. Engineers and by Magetkin Masters, his original consulting engineers. In addition, after having been needled by the Maritime Commission, he hired the firm of J. G. White Engineering, which had built the Delta Shipyard in New Orleans, as a second set of consulting engineers. Also, before choosing the site he had obtained all the records from the Orleans Parish Levee Board concerning the Michaud tract, researched the files of the Louisiana State Board of Engineers, and enlisted the services of Orloff Henry, considered by many to be the foremost foundation engineer in the southern United States.

12. Andrew Higgins to Congressman Herbert C. Bonner, September 1, 1942, in McGuire Collection.

Higgins' new response was informative and calmly addressed the main issues, but it did not express what he wanted to say. Finally, near the end of the letter, he could no longer restrain himself. He stated adamantly, "I have more engineering sense in my little finger than all the big names of the engineering organizations, and I certainly know conditions around New Orleans a damned site better than a lot of engineering firms that would want to charge a fee of a million dollars."[13] Bonner might have been looking for a scapegoat, but Higgins was determined that it was not going to be him.

During August, while the Truman Committee issued its report to Knox and Bonner investigated the Liberty ship contract, another important event occurred. Comparative tests were held of the Higgins LCVP, the Higgins LCPL, and the Bureau of Ships' new LCPR. Trials were conducted at Camp Edwards, Massachusetts, headquarters of the Amphibian Command of the U.S. Engineers Corps. Present to witness the trials was an investigator representing the Truman Committee.

Tests were conducted with each boat carrying a three-man crew and thirty-six fully equipped soldiers. Calm seas prevented holding the proposed rough water trials, but the boats were tested for their handling while landing troops. The LCPL experienced the most difficulty because soldiers had to leap over the sides or across the rounded bow. It required fifty-seven seconds for the men to clear the craft once it reached shore. The bureau's newly designed LCPR with its narrow ramp was able to debark its troops in thirty-two seconds, even though the soldiers had to exit single file through the small ramp opening. Troops on the LCVP with its wide ramp were unloaded in nineteen seconds, making it clearly the most effective of the three, but the bureau was not yet ready to concede another victory to Higgins. It decided to conduct additional tests.

In August, Knox had requested that Truman not release the committee's report because of security considerations. The senator had complied with the request. On September 21, 1942, however, Drew Pearson's nationally syndicated column, "The Washington Merry-Go-Round," printed a portion of the telephone conversation between Commander Roth and Captain Crecca. The following day, Pearson's column included a description of the May 25 contest between the Higgins and bureau lighters. By the time the columnist leaked this information to the public, shipyards across the nation had already discarded the bureau's

13. Andrew Higgins to [?], September 1, 1942, *ibid.*

tank lighter plans and were producing LCMs according to Higgins' specifications.

Pearson also included in his column a description of the boat builder from the bayous. The columnist viewed Higgins as "very disagreeable, likes to write insulting letters to admirals, gets on almost everyone's nerves, but is a genius when it comes to small boat design." As a producer of small boats Pearson rated him "at the top." He claimed that because "Higgins got on the Navy's nerves he was rebuffed. And as a result the positions of Russia, Great Britain and the United States today all have suffered." [14]

In lieu of the unpublished committee report, the newspaper article served the purpose of informing the public that the tank lighter controversy was over. The outspoken Higgins had challenged the navy in a head-to-head competition and had proved his craft's superiority.

It is true that Higgins irritated more than his share of swivel-chair admirals, that the bureau initially opposed his expansion, and that the Maritime Commission canceled his contract. But as a result of his determination, on Sunday, September 13, 1942, a triple ceremony was held at the recently completed Industrial Canal facility. The new plant was officially dedicated, the company and its workers were awarded the Army-Navy "E" for exceptional production, and the City Park facility celebrated its first anniversary.

The event was covered by the National Broadcasting Company with announcer Everett Mitchell describing the ceremony to millions of listeners the world over. On the grounds five thousand spectators gathered to take part in the festivities. Serving as master of ceremony was Higgins' longtime friend from his earlier lumber days in Mobile and his most powerful spokesman in Washington, Alabama's congressman Frank Boykin. Higgins often described Boykin as Alabama's first congressman and unofficially Louisiana's ninth. It was to Boykin, head of the Merchant Marine and Fisheries Committee, that Higgins turned when he was in need of congressional help. [15]

Higgins depended on Boykin because of their friendship and because

14. Drew Pearson, "The Washington Merry-Go-Round," Washington *Post,* September 21, 1942, Sec. 2, p. 5.

15. "Army and Navy 'E'," *Eureka News Bulletin,* I (August–September, 1942), 1, 50; "Presentation Ceremony of Army-Navy 'E' to Men of Higgins," *Eureka News Bulletin,* I (October, 1942), 1–4, 13, 16, 36, 45, 51, 53.

he had little faith in Louisiana's Washington delegation. An article published in the New Orleans *States* in 1940 reported that Higgins had been awarded a navy contract because of his own efforts. The reporter felt it was important for local readers to be aware that the industrialist received no aid from Louisiana's congressional delegation, which, according to the journalist, was now trying to "grab the credit." The writer continued: "Those weak sisters proved so ineffective in other directions that he [Higgins] knew it would be a loss of time to invoke their aid. The best they have ever done is to claim an undeserved merit." [16]

Higgins' earlier lack of faith in Louisiana's representatives, his longtime friendship with Boykin, and the fact that his assistant George Rappleyea had worked for Boykin before coming to Higgins made it natural for the industrialist to look to Alabama's congressman instead of his own. It was also natural for him to want his friend to share the national spotlight by serving as master of ceremonies at the September 13 event.

Boykin introduced the speakers, including Marine Corps general E. P. Moses, who had been instrumental in helping Higgins develop the first LCVP and tank lighter. Also present were Rear Admiral Frank Leighton, commandant of the Eighth Naval District, Brigadier General Guerre, Brigadier General Dillion, Captain Petrie and Commander Bevins of the Royal Navy, and Louisiana's governor Sam Jones.

Moses spoke to the enthusiastic crowd from a flag-draped platform atop the flat roof of the white two-story administration building. As the packed crowd cheered, he told them, "I have been in the Marine Corps now forty years as an officer, and I say that I have never taken part in maneuvers where I thought we were landing in any craft superior to the Higgins 'Eurekas.'" He ended by offering the thousands of workers and spectators a catchphrase he felt they could take pride in—"From the Industrial Canal to Guadalcanal." [17]

Next, Boykin introduced Governor Jones as a great friend of Andrew Higgins and one of the great men of America. Jones commended the industrialist for his accomplishments and compared him to the man for whom he was named, Andrew Jackson. According to the governor: "Both these Andrew Jacksons were red-blooded, two-fisted fighters. The

16. "Shipbuilding Here," New Orleans *States,* September 27, 1940, p. 6.

17. "Army and Navy 'E'," 1, 5; "Presentation Ceremony of Army-Navy 'E' to Men of Higgins," 1–4, 13, 16, 36, 45.

first wrote glorious history in the Battle of New Orleans. The second writes glorious history in the battle of the world." Jones then applauded the shipbuilder for taking ten thousand untrained people and turning them into some of the finest boat builders in the world. He praised Higgins for "opening up new horizons for Louisiana's resources, her manpower and her genius."

Then came the main speaker of the day, Admiral Henry A. Wiley, who until 1936 was commander in chief of the United States Fleet and later served as a member of the Maritime Commission. Wiley praised the company for building the boats that landed the marines on the Solomon Islands and the commandos on Europe's western shores and that were playing an important role the world over. He then congratulated the workers for their production record and for the incredible feat of having launched thirty-six boats in a single day, which he acknowledged "was just right in line with their regular performance."

Wiley, serving as the representative for the army and navy, unfurled a flag that had in its center a large *E*. The *E* stood for excellence and was the highest award the services bestowed upon a company. As the admiral and Higgins held the flag before the wildly cheering audience, Wiley told the industrialist: "I take great pleasure in presenting to you in the name of the armed services of the United States this flag. It shows appreciation for a job well done. Keep it flying."

The pennant was hoisted to the top of the flagstaff by soldiers of the Amphibian Command of the United States Engineers, presently enrolled as students at the Higgins Boat Operators School. Higgins then proceeded to the microphone. He thanked friends and distinguished guests for attending and then acknowledged the presence of "the leader of the State, members of Congress of the United States, the Army, the Navy and our own beloved Marine Corps." At the mention of the Marine Corps, the crowd broke into roaring applause.

As the applause subsided, Higgins told the audience that "it is healthy for a group of people to know that their individual and collective effort and work is acknowledged as well done. But let us think mostly and constantly of the needs of the men who are doing the fighting and the dying. No effort or sacrifice is too great." He reminded them to think of the "sons of the five hundred of our own men from our own plants who have gone cheerfully when called to the forces."

As the enthusiastic cheering faded, General Richard Donovan of the

U.S. Army came to the podium. Donovan was to present lapel pins to the workers in recognition of their accomplishment. Chosen to represent the employees was Henry J. "Red" Barbe of the City Park plant. Accepting the pins, Barbe pledged continued hard work to "give our fighting forces the boats and the weapons they need to lick the enemy." He also informed the millions of radio listeners that relations between the workers and management of Higgins "are perhaps the best in the country. Here management and labor are truly partners." The presentation portion of the ceremony concluded with the 125-piece Higgins band playing "America."

Higgins, Boykin, General Moses, and the other distinguished guests moved from the platform to the deck of PT 73 docked in the Industrial Canal. Along with thousands of spectators on shore, they witnessed a "marine pageant and naval combat motor boat rodeo."[18] Boats hurtled logs and exhibited their maneuverability to the crowd. Then Captain McDerby and eleven of his instructors surprised Higgins as they slowly cruised down the Industrial Canal in twelve LCPLs in the form of an E.

Festivities continued with the employees' families touring the wharves and the plant. Boats were on exhibit, and for many this was the first time they were able to see at close hand the work of their fathers, sons, and brothers. The crowd listened to the Higgins band play such tunes as "The Amphibian Engineers' Song," written by band members Al Hirt and Louis Escobedo, and the "Higgins Victory March." After the disappointing cancellation of the Michaud contract, this celebration served as a much needed morale booster for management and labor.

When the Maritime Commission canceled Higgins' Liberty ship contract in July, the industrialist had spoken harshly of President Roosevelt, but the wound healed quickly. On September 29, 1942, Higgins served as host when the president made a special stopover in New Orleans on his two-week cross-country tour of defense plants.

The president's railroad car was pulled onto the City Park plant's spur track, and Roosevelt and his aides were met at a specially arranged platform by Higgins and his four sons. Then, unannounced, a three-car procession drove through the plant. The president, riding in the front seat of young Roland Higgins' convertible, had a clear view of the facilities. The open car also made it possible for the employees to see their commander

18. Caption, *Eureka News Bulletin*, I (October, 1942), 51.

in chief. The night before, workers had been instructed to widen a door opening by three feet and to move machinery so that enough space was available for a vehicle to pass. No reason had been given for the sudden modifications. Once FDR's train pulled up to the plant's track, it did not take long for the word to spread that the president of the United States had arrived.

As the convertible traveled through the building, Roosevelt was shown the six-hundred-foot-long assembly bay where 36-foot LCVPs were produced. Here, four production lines were set side by side. Boats were inverted at the start of the line and frames were formed by the use of jigs and templets. Then, as the craft moved down the bay, plywood and planking were applied. Once this was completed, a crane with specially designed fabric slings turned the boats right side up. Workers not able to finish their task in the allotted time remained with the boat as it moved to the next station. A crew was not allowed to halt the progress of the line to complete its task.

FDR then toured the production bay, where the deadly PT boats were fabricated. Here he saw two production lines side by side with raised walkways between them to allow workers to have access from above, below, and on all sides at the same time. When a boat was completed and reached the end of the line, it was lifted by crane onto an awaiting railroad car and transported to Bayou St. John for testing.

Higgins' City Park plant was the only location Roosevelt visited in Louisiana, and during his hour tour he appeared to be impressed. As the procession moved through the plant, workers dressed in overalls and hard hats, in guard uniforms, and in white painter's caps stood atop PT boats, LCVPs, or on the ground along the route to catch a glimpse of their president. Members of the Higgins band had been instructed to bring their instruments to work, and as the tour approached their station they played "Hail to the Chief," followed by the popular "Anchors Aweigh." The president, enjoying the music, kept time by tapping his fingers on the side of the car. Next, as FDR quietly read the lyrics, the band played its final selection, the "Higgins Victory March."

Higgins stood up in the convertible and yelled to his men: "All right, everybody! For the world's greatest man, three cheers!" The men's voices echoed throughout the building as their boss led the ovation. After completing the last cheer, Higgins shouted, "And now, the President would like to see how quickly you can get back to work." The workers gave an approving smile and returned to their stations. At the end of the tour, Roosevelt, Higgins, and a late-arriving Governor Jones entered into a lengthy discussion and thumbed through a scrapbook of the Michaud facility. Workers speculated that they were discussing the completion of the facility for a new project. At the conclusion of their conversation, Roosevelt slowly boarded the train, waved good-bye, and proceeded to his next destination, Camp Shelby in Mississippi. No announcement was made as to what was discussed.[19]

On October 14, not long after FDR's visit, encouraging words for Higgins and the city of New Orleans were expressed by Donald Nelson, chief of the War Production Board. Appearing before an investigating committee of the AFL looking into the Michaud controversy, Nelson exclaimed that Andrew Higgins "must come into this war effort in a bigger way . . . I am going to do everything I can to see that that takes place. I feel that it is my duty to see that the facilities involved in the cancellation of the Higgins contract are utilized for the war effort and along that line we now have the facilities under consideration."[20]

In September, Roosevelt had visited Higgins in an attempt to restore good relations. During October, Donald Nelson was diligently trying to find a use for the partially completed Michaud facility. And on October 16, Adlai E. Stevenson, general counselor to the secretary of the navy, wrote a memorandum to Knox preparing him for Seward's upcoming report on the tank lighter controversy. Higgins had become a time-consuming problem for Washington's bureaucrats.

Stevenson, in his attempt at damage control, reported to Knox, "I suspect the report will be somewhat critical of BuShips conduct of tank lighter procurement and may also make some general recommendations for reorganization of BuShips." With that in mind, he advised the secretary to "transmit the report to Senators Truman and Walsh with a letter of transmittal commenting on the report and pointing out that after long study, professional advice, consultation, etc., certain organizational changes have been made in BuShips." Next, Stevenson recommended that Knox ask Senator Truman to lunch. This would give him an opportunity to discuss the report personally with the senator. Such a move

19. "President Roosevelt Pays Special Visit to Higgins; City Park Plant Only N.O. Stop," *Eureka News Bulletin,* I (November, 1942), 4.
20. "Nelson Considers Utilizing Higgins," New York *Times,* October 15, 1942, p. 14.

might avoid more formal discussions before the committee. It would also afford him an opportunity to comment casually on the personnel changes in the bureau, which is what Stevenson felt Fulton and Truman were really interested in.[21]

On October 18, two days after Knox received Stevenson's memorandum, a small article about the Bureau of Ships appeared in section 5 of the New York *Times*. The title near the bottom of the page read, "Younger Men Take Ship Bureau Posts." The story acknowledged that the bureau had been reorganized and that younger men had been promoted to its key positions. Fifty-year-old Captain Edward L. Cochrane succeeded sixty-one-year-old Rear Admiral Alexander H. Van Keuren as bureau chief. Forty-six-year-old Captain Earl Mills had been appointed assistant chief to succeed fifty-seven-year-old Admiral Claude A. Jones.[22]

As far as Higgins was concerned, both were acceptable appointments. In his statement of September 24, 1942 (quoted in full in Chapter 4), he had referred to Cochrane as a fine officer and a gentleman, very capable at repairing large ships but not extremely competent in small boat design. He accepted that Cochrane was a bureaucrat, but to him all construction officers fell into that category. Cochrane had impressed Sam Eaton, Higgins' Washington representative, and Eaton had informed his boss that Cochrane was hardworking, serious, and, perhaps most important, above reproach. Captain Earl Mills was a young officer who had caught Higgins' attention several times. He considered Mills a "go getter," extremely competent and worthwhile.[23]

According to the *Times* story, the changes were effective November 1, and Admiral Van Keuren and Admiral Jones were both assuming new positions. Van Keuren became the director of the Naval Research Laboratory, succeeding fifty-eight-year-old Rear Admiral Harold G. Bowen, who had been assigned to duty in the office of the under secretary of the navy. Jones's new duty was assistant to the chief of the Office of Procurement and Material.[24]

21. "Memorandum for Colonel Knox," October 16, 1942, in Frank Knox Correspondence Files, 1940–44, 8–1 to 12–1, Box 5, Record Group 80, National Archives.

22. "Younger Men Take Ship Bureau Posts," New York *Times,* October 18, 1942, Sec. 5, p. 10.

23. Higgins' "Statement," 17.

24. "Younger Men Take Ship Bureau Posts," New York *Times,* October 18, Sec. 5, p. 10.

While Knox had been reorganizing the bureau, Donald Nelson had been working tirelessly to find a way to use the Michaud facility. Finally, on October 29, eleven days after the bureau shake-up, Higgins announced that the War Department had given him a letter of intent ordering twelve hundred C-76 plywood cargo planes for the Army Air Corps.[25] At that time, the proposed contract, totaling over $212 million was the largest in aviation history.[26] For the redesigning and completing of Michaud as an aircraft factory $30 million of the fee was to be allocated. At the same time, Higgins received a contract to manufacture marine engines for the U.S. Army.

Higgins claimed that during the negotiations he refused the standard contract and "insisted on a percentage less than half of what was offered," which he claimed "formed the basis for the Army Air Corps' renegotiating contracts with other aircraft manufacturers and translated into tremendous savings for the government." It was also responsible for his unpopularity in certain aircraft industry circles.[27]

His competitors might have been upset, but the people of New Orleans were elated. On Monday evening, November 9, when Higgins and his wife, Angele, returned home after six weeks in Washington, they were met at the train station by thousands of cheering employees and appreciative citizens. The gathering surpassed the earlier outpouring of support that had greeted him when he returned home with the Liberty ship contract.[28]

To head the new Higgins Aircraft Company, Higgins chose Colonel John H. Jouett, president of the Aeronautical Chamber of Commerce of America. Jouett had previously served as head of the aeronautical division of Standard Oil, which operated a fleet of planes out of the Menefee Airport in New Orleans, and also had held the position of president of Fairchild Airplane Corporation. During his earlier military career Jouett was one of the few American officers to simultaneously hold the four ratings of balloon observer, airship pilot, military airplane pilot, and airplane observer. He had also commanded the first American Attack Group to be created as such and had been aviation adviser to the Republic of China and personal adviser to General Chiang Kai-shek on aviation matters. When Higgins convinced Jouett to join Higgins Aircraft, he

25. Caption, *Eureka News Bulletin*, I (November, 1942), 5.
26. "Higgins Outlines Big Plane Program," New York *Times*, November 7, 1942, p. 9.
27. "Revisal," 62.
28. Caption, *Eureka News Bulletin*, I (December, 1942), 11.

hired the man he considered the most qualified available to manage his new plant, a man skilled in both the aviation and the administrative aspects of aircraft production.[29]

On November 7, nine days after Nelson and Higgins announced the rebirth of the Michaud facility, Seward submitted his report to the navy. Stevenson was correct that it was not particularly favorable to the Bureau of Ships. The investigation had uncovered several problems, including an organizational structure that was cumbersome and not conducive to quick and objective decisions. Bureau boards regularly exchanged information via written correspondence creating a "slow going procedure" that had not been streamlined even as war approached.

Seward also found that bureau procedures lacked adequate safeguards to ensure proper consideration of designs and ideas from outside sources. He felt this would not have been a problem if several positions within the Bureau of Ships had been filled with well-trained civilians instead of military personnel. Referring to the development of the bureau's tank lighter, the professor reported that design decisions had been made by persons who had never seen a lighter in actual operation. Additionally, the bureau official responsible for the engine room layout of the lighter had never personally seen a bureau lighter before the Truman Committee's investigation.

Seward reported that "the treatment accorded Mr. Higgins was unfortunate and attributable to a clash between strong personalities and dramatically opposed systems of procedure." He admitted that the industrialist had been given only piecemeal orders, making it difficult for him to maintain a flow of continuous production and thereby reduce his cost. The professor also found to no one's surprise that the Higgins lighter was superior to the bureau's. Interestingly, even after all he had uncovered, Seward did not agree that Higgins had received "biased and prejudiced treatment." He referred to the treatment as "simply unfortunate." In reference to the earlier charges that the bureau officials attempted to misinform the Truman Committee, the professor contended that the bureau's witnesses were simply uninformed and should not have testified until they had reviewed the facts.

Seward had recommended a reorganization of the Bureau of Ships.

29. "Higgins Accepts Contract for Cargo Planes," *Eureka News Bulletin*, I (November, 1942), 5.

The first step in the process had already begun with the promotion of Captain Cochrane. Soon after assuming his new position as bureau chief, Cochrane was nominated by President Roosevelt to the rank of rear admiral. Before his nomination hearing, his military record was investigated by the navy's legal counsel, Adlai Stevenson, who stated in a memorandum to the under secretary of the navy, "I believe the only grounds for objection to Captain Cochrane are" Cochrane's involvement in the bureau versus Higgins in the tank lighter controversy, his association with the "infantry landing craft program," which Stevenson reported was "Higgins inspired," and an "alleged delay in advising Admiral King about a proposed small troop transport." Two out of the three and possibly all three of the areas of concern involved Higgins. Nevertheless, Stevenson informed the under secretary that the professor's report was not prejudicial to Cochrane. It would be critical of the bureau but not directly of the captain.[30]

The Truman Committee read the report and found it lacked the desired severe reprimand. The committee responded: "Professor Seward's conclusions, critical as they are of the Bureau of Ships, were apparently reached after an examination of the files of the Bureau and Higgins Industries, Inc. If these additional sources [Marine Corps and U.S. Army records] had been examined by Professor Seward as was done by committee investigators, an even more critical report of the tank lighter program would have been forthcoming." The tank lighter controversy was put to rest. Cochrane assumed the position of bureau chief and received the promotion to the rank of rear admiral, and Truman, at Knox's request, did not release the transcripts of the committee's investigation until 1944.[31]

The announcement in October that Michaud was going to be completed to produce airplanes came as a great surprise to the employees of Higgins Industries. But an even more startling revelation appeared on page 23 of the November issue of the *Eureka*. In bold letters across the top of the page was the title "Higgins the Boatbuilder Begins Training of Women." The article began, "This report is to inform Higgins Personnel

30. Adlai Stevenson to Under Secretary of Navy, November 6, 1942, in Frank Knox Correspondence Files, 1940–44, 8–1 to 12–1, Box 5, Record Group 80, National Archives; *Senate Documents*, 78th Congress, 2nd sess., No. 71, Report 10, Part 15, *Investigation of the National Defense Program*, 133–37.
31. *Ibid.*, 137.

of the introduction of training for women war workers in our plants." It explained to its readers that at present the company was only trying to ascertain what facilities were available for training women for shipyard employment. Management stated, "We know the placing of these women must be done on a very small scale, and the absorption by the shipyard must be slow, in order not to disturb production; and to acquaint both the women placed in our plants with their duties as well as to accustom the men on the job to these women being used in the shipyard."

The plan was to train and place not more than twenty women each in the electrical unit, the machine shop, welding, and ship carpentry. These eighty women were to serve as a test unit to see if females could successfully adapt to a shipyard environment. As all workers did, they had to pass physical skills tests on samples to determine their proficiency rating. Welders, for instance, would be rated third class, second class, or first class. It was the rating, not the sex of the employee, that determined the rate of pay. Women received the same union wage scale as their male counterparts.

Selection of the new employees was handled by J. T. Ringer of the United States Education Service and Salomi D. Sevier, Higgins' coordinator of vocational training for women war workers. Articles in the *Eureka* assured male workers that the applicants were to be thoroughly interviewed and great care would be taken to select only those candidates who had a high possibility of success.

Prospective female employees were expected to have no less than an eighth grade education, but prior work experience or training would be considered and possibly substituted in place of a formal education. The women must have good sight in both eyes, normal blood pressure, no more than a 10 percent weight variation from normal, and be between the ages of nineteen and forty-five. They were to receive the same instruction given male employees so that their skills would be proficient enough to allow them to replace their male counterparts without a loss in production. They were projected to be used in operational work in shops and for fabrication but not directly in or on ships.

The company stressed that the women's part in shipbuilding was small and their introduction would be slow. But unless the world situation changed, as more men were called into the service, their places would have to be taken by women. To help ensure the acceptance of females in the workplace, company policy dictated that if at all possible, when a women was hired, she should be the wife or sweetheart of the man who had just been drafted.

During September, preparations were completed, and the Nicholls Vocational School in New Orleans was chosen to instruct forty women in ship carpentry. Shift A received instruction from 6:00 P.M. to midnight and Shift B from midnight to 6:00 A.M. At the National Youth Administration building twenty-three welding candidates received two hundred hours of classwork, training from 8:30 A.M. to 4:30 P.M. daily. Additionally, twenty-three future woodworkers and ten machine shop trainees followed the same daily schedule. At another New Orleans location, eight trainees in electric welding, one in acetylene welding, nine in machine shop skills, and nine in sheet metal received instruction. Across the Mississippi River from New Orleans in Gretna, ten female trainees studied general welding, and in Houma thirteen were taught electric welding. All instruction was handled through National Defense classes monitored by Higgins Industries.

Articles in the *Eureka* also attempted to reassure the men of Higgins by stressing that "woman's most honored place is in keeping the home fires of the nation burning, upon which the world depends, and she is by far much happier in this natural environment. She is taking this training with no intention of replacing man on a permanent basis, but to relieve a man only for the duration and then return to her home." [32] The fact that there were no plans to employ females in the postwar plants considerably eased the situation. It was also hard to criticize a woman for trying to step in and fill the position that her husband or boyfriend had once held.

In early November, as women were being interviewed as potential trainees, Higgins wondered if he would have enough work to keep his present crews busy. His navy contracts were due for completion by early summer, and there were no future landing craft orders. He feared that before the navy awarded him another contract he would have to lay off his skilled labor force. If that happened, when orders finally arrived, his workers would be dispersed and employed elsewhere. The navy, however, sent a telegram instructing Higgins to build three hundred bureau-

32. "Higgins the Boatbuilder Begins Training of Women," *Eureka News Bulletin*, I (November, 1942), 23; "Job Vacancies to be Filled by Employees' Women Relatives," *Eureka News Bulletin*, II (May, 1943), 3.

designed LCPRs. Higgins had always been critical of this boat and argued that it placed troops in unnecessary danger by forcing them through a narrow ramp opening. He predicted that as Allied soldiers exited single file from the craft the enemy would pick them off "like clay pigeons."

Higgins ignored the telegram. He viewed it as an attempt by vindictive navy personnel to ram the small ramp boat down his throat because the bureau "could not swallow its prestige and officially acknowledge that the Navy was not capable of designing the type of equipment that it actually needed and had to accept something that an outsider, a civilian, had produced." Higgins decided that he would rather close his plants than build a boat that would result in needless casualties. He claimed that if his refusal to build "worthless equipment, dangerous equipment, was 'lese majeste,'" he pleaded guilty to the charge. But he added, "The motives that prompted him to do so should justify the tactics that he adopted."[33]

Because the navy chose not to use his facilities fully, Higgins openly sought other military business. In December, 1942, he was approached by the army, which was in desperate need of a fleet of specially designed cargo ships. During the late 1930s and early 1940s he had focused his attention on designing and producing craft for the navy. In late December, because of the actions of the Bureau of Ships, he began to look to the army.[34]

33. "Report," Supplement A, 12.
34. "Revisal," 36–37.

7

BLOOD IS ON THEIR HANDS

As 1942 drew to a close, Andrew Higgins was not the only member of his family to look toward the army. On December 10, Roland, Higgins' youngest son, was inducted into the service. Weeks earlier the twenty-one-year-old had resigned as superintendent of landing boat construction at Higgins Industries, a war industry position that had deferred him from the draft. On the night of the induction, Higgins told reporters that Roland "was anxious to get into the service and we are proud of him."[1]

Both Private Higgins and his father prepared for their army experience. Roland's life centered around amphibious training with the engineers, while his father's focused on designing a small, highly maneuverable ship to fulfill the army's needs in the Pacific. In late 1941 Higgins had been invited to study plans and submit a bid on a 150-foot boat known as a Retriever. After examining the drawings, he issued a statement that he had no interest in bidding on the contract. He considered the boat poorly designed and predicted that if the plans were not revised the result would be a slow boat that was incapable of carrying the required loads. An additional problem was that the ship was too short to handle the derrick equipment shown in the designs. He stated, "In a nutshell, we did not want to build something we thought would not serve a good purpose."[2]

Higgins kept abreast of the progress made by others producing the Retriever, but nothing changed his opinion that the ship was the product

1. "Roland Higgins Off to War; Quits Job For Service," *Eureka News Bulletin,* II (January, 1943), 5.
2. "Revisal," 66.

of an inferior design. In late December, 1942, at the invitation of the Transportation Section of the army, he attended the trials of a Retriever that was built near New Orleans. After observing the ship maneuver in the Mississippi River, the industrialist was convinced that his earlier assessment had been correct.

Higgins recommended to the army a new design that he suggested was far superior to that of the Retriever. His proposed ship was a 200-foot vessel with a 34-foot beam capable of transporting approximately 450 tons of cargo while not drawing more than the specified eight-foot draft. It was to be powered by diesel engines of sufficient horsepower to meet the qualifying speed of twelve knots when fully loaded, and its design ensured that it would be highly maneuverable. The military was in need of a ship capable of transporting supplies and equipment through the shallow inlets of the South Pacific and participating when necessary in rescue and salvage operations. Higgins suggested that his ship would be ideal for such assignments.

The army was impressed with the shipbuilder's designs but informed him that the boat's beam had to remain 32 feet, not 34, and the 200-foot length was unacceptable. The vessel had to maintain the general characteristics of a small ship. Higgins' engineers finally developed a scale model of a 158-foot ship for tank tests but were unsatisfied with the results. They insisted that the ship should be at least 168 feet in length and finally convinced the army to modify its requirement.

The final challenge was to make certain the vessel could sustain a speed of twelve knots carrying a full load and not exceed the maximum eight-foot draft. The engineers worked day and night on the plans and enlisted the cooperation of the naval testing tank at the University of Michigan. By the latter part of January all problems were resolved, and the designs were submitted for inspection. The army accepted Higgins' ideas but added improvements and equipment that was not standard on the 150-foot Retriever.

A competitor informed Higgins that even though he had received $490,000 per Retriever, his company had lost money on the contract. Higgins estimated that his 170-foot island hoppers would cost $340,000, provided the army ordered the two hundred boats it originally mentioned. He had received a letter of intent for one hundred boats from the military and hoped that his projections were correct.

Higgins now faced the problems of where to build the ships and how to finance the project. His choices were limited. The only location he had that was large enough was the Industrial Canal plant, but the facility had to be expanded over ground containing quicksand, and such an expansion was costly. Funding was unavailable through the Defense Plant Corporation so he reasoned that his only option was to use operating capital.[3]

While Higgins prepared for his new shipbuilding challenge for the army, he also worked on finalizing his agreement with the Army Air Corps, which had acquired the title to the Michaud site. But the Maritime Commission had hired laborers and was hurriedly dismantling and carting off as much of the facility as possible. Higgins was ready to start converting the site to aircraft production, but the commission would not halt the dismantling of the plant. Finally, on Monday, January 11, the commission's crews withdrew, and at noon the following day the contract between Higgins, the Army Air Corps, and the Defense Plant Corporation was signed in Washington. At 1:00 P.M. construction workers began converting the plant from a partially completed shipyard to an aircraft production facility. Higgins estimated that the total loss to the taxpayers because of the cancellation of the Liberty ship contract would now be surprisingly small, possibly less than a million dollars.

In his public announcement of the contract, Higgins expressed hope that the city of New Orleans would give the project its wholehearted support. He predicted that Michaud would continue to be a major employer and be of importance to the city long after the war was won. He also used the opportunity to take a parting shot at the Maritime Commission. "I am happy that I am to build these cargo planes," he stated, "because they will serve their purpose so much better than the slower and more vulnerable Liberty Ships."[4]

As Higgins worked on the problems of the present he was called upon to help honor those who had assisted him in solving the challenges of his past. On Tuesday, February 9, 1943, he served as the principal speaker at a public affairs luncheon given by the Omaha Chamber of Commerce. The purpose of the occasion was to honor the memories of John and Edward Creighton, the founders of Creighton University. Higgins' speech offers an insight into his early life and his views of the war.

3. *Ibid.*, 66–70.
4. "Higgins Industries Gets Green Light on the Building of 1200 Cargo Planes," *Eureka News Bulletin*, II (February, 1943), 1.

In his opening remarks he explained that he had found at Creighton what he had not found elsewhere, "friendship, and fatherly guidance, and advice." He found "no barriers raised, no prohibitions, no proselytizing," only "full freedom of thought and appreciation of one's honest concept of religious belief." His education had instilled in him strict discipline, confidence, reliance, and faith. The fathers who taught at the school had opened great vistas for exploration, introduced the students to new worlds to conquer, and impressed upon their pupils the need for engineering skills. He described his teachers as "fathers" in every sense of the word.[5]

Looking to the future, he stressed that when the soldiers returned home they were not going to be satisfied with selling apples on a street corner. They would expect conditions to be better than their fathers had found after their victory in World War I. It was time for all men "to crusade, to plan, to engineer and to demand that those representing us in government be constructive, and lay aside party strife, personal or political ambitions and greed; to see to it that this country for which our boys are fighting and dying, will be a better place in which to live, than it has ever been before."

He saw no reason why the nation should not have a greater distribution of wealth and a universal opportunity for every person to acquire an education or training to the extent of his or her abilities. He insisted that once the training was completed there must be work and an assured income for the individual. It was sad that it took a national peril and war to reveal the capabilities of a people and of a nation. Higgins reminded his audience that when there is need, the money to meet the need can be found. He deemed it unfortunate that in the past there had been so much "prattling about the balanced budgets, concern for the gold-reserve; alarm about the national debt." This argument had been used to maintain the status quo. He insisted that "the debt will be increased; the budget will continue to be unbalanced; but the debt is our own—it is owing to the American people—and, thank God, very well distributed."

In time of war he believed it was necessary to enlarge this debt to produce those goods needed to assure the peace. But he exclaimed,

5. "A. J. Higgins Visits Omaha," *Eureka News Bulletin,* II (March, 1943), 1–4. Quotations in the following paragraphs are from this source.

"Should we fear to attempt tasks as great as, or even greater than our accomplishments for the war?" He reasoned that the vast plants and other enterprises created to produce the necessary war products should be converted and even enlarged to provide greater employment in a post-war world. They could be redesigned to produce usable articles needed to advance civilization and improve the quality of life.

He proposed that once the war was over the time would be right to undertake such great challenges as the creation of super-railroads, super-highways, and great vocational schools and to eliminate slums. Higgins also saw this as the time to use America's enormous engineering and labor surplus to convert the great central West into a paradise. The nation should use its resources to eliminate the danger of drought and the destruction of property and health caused by the dust storms. The results achieved would be a productivity far greater in value than the cost to the national debt.

Another point he stressed was that as a businessman he was not alarmed by the idea of forced limitation of working hours during peacetime. He agreed that wage scales should be as high as or higher than wartime wages and that wages should increase as labor hours decreased. "The abundance in the land, the technology, the productivity, the need of the rest of the world and our own need and consumption of our production, would balance and determine the labor hours and the wage scales." If the United States maintained a high standard of living and controlled the economy by limiting the hours worked, people would not have to accept menial jobs to survive. And if by the ingenuity of the American people more could be produced with less labor, then the government should make certain that labor time gained was directed toward additional training or education.

Higgins closed his address by stating: "Hitler and his gang set the stage on which they opened the diabolic pageant of Hell—War. The theme of his dream was 'Death to Freedom and Slavery to Mankind.' We and our allies did not set the stage; we did not write the script; but by the Eternal, and with God's help and our own determination and sacrifice, we shall write the last act and raise the curtain for 'Victory,' with the stage set for 'Liberty, Justice and Equality for all mankind!'"

His speech was well received and set the tone for a successful return home, his first visit since 1906. The trip gave him an opportunity to renew old friendships and to show Angele the houses and neighborhoods in which he had spent his youth. The voyage into the past was interesting, but his present responsibilities dictated that he return to New Orleans. The United States was in the midst of war, and his company was preparing for its new challenge of building ships and airplanes for the army.

As Higgins moved forward in his preparations to build C-76s it was only natural that people compared him to Henry J. Kaiser. Both were Horatio Alger success stories. Kaiser had quit school in the eighth grade, Higgins in the eleventh. Both shattered production records in the maritime industry—Kaiser with Liberty ships, Higgins with landing craft and freight supply (FS) vessels. Both became national legends, often featured in newspapers and magazines. By D-Day their reputations rivaled that of any national hero. Because of their media exposure both were resented by their fellow industrialists. Neither was accepted by the close-knit fraternity of old-line shipbuilders.

They thought big and did things on a massive scale. Yet they understood the needs of their individual workers. Higgins was perhaps more in touch with his employees because he frequently went into his yards and talked with supervisors, foremen, and laborers. He practiced a hands-on approach to management. He also had a speaker system installed throughout his plants so that when the urge struck he could address his workers with his own version of the "fireside chat."

Both were shipbuilders turned aircraft producers. Kaiser had received an order for three 7-engine experimental airplanes of monumental proportions of his and Howard Hughes's design. Higgins' contract called for twelve hundred C-76 plywood Curtis Commando transports. The twin-engine C-76 was not an experimental craft but a plane that had already been designed and was presently in operation. Higgins was chosen by the Army Air Corps, not as a designer of a new experimental craft but as a production genius to produce an already developed model. It would seem that the similarities and common problems the two men shared would have drawn them toward friendship. Their competitive spirit and egos kept them apart.

Higgins served as president of Higgins Aircraft and Colonel Jouett as a vice-president and general manager of the company. Higgins' son Frank held the title of vice-president in charge of aircraft production and related activities. When questioned as to whether Higgins Aircraft would be ca-

pable of producing airplanes, Frank responded, "We'll turn out the airplanes all right, but we're going to use men who know as much about
planes as we know about boats."[6]

One of the knowledgeable men brought into the organization was
George Allwood, who was hired away from Howard Hughes's organization to accept the position of chief engineer at Higgins Aircraft. At
Hughes, Allwood had served as project manager of all subcontracting.
Previously he had been chief engineer for Duramold and before that chief
engineer for Fairchild Corporation. Allwood had over fifteen years of
experience in the development of plywood aircraft.

Working on a separate and secret project for Higgins Aircraft were
designers Giuseppe Bellanca and Harry Atwood. Higgins might have
been chosen to produce an already existing plane, but rumor had it that
Bellanca and Atwood were designing a transoceanic cargo plane in which
the wings were used for storage space. It was to be revolutionary but not
the pure all-wing aircraft that many were attempting to design.

Both Bellanca and Atwood had extensive aircraft knowledge that
made them valuable to such a project. Bellanca had achieved fame as the
designer of the aircraft that had carried Clarence Chamberlain and Char-
lie Levine from Roosevelt Field in New York to Berlin on the first cross-
Atlantic flight to carry a passenger. He had also designed the aircraft
flown by Clyde E. Pangborn and Hugh Herndon on the first trans-Pacific
flight. Bellanca had come to the United States from Italy in 1911 and
shortly thereafter formed the Bellanca Aeroplane Company, which later
became the Bellanca Aircraft Corporation of Wilmington, Delaware.

During the infancy days of his company he had earned extra money
by serving as a flight instructor at Roosevelt Field in New York. Here he
had taught a young attorney, Fiorello La Guardia, the art of flying. La
Guardia had reciprocated by giving his instructor lessons in driving an
automobile. The advent of war had halted Bellanca's production of commercial passenger planes. When Higgins invited him to join a major new
war-related project that had giant postwar possibilities, the offer proved
too enticing to pass up.

Bellanca had been hired for his design capabilities. Atwood was chosen because of his expertise in the development of a special woven ply-

6. "What About Higgins in Aviation?" *Eureka News Bulletin,* II (January, 1943), 1–3.

wood that was to be used in making the experimental aircraft. For the new product, woods that were plentiful in Louisiana would be used so as to eliminate the need for hard-to-get imported mahogany.[7]

Another project scheduled for development at Michaud was the Higgins helicopter. Higgins informed the public that his postwar helicopter was planned as "something like the jalopy, in the automobile business." He expected it to be affordable to the general public and retail for approximately $1,500. To head the design and development he chose Enea Bossi, a naturalized American citizen, who in 1909 had built Italy's first airplane.[8]

Higgins' approach to aviation seemed realistic: he would hire the most qualified men available and enter the industry with a contract to produce an already proven airplane. Then he would develop the plant and train the work force while the research department designed the experimental aircraft that he hoped would keep the plant thriving in a postwar world. According to Jouett, Higgins was "in aviation for keeps."[9]

In March, when Higgins was preparaing to produce planes and ships for the army, he was notified of a tragedy that had occurred in Florida. During a landing operation several soldiers had died after debarking from an LCPR, the Bureau of Ships craft that he had so adamantly opposed and had refused to build. Once in Washington and then again in New Orleans Higgins had warned naval officers that if they continued to insist on modifying his company's designs simply to "gratify their vanity," the "blood of American boys would be on their hands."

Very extensive and elaborate training exercises had been held near St. Marks, Florida. On the night of the accident, a storm suddenly formed in the Gulf with wind gusts exceeding forty-five miles per hour. Several hundred landing boats participating in the operation were sixty to seventy miles offshore in the midst of the violent weather. Waves reached heights of twelve to fifteen feet as the boats began making their way toward their target landing sites. Despite the hazardous conditions the craft maintained their formation and reached their objectives as planned.

The boats negotiated the inlet, then proceeded toward their assigned

7. "Bellanca, Famous Aircraft Designer, Joins Higgins," *Eureka News Bulletin*, II (February, 1943), 1.

8. "Higgins Reveals Plans for Cheap Helicopter, All-Wing Cargo Plane," *Eureka News Bulletin*, II (March, 1943), 15; Caption, *Eureka News Bulletin*, II (November, 1943), 7.

9. "What About Higgins in Aviation?" 5.

beaches. In the darkness of the night the bow of one of the boats grounded. The coxswain, believing that he had reached shore, lowered the LCPR's ramp, and the troops rapidly debarked. The boat had stalled on a hard outer sandbar. Nineteen soldiers laden with heavy equipment and unaware of the deep trench between the bar and the shore charged from the LCPR into deep water. Fourteen drowned before they could break free from their packs.

Higgins was outraged when he heard of the tragedy and vented his anger in a letter to his Washington representative, Sam Eaton. Carbon copies were forwarded to Major General Holland Smith and Colonel A. G. Trudeau. The letter reminded Eaton, Smith, and Trudeau that this was the craft Higgins had refused to produce and the type of accident that he had predicted would occur. According to Higgins, the boats were developed by Chris Craft, "aided and abetted by the Hull Design Section—Commander Heiser, Kearnes, and DeKay—with a strong approval of Captain Ross Daggett, or possibly the boat was developed in the Hull Design Section of the Bureau." He claimed that when he objected to building the LCPR, it resulted in "considerable animosity" toward him by the officers mentioned.[10]

He reminded Eaton that he had always been opposed to the narrow ramp because it created an unnecessary hazard for troops debarking. He had also opposed the use of Buda engines because in his estimation they did not produce the power necessary to push a loaded boat over a sandbar. Another drawback of the craft was the extra framing required for the narrow ramp. The framing, combined with the double machine gun mounts, made the boat's bow heavy, or "nosey." A landing boat should approach the sandbars bow high, clear the shallows, cross the trenches caused by the undertow, then land dry on the beach. The bow-heavy, underpowered LCPR was incapable of doing this. It was the nosey condition and the lack of power that Higgins believed had caused the boat to ground on the bar and was responsible for the needless death of the fourteen soldiers.

Higgins claimed to have received personal accounts from soldiers who had landed in North Africa, all of whom reported that what had happened in Florida had happened time and again during combat operations.

10. "Report," Supplement B, 1–5. Quotations in the next three paragraphs are from this source.

In his letter, Higgins wrote, "I sometimes wonder if the considerable information that comes to me from our grand boys that are in the services, who send messages of praise and criticism, if any appreciable part of such information that I get, goes as accurately to the Admirals and the Generals in the services that direct the war effort." He answered his own question: "I sometimes think they do not get as much information as I do, or such as they get officially, is so official that a proper analysis or an appreciation of the facts cannot be officially conveyed."

Higgins wrote that he had been "forthright to the point of being brutal" in his opposition to this craft. He had warned those in decision-making positions not to have "the blood of their countrymen on their hands." He wrote, "I felt that all the officers that made the mistake of promoting and insisting on this type of boat, merely to have something of their own development perpetuated, that these officers should be sent out into the fighting so they would have the chance to experience that which the boys do when they have to use poor equipment." Higgins closed by telling Eaton that he would not fail to remind those officers when he again came in contact with them of his warnings and express to them that "the death of these boys, and the death of many others, which may have occurred or which will occur, if these boats are used, should be upon their heads."

Higgins did more than send the letter to Eaton; he immediately sent McDerby to Florida. The purpose of the trip was investigative and instructional. He wanted to know for sure what had happened, and he wanted his chief instructor to hold refresher courses for the instructors in Florida. He hoped that such a needless loss of life could be prevented in the future.[11]

In March the Bureau of Ships finally awarded Higgins a contract for 352 LCMs. It was not as large an order as he desired, but it allowed his crews at the Industrial Canal plant to continue with uninterrupted production. In May, when the City Park plant completed the last of the thousand LCVPs ordered by the navy the previous November, Higgins received a new contract for an additional two thousand ramped personnel landing craft.[12] This contract represented an admission of defeat by the

11. Richard A. McDerby, interview, August 30, 1992.

12. "Higgins Industries—Small Landing Craft Contracts," in Papers of Mark Andrews, Chief of Procurement, Harry S. Truman Library, Independence, Missouri.

Bureau of Ships, which after much criticism finally discarded its LCPR design.

General Holland Smith had said the navy would never give up as long as it had a shot left in the locker. The LCPR was its last shot, and it had proven unsuccessful. Higgins' war with the bureau was finally over. Instead of having to compete against the navy, he now concentrated on producing the craft it needed to assure a victory over Germany and Japan. The rugged industrialist noted the turning point in his relationship with the bureau in a letter to General Smith. Higgins wrote, "I would not care to appear as if I was disgruntled with the Navy, for after 1942, we got along excellently."[13]

There were two basic reasons for the change in the relationship. First, Higgins had met head-on and defeated the bureau-designed boats with his LCP, LCPL, LCM, and LCVP. His PT boats and LCS (landing craft support) boats were also successful. After his decisive victories, he could afford to be charitable in his remarks about his competitor. The second reason was the change of command. Cochrane had set a new tone for the bureau's relationship with Higgins. An example of this change was a letter the admiral had written on April 14 to the U.S. Navy's supervisor of shipbuilding in New Orleans praising the personnel of Higgins Industries for their successful efforts to meet assigned quotas by certain deadlines.[14]

Also in April, 1943, Brigadier General Daniel Noce, commander of the army's Engineers Amphibian Command had written the industrialist to inform him that the class presently being trained at the Higgins Boat Operators School was to be the last sent from his command because the engineers were not scheduled to train any additional landing boat crews. Noce thanked Higgins for all the courtesies and help that had been extended over the past year and closed by saying, "Your only reward, as far as I can see it, will be your knowledge that through your assistance our battle efficiency will be improved and the knowledge that your help is sincerely appreciated by myself and the officers and soldiers in my command who have benefitted by these efforts."[15]

As the engineers prepared to withdraw their operations from New

13. Higgins to Smith, February 3, 1948, in History and Museums Division, USMC, Washington, D.C.

14. Chief of Bureau of Ships to Supervisor of Shipbuilding, April 14, 1943, in Strahan Personal Collection.

15. General Daniel Noce to Andrew Higgins, April 30, 1943, *ibid.*

Orleans, Higgins had already taken steps to convert part of the school to training men for the Rescue Fleet of the army air force. In a letter to Colonel J. H. Houghton dated April 28, 1943, Higgins laid out the curriculum for six weeks of instruction for the Quartermaster Rescue Boat Operational Training Unit. He based his course on knowledge gained from having built hundreds of rescue boats for the Royal Air Force and from his experiences with his present Boat Operators School, which he explained he would continue to operate for the training of Coast Guard personnel.

Higgins explained that he was familiar with the problems and the curriculum of the Royal Air Force's Sea Air Rescue School. His courses would cover many of the same topics. In addition, he would teach the operators the tricks of small boat navigation, which he had learned over the years from "rum runners, fishermen, and Coast Guardsmen." He suggested that the most important of the 108 sessions of the course might very well be the introductory address in which he would instill in the men the spirit that the rescue service was the most "thrilling, most efficient and the best auxiliary service of the air corps of any nation."[16]

While Higgins was restructuring his boat school, he also focused attention on producing LCVPs, LCMs, LCSs, and PT boats for the navy. He had begun production of FP ships for the army and was overseeing the rebuilding of Michaud as an aircraft facility. He was making progress, especially with the FP ships. The army had given him a letter of intent for one hundred vessels and a verbal assurance that the order would be increased to two hundred. This was all he needed. He jumped the gun and began expanding the Industrial Canal plant. A movable assembly line similar to the one that had been projected for Michaud was designed for the shipyard. Production of the ships began while the ways on which they would be built were being constructed. On March 3, 1943, the workers laid the keel for Higgins' first 170-foot ship, FP-*135*. This was followed on March 16 with the keel for FP-*136* and on April 19 with the keel for FP-*137*.[17] In typical Higgins fashion, production had begun, but the shipyard itself was under construction and the contract to

16. Andrew Higgins to Colonel J. H. Houghton, April 28, 1943, in National Defense Committee Files, Records of the Special Committee of the Senate to Investigate the National Defense Program, Sen. 79A F30, OP-33, Record Group 46, Shipyards and Other Companies, National Archives.

17. Higgins Industries Production Ledger, in Strahan Personal Collection.

produce the ships was not officially awarded until April 23, over a month after the first keel had been laid.

As production on the FP ships began, Higgins, along with three other shipbuilders, was called to Washington to appear before the Truman Committee. The committee's job generally was to uncover problems in war-related industries, but this time it had scoured the country to find four corporate heads whom it believed to have exceptional production records and high morale in their plants. These four men were called to testify before the committee and submit to cross-examination so that an understanding might be gained as to why they succeeded while others failed.

The men chosen were Homer Ferguson, president of Newport News Shipbuilding Company; Roger Williams, general manager of the Carolina Shipbuilding Company, which held the record for production of Liberty ships on the East Coast; Henry Kaiser, who held the record for production of Liberty ships on the West Coast; and Higgins, who had established unbeatable records in the production of landing craft and small war-related boats.

In the case of Higgins, the committee was astonished at a letter it had received from Holt Ross of the AFL. Ross wrote that he had heard that Higgins was called to testify and wished to take the opportunity to let everyone in America know of Higgins' "miraculous achievements." The labor leader informed the senators that "in the first place, we of organized labor feel that full credit should go to Mr. Higgins himself for his genius as an inventor and producer, as well as his untiring energy and unquestionable patriotism." He continued: "Labor has an abiding confidence in Mr. Higgins and the teamwork between him and his employees is remarkable. There are never any disputes and his employees are at all times exceedingly anxious to break production records over and over."[18]

Higgins appreciated the wholehearted support but had to admit that disagreements did sometimes occur. He explained that when this happened, management and labor got together in the soundproof conference room and both sides let their hair down, "but when they came out of that room the disputes were history and harmony prevailed." In closing the investigative session, Senator James M. Mead of New York noted that

---

18. "Truman Committee of Congress Pays Tribute to the 'Men of Higgins,'" *Eureka News Bulletin,* II (April, 1943), 1.

it was the organizational ability of these men, their genius in leadership, and their farsightedness that made them stand out so far ahead of their competitors. They faced the same common problems in their field that others faced, yet they had succeeded where others had failed. Mead suggested that many companies stressed common ailments as a reason for the lack of their success when instead they should have emphasized the need for sound management. He said that the men who had been called before the committee had not run to Washington or the press every time they encountered a problem. They met it head-on and solved it on the job, and that was the reason for their exceptional record. In his final analysis, Mead suggested that to solve the problems of American industry "what we need probably is more Higginses." [19]

Mead was not the only one to take notice of Higgins' abilities during May. In a front-page story published in the German newspaper *Voelkischer Boebachter,* Hitler made mention of the American industrialist and the boats he had developed. This incredible piece of Nazi propaganda informed its readers that in America Higgins was referred to as the "new Noah" and that he was about to solve problems even more complicated than those confronted by the biblical Noah during the great flood. The newspaper suggested that the inventor of this new "Alligator Ark" planned to use his craft under the pretense of opening the dense jungles of South America to United States trade, but in reality he was transporting building materials into the vast jungle regions of South America to help turn the land into a continent of synagogues.

The article reported that Higgins was a true self-made man, who understood the power of advertisement and in this respect even surpassed the Jewish shipbuilder Kaiser. Accused of being partners with Higgins in this South American expansion project were Roosevelt and cartoonist Walt Disney. Roosevelt was described as a man who had his chair pushed into the map room of the White House several times a day and gazed for hours at his globe and secret maps, dreaming of a new American empire. The Nazi newspaper claimed that the world press was aware of this and frequently made mention of Roosevelt's cartomania.

Disney and his characters were included in the expansionist scenario because the paper claimed that Donald Duck symbolized "in its youthful impudence the Yankees," and his samba-dancing parrot friend represented Brazil. The "snarling, stubborn dog" dressed in the gaucho attire,

19. *Ibid.,* 2.

which appeared at various times with Donald and the parrot, represented Argentina, while the baby airplane that appeared in the cartoons stood for American imperialism.[20]

Gladstone Williams, a nationally syndicated American columnist, responded to the absurd German propaganda: "The Higgins boats, as they now have come to be known throughout the world, will not be used for a Zionist colonization scheme in South America, as Hitler's newspaper claims. Germany will be the Mount Ararat on which they will land in the final invasion which will come as a prelude to peace." Williams did agree with one statement in the article—Higgins could be called the "new Noah." His shipyards' phenomenal production records, the reporter reasoned, gave him fair claim to such a title.[21]

While the Nazis were spreading propaganda about Higgins' South American intentions, others in the United States were circulating rumors that his shipbuilding contract with the army was going to be canceled. Higgins insisted that this rumor was spread because his competitors were alarmed that he was actually going to produce the FP ships as rapidly as predicted and at the contract price. He suggested that because the construction process was proving successful, lies were being circulated that the ships were not well designed, that they would turn over and sink, and that the contract was to be terminated.

To those who told him of the rumors Higgins explained that he was almost immune to gossip about cancellation and change. In his opinion, the constant threat of losing his contract, whether it was for landing craft or Liberty ships, had been healthy though irritating. In his words it had made him "a little tough, maybe even belligerent." He claimed that others were condemning him and his company as opportunists, blowhards, braggarts, or notoriety seekers. To these accusations, as well as to the cancellation rumors, he responded, "I will here confess that we admit that we are good, and it's a damned good thing we are, and it's a very good thing that we are well regarded by the American public, by the labor unions, and by the boys that are doing the fighting and dying, and, if some of these obstructionists actually consummate what is rumored, we are prepared to take our case to the American people."[22]

20. "Who's Afraid of the Big Bad Wolf? Who's Afraid of the Men of Higgins? No One Less Than Adolf Hitler Himself!" *Eureka News Bulletin,* II (August, 1943), 2.

21. "Washington Comments on Hitler's Editorial About Higgins Activities in South America," *Eureka News Bulletin,* II (October, 1943), 39.

22. "Revisal," 70–71.

Higgins strongly believed that an attempt was under way to cancel his contract, and he suspected the culprit behind it was William Francis Gibbs. Gibbs was a lawyer, engineer, and head of the New York firm Gibbs and Cox, which specialized in designing Liberty ships, destroyers, tankers, cruisers, and large tank landing ships. During a twenty-four-hour period Gibbs's massive organization turned out thousands of blueprints, issued up to 6,700 purchase orders, and spent approximately a million dollars on materials for the production of various ships.

Gibbs was also well-known because he served as a consultant in redesigning shipyards. He helped to increase output and lower man-hours by introducing mass-production techniques. It was natural for Higgins and Gibbs to be competitors, but one major problem was that they were not competitors on an equal playing field. Gibbs also served as coordinator of shipbuilding for the War Production Board.

Higgins assumed that Gibbs had been appointed to the position because of his highly placed contacts. In a letter to Clarke Salmon, head of Bauerlein Advertising in New Orleans, Higgins stated, "It is none the less a fact that possibly through the Wall Street influence, Assistant Secretary of the Navy Forrestal, and Admiral King, who is reported as being very close and friendly with Gibbs, Gibbs was appointed as Supervisor or Co-ordinator of Shipbuilding for the War Production Board." Higgins continued: "This makes a pretty kettle of fish. Here is this man Gibbs, whose organization is stretched very, very thin, with a tremendous amount of work they have received on a silver platter, and who is power hungry, and profit and money hungry, in the War Production Board, and possibly balanced with (could it be opposed by) Joe Powell, another great patriot, Co-ordinator of Shipbuilding for the Navy, and Special Assistant to the Secretary of the Navy." Higgins surmised, "With these two great disinterested people, each drawing a dollar a year, controlling and/or hamstringing the shipbuilding program, the people of the armed forces are not going to have much of a chance."[23]

Higgins suggested that it was "incongruous" for Gibbs to serve as coordinator of the War Production Board and that his position there exposed both Gibbs and the administration to criticism. He considered it highly inappropriate for a man who virtually held the responsibility of approving designs for government departments to be the head of a com-

23. Andrew Higgins to Clarke Salmon, May 1, 1943, in Strahan Personal Collection.

pany that executed a great many of these designs for the navy. He also considered it inexcusable for the president of a company to accept a dollar a year as head of an agency that gave him the power to impose his will and his designs on his competitors. He firmly believed that Gibbs was using his position to question the construction of the FP ships and to initiate steps to effect a cancellation of that contract. Higgins considered the entire situation to be a "cruelty to Mr. Donald Nelson, and his excellent second in command, Mr. Charles E. Wilson, that they have to be burdened with a man with this power, even if he was endowed with unquestioned patriotism and unquestioned impulses, attributes that it is said he does not possess." Higgins was convinced that Gibbs had been assisted in the alleged cancellation attempt by Under Secretary of the Navy James Forrestal and perhaps even by Admiral King. He was not certain whether jealousy had prompted their action or if there was another motive. In his letter to Salmon he related that because of his fast action the attempt had been defeated but that the three would try a new line of attack.[24]

The action Higgins referred to was the placing of a full-page ad in the *Times Picayune*, the New York *Times*, and several other major publications on April 27. Instead of waiting until the contract had been canceled, he took the offensive. The ad read in bold script across the top of the page "A Pledge," and below it was written in a giant headline "100-SHIP ORDER TO HIGGINS." In a paragraph placed midway down the left side of the page the public was informed that the ships awarded to Higgins under the contract of January 11, 1943, were now under construction in a plant facility that had been built without government subsidy. Materials and subcontracts for fabrications amounting to approximately $20 million (representing more than half of the contract) had been made, were on hand, or were arriving according to a well-regulated schedule. Higgins informed the readers that he had not encountered any difficulties in procurement because the War Production Board was functioning efficiently. The paragraph concluded with a pledge to build the "ships faster, better and cheaper than previously conceived to be possible." Midway down the page on the right-hand side were two large reprints of Western Union telegrams and a statement from labor. A telegram from the Bureau of Ships stated, "The Bureau of Ships is following with Admiration the

24. *Ibid.*

efforts you, the officials and workers of the Higgins Industries are putting forth to accomplish the heavy task we have imposed upon you." In the second telegram the president of the AFL stated, "Delighted to see War Department announcement of award of contract to Higgins Industries for rapid construction of 100 small cargo vessels thus affording Higgins and labor an opportunity to demonstrate and prove their efficiency in line production on ships, an opportunity denied them when the Maritime Commission canceled their Liberty Ship order." The third reprinted statement was a simple pledge from the AFL Shipbuilding and Associated Trades Union. It promised: "Rain or shine—night or day—the task will be completed on or before schedule. We are aware of the need. We will not let our armed forces down."[25]

Higgins reasoned that his ad had prevented the cancellation but that his opponents were now attempting to have the contract modified and transferred to another department, possibly the navy or the Maritime Commission, where they could exert more influence. He was certain that his production was going to be suspended and possibly the firm of Gibbs and Cox would to be called in to redesign the ships, and as a result he would not be able to produce them as rapidly or cheaply as planned. He was adamant that he would not submit to such a move.

The rumors of Gibbs and the cancellation attempt brought back earlier hard feelings that Higgins had had for the War Production Board's coordinator of shipbuilding. Gibbs had been featured on the front cover of *Time* magazine in September, 1942. Behind the close-up drawing of Gibbs appeared silhouettes of Higgins LCPLs and LCMs. To Higgins the picture inferred that all the boats on the cover had been designed by Gibbs. It was as if someone had stabbed him in the heart with a knife.

Gibbs, the cancellation attempt, and the cover of *Time* were the main topics Higgins covered in his letter to Salmon. He admitted that many of his friends had described Gibbs as an able man, a good businessman, and a good politician, but he added, "Of course, I have heard a lot of criticism, and statements have been made from time to time that he and his associates make more mistakes in design that outdo the Annapolis graduates or the civilians in the Navy Department." Another criticism Higgins levied against Gibbs was that he took credit for designs he had not done and that he had perfected "the art of freeing himself, and his firm, of

25. "A Pledge," *Eureka News Bulletin*, II (May, 1943), inside front cover.

numerous bad, as well as poor designs." According to Higgins, Gibbs accomplished this by involving his customer, who in most cases was the navy. He would then blame the customer for the vessel's poor performance should it not meet acceptable standards. Higgins also mentioned several large landing boats that he claimed were originally his concept but that were mysteriously being produced by his competitors. He then charged that his ideas had been taken by the navy and turned over to selected companies for development. Three such designs were for tank carriers of 105, 150, and 298 feet. It was the theft of his 298-foot "Atlantic tank carrier" concept that upset Higgins the most. He claimed that his idea had been heavily modified and then several boats of this new design were built on the Ohio River and later turned over to the British. The British, according to Higgins, had shown their sense of humor by changing the unofficial lettering to "D.T.," insinuating that the crew would get "delirium tremens in normal operations, but that the boats themselves would be a *death trap* either in bad weather, or in attempting to make a landing." Higgins credited Gibbs with the designing of the DTs, though he claimed the original idea was his own.[26]

The DT referred to by Higgins actually went under the designation of LST (landing ship tank). Higgins insisted that his Atlantic tank carrier was the "grand-daddy" of the LST, which he had originally designed in 1940 during the early stages of the emergency. Then, as the battle over London was raging and the ports of London, Liverpool, and Glasgow were being bombed by the Nazis, he renewed his efforts to have it developed. His premise was that large American merchant ships could deliver supplies to Iceland and then this 298-foot version of his Eureka could transfer the cargoes to the many coves of Scotland. The goods would be unloaded and transported overland to Britain.[27]

In his letter he insisted that he tried to interest the U.S. Navy in his idea but did not receive an "attentive ear." Therefore, he turned to the British, who appeared enthusiastic about the concept. Shortly after their initial contact, six English representatives arrived in New Orleans to investigate the craft's design. After the opening rounds of talk, three members of the delegation flew back to England while the other three remained for additional deliberations.

26. Higgins to Salmon, May 1, 1943, in Strahan Personal Collection.
27. Caption, *Eureka News Bulletin,* III (January–March, 1944), 137.

British prime minister Winston Churchill was supposedly informed by the returning representatives of the proposed vessel. Later, during a December, 1941, visit to Washington, the prime minister was said to have spoken with FDR about manufacturing such a craft. According to Higgins, Roosevelt "called the Navy in and gave them Hell, giving them instructions to have these classes and sizes and types of boats built." Higgins also argued that the Bureau of Ships, with which he was not on the best of terms at the time, prevented him from participating in the final designing and manufacturing of the Atlantic tank carrier (LST), even though the initial idea and plans were his. He maintained that Joseph W. Powell (deputy chief of procurement and materials for the Navy Department), Forrestal, Captain Claude Jones, and possibly Captain Rawlings had decided that he should not be involved in the project. Higgins claimed they even had a classmate of Sam Eaton's, a Commander Lemler, call Eaton and tell him that if he caught wind of what was going on not to mention anything to his boss. They supposedly told Eaton that they had already decided who was going to build the LSTs and that they wanted to keep Higgins in the background but still available to build small boats.[28]

It was the rumor that Gibbs was involved in the attempt to cancel his army contract that had brought the cover of *Time* magazine and the Atlantic tank carrier to mind. These thoughts from the past had made Higgins determined not to allow Gibbs and his associates once more to gain the upper hand. Precautions had been taken, and for the moment he felt that his contract was relatively secure. He now devoted time to overseeing the production of landing craft and PT boats, construction of his new airplane plant, building FP ships, and organizing the Higgins-Tucker Engine Company plant to manufacture marine engines for the army.

To assist in the development of engines at Higgins-Tucker, Higgins brought in as chief test engineer one of the most knowledgeable men in the field, Arthur Chevrolet. Arthur and his brother Louis had founded the Chevrolet Car Company in 1911. In 1916, when W. C. Durant, the financier of the company, decided to sell out to General Motors, the Chevrolets were left "out in the cold." The brothers first used their tal-

28. Andrew Higgins to Rudolph Halley, July 13, 1943, in National Defense Committee Files, Records of the Special Committee of the Senate to Investigate the National Defense Program, Sen. 79A F30, OP-33, Record Group 46, Shipyards and Other Companies, National Archives.

ents to build racing engines for Indianapolis 500 cars and later became involved in the development of airplane engines.

The difficult financial climate in 1932 forced them to end their partnership. Arthur found employment for two years as a research engineer for Cummings-Diesel, then accepted the challenge of helping Preston Tucker develop an engine called the Mighty Miller. The small engine, designed for use in midget auto racing cars, was renowned for its tremendous speed. Chevrolet returned to Cummings in 1936 and remained until Higgins convinced him in 1943 to come to Higgins-Tucker to help develop a new marine engine. The challenge proved too much to resist. Arthur and Louis had developed racing car engines and airplane engines, and Higgins had total faith that Arthur would work the same miracles with the new marine diesels. Unfortunately, Louis would not be able to assist in the task; he had died in late 1941.[29]

Chosen to join Chevrolet at the plant as head of the production line was Henry H. Smith, an engine manufacturing specialist. Smith had received his early training from the Packard Company and had also worked for General Motors in the Brown-Lipe-Chapin Division, the Fisher Body Division, and the Aircraft Division. Recently, he had been employed at the Higgins-Tucker plant in Ypsilanti, Michigan, which was one of Tucker's original facilities. Smith was transferred to New Orleans to implement the production techniques necessary to mass produce Chevrolet's marine engine.[30]

As Smith organized for the quantity manufacturing of marine engines, Graham Haddock, superintendent of the Industrial Canal plant, attempted to solve the problems related to the mass production of tank lighters. Before the North African invasions in November, 1942, U.S. tanks had used gasoline engines. The military discovered that these engines were not suited for the hot, sandy terrain they were about to encounter. The solution seemed simple—convert to diesel engines. But the diesels under production were already allocated for use in landing boats. Washington changed the orders and gave tanks a higher priority rating. The Bureau of Ships informed Higgins that for an unspecified period of time he would not receive engines.

29. "Famous Automobile Manufacturer Joins Higgins-Tucker," *Eureka News Bulletin*, II (June, 1943), 2.

30. "A Speedy Production Line Assured at Higgins-Tucker," *Eureka News Bulletin*, II (June, 1943), 3.

Decisions had to be made. Higgins mass produced his boats on a production line, and when they reached the designated station the engines had to be installed. When the last available engine was mounted in a boat, the production line would come to an immediate halt. Work could not continue because the system was designed so that each step built on the preceding one.

In the midst of the war, Higgins Industries was about to stop production. If this happened, workers would have to find employment elsewhere until engines were received. Higgins realized that it would be impossible to reassemble the work force. There had to be an answer; surely something could be done.

A simple but very effective solution was developed. A mock-up engine was constructed from several pieces of six-inch pipe. The necessary connecting features of the real engine were duplicated on the mock-up so that the boat could proceed down the line. The fittings, wiring, and mounts were all installed so that when the real engines arrived, all the workers had to do was drop the diesels in place and connect the matching features. As the engine compartment on each boat was completed, the mock-ups were removed and put in the next craft coming down the line.

In May the City Park plant had approximately 700 boats (LCVPs and LCPLs) tied up in Bayou St. John without engines. The Industrial Canal plant had about 375 LCMs lining both sides of the waterway near the plant. Then, on very short notice, the bureau informed Higgins that engines would soon arrive and a specified number of boats had to be shipped by a certain date to various ports of embarkation.

The boats were constructed and floating in the bayou, but mechanics had to install engines and pipe fitters and electricians needed access to complete their tasks. All this had to be accomplished within the bureau's timetable, but how and where? Graham Haddock suggested using the canal as a production line. The idea was brilliantly simple but highly effective. For almost two blocks along the wharf electrical outlets were installed, oxyacetylene lines and welding machines were placed under protective shelters, and substock rooms were constructed for machinists, pipe fitters, and installation mechanics. Anywhere from fifteen to twenty boats were handled at a time.

At the beginning of the line the shipfitters installed the battery and vent boxes. The boat then moved to the machinists, who were responsible for the clutch controls, steering gear, and aligning the motors. After they were finished, the boat was pulled down the line to the electricians and then to the installation mechanics, who were responsible for the bilge system, fuel pumps, and the remainder of the work on the boat.

Once the boat was completed, it was sent further down the wharf for dock trials. Here the engines were tested before the trial run. The water production line functioned so well that at one point the Industrial Canal plant was delivering as many as eighteen LCMs a day and the City Park workers were turning out up to thirty-six boats during a twenty-four-hour period at Bayou St. John. The increased production created a problem for the navy inspectors. Before acceptance by the military, all boats had to be submitted to a four-hour trial run. With fifty-four boats a day ready for shipment there was a shortage of inspectors. The only way the regulations could be followed was to have one inspector go out with four or five boats at a time and transfer from boat to boat as all of them traveled the test course together.

Once the boat had been accepted, it was brought back to the plant, taken out of the water, the bottom repainted, and the boat lowered back into the canal. Two slings were placed around the craft and used to turn it on its side. Once this was accomplished, the boat was lifted from the canal and placed sideways on a flatcar for shipment. To ship the eighteen boats at the Industrial Canal, the one crane located at dockside had to lift each boat three times during the course of the day, which meant a total of fifty-four lifts during a twenty-four-hour period, plus the eighteen lifts necessary to put new boats in the water to replace the completed craft. The crane was either loading or unloading a boat approximately every twenty minutes twenty-four hours a day.

Another problem Haddock had to confront was that the plant had only one railroad line. On this line eighteen empty gondola cars had to be brought in each day to be used in loading boats, eighteen other cars with LCMs already aboard had to be transferred out, while at the same time shipments of sand, gravel, and concrete were being delivered for use in building the new ways on which the FP ships were to be produced.

While all of this was occurring, carloads of steel were being delivered for use in building landing craft and at least four carloads of engines per day had to be unloaded. To make matters worse, at one point there was a backlog of seventy carloads of steel for the FP ships stationed at a nearby railroad terminal waiting to be dropped off. This massive bottleneck made Higgins delinquent in getting cars back to the Louisville and

Nashville Railroad. The company threatened an embargo, but the navy quickly put a stop to that idea. Higgins promised that once the navy's emergency delivery had been fulfilled, he would dedicate 100 percent of his effort to unloading the steel. He fulfilled his promise by having his crews unload the seventy cars on undeveloped property across from his plant. It took three days to accomplish the task and then three months to unscramble the jumbled mess.[31]

In the midst of this hectic period, on May 13 Higgins was called to Omaha to accept an honorary doctorate of laws degree from Creighton University. During the presentation ceremonies, the dean of the College of Commerce read to the graduates and guests from the citation covering the degree: "Tradition honors the men who go down to the sea in ships. Today we honor a man who sends ships down to the sea. By his daring and courage and inspired leadership in our fight for freedom, he is no longer a citizen of any one city or state but of all America, and merits from his Alma Mater the degree of Doctors of Laws *honoris causa*." It was a ceremony in which Creighton honored one of its family members it felt richly deserved recognition. Higgins was not an alumnus of the university; in fact, he had never taken a college-level course. He had attended Creighton Prep from 1901 through 1903 and left before studying humanities, which was equivalent to the fourth year of high school. The level at which he had participated mattered not to the university's faculty. Higgins had once been a part of Creighton's program, was still a part of its family, and was deserving of the award.[32]

Not long after returning home from Nebraska, Higgins was visited by the noted English author Hillary St. George Saunders. Saunders, known as the assistant librarian in the House of Commons and also as the official recorder of the Combined Operations Command of Lord Louis Mountbatten, traveled to New Orleans to interview the boat builder for an upcoming book on great American industrialists. Previously he had published such works as *Battle for Britain, Coastal Command, Front Line,* and *Combined Operations.* The latter book told the story of the famous British commando units directed by Lord Mountbatten. Before Saunders'

---

31. Graham Haddock, interview, July 25, 1992; "Higgins Speeds Work on Tank Lighters with New Water Production Line," *Eureka News Bulletin,* II (June, 1943), 58.

32. "Andrew Jackson Higgins Honored," *Eureka News Bulletin,* II (June, 1943), 1; Records of Andrew Jackson Higgins, in University Relations Central Files, Creighton University, Omaha, Nebraska; "Andrew J. Higgins" (Clipping, *ibid.*).

visit to New Orleans, Mountbatten had instructed the author to deliver a message personally to Higgins. He wished the builder to know that without the equipment his company was producing, the commando units "could not function." Saunders visited Higgins at the Industrial Canal plant. Upon opening the door to the second floor office, he saw the builder standing outlined in front of a window overlooking the canal. In his book he explained that he found it difficult to describe "this most remarkable man—the most outstanding figure" he met in the United States. He recalled that he had interviewed "many business men and not a few captains of industry in America. They all had drive, most of them vision, and a few genius." Saunders wrote, "Mr. Higgins possesses all three."[33]

Saunders, like the faculty at Creighton, thought that Higgins richly deserved the recognition he was finally receiving. National reports on the invasions of the Solomons, the raids at Dieppe, the landings in North Africa, and the reoccupation of the Aleutian Islands all referred to the amphibious boats used in the operations, not by their military designation, LCM, LCVP, or LCPL, but as "Higgins boats."

Ships built by Kaiser sailed under names issued by the navy or the Maritime Commission, the airplanes manufactured by the major producers were known by a letter and numerical designation such as B-17, B-29, or an official nickname such as the Flying Fortress, but not by the name of the manufacturer, as was the case with the LCPL, LCVP, and LCM. Instead of using the military designations for landing craft, writers and soldiers alike simply referred to the amphibious craft as Higgins boats.

Higgins had achieved an international reputation because of his craft and his company's performance. Writers from the local press, to nationally syndicated columnists, to Saunders, to Hitler's own publication had paid tribute to his incredible accomplishments. His record from Pearl Harbor to June, 1943, had established him as the world leader in small-boat design and development. In July his company's performance and its radically new production techniques were so outstanding that even his staunchest critics wondered if Higgins might not truly be the "new Noah."

33. "British Author Lauds Higgins as Outstanding Industrialist," *Eureka News Bulletin*, III (January–March, 1944), 71.

8

THE COMPLETION OF MICHAUD

Higgins-Tucker Engine Company was nearing completion of its New Orleans plant in June, 1943. To facilitate a smooth start, Higgins and Tucker transferred several workers from Tucker's original plant in Ypsilanti, Michigan, to the new southern location. To welcome the employees, Higgins threw a party in their honor. Chosen as the site was the second floor banquet room of Broussard's Restaurant, located in the heart of the French Quarter.

Attending the event were Higgins and key members of his local organization and Tucker and his transferred staff. The well over a hundred guests spent the evening casually talking and becoming acquainted. All was going exceedingly well. The elaborate decorations, the food, the drinks, the floor show featuring dancing girls, and the atmosphere of the French Quarter had everyone in a festive mood. As the crowd dispersed and headed down the stairs, however, one of "Tucker's men" made a smart remark about Higgins.

Ted Sprague, standing on the step in front of the man, took great offense at the comment. Immediately, he turned and decked the offender. Sprague recalled, "I really admired Mr. Higgins and to have some jerk from up around Detroit making remarks about him was just more than I could stand." An event that was supposed to have blended the two companies turned into a brawl. Fifty people were jammed in the stairwell with approximately ten employees from each side actively involved in the fight. The rest were either trying to stop the melee or escape before they became casualties. Order was restored, but the corporate marriage had started with a rocky beginning.[1]

1. Ted Sprague, interview, August 2, 1992.

Higgins never questioned Sprague about the evening, but the young engineer was certain his boss had been informed about the incident. It was one of the few times that Sprague came in contact with the staff of the engine company. During the spring he had been deeply involved as the design engineer on a new experimental 70-foot PT boat nicknamed the *Hellcat*. The boat, completed in early summer, underwent builder's trials on Lake Pontchartrain on June 30, 1943. Present to witness the tests were navy representatives from the Miami Shakedown detail.

The shakedown had been established to help newly chosen PT crews learn to function as a team. Originally, all PT crews were sent to the navy's training center in Melville, Rhode Island, but the military decided to create a second combat training center in Miami as an adjunct to the Submarine Chaser Training Center. Here all crews headed for the Pacific via the Panama Canal were to receive their training. Commanding officer for the new unit was Lieutenant Commander Alan R. Montgomery, who had seen combat with Squadron 3 at Guadalcanal.

The *Hellcat* performed well during the trials on Lake Pontchartrain, reaching speeds of forty-six knots and reversing its course in nine seconds. The craft's design included a new lower silhouette and offered far greater visibility from the cockpit than earlier models had. At idle speeds the boat threw very little wake, which made it hard to see from the air. Both features were advantageous in a boat designed for hit-and-run tactics. The officers witnessing the trials noted the dramatic improvements and forwarded a highly favorable report to the Bureau of Ships.[2]

While Sprague continued conducting tests of the *Hellcat*, Higgins' plants rapidly turned out landing boats. Once completed, they were docked along the banks of the Industrial Canal and Bayou St. John. At one point more than three hundred craft were tied up and waiting for shipment. Higgins discovered that a similar number of boats had been built by other shipyards and were in storage on the West Coast. The military was in desperate need of tank lighters in its theaters of operations but had no means available to transport the craft. A bottleneck had been created because production had surpassed shipping capabilities.

The lighter was so large that only four to six could be transported on the deck of a cargo ship. To add to the problem, deck space had been designated for shipment of higher-priority aircraft. Months earlier Hig-

2. Bulkley, *At Close Quarters*, 76–78.

gins had predicted the problem and recommended a unique procedure to the navy. He had suggested completely building the lighter and then cutting it into nineteen sections using an oxyacetylene torch. Rough edges were to be ground, cleaned, and repainted and the various sections marked and crated for shipment. The crates could then be shipped in the cargo holds of transports, where space was more readily available. The lighters would be reassembled at predetermined points by military personnel.

In June the navy sent two junior officers to New Orleans to investigate the procedure. The young officers sat in Higgins' office and informed him that his idea was "impractical." In disgust Higgins left the meeting. He proceeded to the yard below, where he ordered his men to cut a lighter into sections, as had previously been discussed, then reassemble it for testing. To the amazement of the officers, the impractical was accomplished while they watched. Changing their opinion, they recommended to their superiors that the program be implemented.

The U.S. Engineers Amphibian Command, the prime user of the craft, immediately supported the experiment. Representatives were dispatched to seek Higgins' assistance in training their personnel. Engineers had to be taught to reassemble the lighters, and Higgins' plants seemed to be the most logical place for that to occur.

At the request of the engineers, Higgins arranged for six hundred officers and noncommissioned officers to spend thirty days working on the assembly line with his skilled craftsmen. The soldiers were taught the various techniques necessary to reassemble the lighters. Duplicate jigs, molds, and forms were built and given to the engineers to assist them at their overseas bases.

One young officer assigned to the program was Second Lieutenant Roland Higgins, Higgins' son. Roland had entered the military as a private and on his own merit had qualified and later received an appointment to Officers' Training School. After graduation he had requested duty with the U.S. Engineers Amphibian Command. He had hoped for combat duty, but he was too valuable to the engineers because of his tremendous knowledge of landing boats and tank lighters. Roland's orders for the moment put him back in the same plant that he had left only months before.[3]

3. "Revisal," 37–38; "A 'Knock-Down' Cruise," *Airlines*, May, 1944, pp. 34, 55.

July marked another special but unheralded occasion, the completion of Higgins' first 170-foot cargo vessel for the army, FP 135. The keel had been laid on March 3, 1943, and on July 21 the boat slid down the ways and into the water. The plant was not complete, but the launchings had begun. No special ceremonies marked the event because the workers were too busy trying to maintain their production schedule. With the number of PTs and landing boats being produced, this was simply one more ship in the canal.[4]

The only acknowledgment of the launching was a story released by Higgins' newly hired public relations man, Dave McGuire. The press release on the event pleased Higgins, but McGuire's initial experiences had him wondering if accepting the position had been the right decision. In a letter to a friend the day after the launching, he wrote: "I am in the process of getting acclimated at Higgins Industries, Inc., as a public relations man and liaison man between Higgins and Clarke Salmon, who handles his advertising and is paid to counsel and guide Andrew Jackson on public relations. The situation is complicated by three factors. First the Higgins clan, a rough lusty clan surrounded by satellites who resent outsiders coming in—especially a public relations guy who will have to be close to the boss."[5]

"Secondly," he continued, "Higgins may not want the kind of public relations that I'll want to give him—and he may not want honest, direct comment. I have been told by one person who should know that the only way to be successful in this giant, mushrooming industrial empire is to kiss the ass of Higgins and his four sons and Gottesman, his treasurer. If that's a prerequisite then I won't be in the job very long."

The third factor was George Washington Rappelyea. McGuire saw him as "a sort of general assistant to Higgins, editor of the House organ, etc. who fancies himself as a public relations man and is very jealous of anyone coming in and getting next to Higgins. The office politics, the intrigue and the maneuvers that go on in this screwball outfit make the government agencies look like amateurs. Life was tranquil and peaceful in OWI compared to this. . . . In my brief contacts with GOD, he has been very pleasant."

4. "First of Hundreds of Higgins Army Cargo Ships Launched," *Eureka News Bulletin,* II (August, 1943), 1.

5. Dave McGuire to Smith, July 22, 1943, in McGuire Collection. Quotations in the following paragraphs are from this source.

When McGuire initially reported to the plant to assume his new position, he discovered that there was no office manager, no one to assist him in getting settled. He had not been assigned an office and was uncertain who was to handle the problem. He decided to discuss it with the plant manager, Ed Higgins, Higgins' oldest son. Of his encounter with Ed, McGuire wrote: "He was looking through a telescope watching some women war workers at Delta (shipyard) several miles down the Canal. Finally, after several minutes, he looked up but said nothing and returned to his telescope. A minute or two later he looked back at me somewhat irritated. I introduced myself, said I would be handling public relations and working with Salmon and Rappleyea, etc., and that I would probably be calling on him. He mumbled something and shook hands because he had to. No welcome to our organization, no offer of cooperation, no nothing. So I said I'm glad to know you, Mr. Higgins, but he was back at his telescope and didn't even hear me." To solve his office problem, McGuire simply found a room that was unused and declared squatter's rights.

On August 3, as McGuire settled in his new surroundings, the Industrial Canal plant prepared to complete its second FP ship. News also arrived that the War Department had restructured its contract with Higgins Aircraft. In place of the small wooden C-76 cargo planes, Higgins was to construct the larger aluminum C-46 Commandos. The announcement from Washington explained that aluminum was no longer in short supply. Metal was now more readily available than wood.[6] What it did not announce was that wood was being diverted to the production of landing craft, much of it being used not far away at Higgins' shipyards.

Higgins had prepared for the manufacturing of plywood planes. A giant oven known as an autoclave, in which layers of wood and glue are heated to form bonded wood, had been installed at Michaud. The bonded wood was needed in the production of molded aircraft bodies. Higgins, over the objections of Senator Alexander Wiley of Wisconsin, had also built his own plywood mill. Wiley had vigorously protested to WPB chairman Donald Nelson that the plywood plant should not be allowed to be constructed.

Before Higgins' plywood and veneer mill was built, logs were shipped

6. "Large Crowd Attends Higgins Aircraft Plant Dedication," *Eureka News Bulletin*, II (November, 1943), 3.

from the South to Wisconsin, made into plywood, and then shipped back to New Orleans. At times, the plant had to wait weeks for a supply of lumber. The industrialist argued that to mass produce aircraft he had to be able to manufacture his own plywood. Higgins won the battle, and the facility was built next to Michaud.

Once his contract was restructured, the plywood plant was of little use in cargo plane production but was of great use in boat building. Aluminum construction required untooling and then retooling Michaud and even hiring a different type of employee. Neither Higgins nor the War Department foresaw any major problems, and both believed the aircraft facility could readily adjust.

On Friday, August 6, three days after the War Department's announcement, a special group of visitors arrived in New Orleans. Senator Truman and several members of his committee were touring the South investigating the decline in aircraft production. For Higgins this was the perfect opportunity to showcase his company's capabilities.

Saturday morning, Higgins, accompanied by McGuire, took the senators on a tour of the various plants. Later that afternoon, in honor of their visit, a formal ceremony was staged for the launching of Higgins' second FP ship. As part of the festivities a marine pageant displaying the various Higgins boats was put on in the canal and Archbishop Joseph Francis Rummel delivered a special prayer blessing a torpedo squadron and crew.[7]

During the ceremonies, Senator Homer Ferguson of Michigan, a member of the committee, spoke to the thousands of workers. In announcing July's production figures he acknowledged that Higgins Industries had shipped more than 700 boats during the month. Included in the figure were 600 landing craft and 118 tank lighters. The senator praised the workers and said: "The production and performance is unequaled . . . Andrew Jackson Higgins can be said to be the number one boat producer in the nation. The men and women of Higgins are doing the impossible and they are doing it well."[8]

Senator Harley M. Kilgore of West Virginia approached the microphone and told the employees and the radio audience that "shipping out

7. "Higgins Output Leading Nation, Senator Reveals," *Eureka News Bulletin*, II (September, 1943), 1–3.

8. *Ibid.*

more than 700 various types of landing craft to the Navy in 30 days represents a gigantic task—a gargantuan job. But it was done and done well—and nobody appears any the worse for it except possibly the Japs and the Germans."[9]

The tour and the festivities at the plant gave McGuire an opportunity to observe Higgins in a variety of situations. He wrote to a friend after the ceremonies: "The Senators were sincerely impressed by what they saw here—the quantity and quality production, the excellent labor relations, etc. I was impressed too, on this jaunt with the Senators, because it was my best close-up of Higgins and of the plants he operates. His men have a deep respect and affection for him. In any of the 5 plants we visited—City Park, Industrial Canal, Higgins-Tucker Engine Company, Bayou St. John, and the Higgins Aircraft Plant at Michaud, as well as the new plywood plant—Higgins can explain the theory and the practical application of any machine or operation. He knows woods, metals and machinery. His vision is unlimited." McGuire continued: "I don't think I made a mistake in accepting this job over the OPA deal in Dallas. This is an opportunity to learn industrial public relations and to be associated with a man who is without a doubt the most amazing and colorful character since Huey Long. Higgins might not like the comparison, but he has many of Huey's characteristics—brilliance, imagination, great physical endurance and vigor, a remarkable memory and great ego."[10]

A few weeks later, McGuire wrote to another friend, Owen R. Hutchinson. He explained: "I have an intense admiration for Higgins as a production man, as an inventive genius and as a practical dreamer with a vast imagination who can translate human needs into realities. The production side of his organization is tops. It's wonderful." Nevertheless, he stated: "The administrative side stinks. It simply hasn't kept pace with the fast and great growth of the small boat business into an industrial empire. In 5 weeks at Higgins I have seen as much confusion, indecision, duplication, lack of coordination and orderly system, as I observed among the war agencies. The Higgins bureaucracy, run by a tight little clique that retains among itself power and authority instead of wanting new blood and delegation of responsibilities, is as bad or worse as any I

9. "Truman Committee Member Praises Higgins Workers," *Eureka News Bulletin*, II (September, 1943), 1, 3, 4.
10. Dave McGuire to L. L. Sisk, August 9, 1943, in McGuire Collection.

have seen in government." McGuire contended that Higgins himself was responsible for many of the company's problems. He considered him a poor administrator. His biggest fault was that he tried to keep too much under his own control, with the result that poor planning caused great confusion. Sometimes the wrong person was told to carry out a directive or the same directive was given to two or more persons. McGuire thought the latter occurred frequently.[11]

McGuire was not the only one to write about Higgins during the summer. National publications such as *Fortune* and *Life* did feature stories on him. In its July issue, *Fortune* described Higgins as "having a stocky build, a pleasantly malicious expression, and a ruddy visage." It claimed that he normally wore dark gabardine shirts and was not afraid to call someone he disliked an s.o.b. to his face. It also reported that Higgins knew all of his foremen personally and pretended to know the name of each of his twelve thousand workers. The article did point out that Higgins' low administrative and sales expenses "highlight a potential handicap in his postwar setup; he may not have the organization to swing so vast a business in normal times. Higgins Industries is now more of a production department of a corporation than a corporation." The article also asked: "Can Higgins continue to be the sole sparkplug? If so, what will happen if he dies? To whom will he delegate authority when it becomes necessary to ramify the management functions? Can his research system compete with the more formal conventional methods? To what extent are his sons being groomed to take places beside him?"[12] The writer saw many of the same problems that McGuire later recognized.

In its August issue, *Life* described Higgins as having "the characteristic bluntness of the oldtime American frontiersman" and of resembling "the conventional captain of industry about as much as a Commando resembles a desk sergeant."[13]

Mill and Factory, a trade publication, was also interested in doing a story on Higgins. Its editor, Harvey Conover, wrote the shipbuilder during August requesting answers to several questions. His first inquiry concerned manpower shortages. Higgins responded: "Yes, we have a manpower shortage. The draft boards are disregarding our request for

11. Dave McGuire to Owen R. (Buck) Hutchinson, n.d., *ibid.*
12. "The Boss," 101, 216.
13. Burck, "Mr. Higgins and His Wonderful Boats," 100.

deferment of skilled men that we have difficulty in replacing within a reasonable length of time. The draft boards are taking young engineers and draftsmen that we just cannot replace."[14]

Next, Conover wanted to know if there was a material shortage. Higgins answered: "Material shortages: Yes we are short of materials. Something will be critical today, and something else won't be so critical. We have change orders. By the time a change order goes into effect, the thing that is critical today might be plentiful when the change has been approved. Accordingly, our inventories in our warehouses increase. We are not permitted to use the critical, or the non-critical materials covered by the change."

When asked about government procedures, he stated: "We only build things of our own design; but, a lot of people who don't know anything about it make us change our own designs. This includes changing specifications, and, of course, this all comes under the caption of 'red tape.'"

On labor relations he said: "Oh yes, we have labor relations and plenty of them. We will ignore a discussion." On absenteeism, "Yes, we have plenty of this too, but less than anyone else." Labor turnover: "Terrific." Strikes: "No—there had better be no strikes." Overconfidence of workers: "We don't understand this, but we do understand the psychology of 'The War is Won' group. This group might also come under the category of, 'Are we working ourselves out of a job?' Some of them could come under the heading of, 'I hope this war lasts long enough', or how about, 'If we work harder, we may be looking for jobs'."

To the question about "cut backs" Higgins responded: "Cut-Backs: Oh yes, our back is cut until it is bleeding." Concerning running at top capacity he wrote, "We have never been able to run at top capacity." In reference to "Impossible to increase production," he answered, "Well, in spite of hell and high water, we have increased it—so much so that in the month just passed (July) we built more marine units than all the other shipbuilding plants, large, medium, and small, in the United States, combined."

Higgins related that though production records were restricted, the navy had permitted him to announce that during the month of July, 1943, his company had built and delivered to the navy over seven hundred var-

14. Andrew Higgins to Harvey Conover, August 12, 1943, in McGuire Collection. Quotations in the following five paragraphs are from this source.

ious types of craft. He wrote: "This figure does not include craft built for the Army and other government departments. Neither did it include 248 vessels that were built and on hand for the Navy, but which were not delivered, or shipped. . . . In spite of all the problems we cannot complain, inasmuch as we are out-producing all the balance of the country put together—but, we are not running at full capacity."

While the magazines were greatly interested in Higgins, the navy was greatly interested in his new 70-foot experimental PT boat. On August 26, the navy purchased the *Hellcat* and designated it PT 564.[15] Lieutenant Robert Searles took command of the boat in New Orleans, and accompanied by Sprague and a navy crew, sailed the PT under its own power nonstop to Florida without refueling. The standard 78-foot Higgins PTs going from New Orleans to Miami had to refuel at Pensacola, Tampa, and Key West. According to Searles, "This tells you something about the improved design of the 564." From the time the boat left the Industrial Canal plant to its arrival at Biscayne Bay it averaged thirty-four knots. The experimental 70-foot boat had a tremendous range even with its three Packard V-12 engines. Sprague recalled almost fifty years later, "It was really a record run."

Lieutenant Searles was assigned the task of putting the *Hellcat* through its trials in Florida. Searles had been a member of Squadron 3, commanding PT 38, and had seen active duty at Guadalcanal. After his Pacific duty he was assigned to the shakedown as a combat instructor. He later saw action in the English Channel as commander of Squadron 30. Searles was very familiar with both the Elco and Higgins PTs. When asked by the author to compare the speed of the *Hellcat* to that of the standard Higgins PT boats or to the Elco boats, he replied, "There is no comparison." During the trials, the *Hellcat* reached the amazing speed of fifty-four knots.[16]

Accompanying Searles on one of the trial runs as an observer was Irwin Chase, the designer and mainspring of Elco's PT boat program. The lieutenant put the *Hellcat* through its maneuvers, which he said "on this occasion were time tests for mobility. That is going full speed and bringing the helm hard over. Testing to see how fast it turned and then how fast it could get back up to speed after it had made a 180 degree turn."

---

15. Bulkley, *At Close Quarters,* 76.
16. Robert Searles, interview, August 16, 1992.

Chase was sitting aft, which was generally the most secure place on the boat. Searles recalled: "Chase had a stop watch and we got to the point where it was three, two, one, turn. I put the wheel hard over. The boat fit into the turn so readily, so accurately, so fast, that it threw him right on his ass. The boat came around and came up to speed way quicker than any Elco or standard Higgins. It was excellent for agility, mobility." [17]

Sprague recalled the tests saying, "In Miami, we ran the *Hellcat* against Elco's best boats and beat them." "Matter of fact," he commented, "Irwin Chase was so impressed with our boat that he offered me a job. I told him, 'Hell no, I'm a Higgins man.'" Competition between the two companies was fierce.

Upon Sprague's return to New Orleans, he was assigned as project engineer for the Higgins helicopter. Bossi had already begun designing the aircraft, and construction was scheduled to take place at the Delgado Trades School next to the City Park plant. Two instructors on the school's staff had previously built airplanes and were well acquainted with what Bossi was attempting to accomplish. The young engineer served as a liaison between Higgins and Bossi. He recalled: "Sometimes things grab you and you really go to town on them—this never really appealed to me. To like boats, to love them you might say, the helicopter just didn't have it. It was such a hell of a looking thing in the first place. Bossi knew what he wanted. I was sort of a fifth wheel. I didn't have a hell of a lot to contribute to it." [18]

While Sprague tried to become enthusiastic about the helicopter, the Higgins plants continued to turn out landing boats in record numbers. An article by Associated Press Washington correspondent Hamilton Faron, published September 20, 1943, on the front page of the *Times Picayune*, revealed that the navy at present had 14,072 vessels, including 613 warships. Only three years earlier the total number of vessels in the U.S. Navy was 1,076, of which 383 were larger fighting ships. The story claimed that of the navy's 14,072 vessels, 12,964 were boats designed by Higgins. Therefore, 92 percent of the U.S. Navy's vessels at the time of the announcement were Higgins boats. [19] Of the 12,964 boats, more than 8,000 had been built by Higgins in New Orleans—meaning that Higgins Industries built over 56 percent of the U.S. Navy's boats and ships. The

17. *Ibid.*
18. Ted Sprague, interview, August 4, 1992.
19. "Landing Boats Represent 92% of U.S. Navy," *Eureka News Bulletin*, II (October, 1943), 1.

figure did not include LCS boats or PTs; if they are included, the total rises to over 63 percent.

Boats were what Sprague wanted to design, and he soon received a reprieve from the helicopter. Within six weeks of delivering the *Hellcat* he was recalled to Florida. A new commander and crew had taken the boat beyond its limits. Sprague explained: "The guys in Miami monkeying around blew up one of the engines. . . . Blew a hole in the bottom four feet by four feet—pretty near lost it." Upon investigation, he discovered that the crew had decided that they could get more speed out of the boat. On each engine there was an automatic cutoff switch to protect it if it surpassed 2,500 revolutions per minute. The cutoff switches had not functioned because someone had taped them down. The crew had taken the boat out and were cruising at speeds of approximately fifty knots. As long as the propeller was in the water, the resistance held down the number of revolutions. Sprague explained: "The swell in the Gulf Stream is pretty darn mean. The boat came out of the water and one of the engines ran wild. A casting in the clutch blew apart. When it did, it blew the whole clutch housing apart which was full of oil and oil vapor. This was ignited by the sparks." The explosion blew the four-foot hole in the bottom. The boat was equipped with an unusual feature, a drainage system and watertight bulkheads. Each section could be individually sealed. The crew had been instructed in the procedure but had failed to secure the damaged section. When the boat put into port, the deck was awash. New engines had to be installed, the radar system replaced, and practically everything that had been underwater repaired. Sprague remained in Miami for almost six weeks supervising the work at a local shipyard.[20]

While the *Hellcat* was being repaired in Florida, Higgins was in New Orleans working to institute a learn-as-you-earn program to train fifteen hundred welders and related craftsmen a month for the Industrial Canal plant. In conjunction with the U.S. Army, the War Manpower Commission, and the Louisiana State Department of Education, Higgins planned to set up training centers in twenty cities across the state. Arrangements had been made for the state school system in those locations to assist in the program. Higgins needed a constant influx of employees to replace those who were drafted or joined the service. Increased production related to the FP contract also called for a larger work force.

A statewide advertising campaign was instituted to attract men in

20. Ted Sprague, interview, August 4, 1992.

white-collar positions, in nondeferrable jobs, and those who were partially disabled. A salary of fifty cents an hour was offered during training, and in New Orleans three centers offered instruction day and night. Transportation was provided for workers living within a hundred miles. Higgins, unlike Henry Ford at Willow Run, made every effort to see that his employees could get to their jobs. Ford took the approach that his company could do little if anything to see that workers had transportation. Higgins, on the other hand, sent company buses to outlying areas to bring employees to work.[21]

When Higgins began the program for the Industrial Canal plant, he also began hiring tremendous numbers of employees for Michaud. Highly skilled aircraft workers were harder to find than he had anticipated. Even though the total staff was not yet hired, official dedication ceremonies for Michaud were held October 24, 1943. Speeches were given by Governor Sam Jones, Higgins, and representatives of the army air force, the city of New Orleans, and the Defense Plant Corporation. The Higgins one-hundred-piece company band provided music for the festive event, and the grounds were open to the public. Displays such as the seven thousandth LCVP and the one thousandth LCM built by Higgins were on hand for the guests to view.

Higgins proudly announced in his speech that the plant had been completed ahead of schedule and that the cost had been held within the projected estimate of $27 million.[22] He informed his listeners that not one hour of double time had been paid during the construction. Ending his address he said, "When the time comes for investigations we hope we can be then as we are now, with clean hands before the public." Governor Jones told the crowd that "the plant marked the turning of an economic corner in the life of the state . . . that it meant better things for the people in peace if the vision of the builder is kept in mind." Colonel Bryant L. Boatner, representing the army air force, called Michaud "a monument to far-sighted men and to American Industry." In many respects Boatner was correct. Michaud was originally designed to build Liberty ships but was officially dedicated to produce C-46 cargo planes and wing panels for the Curtis-Wright C-46 plants in Louisville and St. Louis. Wing panel production had actually begun several weeks before.

21. "To Train Thousands," *Eureka News Bulletin*, II (October, 1943), 7.
22. "New Higgins Plant Dedicated," New York *Times*, October 25, 1943, p. 8.

It had taken creativity and determination to salvage what could have been an enormous waste of manpower and material. The converted facility served as an example of the flexibility of American industry. But it was not the flexibility of Higgins that impressed those attending the dedication ceremony—it was the enormous size of the plant that left them in awe.

Michaud could simultaneously house a dozen football games and a half dozen baseball games inside its main building. The machine shop alone was over four blocks long. The plant had more floor space under a single roof than any other manufacturing facility in the nation except Ford's plant at Willow Run. It was "a monument to American Industry," but to New Orleans it was a source of employment for a projected twenty thousand workers.[23]

It was an opportunity for thousands of people to learn new skills. But not everyone in the state applauded Higgins' new accomplishment. Butlers, maids, bartenders, farm help, sugarcane cutters, and thousands of other workers left their old jobs, lured by higher pay at Michaud. The completion of the plant, as had been the case when other Higgins yards were expanded, forced employers to raise wages or lose their laborers.

On October 26, the day after the dedication of the aircraft plant, Higgins turned his attention to what he considered another important issue, the restructuring of his company's magazine. The *Eureka,* like the boat it was named after, was of superior quality. Even without a full-time staff, Rappleyea was publishing a magazine of professional standards. Its cover, photography, printing, and layouts were comparable to those of many commercially printed publications of the period. Higgins recognized the direction his house organ had taken and circulated an interoffice memorandum discussing the issue. He stated: "All praises to George Rappleyea for editing and publishing the 'Eureka News Bulletin.' This magazine, however, has become national if not international in its importance, scope, and coverage. It is a misnomer to print on the 'Eureka' the caption that it is an employees' magazine, for getting down to the brass tacks it is not that."[24]

Higgins stressed that "the original purpose of the 'Eureka' was to

23. "Large Crowd Attends Higgins Aircraft Plant Dedication," 1–3.

24. Andrew Higgins to M. Gottesman, A. J. Higgins, Jr., and others, October 26, 1943, in McGuire Collection. Quotations in the following six paragraphs are from this source.

build up morale and to stimulate the workers of the Higgins plants. With the older, more serious type of employees, superintendents, foremen etc., it serves that purpose, but unfortunately there are many newcomers for we are scraping the barrel of the reservoir of manpower, you might say, and while it has good articles, serves a good purpose, and is interesting to many, it is way over the heads of others."

In the memorandum he instructed his staff to begin designing a new company publication, one that would be printed on coarse, cheap paper and have a homespun appearance. He wanted the bulletin to be circulated only to active employees and to labor officials representing the various unions in the company. Its editorial staff was to have one or more key executives but was also to include superintendents, foremen, and representatives chosen from the apprentices and journeymen. Higgins did not want a fancy editorial policy. He just wanted the bulletin to be human and current. "I am not saying whether it should be published every week, or every other week, but I want it timely—and if something happens on a Thursday and the paper comes out on Friday, goddamit I want the thing that happened on Thursday to be printed in the paper that comes off the press the next day."

He believed that the paper should publish the names of those workers who were doing a good job, whether it was sweeping the floor or designing combat craft. It should praise those who had given helpful suggestions to management and print the names of the less industrious employees who "break their ass to get to the clock at knocking off time."

Higgins did not intend for the paper to become a "scandal sheet or bring disrespect or disrepute to either the company or the employees." But it might model itself a bit after the Walter Winchell column. It could come very close to identifying male employees who were having affairs with female employees, and if the situation did not correct itself, it could threaten to print the names of both parties.

He wanted the journal to "give credit where credit is due" and to view with alarm if there was "a bad situation brewing." It should be a source of helpful information. He informed his staff that "if we can get this paper really going, it can grow to be an educational thing. Assuming that it will be properly edited and published, as the different issues come out, let's inspire the workers to save their money and purchase a bond; put some money away for a rainy day; for them to look forward to the company helping them to buy themselves a home; to buy a little piece of ground; to build a church; to get a playground; to educate their children."

He wanted it to inspire the workers to be better citizens "so that if the day should ever come when there wouldn't be enough work for them in the Higgins enterprises, they would have a nest egg to fall back on—and they would be better qualified to fit somewhere in adjusted economies after the war." The staff was organized and plans were formulated to replace the *Eureka* with the new company publication, the *Higgins Worker.*

During November, as the staff of the *Worker* began preparing for its new project, Sprague was finishing an old one. The repairs to the *Hellcat* had been completed, and he returned to New Orleans. Higgins assigned the engineer a new task, the development of an airborne lifeboat that could be dropped from the belly of a B-17 bomber. Its purpose was to help save the lives of pilots downed at sea. "That's the kind of stuff I wanted to do," Sprague recalled. "And if you want to do something you can do it and you can be good at it and work your heart out." The airborne lifeboat originated in England to help rescue pilots downed in the Channel. Britain's 30-foot model was the product of famous English sailboat designer Uffa Foxx and was similar in construction to a canoe. The U.S. Air Force was not enthusiastic about the boat because it was too long to fit under a B-17 without removing the belly turret. According to Sprague, the air force chose not to modify the model because it "did not have enough seaworthy qualities to justify building the same design." [25]

Higgins sent Sprague and John Poche to Wright Field near Dayton, Ohio, to inspect a British boat and to witness a mock rescue attempt. Accompanied by English wing commander Becknell and Captain Pete Dawbarn from Wright Field, they waited near the grassy target area for the B-26 to make its final approach. Poche recalled: "They dropped it with three 26-foot parachutes. The boat hit the ground at 15 to 20 miles an hour. It just flattened." [26] It was not destroyed, but it was seriously damaged.

After watching the unsuccessful drop and closely inspecting the lifeboat, Sprague had a better understanding of the problems he had to over-

25. Ted Sprague, interview, August 2, 1992.
26. John Poche, interview, October 28, 1975.

come. He returned to New Orleans and began designing a model for the B-17.

During the period that Sprague completed his repairs to the *Hellcat* and was assigned the task of designing the lifeboat, Higgins Industries expanded again, this time into the newly modernized eight-story Industries Building at Gravier and South Saratoga streets in downtown New Orleans. The first four floors of the building were renovated to serve as the employment department for Higgins Industries, Higgins Aircraft, Higgins Engine Company, and Higgins Plastics Corporation. White applicants entered from the Saratoga Street entrance and were interviewed in offices on the first floor. Black applicants entered from the Gravier Street entrance and were sent to the second floor to complete their applications.

All potential employees were given a physical examination on the third floor and, once approved, proceeded to the fourth floor for fingerprinting and an identification badge. After the process was completed, the new worker was sent directly to an assigned plant. Higgins thought the centralized location would cut down on "lost time and motion."

The fifth and sixth floors were leased out for office space, and the seventh floor was retained by Higgins for use as meeting rooms. The eighth floor contained a large auditorium and served as a multipurpose facility. It was used as a theater and as a meeting place for such groups as the Higgins American Legion Post, the Power Boat Squadron, and Club La America. Club La America was an organization for those interested in South America and its culture. The auditorium also served as a hall for dances, a gym for basketball tournaments and boxing matches, and an arena for indoor sports.[27]

As the personnel departments settled in their new surroundings, Higgins continued his routine of looking to the future but taking care of today. Publicly, he spoke of such massive projects as a new South American river transportation system and of his helicopter that was to be affordable to the average American. But in his interoffice memos he dealt with the smaller everyday concerns of running a company. Like Winston Churchill, he was a stickler for detail and demanded immediate action. In a note dated November 18, 1943, Higgins remarked on the Indus-

27. "All Higgins Hiring Now Assembled Under One Roof," *Eureka News Bulletin,* II (December, 1943), 1–2.

trial Canal plant and the type of people it now employed. In the memo addressed to A. J. Higgins, Jr., George Hockensmith, Graham Haddock, and all superintendents and foremen he wrote: "The drive out the road to the north, along the top of the old levee is oppressive. I would like for Mr. Hockensmith to get with A. J. Higgins, Jr. and Mr. Gottesman, and whoever else they want in on such a meeting, to decide what should be done with a lot of pipe, ramp gates, and other metal structures that are scattered all over the place. When the war ends, scrap iron will be nothing but scrap iron—it has some value now, so why should we not clear up this litter: salvaging some for sale, and making a contribution of some by giving the scrap iron to those who need it."[28]

During his survey of the yard, he was appalled by the lack of concern for equipment. Winches belonging to the navy were lying around rusting when a work order could have been obtained from a navy supervisor to repaint them. He noted, "The day may come when we will want to buy them—there may be some commercial use for them after the war, and to grease them up and protect them might be worth our while." Higgins also saw diesel engines and generators "improperly covered against dust and rain." He stated, "In many cases the tarpaulins for same have fallen off and are lying along side the engines; and not a Superintendent, nor a Foreman, nor a God-damn laborer gives a damn to stop long enough to put the cover back on the valuable equipment, or order someone else to do it."

His biggest shock came when he took a group of dignitaries on a tour of an FP ship. As he walked on the main deck he happened to look over the side at the yard below. He wrote: "I never want to do this again under similar circumstances. The plant looked like a pig-pen, with greasy rags, paper pie plates, and all kinds of litter all over the place." He questioned: "What kind of people do we have working for us anyway, and what in Hell is the matter with the Superintendents and Foremen? My God are we Americans?—in many cases, not Americans to be proud of. What in the Hell is the matter with people anyway at this plant? Have they no interest in the war? Have they no interest in their Company? Have they no interest in their job? Have they no pride in themselves, that they would

28. Andrew Higgins to Andrew Higgins, Jr., George Hockensmith, Graham Haddock and All Superintendents, All Foremen, November 18, 1943, in McGuire Collection. Quotations in the following four paragraphs are from this source.

permit the amount of loafing, and the litter and the waste to go on? It is absolutely criminal, the way valuable property is permitted to be ruined. . . . My God, what an awful day of reckoning there will be."

To rectify the problem, he instructed A. J. Higgins, Jr., to, "select a chairman and a committee to lay plans for making a record of the men working in this plant. This Committee is to make up an honor-roll of the men who continue to try to do their best, although right along side of them there is a loafer and a no-account. Let's grade the men in this plant, so if and when the war ends, or the work might slack, let's get rid of the no-accounts and loafers; but for the fellows who are really trying, give three cheers."

Higgins wanted his supervisors to realize that when the war was over, he intended to give jobs to returning soldiers and sailors but that he did not want to lose his good men, "the men who put their shoulders to the wheel." The "no-accounts" that were now on his payroll, he insisted, "will drift back into the nothingness from where they came."

Another Higgins memo dated November 27, addressed to "All People Concerned," said: "This is a must, and an A-1 piece of instruction. Any time the word Higgins is reproduced, it must be in the same type of script that we have standardized on. We have an after-the-war position to worry about, and we should capitalize on the name Higgins written in the script that we have adopted, which we know has met with public acceptance and interest, and has a strong advertising value." He ordered that "any sign . . . on any piece of equipment, automobiles, trucks, buildings, water tower, or wherever the word Higgins" appeared be blanked out and rewritten in the type of script that the company had "adopted as a copyrighted name." He noted, "In defiance of my instruction, the last edition of the *Higgins Worker* came out with Higgins printed, and not in the script of Higgins as we have copyrighted the name. Why the hell is this dumbbellism displayed?" He explained, "Now, advertising men who know their stuff, say there is great value in the script in the manner in which we write this word; and by God, I want everybody to see that they don't get forgetful; and this applies to everybody; on order blanks, dray receipts, billboards, letterheads, or any God-damn place our Company name is written, it has to be in this script . . . and God help the man who gives instructions to have anything printed without the name being printed that way; and I don't mean maybe!"[29]

29. A. J. Higgins to "All People Concerned," November 27, 1943, in McGuire Collection.

While Higgins was attempting to take care of the minor problems in his shipyards, a major problem arose at the Higgins-Tucker Engine Company plant. Tucker had arrived with a flair, and many predicted that his teaming with Higgins would make New Orleans the Detroit of the South. Production had not begun on the gasoline-operated marine engines for the U.S. Army when, according to Jack Higgins, Tucker "departed in a hurry."

Jack, Frank P. Higgins' son, worked at the plant as an assistant to Arthur Chevrolet. He was initially hired by his uncle to assist in the drafting department of Higgins Industries during the summer of 1940 while on semester break from Tulane University. In May, 1943, after recovering from a serious illness and surgery that had forced him to resign from school, Jack went to see his uncle about a full-time position. He hoped his engineering major and earlier training would assist him in getting assigned to a related field at one of the plants.

While Jack was waiting in the outer office, his uncle's secretary Elliot Pittman asked him if he had any cigarettes. If so, he should get rid of them. Dr. Alton Oschner had been on a crusade to get Higgins to give up smoking, and Higgins was now attempting to convince everyone else to eliminate the habit.

When Jack entered the office, his uncle was sitting at his desk. He got up and gave Jack a hug. As Higgins started to sit in his chair, he felt his shirt pocket as though he was looking for something. Jack recalled his uncle saying: "'Jackie, Jackie, give me a cigarette.' I said, 'I don't have any, Uncle Andrew.' 'You don't have any?' 'No, sir.' 'You quit?' 'Yes, sir, I'm trying.' 'Good for you. Goddamit, if you'd have given me a cigarette you wouldn't have gotten the job.'" Jack said, "I wasn't hired because I was family or I could fulfill a certain position, I qualified because I just didn't have a cigarette." [30]

Jack was hired and assigned to the experimental department of Higgins-Tucker Engine Company. He recalled that each morning Tucker would arrive at the plant accompanied by a very sexy secretary. Upon entering the building, he would remove his white felt hat and gently hand it to her. She would carry the hat with one hand supporting it from the inside almost as a waiter carries a tray. As her boss walked through the plant, she trailed closely behind, careful not to let the hat get the least bit soiled. Tucker would walk down the assembly line stopping at each po-

30. Jack Higgins, interview, August 12, 1992.

sition and talking to the worker. Jack said: "I doubt that he knew their names, but he came on like he was one of the guys. Suited up, handkerchief, like he just stepped out of a bandbox. He'd make his circuit then go up to his office. That's about as much as I saw of Preston Tucker." Tucker's sudden departure caused much speculation. Jack recalled that it was rumored around the plant that Tucker "was found keeping two sets of books." No proof ever surfaced, but "that's what filtered down the grapevine." Sprague saw Tucker as "a pure promoter . . . strictly a fast talker." Andrée, Higgins' daughter, remembered him as "all fluff and no substance." She said, "When my father realized what Tucker really was he ended the association." Haddock suggested that it could have been the conflict of two strong personalities that caused the relationship to end abruptly.[31] Whatever the reason, Tucker left the company in the fall of 1943, and the December issue of the *Eureka*, giving no explanation, referred to the company as Higgins Engines, Inc.

Another small article appearing in the December issue mentioned the return of the "X-Ray Boat." Several weeks earlier, Higgins had had his workers construct a 36-foot LCVP that was a completed landing craft on one side but simply framing on the other. People could view the boat's inner construction through the unfinished half. The LCVP, carried on a tractor trailer bed, toured thirteen southern states as part of the War Department's ninety-vehicle "Salute to Wood" caravan. It was seen by more than 200,000 onlookers and offered Higgins an opportunity to showcase the quality of his work and keep his name before the public in potential postwar markets.[32]

Another boat that was also well-known along the southern coast of Louisiana and Mississippi was soon to come to Higgins' Industrial Canal plant. On December 27, 1943, Colonel Duval Watkins, head of the New Orleans Port of Embarkation, contacted Higgins. The U.S. Army Transport Service had a serious problem and requested immediate help. A 492-foot C-3 oceangoing cargo ship called the *Sea Scamp* had been built by Ingalls Shipbuilding Corporation in Pascagoula, Mississippi. Almost im-

---

31. *Ibid.*; Ted Sprague, interview, August 2, 1992; Andrée Higgins Stefferud, interview, October 16, 1992; Graham Haddock, interview, September 24, 1991.

32. "X Ray Boat Comes Home," *Eureka News Bulletin,* II (December, 1943), 12, caption.

mediately after completion, it was taken to the Todd-Johnson Shipyard in New Orleans to be converted into a troop carrier. Todd-Johnson had begun work on the ship in August, 1943, but in December, just before Christmas, the workers went on strike. The labor stoppage caused the partially converted ship to miss its convoy. A second convoy was being assembled, but the boat had to be completed and ready to sail from New Orleans by January 13.

The best estimate the army had thus far received for the completion of the ship was thirty-one days. Upon hearing his competitors' projections, Higgins unhesitatingly told Watkins to bring the Sea Scamp to the Industrial Canal plant and then notify Washington that the ship would meet the convoy. To accomplish this, he had to have it completed by January 8.[33]

According to Jack, his uncle "loved to have something that would astound somebody."[34] The Sea Scamp problem met that criterion. If his competition could not complete the ship in thirty-one days, everyone would be amazed when his men accomplished it in twelve.

Higgins called his supervisors to his office and informed them of the project. Haddock recalled: "He got us all together and said, 'All right boys we got a ship coming over here. Todd's on strike so I told them to bring the boat over here.' We said, 'What's got to be done on it?' He said, 'I don't know. I told them we'd finish it and we'll finish it for them.' "[35]

Higgins sent a team of men to the Port of Embarkation to inspect the ship and formulate a plan for its completion. While his workers were assessing the project, Higgins and Colonel Watkins were meeting with thirty or forty representatives from the city's various craft unions to be sure there would not be a conflict between the plant's unions and the uptown closed shops. Once the story was revealed, both parties agreed to relax regulations and work hand in hand without friction or delay.

At 2:30 P.M. on December 27 the Sea Scamp left the Port of Embarkation headed for Higgins' shipyard. On its way down the narrow Industrial Canal the large ship's gun tub caught the eastern section of the Danziger drawbridge, partially destroying the bridge. By 8:00 P.M. the ship had completed its journey and was docking at the Industrial Canal plant.

33. "The Story of the Sea Scamp," Eureka News Bulletin, III (January–March, 1944), 76.
34. Jack Higgins, interview, August 12, 1992.
35. Graham Haddock, interview, September 24, 1991.

Before she was fully secured, more than four hundred men were already boarding her to begin their assigned task.

Haddock remembered when he first saw the ship. "All the troops berthing were lying in the bottom of the cargo holds in piles. The galley equipment had not been installed, and the ventilation systems were pre-fabricated, but stacked in pieces." Also, "Not one life boat had been rigged or tested. No rigging on the cargo booms." He said the one advantage was that "all of the rigging material, the blocks, booms, wire rope, everything was standard Maritime Commission material. So everything we had to rig down our cargo booms on the FS ships (FP ships were later designated FS, freight supply) would also fit the same booms on this ship. All of our life rafts would fit this ship. All the equipment that goes in a life raft is the same, so we took out of our warehouse all the material needed to finish the boat." [36]

On December 30, while the crews outside his office worked hard on LCMs, FS ships, and the *Sea Scamp*, Higgins addressed a memo to George Rappleyea concerning an advertising problem. He wrote: "I chanced to look through the November *Yachting*, and when I saw this, a chill of horror and revulsion went through me. During the next few days, Andrew Jr., Frank Higgins, and Ed Higgins called screaming. Then I get a note from Teddy Sprague. Why the hell did we put an ad in the god-damn Yachting magazine, particularly an edition that was glorifying the Elco boats. They had magnificent pictures of their boats, when they were in the right and correct trim." Higgins was not opposed to advertising, but he was very much opposed to the picture chosen and the issue in which it appeared. He wrote: "When a number of pictures of the *Hellcat* were shown to me in the office, this very same god-damn son-of-a-bitch of a picture was taken by me and I threw it out, and I instructed that the negative of this be destroyed. Look at the god-damn cockeyed position of the skyline, running diagonally up the paper on which the picture is printed. How anybody in our organization could permit any picture of any of our boats be taken when the bow is sticking up and the ass down, is beyond me." He continued: "I raised a hell of a lot of hell with Clarke Salmon. I just come to a memorandum of his on my desk dated December 23rd, and I am sending this to you and you will see that he puts the

36. *Ibid.*; Graham Haddock, interview, June 26, 1975; "The Story of the Sea Scamp," *Eureka News Bulletin*, III (January–March, 1944), 76.

B on you, that you okayed this ad. Where the hell did you get the photograph? Did you actually okay the proof? I would have to see your initials on it to believe it." He threatened: "George if you did approve the proof of this ad, with the photograph of this cockeyed and malformed skyline, I am going to speak to your wife about ʾou. Have you stopped using an eyedropper and gone to guzzling? George, have you taken up strong drink?" [37]

While Higgins tried to prevent such a mistake from happening again, his employees worked around the clock on the *Sea Scamp*. As many as a thousand men were assigned to the boat during any given twenty-four-hour period. On New Years' Eve, as most of the residents of New Orleans prepared to forget the war for an evening, the Higgins employees assigned to the transport continued their race against the clock. [38]

One Higgins employee who was not scheduled to work that night was Captain Richard McDerby. His duties as chief instructor of the boat school were over for the day, and he was looking forward to an exciting evening at a New Year's Eve party. McDerby explained: "We were getting ready to go out just before the sun went down and I got a call saying Mr. Higgins wanted to see me in his office. So I went over and he said, 'Get your boat and bring it over to the Industrial Canal. We're going to load it up with a lot of food and everything in the world. I got the o.k. from the Admiral over at the naval station and we can get into quarantine [a troop transport was anchored downriver from the city in a restricted area before it headed overseas] and aboard this ship.' " [39]

A childhood friend of Higgins' had a son aboard the ship, and Higgins had promised that he would visit the boy before the ship left for overseas. McDerby was accustomed to being called on a moment's notice to serve as Higgins' chauffeur at sea. If his boss wanted to impress visiting dignitaries by giving them a ride on the lake or the river, he always called Mac. It was a matter of pride with the chief instructor that when Higgins went anywhere by boat he was at the helm. On New Year's Eve, as the sun went down, Mac felt a little less honored than usual. Honored or not, McDerby respected and admired Higgins and knew he could never

37. Andrew Higgins to George Rappleyea, December 30, 1943, in Strahan Personal Collection.

38. Graham Haddock, interview, September 24, 1991; Ronald W. Charles, *Troopships of World War II* (Washington, D.C., 1947), 270.

39. Richard A. McDerby, interview, August 30, 1992.

tell him no. He canceled his plans, enlisted the aid of a motor mac, and took the boat to the dock below Higgins' office. The supplies were loaded, and once Higgins was aboard they proceeded down the Industrial Canal, through the locks, and downriver to the quarantine area.

McDerby recalled: "I flashed my lights several times to let them know we were coming in and they flashed back 'o.k.' . . . They let some line down and we tied the boat alongside the ship. The Jacob's ladder was already down and they dropped a net and we filled it up with all the groceries, the liquor, the food, the nuts, you name it and it was there." The sailors hoisted the net and then, to McDerby's surprise, Higgins decided that he wanted to go aboard. Mac said: "That scared the devil out of me because he had to climb up the rope ladder on the side of that ship. He made it up it. When he got up there, he spread everything out. The boy was an enlisted man. Mr. Higgins looked at him and said this is for you. I told your dad I was bringing it. You're leaving tomorrow and I want ya'll to have a big party tonight. If you want, you can invite the officers." Higgins, McDerby, and the motor mac did not get back to the plant until 2:00 A.M. Mac had been at a party all night but not the one he had planned to attend. He readily admitted: "Mr. Higgins was my idol. I didn't mind doing it. I wanted to do everything I could for him, but that was an unpleasant night. . . . I had everything lined up for a big party."[40]

That same New Year's night, crews at the Industrial Canal plant worked feverishly converting the *Sea Scamp* to a troop transport. The job was done, and the ship sailed as promised on January 8. According to Haddock, however, "We were crippled for the next three months because we had taken the material needed to finish twenty little (FS) ships to complete the big troop carrier."[41]

Higgins' willingness to attempt what others considered impossible had depleted the materials needed for the FS vessels and put his crew far behind schedule. But he had faith that his men could overcome the adverse situation. To create the necessary environment for his workers to accomplish feats far greater than they themselves deemed possible, Higgins in 1944 would use psychology and masterful planning.

40. *Ibid.*
41. Graham Haddock, interview, September 24, 1991.

As 1943 came to a close, Higgins looked back on a year filled with accomplishments and controversy. His company had begun production on one hundred 170-foot FS vessels and also had started designing a helicopter for the postwar world. Higgins had condemned the navy for producing the LCPR, in which fourteen soldiers drowned near St. Marks, Florida. During 1943 Higgins' LCVP finally became the standardized vehicle-personnel landing craft, and Hitler denounced Higgins as the "new Noah."

That same year he received an honorary degree from Creighton University, neared completion of the Higgins-Tucker Engine factory, saw his company build the *Hellcat,* began sectionalizing LCMs for shipping overseas, instituted a training program to help provide the workers needed for the Industrial Canal plant, and celebrated the delivery of his seven thousandth LCVP and one thousandth LCM. In 1943 he opened the Industries Building on Gravier Street, began work on the *Sea Scamp,* and saw the sudden departure of Preston Tucker. But perhaps his most satisfying accomplishment was the completion of Michaud. It was a project that he was determined to see through, and it was his stubborn refusal to quit that was responsible for the plant being built. Even for Higgins it was an incredible year.

9

LABOR RACKETS

E arly in January, 1944, as the *Sea Scamp* sailed to meet its convoy, two other Higgins projects were nearing reality. Enea Bossi was ready to test the recently completed Higgins helicopter, and the Higgins Engine Company was preparing to begin mass production of its marine engine. For reasons beyond Higgins' control, engine production had been delayed.[1]

The delay was of major concern to Higgins, but an even greater problem required his immediate attention. Rumors had surfaced that the navy was considering modifying the design of the *Hellcat*. According to his sources, the Bureau of Ships wanted to attach step angles to the boat to give it a hydroplane effect. Elco, the developer of the steps, claimed that when fastened to the bottom and sides of PTs they enhanced the boats' speed and maneuverability. The idea was first tested on Elco's PT 487, which reportedly reached the amazing speed of 55.95 knots and completed a 180-degree turn in six seconds.[2]

Higgins did not want anyone tampering with his design. In an attempt to prevent it, he wrote to the navy's assistant supervisor of shipbuilding assigned to his plants, Lieutenant Commander C. W. Leveau, warning that "a haphazard installation of steps, either flat sections, or steps of conforming radius will make this boat 'tricky' at high speeds."[3]

Higgins also mentioned to Leveau how difficult it was to design PT boats when the navy was not certain what capabilities it wanted incorporated. He explained that "without knowing what the Navy wants, it is

---

1. Andrew Higgins to J. K. Byrne, December 28, 1943, in McGuire Collection; Oakes, "Boat Builder to the United Nations," 19.
2. Bulkley, *At Close Quarters*, 78.
3. Andrew Higgins to C. W. Leveau, January 8, 1944, in Strahan Personal Collection.

hard for us to go into discussions and set up a hypothetical case, or cases, of this or of that." Higgins recalled: "A while back, when the Japanese had their Destroyers running about freely in the Pacific, the boys back from that section told us that what they needed were more PT boats with less weight on them—they even wanted to carry only two torpedoes to enable them to get the last bit of speed; every last bit of maneuverability; to get in there and shoot their wad and get the hell out. They wanted the smallest possible boat and the fastest boat they could get." In contrast to earlier reports Higgins had received, the boys just returning from New Guinea and New Britain told him that instead of speed they wanted armament. PT squadrons were installing 37mm and 1.1 guns that they got from the navy and were also mounting stolen Japanese guns on their boats. They were fitting their PTs with all the firepower they could beg, borrow, or steal. With no Japanese destroyers in the area to fight, they had little need for torpedoes, but they needed guns with which to attack the Japanese barges that were running in the shallow waters. Speed was not necessary because the barges made only approximately nine knots. Higgins summed up his thoughts: "In other words, the Navy should make up their minds whether they want Motor Torpedo Boats or Motor Powered Gun Boats. Maybe they need two classes of vessel. You can't eat your cake and keep it too, and when you make a compromise you can't have the best of both elements." In reference to Elco's experiment with hydroplane steps, the shipbuilder said his competition began experimenting only after the heavier, rugged Higgins boat proved to be as fast as Elco's lighter-weight PTs. He claimed that he had proposed the same idea to the navy in 1939 or 1940 but warned against accepting the idea too quickly.[4]

Elco's experiment appeared to be a major breakthrough. The Bureau of Ships was preparing to issue Elcoplane conversion kits to all PT squadrons when several problems were discovered.[5] In a comparative test against a 78-foot Higgins boat running from Miami to Fort Lauderdale, the Elcoplane boat consumed some forty gallons of gasoline more per hour than did the Higgins boat. The extra consumption greatly reduced the boat's cruising range.[6] In another experiment, four boats from Motor

4. Ibid.
5. Bulkley, At Close Quarters, 78.
6. Higgins to Leveau, January 8, 1944, in Strahan Personal Collection.

Torpedo Squadron 29 equipped with hydroplane steps made a trial run from New York to Miami. Elco's steps proved ideal for high-speed operations, but under normal cruising conditions they caused a 25 percent increase in fuel consumption and a dramatic 75 percent increase in the consumption of lubricating oil.

The steps also made the boats more difficult to steer at normal speeds and lessened their ability to accelerate. The final blow occurred during the Atlantic run when the attached steps warped and the supporting brackets loosened and cracked. The Elcoplane had shown promise, but it died in the experimental stages.[7]

Just as the Elcoplane had problems, so did the *Hellcat*. In the beginning of the war, PTs needed speed and agility. By the time the *Hellcat* went into service, the boats were carrying heavier armament and larger crews. Originally PTs carried two officers and a crew of eight. By mid-1943 they carried three officers and a crew of sixteen. The navy felt that it was impractical to attempt to incorporate the added requirements on a 70-foot hull.

Higgins disagreed. He informed Leveau that "somewhere along the line I have heard that the people in Bureaus in Washington have determined, or surmised or even drawn a conclusion, or otherwise made up their minds that the 70' boat cannot carry a full military load such as has been prescribed for our 78' footer, or the Elco boat. Well, whoever has drawn this conclusion has not referred to the past record, for our 70' boat will carry the same load that our 78' boat, or the Elco boat will carry, and she will be faster." He argued: "Our 70 footer has more battle deck space than has the Elco boat. There are many other advantages;—a smaller boat; a boat that can be transported on the decks of steamers and which can be handled by the derrick equipment on most steamers; a boat that has more maneuverability; a boat that has a lower silhouette; a boat that can punch and dodge and get away; is far more facile than is the Elco boat, and faster than our 78 footer."[8]

Higgins continued: "If the Navy wants something sensible, why the hell don't they listen to people like us who have had years of experience. They don't have to accept what we tell them. If they want to maintain

7. Bulkley, *At Close Quarters*, 76–78.

8. Higgins to Leveau, January 8, 1944, in Strahan Personal Collection. Quotations in the following two paragraphs are from this source.

their dignity, let them order us, from their great wisdom, to build the goddam 70′ boat (prohibited to be referred to as the 'Hellcat') with flattened instead of concave sections. She will still be a good boat at slow, intermediate, or full speeds; with fuel economy."

Realizing his temper was beginning to shorten he wrote: "I had better draw this letter to a conclusion. I am getting disgusted, and I might get worse, and step on somebody's feeling,—but I cannot close without this dirty crack and comment; that I have devoted my life to the design of small boats; that boats of my design hold practically all worthwhile records, many of the records not published; that from a small one we are now a big organization, and that we have as much, in fact more talent than we once had." He closed: "The oil companies and concerns who know how to earn and how to spend a dollar, come to us, but our own Navy does not; that I am forced many times to abide by decisions of young men, many of them who could not get a position with me as a draftsman, let alone a designer, yet many of their senior officers who might know a lot about battleships and cruisers acknowledge to me that they don't know much about smaller boats; yet they are all in position to tell me what to do, and do not ask me for advice. I could keep on ad nauseam."

As Higgins tried to convince Leveau that the Hellcat in its present form was the most effective PT boat ever built, the navy was redefining the purpose of PTs. The Hellcat obviously had much greater maneuverability, acceleration, and speed than the standard torpedo boats, but other factors were now just as important. According to Searles, as the war went along the boats became more and more gunboats and less and less torpedo boats because the PT boat, in the sense that it is a torpedo boat, is a loser's weapon, used when the enemy's navy is on the attack. A PT boat cannot strike out very far. He explained: "Its range is insignificant compared to a carrier, a battleship, a cruiser, or a destroyer. It also only has a one-shot ability to do anything. The others have repeated ability. They also had defensive armament that a PT boat didn't have. The Hellcat would have been ideal at Guadalcanal because of its lower profile, its smaller size, and its speed. The use of torpedo boats dropped off as the Japanese navy started getting defeated time and time again and they couldn't reach out."[9]

9. Robert Searles, interview, August 16, 1992.

The *Hellcat,* according to those who designed and tested it, was the fastest and most maneuverable PT boat to enter the service. But because of the changing requirements of the war, the navy continued to produce the 78-foot Higgins boat and the standard Elco model.

As the debate over PT designs continued, Ted Sprague was busily working on his new project, the airborne lifeboat. In January, 1944, Sprague had an 18-foot dummy lifeboat ready for testing. He transported the craft to Eglin Air Force base near Fort Walton, Florida, for an experimental drop. During the test the shackles holding the boat to the airplane failed to release properly.

The boat should have disengaged when the bombardier activated the bomb salvo. Instead, one set of shackles let go and the other held. When the final set released, the stern went down and the bow lifted and scraped against the belly of the plane, damaging a bomb bay door and ripping off part of the boat's side. Sprague explained that they "repaired the dummy and the bomb shackles and then took the craft up for more test drops." These first tests led to the addition of a catapult system that pushed the boat away from the plane once the bomb salvo was activated.[10]

After concluding the first series of tests, the young designer and his crew returned to New Orleans and built a 30-foot prototype. Like the first, it resembled a canoe but had fins attached to the stern to keep the stern up and prevent the bow from damaging the plane. Tests on the second model suggested that the release problem had been solved.

Sprague's next step was to have his crew hand build a 27-foot boat that could fit under the belly of a B-17. The result was a strong craft composed of oak ribs and triple planking. To make the drop simulate reality, Patterson Air Force Base at Wright Field sent blankets, K-rations, canned water, and an assortment of other items that were to be stocked in the actual lifeboat.

The 27-foot sailboat was loaded beneath the bomber. When it was dropped, three 48-foot parachutes, attached to the boat by a metal ring, were to open and allow the boat to descend slowly. Self-righting chambers were incorporated in the design to assure that the lifeboat would come to rest on the water deck up and hull down. Self-bailing features were built in to keep the craft dry.

10. Ted Sprague, interview, August 2, 1992. The following paragraphs are based on this source.

At five thousand feet the B-17 released the boat. Sprague remembered the test as if it had been yesterday. Smiling, he said: "When the parachutes opened, the ring broke. Down comes the boat. The parachutes floated off toward Miami and the boat just keeps coming down and it lands upside down. It was laying there bobbing in the water like an old rag. The engines went right to the bottom and the fuel tanks broke open." The boat had free-fallen for over four thousand feet, and all that was left was boards floating on the water.

Sprague returned to New Orleans and had his crew start building an identical 27-foot boat using a heavier forged ring. When tested in February, the prototype successfully parachuted down at the proper fifty-degree bow-heavy position. The boat struck the water bow first, submerged about one-third of its length, and then floated up and came to rest on the surface.

After several successful drops, the air force assigned Sprague personnel representing a typical bomber crew. Captain Dawbarn from Wright Field, along with a radioman, a navigator, and a few selected airmen, were chosen to participate in a final test. Their assignment was to sail the lifeboat from Biloxi, Mississippi, to Tampa, Florida—a challenging task because no one on board other than Sprague had any sailing experience. Sprague explained: "The men aboard knew a lot about airplanes, but nothing about boats. We figured that this would probably be a common thing."

It took five days to make the trip by water. The first night out they encountered bad weather. Sprague recalled: "We had a Gibson Girl radio and the radioman would send a signal to let them know we were all right. They weren't getting it for some reason." When the signals were not received, Higgins and Sprague's pregnant wife, Jean, became worried. Higgins was concerned about all the men in the boat but especially about his engineer. He was extremely fond of Sprague. When Ted and Jean were married in February, 1942, Higgins had insisted that the ceremony and reception be held at his Prytania Street home.

To ease Jean's and his own worry Higgins requested that the air force search the Gulf. The planes never spotted the lifeboat because the boat, the sail, and the crew's clothing were camouflaged to blend in with the sea. Sprague said they saw the planes but had no idea that the aircraft were looking for them.

Several days later, the crew arrived safely at McDill Field near Tampa.

Some had suffered slight seasickness, but other than that there were no major problems. As a result of the experiment, the air force discovered that two changes needed to be made. One was in the type and amount of supplies loaded in the boat, and the other dealt with instruction. The air force changed from K-rations to sea rations, and pilots were given instructions on using the lifeboat as part of their training.

Sprague, Dawbarn, and the crew stayed at McDill for a day, then, along with the boat, were transported back to New Orleans. Upon his arrival home, Sprague and Jean left almost immediately for the hospital. That night Jean gave birth to an eight-pound baby girl.

Higgins' shipyards were rapidly turning out LCVPs, LCMs, and PT boats, and Higgins Engine Company was hoping to start production soon. Parts manufactured by other companies and covered by patents still had not arrived. Meanwhile, Higgins Aircraft was finding it difficult to hire highly skilled technicians.

After Michaud had started to retool for aluminum production in the fall of 1943 and Higgins tried to recruit personnel, he discovered that a vicious racket existed. Companies disguising themselves as engineering concerns had cornered the market for technicians with particular skills. These companies, located mostly in Chicago and Detroit, presented themselves to the aircraft industry as labor suppliers. They had machinists, loftsmen, tool designers, and other specialized workers under contract and would lease their services to manufacturers at greatly inflated rates of pay. Higgins Aircraft could not compete with the wages offered by the service companies because of the federal wage stabilization program. The service companies were exempt from such control.

Higgins soon discovered that New Orleans and the surrounding area lacked the skilled labor force needed to staff an aircraft plant. He was forced to subcontract through three of the service companies, a situation that bothered him and that he hoped to eliminate. He planned to work with the service companies only until he could find adequate labor without their help. Simultaneously, he began registering protests with the proper agencies in Washington and requesting permission from the War Manpower Commission to be allowed to recruit workers in other states.

On February 11, 1944, Frank O. Higgins, vice-president of Higgins Aircraft, wrote to Hugh Fulton, counsel to the Truman Committee, concerning the labor racket. He wanted Fulton to be aware of the "deplorable condition" that was seriously retarding his new plant's operations and increasing his production costs. He believed that an investigation would show that the situation was prevalent throughout the aircraft industry and must be similarly affecting other aircraft manufacturers.[11]

Frank informed Fulton that to build C-46 aircraft his plant required certain highly skilled employees. The Wage Stabilization Unit of the United States Treasury Department regulated the salaries that he could pay. He could offer a tool designer $1.75 per hour, a loftsman $1.50, a production planner, jig builder, and tool and die maker all $1.45, and a template maker $1.30. By law he could not vary the scale. He stated, "From the moment that our first airplane contract was announced, we were prematurely besieged with offers from countless engineering service companies throughout the country, to supply engineering talent to us at rates ranging up to $4.50 per man-hour, which we consistently declined, naively believing that we could avoid this exorbitant expense by direct employment."

After months of trying to find high-quality personnel, Frank realized that the numerous engineering concerns had a monopoly on the services of these men. To complete his processing, planning, tool designing, and lofting in time to meet his schedule, he was forced to negotiate with some of the firms. He pointed out that the engineering service companies were exempt from the limits established by the Wage Stabilization Unit. They could offer their employees $2.50 an hour and a maintenance allowance of $48.00 a week. Aircraft manufacturers could not compete. Even more confusing, the U.S. Army Air Force recognized as allowable the $4.50 per hour straight time the service companies charged the employer who used their technicians.

The use of contract labor also created other problems. Employees hired from the service companies often tried to lure potential Higgins employees to sign with their employer first. They would then be assigned to the same plant but at a higher salary. Contract employees also felt immune from company rules and regulations. When violations occurred, Higgins had to have the workers recalled by the service company. They also tended to brag about their high wages. Higgins' employees working

11. "Higgins Exposes Labor Black Markets, Extension of Remarks of Hon. F. Edward Hebert of Louisiana in the House of Representatives," August 7, 1944, pp. 3–8, in F. Edward Hebert Papers, Manuscripts Department, Howard-Tilton Memorial Library, Tulane University. The following paragraphs are based on this source.

alongside the higher-paid help often wanted to be released from Higgins Aircraft so that they too could sign with the service company. Frank told Fulton that "when workmen are forced to stay on the job, in such a frame of mind and under such inequitable conditions, the quality, efficiency and volume of their work is lowered, resulting in an undermining of our entire organization."

Frank argued that the expense of having to deal with the labor brokers "is appalling." At the time the letter was written, Higgins Aircraft had contracts with three engineering service companies for more than four hundred men, whose average combined weekly salary was approximately $105,000. If these same employees were hired direct according to wage stabilization guidelines, the aggregate of their wages would be approximately $35,000 per week. Having to deal with the labor brokers was costing an additional $70,000 per week. He complained: "It is difficult to understand, in these times, how parasitical enterprises with no contracts of their own can maintain a monopoly of hoarded engineering talent at extravagant remuneration and subsist by victimizing aircraft companies with contracts vital to the war effort, who are at their mercy because of the critical shortage of technical personnel."

The aircraft executive offered two methods by which the federal government could solve the problem. First, subcontracts for engineering services could be outlawed and eliminated as a reimbursable item of expense for all government contracts. Then the service companies would have to release their contract labor and the workers would have to accept employment at existing wage stabilization rates. The other solution was to allow the aircraft companies to raise wages so that they could compete on the open market for the skilled technicians. This would not be as economical but it would bring relief to the aircraft industry by placing it in an equitable position. It would help break up the labor pools and eliminate the excessive profits now going to the labor racketeers.

Frank hoped his letter would lead the Truman Committee to investigate the problem. He enclosed a list of every labor broker who had ever contacted him and sent copies of his correspondence to several high-ranking army air force officials, to Chairman Donald Nelson of the War Production Board, and to Charles E. Wilson, executive vice-chairman of the board. On February 16, Fulton replied: "Thank you for your letter of February 11. The Committee is checking into the matter."

In early March, Andrew Higgins sent Colonel Jouett to Washington to protest the labor-hoarding practices. In conferences with high-ranking officials of the WPB, the War Manpower Commission, the War Labor Board, and the comptroller general, Jouett argued that the practices of the service companies violated the letter and the intent of the wage stabilization program. He explained that Higgins had requested that his cost-plus aircraft contract be renegotiated so he would receive a reduced fee. Now his boss was furious because he had to sit back and watch labor racketeers reap excessive profits from the very same contract.

As Jouett made his rounds in Washington, either by coincidence or by design, the Truman Committee finally made public its findings concerning the 1942 tank lighter controversy. According to the committee, the report had been withheld for security reasons. Its release at this time seemed to serve notice, perhaps intentionally, to the labor racketeers that the committee was not going to tolerate abuses in war-related programs, even by government agencies.

During his stay in Washington, Jouett also visited with officers of the army air force. He openly stated his case and attempted to elicit support. He gained the backing of General Oliver P. Echols, who found it hard to believe that in the midst of war the government was allowing such a situation to flourish. Following his meeting with Jouett, he too approached the War Manpower Commission concerning the service companies' questionable practices.

On March 9, Jouett informed Higgins: "Our action has spread like wildfire throughout Government circles and the aircraft industry. The Glenn L. Martin Company has filed a letter of protest against the engineering firms, and one or two others have officially expressed themselves also." The companies had long been opposed to the practice, but no one wanted to be the first to protest. Jouett continued, "At the present moment Higgins Aircraft is hailed as a constructive force." The colonel also informed Higgins that he had spoken with Charles E. Wilson, who, he claimed, "is a thousand percent in favor of the action we are taking. He said that if the racket is not busted up, it will become a national scandal, and he is happy that Higgins is taking the lead." [12]

Jouett continued his campaign and on March 10 wrote to Louisiana's congressman F. Edward Hebert, stating: "I have been in Washington for

12. "Higgins Industries, Inc., New Orleans, Louisiana, March 5, 1944" (Typescript of Truman Committee Report, in McGuire Collection).

several days swinging both fists at a racket which exists and which we are going to break up. There is no need of your help at the moment, but I thought you might be interested in the problem which is fully outlined in the enclosed letter." The colonel explained that while he was attacking the problem on Capitol Hill, Higgins was taking steps to have his own engineering companies incorporated in Michigan and New York on a nonprofit basis. Jouett surmised that this should bring the matter to a head. "There may be some repercussions, but I think the racket is such a scandalous one that nobody will dare try to defend it."[13]

Using information supplied by Andrew Higgins, the Baltimore *Sun* on March 26 published a front-page story entitled "Labor Black Market Operations Described." The paper informed its readers that the War Labor Board would soon take action against a labor racket. According to the article, government officials confirmed the existence of a "widespread 'black market' in skilled labor that is smashing wage ceilings and disrupting industrial relations." The paper gave credit to Frank O. Higgins for putting the Truman Committee on the trail of the labor scandal.[14]

While Higgins fought against the labor racketeers, one longtime ally was retiring from the battles. Major General E. P. Moses of the Marine Corps was reluctantly leaving the service. In a letter to Higgins dated April 6, 1944, the general stated: "It makes me very sad to think that I can no longer take part in this great war. I believe I have sent out about 175,000 young Marines from Parris Island, and we all feel that we have done a fine job here, as those were in great part the boys that took Guadalcanal, Tarawa, Kwajalein and who will march on Tokyo." He reflected: "Looking back over my service since we declared a National Emergency, I can find no period that I enjoyed more than being with you in New Orleans. Even to this day, it seems a marvel to me the way you constructed the first 36-foot ramp boat in twenty-four hours and the steel tank lighter with ramp in forty hours . . . I can recall nearly every minute of the time spent with you on those jobs in New Orleans and only wish that I could live those days over again."[15]

Moses had always been an active supporter of the Higgins boats and,

---

13. Colonel John H. Jouett to F. Edward Hebert, March 10, 1944, in Hebert Papers; "Higgins Exposes Labor Black Markets, Extension of Remarks of Hon. F. Edward Hebert of Louisiana in the House of Representatives," August 7, 1944, p. 9 (Typescript in Hebert Papers).

14. "Higgins Exposes Labor Black Markets," August 7, 1944, p. 10.

15. Moses to Higgins, April 6, 1944, in Strahan Personal Collection.

like General Smith, professed that they could accomplish the impossible. Not everyone had such blind faith. Shortly after receiving Moses' letter, Higgins called McDerby at the boat school and instructed him to come to his office. A movie crew wanted to film a landing boat hitting the beach, and Higgins wanted Mac to handle the affair. Mac still recalls Higgins' instructions: "I want you to put that boat out of the water." The film crew apparently had doubts about the craft's beaching capabilities. McDerby readied his boat and took it to Howes Beach on Lake Pontchartrain, where cameras were being positioned for the shots. Mac recalled: "I went over there and made a few trial runs. These guys had put up a big tower about thirty feet from the water's edge. They were going to film me coming in. I said, 'What side do you want me to come in on, the right side or the left side?' They said, 'No, we want you to come straight in.'" McDerby laughingly stated, "I came straight in and I knocked the tower down. I put the boat completely out of the water where we had to get an LCM to come pull it off the beach. Well, one guy got his leg broken. That afternoon I went into the plant to see Mr. Higgins and he wanted to know how I made out. I said I made out good but you may run me off." McDerby described the incident to his boss by simply saying, "It was a mess." Before going into the details about the tower and the broken leg, he wanted to make certain that Higgins understood that the film crew had chosen, in fact insisted, that he come straight toward the camera. Then he somewhat apologetically said, "I put the boat out of the water, but I don't know whether they got the shot." According to Mac, after Higgins heard the full story he was the happiest man in the world. He said, "Mac, how much are you making? I want to see you get a raise right fast. I wanted to show those son-of-a-bitches what my boat would do and now they know."[16]

While McDerby was toppling camera towers, Sprague was preparing to mass produce the airborne lifeboats at Michaud using the giant autoclave. Higgins was continuing his battle against the labor racketeers, and Haddock was attempting to regain the time lost on the FS program because of the *Sea Scamp*. Partially completed FS vessels were docked all over the canal, but they could not be delivered because the plant lacked the rigging, lifeboats, and several other parts that had been scavenged to complete the troop carrier.

The army had been desperate to have the *Sea Scamp* completed but

16. Richard A. McDerby, interview, August 30, 1992.

now was complaining about the delay in delivery of the FS ships. Haddock, several of his assistants, and other key personnel involved with the ships met to discuss how they could get back on schedule. They came to the conclusion that production could recover all lost time by May 31 if the material was delivered as promised. To accomplish this, Haddock said, "In 42 days we had to deliver 21 ships." He recalled: "We were in the old man's office with the army and presenting our plan and everyone seemed to be happy about it. Except they had a little so and so called Harry Beckanstin, some sort of assistant to Mr. Higgins. He said, 'I don't think you can do it.'" Carl Handlin, who was an assistant plant superintendent, said, "I think we can. I don't see any reason why we can't." At this point, Haddock explained, "Beckanstin reached into his pocket and pulled out his wallet and said, 'I don't know what you got, but what I got here says you can't do it.' Carl replied, 'OK, I'll match it.' Then Beckanstin stated, 'I'll take all the more of that you can bring in.'"

Haddock said that with that remark he and Handlin went into the plant and collared every foreman who had anything to do with FS production and said, "Look, you're putting up a hundred dollars." They then took the money and the IOUs to Higgins' office and had Beckanstin called in. They threw $3,700 in money and pledges on Higgins' desk. The bet was on.[17]

Higgins depended on his workers to accomplish the impossible. During this same period, several members of the Bureau of Ships must have been praying that the impossible would never come to pass. Their prayers had nothing to do with the FS ships but with Higgins. They had heard an incredible, bone-chilling rumor. The grapevine had it that Higgins was being considered for the job of secretary of the navy.

On May 10, the Cleveland *Plain Dealer* carried a story that had been broadcast on the "We the People" national radio program. Secretary of the Navy Frank Knox had died earlier in 1944, and Under Secretary of the Navy Forrestal had taken over as acting secretary. According to law, Forrestal had to step down by May 28. Discussion ensued over who should permanently assume the position. The article mentioned that neither Knox nor Forrestal had had practical experience in the industry with which they did business. Knox had been the publisher of the Chicago *Daily News,* and Forrestal's experience was in investment banking.[18]

17. Graham Haddock, interview, June 26, 1975.

18. Cleveland *Plain Dealer*, May 10, 1944, n.p. (Clipping in McGuire Collection). The following paragraphs are based on this source.

Because of the history of these two men, the paper suggested that Roosevelt might want to choose a "practical" shipbuilder as secretary of the navy, even if he served for only a few weeks. After the Republican convention in June, if Roosevelt desired to continue the wartime "coalition cabinet" he could offer the position to Wendell L. Willkie or Lieutenant Commander Harold Stassen.

The reason the position would not be offered now, according to the story, was that if either man accepted the post before the nominations, his political leverage in the Republican party would be weakened. The article expressed the belief that Roosevelt was too sound a politician to create a stir inside either party during the campaign. The writer assumed the president would appoint a temporary secretary, possibly as early as the middle of May.

Two outstanding candidates were suggested for the position. One was Henry J. Kaiser, though with the war in the Pacific intensifying it might be inadvisable to take him away from his shipyards even for a short time. Therefore, the best practical businessman for the job was Andrew Jackson Higgins, the fiery Louisiana shipbuilder, who had performed production miracles in his New Orleans plants.

The reporter suggested that Higgins' share of the shipbuilding program had tapered off, and he might be free to take the job for a few weeks without seriously affecting his yard's production. Higgins was a Democrat and knew all about navy procurement from the receiving end: "He knows where the body is buried, who has the inside track on naval contracts and why. The long overdue housecleaning job in the navy might best be handled by putting such a man in charge, with practical authority over the procurement end and with intelligence enough not to interfere with naval operations."

The writer felt that "as secretary of the navy for four or five weeks, a man like Higgins could put some of the streamlined efficiency of the shipyards into the department that places the orders and passes on specifications. As a fighting, two-fisted Irish-American, Andrew Jackson Higgins would also have the courage and the temperament, as well as the knowledge, to make the changes in procurement policy and personnel which have hitherto hampered the navy's magnificent war effort. Such changes were exactly what some of the personnel in the Small Boat Division of the bureau must have feared. A sigh of relief was breathed when Forrestal received the permanent appointment.

Relief was also felt at the Industrial Canal plant, but for another reason. At 2:00 P.M. on May 31, ten hours before the deadline, it was announced that the twenty-first FS ship was ready for delivery. Production was back on schedule. As a bonus to the bet, Mr. Higgins threw a party for the superintendents, supervisors, and those most responsible for the incredible feat. The event was held downtown at the New Orleans Athletic Club.

Haddock easily remembered the night. Higgins and several important dignitaries were on hand to help celebrate the occasion. Smiling, Haddock recalled: "When the banquet was over Mr. Higgins said, 'I don't want to inhibit your fun.' So he and his special guests left the party." Higgins had arranged for one last surprise. A four-foot silver platter with a big dome top was carried into the room by several waiters. They placed it on the table in front of Haddock, and when they lifted the cover there was a naked girl. With Bourbon Street only blocks away, it was easy for Higgins to find a stripper to shock his shy and reserved superintendent. Haddock did not elaborate about the girl, but he did remark "I think Mr. Higgins underwrote the bet. If he did, it was the best $3,700 bucks he ever spent. He had a wild way of working, but darn, people would work." [19]

Production of FS ships was again on schedule. Another very important problem was also close to being solved. On June 5, the Department of Justice announced that a federal grand jury had indicted four persons in connection with labor fraud. One of those indicted was Andrew Kalman of Affiliated Engineering Company, one of the service companies that Higgins had contracted with and vigorously complained about in Washington.

According to Associated Press reports, Kalman's company made exorbitant profits by padding payrolls, billing from fictitious time sheets, and charging labor fees for designers who did not exist. The four indictments handed down by the Department of Justice were the first steps taken toward controlling the labor service companies. The action had been taken because Andrew Higgins, Frank Higgins, and Colonel Jouett had forced Washington to address the issue.[20]

Now that the courts were taking action against the labor racketeers, Higgins started devoting time to a new interest—national politics. As

19. Graham Haddock, interview, June 26, 1975.
20. "Higgins Exposes Labor Black Markets," August 7, 1944, p. 12.

usual, he proceeded at full throttle. That one of his choices had not yet been nominated for office was seen as a minor problem. That this proposed candidate openly admitted to Higgins that he was not interested in holding the office was even of less concern. Higgins was not about to let such trivial problems interfere with his plans. His decision had been made, and he was prepared to act.

10

POLITICS

In the early morning hours of June 6, 1944, the largest fleet in the history of the world prepared for the Allied invasion of Europe. Standing ready off the coast of France was an assortment of over five thousand ships: modern troop transports, tugs, old cargo vessels, LSTs, ocean liners, and almost any other boat that could be converted for carrying men and equipment.

The armada was so large that it was scheduled to sail across the Channel in a ten-lane formation stretching out over a distance of twenty miles. Nestled aboard the transports were more than fifteen hundred Higgins LCMs, LCVPs, and LCPLs. Protecting the fleet's perimeters were 702 warships. Minesweepers, cruisers, destroyers, antisubmarine boats, gunboats, battleships, deadly PT boats, and many other small specialized craft were ready to act at the first sign of enemy aggression.[1]

As Higgins boats ferried thousands of men from the ships to hostile shores, their designer was speaking before the Rotary Club of Chicago. His address, broadcast over radio, was lost in the avalanche of news concerning the invasion. On June 10, four days after his speech, Higgins wrote to Truman: "D-Day on June 6th, I am afraid, killed the newspapers' attention to a broadcast I made in Chicago, in the course of which I nominated, in fact, elected you, as Vice-President. In my talk I set forth that I found it was the opinion of the majority of thinking and knowing Americans, that the work of your committee is the most outstanding thing in our war effort . . . while many foolish things had been done, the influence of your Committee has kept down the boodle and loot to a lower percentage than heretofore in our country's war involvements." In closing, Higgins suggested, "Your knowledge of industry, and the high

1. Cornelius Ryan, *The Longest Day* (1959; rpr. New York, 1967), 81–82.

plane on which all of your investigations and decisions, punitive, even though when corrective, made you the best qualified man to be a strong right arm to the President in the future conduct of the war, and the diplomatic war to follow to secure a workable and enduring peace."[2]

Three days later, Truman responded: "Please don't run me for Vice President. I have no ambition to be the Vice President. While it is a most honorable office and any one ought to be honored to fill it I like my job as a United States Senator, and that is where I want to stay."[3]

On June 17, Higgins countered: "Normally I would not want to sentence you to that office, but you would certainly add strength to Roosevelt's ticket, although I believe he will win in a walk, regardless of who his running mate may be." He then suggested to Truman that FDR should allow the vice-president to handle all domestic concerns while he attended to foreign matters. Continuing this line of thinking, Higgins wrote, "You would be the ideal Vice President, for under such an arrangement you could continue to be the power for good, as you are now, heading your excellent Committee."[4]

As of June 17, Roosevelt had not publicly or privately admitted that Vice-President Henry Wallace was not going to be included on the upcoming Democratic ticket. Rumors had surfaced in May that Wallace's candidacy was in trouble. When the president sent him on a mission to China, speculation increased. Roosevelt, it appeared, was giving other potential candidates an opportunity to muster support. In mid-June FDR was still publicly uncommitted to any candidate. He openly encouraged others to seek the vice-presidency while simultaneously trying not to discourage Wallace from pursuing nomination and reelection.[5]

Truman had been approached by friends early in the summer of 1943 about the office, but his response was always an emphatic no. Writing to a friend, he explained: "The Vice President simply presides over the Senate and sits around hoping for a funeral. It is a very high office which consists entirely of honor and I don't have any ambition to hold an office like that."[6]

Higgins was aware of the senator's disinterest in the position but con-

2. Andrew Higgins to Harry Truman, June 10, 1944 (Copy in McGuire Collection).

3. Harry Truman to Andrew Higgins, June 13, 1944, ibid.

4. Andrew Higgins to Harry Truman, June 17, 1944, ibid.

5. James MacGregor Burns, Roosevelt: The Soldier of Freedom, 1940–1945 (New York, 1970), 503.

6. McCullough, Truman, 298–99.

tinued to pressure him to run. He saw Truman as the one person in Washington who understood the needs of business and who the nation could trust. When the tank lighter controversy had occurred in May, 1942, Truman helped force a showdown between the bureau's lighter and Higgins'. When labor racketeering surfaced in the aircraft industry, Higgins turned to Truman's counsel Hugh Fulton to get the committee to investigate. Higgins figured that if Truman would not seek the position on his own, it was up to him to make a public call for his candidacy.

At about the same time Higgins was trying to convince Truman to run for the vice-presidency, he was also promoting two new projects at home. The first was designed to hire and train returning servicemen, especially those wounded in action. Outlines of the program were forwarded to various government departments: the surgeon general's office, the veterans' bureau, and the commanding officers of the various branches of the armed services. In his June 10 letter to Truman, Higgins mentioned that he had hired more than 280 disabled veterans, including some who were totally blind.

His second project concerned ground-breaking ceremonies for an employee housing project being constructed near Michaud. This was an extension of a federal program begun earlier for the workers at the Industrial Canal plant. The massive influx of people to New Orleans in 1943 had created a major housing problem. Potential employees often arrived with little money and no place to stay. Unable to find affordable room and board, they frequently gave up and returned to their farms or small towns. As a temporary measure Higgins built a large two-story bunkhouse on a barge and moored it across from the plant. New employees were fed and housed on board while they searched for permanent quarters.

Housing in a city overwhelmed by a huge number of new workers was difficult to find, especially for those with a family. Many tried commuting from as far away as a hundred miles, but Higgins discovered that this affected both the employees' morale and the quality of their work. To solve the problem, he proposed that the government build furnished houses close to the Industrial Canal plant. In late 1943 his efforts helped convince the Federal Public Housing Authority (FPHA) to construct 900 housing units on Gentilly Boulevard near the shipyard. By July, 1944, 750 "hutments" had been completed and were immediately occupied.

Higgins saw these temporary prefabricated units as the most reasonable solution to his employees' needs. Because they were temporary, at the end of the war, when employment declined and workers returned to their permanent homes, the hutments could be disassembled. Thus New Orleans would not be left with large "ghost cities" as some industrial centers had been at the end of World War I.

Additionally, a hutment cost less than $500 per unit. Rent would more than pay for the construction cost within two years. If the war should end before the mortgages were paid, the units could be sold to the renters or auctioned for salvage. The company had already received several requests from tenants hoping to buy the hutments. Responding to their inquiries, Higgins' employees' realty department manager, Joseph Spiro, sent a letter to W. H. O'Kelly, acting area director of the War Manpower Commission, recommending that the commission consider selling the units to the workers.

The program had been developed through the FPHA because the Federal Housing Administration (FHA), established in 1934, and the National Housing Act, passed in 1937, had not considered the problems that would be encountered by employers such as Higgins. On July 12, 1944, Spiro wrote O'Kelly explaining that the hutments proved to be the answer to the housing situation. "Without their use," he explained, "it would have been impossible to house the men we have employed." According to Spiro, the FHA and the NHA neglected the needs of shipyard workers. The FHA asserted that housing was available in the city, but Spiro knew that many of Higgins' workers could not obtain housing. Contractors refused to rent to large families and preferred white-collar employees over blue-collar shipyard workers. Additionally, many of Higgins' employees could not move into available housing because it was unfurnished and the initial rental cost was too high.[7]

Higgins felt that expanding the FPHA program to Michaud would ease the housing shortage for that plant's personnel. Three hundred hutments were scheduled to be assembled on the west side of the facility on the site of the old Micheaud sugar plantation. On the east side, to accommodate the highly skilled and higher-paid aircraft engineers and technicians, 150 modern brick homes were to be constructed.[8]

In July, as plans to overcome Michaud's housing problems moved forward, the residents of the earlier settlement of hutments near the Industrial Canal decided to change its name from Shipyard Homes to Our-

7. Joseph Spiro, Jr., to W. H. O'Kelly, July 12, 1944, in Hebert Papers.
8. "A. J. Higgins Tells Program for Veterans," *Higgins Worker*, June 23, 1944, p. 3.

town. It was a small act but one that Higgins fully supported. It symbolized to him that the settlement was beginning to take on a community identity.

Higgins sympathized with the problems the residents of Ourtown had to confront. Most of the workers had been uprooted from old neighborhood ties, affiliations, and familiar surroundings. He also understood that as parents they had to believe that their children were happy at home before they could fully dedicate themselves to their work. Higgins instituted a recreation program, which he reasoned, might even nip juvenile delinquency in the bud. Delinquency was on the rise nationally as fathers served in the military and mothers entered the work force or when both parents were employed and children were left at home unsupervised.

In the fall of 1943, Higgins had appointed his sister Joy Montgomery Higgins as director of the company's recreation department. The program originally focused on adult intraplant and interplant championships in baseball, softball, golf, bowling, wrestling, touch football, basketball, and track. The interplant champion then represented the company in the Commercial Athletic Association and Southern Amateur Athletic Union leagues. Higgins had Joy expand the program in the summer of 1944 to encompass the needs of the adults and children of Ourtown. A representative of the recreation department was assigned to the community on a full-time basis.

As the demands on the recreation department expanded, so did the staff. Joy became the director of the company's social services office and William Rinehart was appointed director of athletics and recreation. Al Hessmer, director of the Higgins band, became the head of the musical and social activities program.

Joy had already arranged for a playground to be built for the children of Ourtown, and plans called for building several others in the future. She was also instrumental in having a child care center constructed, in organizing classes in drama, dancing, and music, and in establishing youth leagues in a variety of sports. In addition, Higgins sponsored parent clubs and recreation facilities for the residents. To give the settlement a neighborhood appearance, the company supplied materials for victory gardens. Higgins was determined that the project should be a community of homes, not just temporary housing.[9]

9. Caption, *Eureka News Bulletin,* III (January–March, 1944), 118.

Higgins' approach was much different from that taken by the Ford Motor Company. In 1943, when similar problems affected employees at Willow Run, a Ford representative responded: "What our workers do outside the plant, or how they live, is no concern of ours. The community will have to take care of that." Local 50 of the United Auto Workers eventually helped organize recreation and adult education programs for Willow Run employees.[10] The Fords basically ignored their workers' outside life, whereas Higgins appointed Joy to see to the recreational and educational needs of his workers. He also made available company buses to take his employees' older children to the public schools several miles away, and he took measures to help turn the temporary neighborhood into a true community.

On July 12, the Democrats were making last-minute preparations for their national convention. The discussion among party leaders was not about convention arrangements but whether Roosevelt's health would allow him to complete another term. FDR's physical condition made the vice-presidential nomination far more critical than normal. The convention might well be nominating two presidents, not one. Who the second choice would be was still unclear.

On July 17, two days before the convention was to open, Samuel Jackson, convention chairman, released a letter in which Roosevelt endorsed Wallace. FDR described the vice-president as a friend whom he liked and respected. In closing, he wrote, "For these reasons I personally would vote for his nomination if I were a delegate to the convention." The statement, though officially supportive, was so lukewarm that many considered it a kiss of death.[11]

When the convention opened in Chicago on July 19, Roosevelt was in San Diego secretly preparing to sail aboard the heavy cruiser *Baltimore* for Hawaii. His agenda included meetings with General Douglas MacArthur and Fleet Admiral Chester W. Nimitz. Before departing, FDR delivered his acceptance speech via long distance. Delegates in the convention hall faced an empty podium and listened to the president's address being broadcast over the hall's sound system.[12]

10. Keith Sward, *The Legend of Henry Ford* (New York, 1972), 436.
11. McCullough, *Truman,* 310.
12. *Ibid.,* 316.

As Roosevelt spoke, it still was not clear who should be chosen as his running mate. Wallace was fighting hard to maintain his position, although many at the convention believed that the president preferred James F. Byrnes, once an associate justice of the Supreme Court and presently head of the Office of War Mobilization. Others backed Senate majority leader Alben Barkley, Supreme Court justice William O. Douglas, or Senator Truman.

Truman, still contending that he was not interested in the office, had agreed to nominate Byrnes. He later withdrew the offer after being convinced that he, not Byrnes, was Roosevelt's first choice. Byrnes, feeling betrayed by the president, bitterly withdrew his name from consideration. Finally, on July 21, at 8:14 P.M., after a nine-hour session, the second ballot was tallied and Truman was declared victorious. Roosevelt wired his congratulations.[13]

As Truman reached a milestone in his political career, Higgins reached one in production. On Sunday, July 23, ceremonies were held to commemorate the delivery of the ten thousandth boat built by Higgins Industries for the U.S. Navy. The boat, a 56-foot welded steel tank lighter, was completed Saturday, July 22. It was then loaded onto a decorated platform and transported to the lakefront close to where the Industrial Canal enters Lake Pontchartrain. The LCM was positioned near the VIP platform that had been built especially for the ceremonies.

In honor of the occasion, George Rappleyea had written a script recreating a phase of the invasion of Normandy. McDerby and his students turned the idea into reality as thousands of onlookers sat on the concrete sea wall steps and watched. An FS ship anchored offshore unloaded troops onto LCVPs and LCMs. The craft then assaulted their target beach. PT boats patrolled the shore while airplanes flew overhead as if defending against enemy aircraft.

In the VIP stands were Higgins; Bureau of Ships chief, Rear Admiral E. L. Cochrane; Rear Admiral P. W. Foote, the inspector of naval material from Houston; Holt Ross of the AFL; and several special guests. Higgins had sent an invitation to Mexico's president, Manuel Avila Camacho, but pressing duties at home prevented him from attending. He was represented by Vice-Admiral Othon P. Blanco, under secretary of the

13. *Ibid.*, 318–20.

Mexican navy; Francisco Doria Paz, acting mayor of Mexico City; and high-ranking officials from Mexico's Interior Department and Bureau of Tourism.

The souvenir program given to the guests called the delivery of the ten thousandth ship a milestone. Perhaps even more of a milestone was the sight of Higgins sitting next to Rear Admiral Cochrane. A few years before, the idea of Higgins sharing the same platform with the head of the Bureau of Ships would have been unthinkable. The change in the relationship was mainly owing to the bureau's change in leadership. The bureau of 1944 was a different organization from the one that Higgins had battled only a few years before.

Higgins Industries also had undergone great changes since the company received its first contract from the navy in 1937. Then the company had consisted of only a few men and a small building on St. Charles Avenue. Today, as Higgins sat watching seven different types of landing craft and PT boats perform on the lake, he was the president of an industrial giant. His company encompassed seven plants employing over twenty thousand workers. The facilities occupied more than 100 million square feet of which 5 million were under roof. Over sixty-four different products were now produced by his employees. The best known were the LCPLs, LCVPs, LCMs, LCSs, antisubmarine boats, aircraft rescue boats, FS ships, and PTs, but his company also manufactured wing panels, plywood, plastics, engines, solar stills, pumps, torpedo tubes, radios, and a variety of other related products.

His average employee earned $58 per week; his companies' weekly combined payrolls exceeded $1.16 million. Annually, he paid over $60 million in wages. In dollars and cents Higgins' massive payroll was worth more to the state of Louisiana than the two most important agricultural crops, sugar and rice. Higgins Industries also provided work for 256 subcontractors who employed thousands of additional workers. The annual value of their contracts was over $16 million, of which $5 million went to 110 subcontractors in the city of New Orleans. This figure does not include Higgins Aircraft, which sublet contracts for an estimated $35 million. At the peak of Higgins' production, 69 train cars a day, containing 2,427 tons of material, unloaded their freight at the three main boat plants. During the fifteen months before the ceremony, 25,779 freight cars delivered over 910,098 tons of material to the three plants. Higgins had built ten thousand boats for the U.S. Navy and an additional three thousand for other branches of the service and for the Allies. Simultaneously, twenty-five other companies in the United States were building Higgins boats royalty free.[14]

Cochrane, addressing the crowd over a loudspeaker, expressed the bureau's new feeling toward the industrialist when he stated: "Our landing craft program had its beginning in the field of the smaller types of such craft—landing boats and tank lighters. Unquestionably the pioneer in these fields was Andrew Jackson Higgins." The statement exhibited just how much the relationship had changed. Not forgetting the workers, Cochrane announced, "It is no exaggeration to say that the successes which our amphibious forces have been achieving against the strongholds of the enemy on both sides of the globe could not have been won without the contribution of the men and women of Higgins Industries." The employees presented Cochrane with a special gift, a plate they had designed and fabricated on which was inscribed the inspection record of the ten thousandth boat. Following the presentation, Holt Ross, general representative of the International Laborers Union and a southern representative of the AFL, spoke to the crowd. Ross praised Higgins as "a model employer and a great humanitarian whose workers may well be proud of him."[15]

The symbolic delivery of the LCM to Cochrane did not end the festivities. The following day ceremonies were held at the Industrial Canal plant in conjunction with the launching of the SS Veracruz. Higgins saw Mexico as a potential postwar market. The launching served as an opportunity to solidify connections with a future trading partner. Participating in the ceremonies were distinguished guests from the republic of Mexico. Dr. A. Ortiz Tirado opened the program with Mexico's national anthem, after which thousands of Higgins workers enthusiastically waved flags and cheered "Viva Mexico." Mrs. Andres Horcasitas, wife of the Mexican tourist agent for Louisiana, christened the Veracruz with a bottle of tequila, and Francisco Doria Paz, acting mayor of Mexico City, leaned over and kissed the ship as it slid down the ways. Mexico's undersecretary of the navy, Vice-Admiral Othon P. Blanco, praised the employ-

14. Souvenir program, ceremony for the delivery of Higgins' ten thousandth navy boat, in Strahan Personal Collection.
15. "Navy Officials Pay Tribute to Higgins Ind.," Higgins Worker, July 28, 1944, p. 1.

ees for their work and read a message from Mexico's president, Manuel Avila Camacho.[16]

Higgins followed by reading a telegram just received from Roosevelt concerning the previous day's celebration. The president, still in the Pacific, stated: "I regret exceedingly that I cannot accept your cordial invitation to attend the ceremonies. It gives me however the greatest pleasure to extend hearty congratulations to you and to the loyal men and women who have made possible this outstanding achievement. Keep up the good work. It spells confusion to our enemies and hastens the day when we shall beat them to their knees."[17]

On July 27, three days after the launching of the *Veracruz* and six days after Truman was chosen as the Democrats' vice-presidential candidate, Higgins took time to write the senator: "I preferred to wait until you had received the deluge of congratulations before writing you. You, of course, know where I have stood all along. Incidentally, I have collected quite a number of bets—many of them made over a year ago—that you would be nominated for Vice President. Every one of these bets were cheerfully paid." Higgins closed by stating: "I do not claim to be psychic or occult, or have a crystal ball, but I do have hunches that, in a majority of cases, come true. Even when you earnestly declined support, I knew then that the honor would be forced on you. I have another hunch: It is in the cards that within the next four years you will be President of the United States. I earnestly hope that this will come to you by the resignation of Mr. Roosevelt."[18]

Four days later, Truman responded: "I wish you would not bring up that situation about the cards being stacked for that was one of the things that scared me off and made me hesitate about accepting the nomination. I am in now with both feet, however, and I know we are going to win."[19]

During the period in which Truman and Higgins were corresponding the *Higgins Worker* carried stories on the delivery of the ten thousandth

16. "Thousands See Ship Launched at Canal Plant," *Higgins Worker*, July 28, 1944, p. 1.

17. "Roosevelt Praises Higgins Achievements," *Higgins Worker*, July 28, 1944, p. 1.

18. Andrew Higgins to Harry Truman, July 27, 1944 (Copy in McGuire Collection).

19. Harry Truman to Andrew Higgins, July 31, 1944, *ibid.*

boat, the launching of the *Veracruz,* and Roosevelt's statement of congratulations. Sharing the front page were two other articles the paper deemed important. The first announced that Ourtown was inaugurating regular door-to-door mail delivery and houses would be assigned addresses instead of hutment numbers. The second article explained that Ourtown's Brownie troop was becoming part of the national Girl Scout organization. Investiture ceremonies were to be held in the recreation hall of the Ourtown child care center. Higgins had wanted the temporary housing units to develop into a community. His wish was becoming a reality.[20]

As the Industrial Canal and City Park shipyards were setting production records and Ourtown was taking on the signs of a permanent subdivision, the Michaud plant was caught up in sweeping changes. On August 10, in preparation for a massive offensive in the Pacific, the military announced a shift in production emphasis to superbombers and larger and longer-range troop transports. The change in strategy meant a reduced demand for B-24 Liberator bombers, P-47 Thunderbolt fighters, and C-46 cargo planes.

Michaud, not yet in production, was one of the plants to have its contract canceled. Thus far the facility had produced only one plane. Delays were initially caused by retooling from the C-76 project to the C-46 and later because of the difficulty in finding skilled labor. The announcement by the WPB stressed that the cancellations were not a reflection on the plants whose contracts had been terminated but of a change in the needs of the military. Michaud's mass production of wing panels for the Curtis-Wright plants in Louisville and St. Louis continued, but plans to build complete airplanes were halted.[21]

Higgins was disappointed with the cancellation of the contract, but he had become accustomed to such occurrences. He could not become accustomed to the treatment of prisoners of war being held in Louisiana, however. To express his concern, he wrote to Louisiana's senators, John H. Overton and Allen J. Ellender. Copies were sent to Louisiana congressmen F. Edward Hebert and James H. Morrison and to his longtime friend Congressman Frank Boykin of Alabama. Higgins had heard

20. "Mail Delivery Is Established in Our Town," *Higgins Worker,* July 28, 1944, p. 1; "Ourtown Brownies to be Invested," *Higgins Worker,* July 28, 1944, p. 1.
21. "Orders Increase in Superbombers," New York *Times,* August 11, 1944, p. 6.

that where German prisoners were incarcerated in the same facility with American soldiers of lesser rank, the GIs had to salute the Nazi officers. One or more noncommissioned officers, he insisted, had had their rank degraded "because they refused to salute arrogant German officers." An even more shocking situation was rumored to exist at Camp Van Dorn. American soldiers were sent to the camp as punishment for minor disciplinary offenses. Higgins had been told that these Americans were deprived of their pay while incarcerated. Yet they were forced to work alongside Nazi prisoners, who were receiving ninety cents a day and were "treated with consideration which they abused." American prisoners, he understood, who refused to work with the Nazis reportedly were punished. Higgins argued, "The American soldiers' attitude is that they are in the Army to fight and kill Germans, and not to salute their officers or be degraded alongside of the Nazi scum." Even closer to home Higgins saw what he considered startling treatment of prisoners of war. "Right here in New Orleans, Italian prisoners have the freedom of the streets, and are even entertained at bathing parties on Lake Pontchartrain. All of this coddling of our enemies is excused by the statement that it is required by the laws of war, and the requirements of the Geneva Convention. Is there anyone in this country foolish enough to believe that the Germans are showing our men, officers or privates, like consideration? I think it is time that this thing be protested on the floor of Congress." [22]

Higgins did not have much time to follow up on the prisoner-of-war issue for in August he was called to a meeting at the White House. Roosevelt informed him that he would soon be contacted about participating in "the most vital project of the war." The project carried the highest top secret classification, and for the moment neither he nor anyone else at his plant could be given any information other than the specifications for the parts they were to produce. The president explained that for seven months other companies had being trying to manufacture the parts but without success. Higgins agreed to accept the challenge and recommended that production be carried out at the Michaud facility. Security was to be maintained by explaining that the finely machined parts were for radio and radar communication, and every employee had to agree to an oath of secrecy. [23]

22. Andrew Higgins to Overton, Ellender, Hebert, Morrison, and Boykin, August 21, 1944, in Hebert Papers.

23. Statler Hotel Statement, 17.

232 ANDREW JACKSON HIGGINS

Not long after returning from Washington, Higgins was contacted by Clarke Salmon, head of Bauerlein, Inc., about another project concerning the president. Salmon was Higgins' outside public relations agent, very pro-Roosevelt, and a close friend of Harry Hopkins. During a meeting with Salmon, Higgins was convinced to accept the honorary national presidency of Businessmen for Roosevelt.[24]

In a September 29 interoffice memo to Dave McGuire, George Rappleyea informed him that Higgins was to attend a dinner in Washington on Monday, October 9. "Before he leaves we must organize a 'Businessmen for Roosevelt Association,' with an office as headquarters in the Industries Building." Literature, press releases, and broadcast time all had to be arranged, and a staff had to be organized. Rappleyea instructed McGuire to see him immediately "about getting the ball rolling."[25]

Three days later, on Monday, October 2, Higgins delivered a speech over local radio announcing the formation of the new organization. Listeners were informed that businessmen supporting the president's reelection and the election of Senator Harry Truman as vice-president had been unorganized and acting as individuals. He stressed that in "unity there is strength" and that businessmen should recall Benjamin Franklin's famous saying, "We had better hang together or we will hang separately." Higgins told his audience that he was pro-Roosevelt because FDR was a proven leader, was the most qualified candidate to be commander in chief, had great leadership abilities, and at the peace table "is far better qualified to protect American interests, without injustice to other nations, large or small." Then he requested each listener to stop what he was doing for a moment and see if he could think of a junior officer whom he might want to elevate to take General Eisenhower's place. Or perhaps he knew of a brilliant young recruit who could replace General George C. Marshall. His strategy was to convince his listeners that replacing Roosevelt in the midst of war was just as illogical.[26]

Higgins' next speech was the first of three that he delivered to a national radio audience. On October 5, using five minutes paid for by the Democratic National Committee, he explained why he was helping to reelect Roosevelt: "When I was asked to serve as honorary president of this organization, I accepted because I am a realist—and face facts. . . .

24. "This is an account of . . . ," n.d. (Handwritten note in McGuire Collection).
25. George W. Rappleyea to Dave McGuire and Clarke Salmon, September 29, 1944, *ibid.*
26. "Address by Mr. Andrew J. Higgins," October 2, 1944, *ibid.*

The Democratic party picked the man we all know to have the greatest ability and experience for the job, while the Republicans repudiated their great men, amongst them one Wendell Willkie, an acceptable counterpart of Franklin Roosevelt in international affairs, a man who won the public's approval and acclaim, who gained the respect of our allies and successfully impressed them with our war and peace aims." The repudiation of Willkie "leaves us but one choice."[27]

As Higgins delivered his speech, McGuire sat in the new Businessmen for Roosevelt office in the Industries Building. Surrounded by blowup photos and literature advertising the candidacy of Roosevelt and Truman, he took a moment to write a friend about his new political assignment. "I am not enthusiastic about it for two reasons. First, I dislike to embark on lost causes when there is absolutely no chance of success. The results are not likely to be happy for the sponsor or his menials. This is definitely a lost cause. I never knew of a loser one. The business men of New Orleans, by tradition and by recent events, are anti-Roosevelt, and anti-New Deal and even anti-Higgins. Trying to recruit members is like trying to find Nazis in Russia." McGuire had just completed twenty telephone calls to potentially pro-Roosevelt businessmen. His objective was to find ten prominent names he could list as a local committee on the organization's letterhead. He got two yeses and eighteen nos. Both yeses did business with Higgins.[28]

As McGuire was getting the ball rolling in New Orleans, Clarke Salmon was opening a national Businessmen for Roosevelt office in the Roosevelt Hotel in New York City. His responsibility was to coordinate the organization's activities with National Committee chairman Robert Hannegan and treasurer Edwin W. Pauley. Salmon, like McGuire, discovered that the task was not going to be easy. A prominent New Yorker who was asked to serve on the national committee responded, "It is of considerable interest to us that the Administration had to go clear across the country to New Orleans, bypassing all the cities in the eastern part of the United States, before they could find a group of businessmen who would incorporate to support Roosevelt."[29]

Salmon was busily organizing the national effort in New York while

27. "Secure the Future with Roosevelt and Truman," *Higgins Worker,* October 13, 1944, pp. 4–5.
28. Dave McGuire to Smith, n.d., in McGuire Collection.
29. Jack B. McGuire, "Andrew Higgins Plays Presidential Politics," *Journal of the Louisiana Historical Association,* XV (Summer, 1974), 279–80.

Higgins on October 11 was entertaining Truman in New Orleans. The vice-presidential candidate, along with five other senators, was in town to attend the annual meeting of the Mississippi Valley Flood Control Association. The visit gave Higgins and Truman an opportunity to discuss the campaign and for the senator to view the progress that had been made at Michaud. It also gave the men a chance to spend an evening at Higgins' home playing poker, a game that Truman thoroughly enjoyed.[30]

After leaving New Orleans Truman embarked on a cross-country trip that officially opened his campaign.[31] As the vice-presidential candidate made whistle stops in the West, the *Higgins Worker* published an article about his visit to the plants. Also included in the October 13 issue were three other stories of interest. One, titled "Statement Tells Trap Rumor Is Unfounded," clarified remarks that Higgins made in a speech broadcast to the Industrial Canal and City Park plants. In his address he had used the old adage "If you build a better mouse trap than your neighbor, the world will make a beaten path to your door." His intent was to illustrate that if after the war the plants continued to produce boats superior to those built by the competition, work would continue to be plentiful. So many employees misunderstood the analogy that the company issued a simplified explanation on the front page of the paper reassuring its workers that Higgins Industries was not going to produce mousetraps.[32]

A second article, sharing page 5 with a transcript of Higgins' October 5 speech, related that the Office of War Information wanted a photograph of James Murray. In an earlier issue the *Worker* had featured a picture of Murray, a forty-one-year-old armless black welder at the Industrial Canal plant. The paper proudly explained that Murray was the father of two sons serving overseas and had been an employee of Higgins since July 21. He had completed a welding course offered by Xavier University in New Orleans, graduating with an above average rating. The *Worker* had described him as most dependable and industrious at his job. The article and photograph were important for two reasons. First, it featured a person contributing to the war effort despite extreme physical handicaps. Second, it appeared in a company paper in the South. This

30. Truman Guest of A. J. Higgins at Aircraft," *Higgins Worker,* October 13, 1944, p. 1.

31. McCullough, *Truman,* 329.

32. "Statement Tells Trap Rumor Is Unfounded," *Higgins Worker,* October 13, 1944, p. 1.

might have been considered unique by many but not by those at Higgins. The *Eureka* and the *Worker* on several occasions printed stories concerning women or minorities. Articles such as the one about Murray were viewed by the work force as simply another story about a fellow employee.[33]

A third article of interest celebrated the upcoming opening on October 16 of the "Little Red Schoolhouse" in Ourtown. Children in kindergarten and first grade would now have a neighborhood school. The children who were just starting their education had been uprooted from their old neighborhoods, and their lives were confused. The paper suggested that the school would make their lives more stable. The FHA had constructed the building, and the Orleans Parish School Board equipped it and furnished the teachers. The article stated: "We are looking forward to a happy winter. These children can call back memories, when they are grown up, to the days of the Great War when their fathers and mothers, probably both of them, were working in a war plant building boats for Victory, and when they went to the little red school house under the trees." Older children in Ourtown were transported to nearby city schools in Higgins Industries buses.[34]

As the kindergarteners and first graders were preparing for classes in their new school, the presidential candidates were preparing for a strong finish to end their campaigns. Higgins had left New Orleans and arrived in Washington on October 15. He was embarking on a hectic five-week campaign in the Northeast to help reelect the president.

In the weeks preceding the trip to Washington, McGuire and his staff had sent out pamphlets and letters trying to elicit support for Businessmen for Roosevelt. Higgins informed Gladstone Williams, a journalist, that "the reaction I got was frightening. Those who weren't bitterly against Roosevelt, wanted to vote against something, and the only thing they could be against was the party in office."[35]

Higgins even found it difficult to raise money in his own home state. In a letter to a friend, Sylvester Labrot, who had donated $5,000 to Businessmen for Roosevelt, Higgins stated: "I am trying to raise every possible dollar here in Louisiana, but it is a tough proposition, with the

33. "OWI Wants Picture of James Murray," *Higgins Worker*, October 13, 1944, p. 5.
34. "Little Red Schoolhouse Opens Monday for Ourtown Children," *Higgins Worker*, October 13, 1944, p. 6.
35. Andrew Higgins to Gladstone Williams, n.d., in McGuire Collection.

damn bigoted fools down here. They will put out for Mardi Gras, French Opera, and a lot of tom-foolery; but they bemoan high taxes, and they bemoan the slightest inconveniences they have in a time when their country is going through the most terrific war of all time. They have to have something to gripe about, and somebody to gripe at, so they pick Roosevelt." [36]

Higgins became more determined. As the campaign intensified, Businessmen for Roosevelt sent a mailing of 500,000 letters to businessmen in twelve states the party considered key to the election. Radio broadcasts were sponsored in the South, and three network telecasts were paid for with funds raised by the organization.[37] To help assure that Missouri would support the Democratic ticket, Higgins convinced a young Louisiana congressman, Jimmy Morrison, to stump across the state. The industrialist personally supplied his recruit with sound trucks, an expense account, and instructions to give five or six speeches a day in Republican strongholds. Concerning the congressman's effort Higgins wrote to a friend, "Morrison is a better speaker to country folks than was Huey Long." [38]

Other states also needed special attention. The Republicans announced that voters in New Jersey, Ohio, and Michigan were supporting Republican candidate Thomas E. Dewey and that Pennsylvania would soon follow. Herbert Brownell, Jr., the Republican national chairman, claimed that on October 21, Pennsylvania's Democratic chairman, David Lawrence, called Washington for immediate help before his state was lost.

In a statement from national party headquarters Brownell reported: "Look who came in with Mr. Lawrence—a couple of 'economic royalists.' Isn't this the Andrew J. Higgins who was paid $40,000,000 to drive 4,000,000 useless piles in a Louisiana swamp? It was intended to be a shipyard but was abandoned when someone discovered that ships could not be built in the middle of the mud. Isn't this the J. Louis Reynolds, to whom the New Deal loaned millions of Government money to go into war contracting?" Higgins was furious when he heard of Brownell's comments. "First of all," he told a reporter, "it wasn't $40,000,000 and the place was completed and is in successful operation building equipment

36. Andrew Higgins to Sylvester Labrot, October 15, 1944, *ibid.*
37. McGuire, "Andrew Higgins Plays Presidential Politics," 280.
38. Congressman Jimmy Morrison, interview, September 21, 1991; Higgins to Williams, n.d., in McGuire Collection.

vitally needed in the war. It was completed at less than its estimate."
Campaigning now took on a new dimension. No longer was it simply
enough to reelect Roosevelt; Higgins wanted to defeat the Republicans.
The situation had become personal.[39]

Through its tireless efforts, Businessmen for Roosevelt raised approximately $19,000 in the New Orleans area and a total of about $60,000 to
$70,000 nationally. The funds were used to finance mailings and broad-
casts and to outfit Truman's campaign train.

In late October, when the Democratic party needed money to sponsor
a nationwide broadcast by Roosevelt from Shibe Park in Philadelphia,
Higgins personally raised the $20,000 to underwrite the event. The total
included $5,000 in contributions from Higgins, his son Frank, his sister
Joy, and George Rappleyea. Because of his efforts to raise the money and
his position as head of Businessmen for Roosevelt, Higgins was chosen
to introduce the president at the rally. Between October 28 and 31 Higgins also stumped for the ticket in South Boston, Lynn, and Lawrence,
Massachusetts.

During his visit to Boston, Higgins joined Truman for a press conference. Questioned about the president's health, Higgins responded:
"People, knowing I have been with the President, ask me in whispers,
'How is his health?' Well, I say, damn good! He is wearing down the
young, tough guys with and around him." Stressing FDR's vitality, he
continued: "Sixty miles through cold, during rain, in New York! I got
sniffles, he did not. In Philadelphia, high winds and cold. I froze and
shivered with a heavy coat. Roosevelt threw off his cape. You heard his
speech—45 minutes. Sick men can't do that! All this talk about the Commander in Chief in ill health is pure unadulterated bunk, part of a dirty,
underhanded whispering campaign."[40]

Following his speaking engagements in Massachusetts, Higgins headed
to New York and Madison Square Garden for an "Everybody for Roosevelt Rally." He later commented: "Unlike the hatchet-man Ickes, over
and above this, I was on a vacation, traveling with my wife, and I bore all
of my own expenses, which were considerable on my vacation. Mr. Ickes'
wife gave $500.00, but he said he was giving enough in his campaign;
yet the raspy ass spoke eleven minutes overtime at Madison Square Gar-

39. "Brownell claims Ohio and Michigan," New York *Times*, October 21, 1944, p. 9.
40. McGuire, "Andrew Higgins Plays Presidential Politics," 281.

den, and the money that paid for that broadcast came out of my pocket, or went through my pocket. I deny, for I will always deny, and can always prove, that I did not contribute more than $5,000. Ickes took enough time so that my speech, which was the best received at Madison Square Garden, only had one minute over the radio. I doubt if there is any one who can prove to me that Ickes gained one more vote than he lost for Roosevelt."[41]

After delivering more than twenty-nine speeches during a four-state campaign tour that included Maryland, New York, Pennsylvania, and Massachusetts, Higgins returned to New Orleans. In discussing the trip with McGuire he confided: "My God, the president looks ghastly. There's no doubt in my mind that Truman will be president within the next year."[42]

Publicly, Higgins had called charges that Roosevelt was ill "bunk," but in private, as with McGuire, he admitted the truth. He felt strongly that the country should retain its present leadership in the midst of war but that if FDR could not finish his term, Truman was certainly the best man to hold the office.

Higgins' last effort for the campaign was to order that a memorandum be posted in his plants encouraging all employees able to do so to exercise their privilege and vote on November 7. He pointed out that in this election the women's vote assumed a greater importance than in previous years. Higgins encouraged those women who were qualified to do so to "make it a special point to go to the polls and vote for the candidate they believe best qualified to direct our Nation's affairs over the next four years."[43]

The election results delighted Higgins. He had campaigned hard for the ticket and believed he had been partially responsible for Truman's appearance on it. On November 8, he wrote the newly elected vice-president: "Thank God the country had good sense . . . I know you are glad the campaign is over. It certainly was a stinker. This is the first time I ever got active in political campaigning. I never did like the Republicans, but I really got right down to good hating business this time." Higgins admitted, "I am afraid I would have been a bad loser if Dewey had

41. Higgins to Williams, n.d., in McGuire Collection.

42. McGuire, "Andrew Higgins Plays Presidential Politics," 281; Statler Hotel Statement, 19.

43. "Attention All Employees," n.d. (Memo in McGuire Collection).

won, and, and, as far as that goes, I might have been better off moving to South America, for I increased my s—— list tremendously, and I guess I accumulated a lot more enemies."[44]

On November 14, Truman responded: "Thank you for yours of the Eighth, but you needn't be in any doubt as to how to address me. . . . You always called me Harry—keep it up . . . and all of us appreciated your efforts in the campaign."[45]

A friend living in the nation's capital wrote McGuire: "Mr. Higgins undoubtedly rendered yeoman service in the campaign. The impression in Washington was that he and his name carried a tremendous amount of weight and almost certainly influenced many business men either to support the president, or at least not to oppose him." General Holland Smith wrote Higgins, "I note that you did some campaigning for Roosevelt, and I congratulate you because I know you did a damn good job just like you do in everything you tackle."[46]

Higgins was pleased with his effort. He had delivered numerous speeches during his five weeks of campaigning and had been responsible for raising over $106,000. Included in the figure was $60,000 to $70,000 from Businessmen for Roosevelt. Accounting for the rest of the funds, Higgins claimed that he did not contribute more than the $5,000 legal limit. But he admitted, "I have a big family, and a large number of associates and a wide acquaintance." Higgins enjoyed the political arena but was not thrilled with everyone or everything he encountered during the campaign. He had earlier admitted to disliking Secretary of the Interior Harold Ickes, and in a letter to a friend he wrote: "Another man who gripes me is Kaiser. He contributed to a nonpartisan outfit, which was organized ostensibly for the pretext of getting out the vote. . . . After he sat at the Teamster's dinner, when Roosevelt first spoke, Kaiser got excited and was afraid he would hurt himself, so he wallowed his fat belly around, and tried to sit in at a Republican dinner, to prove how nonpartisan he was." Higgins stressed that Kaiser "refused to give a dime, and there is no proof that he gave a dime to the Roosevelt campaign; but his press agents are now spouting off what great assistance he gave the President; and his press agents also see that there is an announcement

44. Andrew Higgins to Harry Truman, November 8, 1944, *ibid.*

45. Harry Truman to Andrew Higgins, November 14, 1944, *ibid.*

46. [?] to Dave McGuire, November 20, 1944, General Holland Smith to Andrew Higgins, November 22, 1944, both *ibid.*

about once a week that he had a luncheon engagement with the President." Feeling slighted, Higgins commented, "So far, the only acknowledgment that I have had, that I was active in the campaign, was two short paragraphs from Senator Truman, telling me to still call him Harry."[47] Roosevelt would eventually acknowledge Higgins' support, but in mid-November the war, his fourth term, and his health were of primary importance.

With the presidential campaign over, Higgins focused his attention closer to home. His immediate concern was eliminating the problems created by having thirteen separate AFL-affiliated trade unions operating in his plants. What he initially viewed as a time-consuming nuisance was about to erupt into a major labor versus management confrontation. During 1945 the conflict drew national attention and concluded in Higgins fighting the AFL in the final labor dispute in his company's history.

47. Higgins to Williams, n.d., *ibid.*

Workers unload crated LCMs and prepare to reassemble the boats in a South Pacific jungle shipyard.

Courtesy Higgins Family

An aerial view of Bayou St. John shows LCVPs, PT boats, and LCSs awaiting shipment.

Courtesy Graham Haddock

Higgins, third from right, adds another star to the Army-Navy "E" Award during a ceremony on July 23, 1944, commemorating the delivery of the ten thousandth boat built by Higgins Industries for the U.S. Navy. With him (from left) are Lieutenant Commander C. W. Leveau, U.S. Navy supervisor of shipbuilding at Higgins Industries; Captain L. L. Border; Rear Admiral E. L. Cochrane, chief of the Bureau of Ships; Rear Admiral P. W. Foote; and Rear Admiral James Pine.

Courtesy Eisenhower Center, University of New Orleans

Students from the Higgins Boat Operators School group their boats to form an E as they move past crowds on hand to celebrate the one-year anniversary of the City Park plant, the dedication of the Industrial Canal plant, and the company's receiving the Army-Navy "E" Award, on September 13, 1942.

Courtesy Richard McDerby

Troops disembark from a Higgins LCVP during an amphibious assault.

Courtesy Higgins Family

LCVPs are transported overland to be used in crossing a river in Europe. The boat cradle here is the same type Higgins used to move his boats from the St. Charles Avenue plant to hoists on the Mississippi River.

Courtesy Graham Haddock

Higgins takes President Franklin Roosevelt on a tour of the City Park plant on September 19, 1942. Also on the tour were Rear Admiral Frank Leighton, left, and Governor Sam Jones of Louisiana, second from left.

Courtesy Herald Braud

The *Hellcat* was considered the fastest PT boat to enter the service during World War II.

Courtesy Higgins Family

The Higgins airborne droppable lifeboat was catapulted from bombers to pilots downed at sea.

Courtesy Higgins Family

Once aboard the lifeboat, the downed crew would install the sail, unpack dry clothes, food, and medical supplies, and sail toward safety.

Courtesy Higgins Family

A reenactment of the invasion of Normandy was part of the festivities celebrating the delivery of the ten thousandth Higgins boat to the U.S. Navy.

Courtesy Eisenhower Center, University of New Orleans

Archbishop Joseph Francis Rummel blesses PT Squadron 23 on August 7, 1943.

Courtesy Higgins Family

Higgins with vice-presidential candidate Harry Truman during the 1944 presidential campaign. Higgins was a strong support of the Roosevelt-Truman ticket and served as national president of Businessmen for Roosevelt.

Courtesy Higgins Family

The only C-46 built at Higgins' Michaud facility.

Courtesy Higgins Family

Higgins was also involved in helicopter design.

Courtesy Higgins Family

The *Veracruz*, a Higgins FS ship, is launched in New Orleans. Higgins' FS ships were built on the only moving production line for cargo ships in the United States.

Courtesy Higgins Family

This photograph, taken a few weeks after the end of World War II, shows the last Higgins boat for the U.S. Armed Forces coming off the assembly line.

Courtesy Higgins Family

The *Angele Higgins* was to be the first ship in Higgins' proposed steamship service, which was to tie the Gulf Coast to Central and South America. The *Angele Higgins* was a specially designed shallow-draft boat that could enter harbors that were inaccessible to conventional commercial ships.

Courtesy Higgins Family

Mrs. Andrew J. Higgins

Courtesy Higgins Family

Andrew J. Higgins

Courtesy Higgins Family

11

THE BEGINNING OF THE END

Jurisdictional disputes between various trade unions had for some time been a nagging problem for the management of Higgins Industries. By the fall of 1944, the disagreements were so frequent that they were affecting production. In hopes of solving the problem, Higgins had Morris Gottesman, secretary and treasurer of the firm, write to William Green, president of the American Federation of Labor, to try to arrange a meeting with the union's national leadership.

In his November 17 letter, Gottesman reminded Green that Higgins was the first major company in New Orleans to sign agreements with the international unions affiliated with the AFL. He argued that Higgins had willingly broadened the contract to include the Gulf Zone Stabilization Agreement and had abided by its conditions though his competitors were paying lower wages and maintaining less favorable working conditions.

He admitted that when the original closed shop agreement was signed in September, 1940, Higgins had conceded that every employee would have to join the union representing his craft. At the time, however, only a few AFL craft unions and three hundred employees were involved. Presently, there were thirteen different AFL trade unions and over twenty thousand workers. The disputes between the various crafts were creating conditions that resulted in high production costs and the company's inability to participate successfully in the government's bidding process. Gottesman suggested that to be able to bid competitively, yet continue to offer the highest possible pay for employees, the company needed the union's help.

He requested that the contract, which was scheduled to expire on January 1, 1945, be abrogated and a new one written. This new agreement should be structured so that a committee of union representatives

255

would be authorized to represent workers in all crafts employed in the plants. The committee should handle all jurisdictional disputes among the crafts and be the only unit with which management would bargain.

Higgins hoped the letter would lead to face-to-face discussions resulting in a workable solution. The timing seemed ideal because the AFL was scheduled to open its national convention in New Orleans in a matter of days. Gottesman closed his letter by stating, "In the interest of Labor as well in the interests of this Company, we ask that serious consideration be given to this request at this time, when all of you gentlemen who have the interests of Labor at heart are assembled in our City."[1] According to Stuart Hellman, Higgins' director of industrial relations, the AFL received the letter with little enthusiasm. Its national leaders failed to find time to meet with Higgins and discuss his company's problems.[2]

As Higgins awaited Green's reply, a partially completed C-1-M-AV-1 military cargo ship arrived and sat docked at the Industrial Canal. The vessel had been brought down from the Great Lakes via the Chicago Sanitary and Ship Canal to the Des Plaines River, then to the Mississippi River and to New Orleans. It was brought to the southern ice-free port before it was stranded by winter conditions.

The ship had been completed, but to enable it to pass under low bridges the mast and riggings had been detached. The pilothouse was cut off and set down in the hold. The second level was removed and placed on the main deck. Once the ship was in New Orleans, the structures had to be reattached and the ship had to undergo sea trials. Another eighty to one hundred vessels were also preparing to move south, and similar work would have to be performed on them. Higgins Industries, because of its location and reputation, had been chosen by the Maritime Commission as one of the companies to receive a portion of the contract.

The commission, as the regulatory agency in charge of the project, designated the work as "new construction." Under that listing, Higgins was required to pay time and a half for all overtime as prescribed by the Gulf Zone Stabilization Agreement. The New Orleans Metal Trades unions viewed the work as repair and conversion and demanded double time.

On November 27, as a result of the Maritime Commission's ruling, Higgins received a telegram from the Metal Trades Council (MTC) in-

1. Morris Gottesman to William Green, November 17, 1944, in McGuire Collection.
2. Stuart Hellman to F. Edward Hebert, June 8, 1945, in Hebert Papers.

forming him that the MTC had instructed its members to discontinue all repair and reconversion work at the Higgins plants. A conference call between Higgins, the union, and the commission was held the following day, but the union refused to change its demand. Higgins tried to break the deadlock by offering to pay whatever rate was finally negotiated between the commission and the union, requesting only that work on the C-1-M-AV-1 vessel continue. The union rejected Higgins' offer, and on November 28 its local leadership designated the vessel a "hot ship," placing it off-limits to its members.[3]

Two days later, while work on the ship continued, a foreman called plant manager Ed Higgins and reported that Nick Tedesco, a company employee, was walking around the yard talking to various workers on the dock, the derricks, and the hot ship. Ed reported the suspicious behavior to his father.

Higgins immediately called his rigging superintendent, J. W. Atkins, to his office. Atkins told Higgins that Tedesco was presenting himself to the men as a union business manager with authority to act in behalf of the ship riggers and two or three different unions. Tedesco had instructed the men not to work on the ship. Those not following his instructions were threatened with the loss of their jobs and of their union membership.

Higgins requested that Tedesco report to the administration building immediately. Pinned on his jacket was one of the company badges issued to union managers allowing them access to the yards. Recognizing Tedesco as an employee on the night shift, Higgins asked about his employee badge. The worker responded that it was in his pocket; he switched badges when he switched jobs.

The conversation was interrupted by the arrival of five or six business managers representing other crafts. Simultaneously, a call came in from a Mr. Campbell, who claimed that he, not Tedesco, was the official representative of the riggers. Higgins gave Tedesco a choice—he could either work for the union or he could work for the company, but he could not work for one during the day and the other at night. He reasoned: "I did not think it was fair to deprive him of sleep, or time for rest. He asked me did I have any hard feeling toward him. I said, 'absolutely not'. If you are doing a good job for the unions, and they identify you as their legal

---

3. Stuart Hellman to Charles G. Ross, November 12, 1945, p. 3, in Truman Papers.

representative, so long as you are their representative, I will deal with
you as such." While Higgins and Tedesco talked, another "walking delegate," a member of the Boiler Makers local, was circulating throughout
the yard. This delegate, named Adler, was threatening to have the time
card of anyone working on the hot ship pulled from the rack, thus denying the worker his wages. He also declared that he would have the
offender discharged and run out of the union. Higgins demanded that the
delegate be brought to his office. Adler admitted that he had usurped
management's authority when he threatened to pull the time cards. In his
defense, he claimed that he was following orders. Higgins considered the
facts, allowed Adler to keep his badge, but warned him never again to
interfere with management.[4]

Higgins was caught in the middle. He desperately wanted to retain the
contract, especially because by the spring of 1945 the Industrial Canal
plant would complete the last of the 170-foot army FS ships. But neither
the local union leaders nor the Maritime Commission would reconsider
their positions on overtime pay. As a result of the dispute, the commission
canceled the contract, causing Higgins to lose the hot ship and as many
as thirty to fifty others heading toward New Orleans. It was a no-win
situation. Higgins lost potential profits, the Maritime Commission lost a
contractor that it desperately needed to complete the ships, and the workers lost two thousand jobs.

Higgins found the MTC's stance incomprehensible. A union that supposedly existed to protect labor was taking an action that directly hurt
its membership and the company. Angered over the loss of the contract,
on November 30 he informed the signatory unions of the 1940 AFL
agreement that as of January 1, 1945, their contract with Higgins Industries would be canceled. He based this decision on two beliefs: first, that
the union had breached the agreement when it pulled its workers off the
C-1-M-AV-1 vessel, and second, that the terms of the contract permitted
cancellation after a thirty-day notice. The union, contesting Higgins' action, contacted the War Labor Board's Shipbuilding Commission. A hearing was scheduled in Washington for December 30, 1944.[5]

As the AFL prepared its case against Higgins, Radio Reader's Digest

4. Andrew Higgins to Montgomery, Fenner & Brown Attorney-At-Law, December 15,
1944, in McGuire Collection.
5. Hellman to Ross, November 12, 1945, p. 4, in Truman Papers.

prepared a national broadcast about the industrialist over the CBS network. The program began: "We Americans walk big, we talk big, we think big. When we invent legends they are big legends; no story-book fairies for us. We think up giants." It spoke of such legends as Davy Crockett, who was craftier in the woods than any Indian; John Henry, the steel-driving man; and Paul Bunyan, who by dragging his ax behind him had created the Grand Canyon. Then the announcer stated: "American giants still walk the American earth. This is about one of them. This giant's name is Andrew Jackson Higgins." The program focused on the remarkable feat that Higgins and his company had accomplished in designing and building the first tank lighters. It ended with Higgins discussing his company's postwar plans. Higgins, never mentioning his labor problem, stated: "There should be no unemployment in our plants or throughout the land. Americans can keep right on going and doing, working and achieving victories in peace as in war, making useful things for peaceful times. For, unless we Americans lose our faith and courage, we with others will see to it that these vast plants will not be roosts for bats!"[6]

Work continued at the Higgins shipyards on LCVPs, LCMs, FS ships, LCSs, air-sea rescue craft, and PT boats. At Michaud the C-46 contract had been canceled, but Higgins Aircraft continued to produce wing panels. Higgins Plastics, also at Michaud, was producing airborne lifeboats, and its carbon division was machining parts reportedly for radar and radio communication equipment but actually for the atomic bomb.

The plastics company had also been awarded a vehicle repair contract and a munitions contract. Thousands of battle-worn jeeps and trucks were arriving from all over the world, being overhauled, repainted, and shipped back to the army for reassignment. The munitions contract awarded by the army Ordnance Department called for five production lines to be installed at Michaud to produce more than a million 105mm shells per month.[7]

By mid-December, 1944, the carbon division, under the supervision of George L. Baum, was in full production. The hand-picked crew was a strange assortment of workers. Instead of the highly trained technical

6. "Dramatization of the Story of Higgins," December 3, 1944 (Transcript for "Radio Reader's Digest," in McGuire Collection).

7. Dave McGuire to Lieutenant Hale Boggs, December 9, 1944, *ibid.*

personnel one might imagine, the division was staffed by a conglomeration of grandmothers and grandfathers, wives and mothers, men and boys. They had been told that their work was top secret, but they had no idea of the project's importance. The absence of heavy security measures made the work appear less significant than it actually was. Employees at the plant viewed the new division as simply another project for Michaud, unique but no stranger than building lifeboats to be dropped from B-17s or manufacturing wing panels in a plant originally designed to build Liberty ships.

During December the "Carbonites," so nicknamed because of the fine black dust that covered them, worked feverishly to maintain production deadlines. Normal work schedules included ten-hour days six days a week and often Sundays. The crew worked through Christmas Eve, dispersed for several hours, and then returned and worked a full shift on Christmas Day. Once an order was completed, the company notified the army, which sent a plane to transport the finely machined carbon pieces to a classified destination.[8]

Carbonites were not the only ones who worked on Christmas Day. Several employees of Higgins Engine Company were busy at their plant. By the fall of 1944, production had finally begun on the Higgins 200 marine engine. On Christmas Day the engine company was in the midst of a government-required thousand-hour continuous endurance test on one of its motors. Jack Higgins, Higgins' nephew, was in charge of the test, and it was his responsibility to see that it ran smoothly. As he sat at his parents' table eating Christmas dinner, he received a call from Joe Dugas, manager of the engine company. Dugas told Jack that everything was running smoothly until at approximately eight hundred hours into the test, when the engine ran out of gas. Jack recalled: "I could have thought of a lot of things I didn't want to hear and that was right at the top. Boy, I caught it. I was supposed to be in charge. I had a guy designated to check the outside tank, and he didn't do it so it was my fault." He immediately called Shell Oil Company, and within an hour the tanks were refilled and the engine restarted. The almost continuous endurance test proceeded from the point it had abruptly stopped.[9]

As the engine company and carbon division continued their produc-

8. "Orleanians, from Youths to Grandmothers, Help Build Atom Bombs," New Orleans *Times-Picayune/States,* August 12, 1945, Sec. 2, p. 4.
9. Jack Higgins, interview, August 12, 1992.

tion, in Europe German field marshal Gerd von Rundstedt, supreme Nazi commander in the west, poured every bit of German strength he could muster into a last-ditch counterattack in hopes of changing the war. As the Battle of the Bulge was being fought on the frozen ground of Europe, Higgins focused on the postwar world.

In a December 27 interoffice communication to all "Key Men and Heads of Departments," he reminded his staff that despite the grave situation in Europe, "We must prudently look forward to the shock of its termination, readjustments, and the economies that must be effected." He noted that during the latter part of 1944, the company had reduced the price on everything it manufactured for the government and had lowered its cost of production to virtually the minimum. He explained, however, that "we have not become consciously zealous of reducing our overhead." To emphasize his point, he referred to the traveling, entertainment, and out-of-town expenses charged by company executives. He was particularly concerned that on several occasions when he inquired as to the whereabouts of key personnel he was told that they were in Washington or New York on business, but no one seemed to know why. He instructed his staff that as of the date of the communique more than "one mind" must decide whether such an investment in time and travel was in order. No matter how high ranking the staff member, he was to consult with his associates, and certainly with his boss, if he had one, as to the necessity of such a trip. Higgins thought the new policy should "invoke no displeasure," for he claimed that before he traveled he debated with his subordinates about the advisability of the trip. He reasoned that "certainly everyone knows when I intend to leave, what I am going for, and when I expect to return, so I am only giving these instructions to do what I, myself, practice." [10]

Higgins was still waiting for the ruling of the Shipbuilding Commission of the National War Labor Board (WLB). The hearing, held on December 30, resulted in issuance of an interim order that directed Higgins Industries to maintain its 1940 contract with the AFL "status quo" until the commission had time to conduct a full study of the transcript of the hearing and render a decision. Higgins, still upset over the hot ship incident, begrudgingly agreed to abide by the directive. [11]

10. Andrew Higgins to All Key Men and Heads of Departments of All Higgins Plants, December 27, 1944, in McGuire Collection.
11. Stuart Hellman to William H. McPherson, May 2, 1945, in Hebert Papers.

The new year brought new hope of finding a solution to the labor problems and also a belated letter of appreciation from the president, who wrote Higgins on January 3: "The Businessmen for Roosevelt, Incorporated, did such a great job during the recent campaign that I have wanted to tell you personally how much I appreciated the efforts of each and every one of your group. Not having been able to arrange to see you at once, I do not want more time to pass without going on record with this expression of my gratitude for the significant part you and your associates had in getting the real issue before the people." Roosevelt concluded: "It is my hope that you and your coworkers of the committee will not abandon your efforts to develop among the business community a broader understanding of the principles of government and social progress for which we stood during the campaign. These principles must continue with renewed vigor if the victory which we will ultimately achieve in battle is to have meaning in the years ahead."[12]

The letter helped soothe Higgins' feeling that he was unappreciated, but like Roosevelt earlier, he now had more pressing problems. As production lines continued to mass produce LCMs, LCVPs, PT boats, and other small specialized craft, Higgins awaited the Shipbuilding Commission's final ruling. By February 1, the commission still had not decided whether Higgins could cancel his 1940 agreement with the AFL. Eager to find a solution, the New Orleans Metal Trades Council approached the company about signing an amendatory agreement to the original contract. Higgins, also wanting to settle the issue, agreed to negotiate. Both sides immediately wired the commission requesting that it withhold a decision pending completion of the current negotiations.

Meetings between the company and the MTC continued for approximately six weeks. By the end of that period, the union agreed with all of the articles in the company's newly proposed contract except for the last paragraph of Article VI. The section, entitled "Union Membership," stated that the new agreement would not apply to World War II veterans who had been in foreign service and had never previously belonged to any union. In such cases, the employer would request that they join the union but would not make compliance with this request a condition of employment.

The union adamantly rejected Article VI. Negotiations became dead-

---

12. Franklin Roosevelt to Andrew Higgins, January 3, 1945, in McGuire Collection.

locked. Stuart Hellman wrote the union leadership on March 12 that management was aware of the advantages the workers received when represented by unions in collective bargaining. But he insisted that the company was unwilling to make that decision for the returning overseas veterans. "The Government," he wrote, "under the G.I. Bill of Rights, permits the returning veteran to work anywhere without referral. Shall Labor or Management do less?" [13]

Also on March 12, the final FS vessel was undergoing its dock trial at the Industrial Canal plant. The company had built the ways on which to produce the ships and one hundred vessels in approximately 105 weeks. To Higgins, this proved that his earlier concept for mass producing Liberty ships at Michaud would have been successful. [14]

Two days later, as the last FS ship underwent its river trial, an article appeared in the March 14 issue of the San Francisco publication *Peoples World*. The story, titled "Ship Tycoon Higgins, the Ford of Dixie?" included an interview with the industrialist concerning his company's labor woes. The article noted that Higgins, once considered by labor as one of its few friends among the top industrialists, was now turning away both from the cooperative labor-management program of the unions and from President Roosevelt's full employment program.

According to the article, Higgins now favored legislation that would outlaw the closed shop. Additionally, he favored the compulsory incorporation of unions. The story quoted him as stating: "The unions should be subject to public authority like any other corporation. I've had so damn much trouble with so many craft unions and conflicting jurisdictions that if it weren't for the war, I'd shut up shop and go home." When the writer asked if he thought cooperation among labor, management, and government should continue into the postwar period, Higgins snapped: "Not if you have to depend upon unions for the labor cooperation. I've been a friend of labor but I'm beginning to realize that you can't cooperate with the unions although a working man would be a damned fool not to join a union. Labor can contribute to the maintenance of prosperity only by stopping all jurisdictional strife and by seeing that one

13. Stuart Hellman to "All Crafts Affiliated with the New Orleans Metal Trades Council of the American Federation of Labor," March 12, 1945, in Hebert Papers.

14. "War Department—Transportation Corps 170′ & 180′ Army Vessels—Higgins Industries Inc." (Production schedule in Strahan Personal Collection).

craft cooperates with another craft so that industry won't lose production time while craft disputes are being settled."[15]

With work continuing at the plant but negotiations deadlocked, Higgins asked the Shipbuilding Commission to hear the new dispute concerning the veterans clause. He reasoned that because his original case, pertaining to his 1940 agreement with the AFL, was certified to the Shipbuilding Commission, it was only logical for the commission also to hear the new case concerning the veterans clause. The commission agreed, but the union immediately objected, arguing that the veterans clause was a separate issue. The AFL charged that the case had to be handled by the Conciliation Service of the U.S. Department of Labor.

On March 27, the Shipbuilding Commission turned the case over to the Conciliation Service as the AFL demanded. Hellman immediately requested that the dispute over veterans be certified back to the Shipbuilding Commission. The service was in the process of complying with the request when the unions again objected, with the result that the Department of Labor took no action. Hellman next appealed directly to the secretary of labor.[16]

As Hellman patiently awaited a ruling on the canceling of the 1940 labor agreement and a reply from the secretary concerning the veterans clause, Higgins was trying to take care of a small detail in one of his company's departments. Even as the head of an industrial giant, he operated with a hands-on approach at all levels of his company.

Unlike Henry Ford, who at Willow Run had no interest in soliciting technical ideas from his workers, Higgins had a very different approach. Every afternoon, at the end of the first shift, his sons, foremen, department heads, superintendents, and any other interested person could drop by his office, have a drink, and discuss with him or others present their problems or ideas. As Ted Sprague recalled:"We'd just sit in there and talk. That way he really knew what was going on. He listened. He might raise hell after you got through telling him what you thought, but he listened. He had a big ego, but he didn't feel like he was so damn smart he couldn't learn something. If you knew something he didn't know, and you told him, then he was happy to know it. He didn't put anybody down unless they got way out of line."[17]

15. "Ship Tycoon Higgins, the Ford of Dixie?" *Peoples World*, March 19, 1945, n.p. (Typed copy in McGuire Collection).

16. Hellman to Ross, November 12, 1945, pp. 5–6, in Truman Papers.

17. Ted Sprague, interview, August 2, 1992.

One detail that Higgins was involved in was an attempt to get his advertising department to become imaginative and aggressive in its approach to publicity. In an interoffice memo dated March 31, he told his staff to get "the Navy people and let them send out some pictures; let the Navy play up the fact they supported the Army in crossing such an inland river as the Rhine, and by cultivating some of our new found friends, ex-Hollywood moving picture people, maybe they would release pictures glorifying the Navy, and accidentally mention that the boats were Higgins boats."[18]

In another memo he noted: "Our drawings in all our literature and our advertisements have an amateurish appearance. . . . It might have paid us a little bit more in dividends, presently and in the future, had we given some thought, or commissioned some competent painter, to reproduce some striking action scene that would not necessarily be an advertisement of our boats, but be a picture the reproduction of which people would like to frame and have in their home, and indirectly be a constant advertisement of our boats." He also suggested a more direct approach to advertising that could be accomplished immediately. Because most government restrictions concerning the physical plants had been removed, Higgins thought it would be a good idea to paint the company name on the side of the buildings so that it would be visible to persons traveling nearby on Southern Railway passenger trains. He also recommended painting the name on the roof, stating, "There are not a great many people who fly over our plants, but as time goes on, more will, so it wouldn't hurt to have Higgins on the roof."[19]

Higgins took a moment from his busy schedule to write to Vice-President Truman. His letter of March 31 concerned a telephone call he had received inquiring into the competency and accomplishments of Rear Admiral Edward L. Cochrane, chief of the Bureau of Ships. The inquiry was in response to the submission of Cochrane's name to the Senate for approval for advancement in rank from rear admiral to vice-admiral.

During the July, 1944, ceremony commemorating the delivery of Higgins' ten thousandth boat to the navy, Cochrane had praised the industrialist and called him a "pioneer" in the development of the landing craft. Higgins now had an opportunity to return the compliment. In

18. Andrew Higgins to Harry Lafond and others, March 31, 1945, in McGuire Collection.
19. Andrew Higgins to A. J. Higgins, Jr., and others, April 2, 1945, *ibid.*

his letter he told Truman, "Certainly, you know what a job Admiral Cochrane inherited, and somewhat, for the same reason, you will appreciate that I am in a good position to judge the accomplishments in the improvements of the Bureau of Ships, since the administration of Admiral Cochrane, and to this I can attest, in the highest terms, commendation." While lobbying for Cochrane's promotion, Higgins took the opportunity to praise two other naval officers whom he felt were worthy of higher ranks, Admiral Earl Mills and Captain N. Morgan Watt, Jr. Higgins thought that Mills, who was Cochrane's assistant, deserved some credit for the improvements in the bureau and, like Cochrane, should be promoted to vice-admiral. He suggested that Watt was doing an excellent job serving on temporary duty with the Maritime Commission. Several different sources had informed him that Watt handled matters expeditiously and had brought new blood to the commission. The captain, Higgins insisted, was "a man who would be outstanding anywhere— Navy, Maritime Commission, he would be a great industrialist; or in any place he would be put, he would serve outstandingly well." Higgins argued that "all of these men are deserving. They didn't have the opportunity of serving in the limelight, in glamorous action with the fleet, the serving of which, they again would be most competent; but the fleet couldn't have done what it has, had it not been largely for the actions of these three men." In closing, Higgins told Truman that he and Angele were leaving for Washington on April 9 in response to several invitations that he had received, one of which was for the Jeffersonian dinner to be held on the twelfth. "While there, I would like to have you and your family with us for dinner some evening. Otherwise, I want to discuss a number of matters with you, and particularly the substance of this letter."[20]

A meeting was scheduled for the evening of April 12 in Higgins' Washington hotel suite with several senators and the vice-president. The meeting occurred, but Roosevelt died earlier that day, and Truman was unable to attend. The new president, however, sent Colonel Harry Vaughan to express his regret that he could not keep the appointment.

Higgins later wrote to Vaughan: "You can hardly realize the tremendous impression it made on all that President Truman could think of, and remember the appointment, with all the tragedy and momentous things upon him; that he should think of such a small detail. All of the Senators

20. Andrew Higgins to Harry Truman, March 31, 1945, in Hebert Papers.

present exclaimed, 'Well, that's Harry Truman for you!'" He also informed the colonel that "after you left, we drank a toast to him and I proposed there and then that the Republican senators present should get *all* the Republican senators to forget petty partisanship and to give the new, typically grass root American man, so well qualified and providentially placed in the Presidency, their full cooperation. It was gratifying that the very next morning they took this up with senators" Arthur Vandenberg of Michigan and Harold Burton of Ohio. "I hope they will remember their vows for a long time." [21]

On April 26, shortly after Higgins returned to New Orleans, Stuart Hellman received a letter from the acting director of the U.S. Conciliation Service, Howard T. Colvin. Colvin stated that Executive Order 9017, which created the WLB, defined disputes that the Department of Labor was authorized to certify to the WLB as "labor disputes which might interrupt work which contributes to the effective prosecution of the war." In essence, Colvin told Hellman that to get a ruling on whether Higgins Industries could cancel its 1940 labor agreement with the AFL and whether it could hire veterans without requiring them to join a union, a work stoppage would have to be threatened or actually occur. Higgins was astounded by this response. Neither management nor the union wanted a work stoppage in the midst of war.

On May 7, as the company contemplated its next move, Associated Press correspondent Edward Kennedy broke the story to the world that Germany had surrendered. Kennedy's article was accurate, but because of its premature release he was ordered back to the United States. On May 8, President Truman informed America while King George announced to Britain that the Axis powers had fallen.[22]

As the nation celebrated victory in Europe, Higgins wrote to Colonel Vaughan. His object was to get the colonel to discuss with Truman a change in battlefield policy. Higgins wanted the president to consider chemical warfare. He argued that "most of us realize that the use of gas when we were fighting the Germans was debatable, merely as to the effect of counter measures by the Germans against our ally, the English—but no such argument can be set up in our fight against Japan." [23]

He advised Vaughan that a secret Gallup poll had been taken some-

21. Andrew Higgins to Colonel Harry Vaughan, May 8, 1945, in McGuire Collection.
22. Francis Trevelyan Miller, *History of World War II* (Philadelphia, 1945), 963.
23. Higgins to Vaughan, May 8, 1945, in McGuire Collection. Quotations in the following paragraphs are from this source.

time before concerning the use of gas against both the Germans and the Japanese. Though never explaining how he acquired the results of the poll or offering any documentation of its accuracy, he claimed that over 70 percent of those polled were in favor of the use of gas. He concluded, "I am sure that if the true wishes of all of the American people could be polled that 95 percent of them would be in favor of the use of gas, or anything else, to quickly end the war and to help the Japs in their professed desire to join their ancestors."

Higgins noted that many would say that the use of chemicals "would be ghastly—but War in any form is ghastly—and the more terrible we make it, the better effect it will have on any nation hereafter wanting to expose themselves to the horrors resulting from war." He found it difficult to distinguish between burning the "Japs' a——s off with flame throwers" or "smothering them with noxious or lethal gases, or burning their a—— off with Mustard Gas." He wrote, "I would sooner burn them to death as we have been doing, but more Americans get killed attacking them with flame throwers than would be the case if we dropped the more merciful form of destruction on them from high altitudes."

His final suggestion was that the Office of War Information and the other departments of government "disregard the 'screw ball' opinions of the short-haired women and the long haired men; the professors and the 'pansies' and the idealists and to let the OWI, and the Army and the Navy release all the horrible pictures that they have in their files showing Jap atrocities and showing even more of the atrocities committed by the Germans than they have shown so far."

Higgins claimed that releasing the photos would cause a "clamor throughout the country to save American lives by going to chemical warfare." He suggested that had "a little Phosgene" been used on Iwo Jima, the Japanese would have been defeated in twenty-five minutes and some "grand American boys" would still be alive. "Think of the tremendous cost that the continuation of the war is piling up, and think of the many American lives that could be saved. Let's blot the Japs out and to hell with all the 'fancy pants', the dilettantes with the cream puff ideals."

Higgins had one more request. He wanted the president to "pass down the line instructions that the goddam coddling of German prisoners be brought to an end. The Army says this is not so, but damn it, I know it is so. Recently, there was a bunch of German prisoners of war working on the levees during the high flood stage of the Mississippi River, and I know, first hand, how difficult it was to handle this arrogant bunch of bastards." He closed: "Others beside General Sherman said that 'War is Hell', and if Harry S. Truman makes Hell on Earth a little bit surer he will have the support of the American people and the Civilized World, even though he orders that war be not quite as 'civilized' as a lot of silly idealists would have it." No reply from either President Truman or Colonel Vaughan has been found to Higgins' remarkable letter.

As the Allies celebrated V-E Day and Higgins passed on his suggestions to Vaughan, McDerby was busy preparing for his part in the "Mighty Seventh War Loan Drive," starting June 3, in Denison, Texas, the birthplace of Dwight Eisenhower. The Treasury Department had decided to stage a mock invasion in hopes of attracting potential bond purchasers. The scene was to be repeated in several river towns from Denison to New Orleans. As an added incentive, all patriotic citizens who purchased bonds were taken for a ride aboard the LCPLs.

The "Mighty Seventh" was just the sort of scene that Higgins loved—thousands of spectators and plenty of headlines. An LCM and an LCPL would navigate the rugged 950 miles from New Orleans up the Mississippi, then up the Red River, whose shallow water and sandbars had prevented navigation by a boat the size of the 56-foot LCM for over forty years. Seven additional LCPLs were to be shipped on trucks overland to participate in the show. To make certain that the trip was possible, several weeks earlier Mac had made the run in a 36-foot LCPL, but he had hidden it downriver from Denison so it would remain undetected. A prearranged army escort picked him up and drove him to the military base in Sherman, Texas, where he rested and purchased supplies before heading back to New Orleans.

Captain McDerby, in his LCPL command boat the *Okinawa*, along with the 56-foot LCM, officially left New Orleans on May 14 for the June 3 event on Lake Texoma. Higgins was to join Mac in Denison and take part in the ceremonies, which also included actor Robert Young and Pfc. René A. Gagnon and PM 2/c James Bradley, two of the famous Iwo Jima flag raisers.

Once McDerby was on his way, Higgins turned his attention back to his company's labor dispute. On May 16, he wrote to the Shipbuilding Commission: "Having followed the few processes open to us in a sincere effort to settle the differences between the Unions and ourselves, and having been thwarted by the very agencies established to aid us, we feel that there is no course left but to respectfully request that the Shipbuilding Commission render its decision on the original dispute." Higgins at least wanted to get a ruling stating that he was within his legal rights in canceling his 1940 agreement with the Metal Trades Council.[24]

As he awaited the commission's reply and made preparations to leave for Lake Texoma, he took time to host a reception in honor of several visiting dignitaries. In attendance were some Hollywood filmmakers who happened to be in town. During the party, they suggested making a movie dramatizing the story of the Higgins airborne lifeboat. Higgins thought it was an excellent idea.

In relating the story to his key employees in a May 29 interoffice memo, Higgins stated: "I forget who the damn fool was,—one of the guests—put up the argument to the moving picture people that it would be indelicate for them to mention this as the Higgins Airborne Lifeboat." Higgins told his staff that "modesty is a very becoming trait, but a lot of people are so goddam modest they don't eat well! . . . I have heard that members of our own organization have lately become fancy pants and consider it indelicate and immodest to take advantage of our accomplishments, and refused advertising, or to feature too boldly, and of course accurately, what we have done. I don't want anybody in our Advertising or Sales Department to acquire any such ideas, for we have no place for shrinking violets in our organization." Having made his point, he again focused on the idea of the movie. "The Army Air Forces are hungry for publicity to show that, in addition to devising efficient war machines, they have also been concerned about rescue. The public will eat up stuff pertaining to rescue . . . I want replies from the people this is addressed to, as to what they are going to do to get these big producers to put over a super duper, mammoth, colossal picture with the airborne lifeboat the chief motive."[25]

The Hollywood production would demonstrate the durability of the wartime model and keep the company name before the public. It was a promotion that Higgins hoped would create postwar sales. Ted Sprague and Frank O. Higgins had already begun redesigning the airborne lifeboat into a pleasure sailboat featuring a streamlined molded cabin.

24. Hellman to Ross, November 12, 1945, p. 6, in Truman Papers.
25. Andrew Higgins to Dave McGuire and others, May 29, 1945, in McGuire Collection.

On May 30, the day after Higgins sent his memo and just before he left for Texas, the Shipbuilding Commission issued its "Directive Order" concerning the cancellation of the company's 1940 agreement with the AFL. The commission ruled that the contract between the parties was terminated as of January 1, 1945, pursuant to written notice given by Higgins Industries on December 1, 1944. The commission also informed both parties, however, that although management had the right to cancel the contract, the terms of the agreement were to be extended for thirty days. During this time the union could appeal to the proper government agencies "for a determination of representation status."

After studying the directive, the local union leaders approached the company on June 2, requesting answers to two questions. First, would Higgins Industries sign the proposed amendatory agreement that excluded the veterans clause? Second, would the company recognize the New Orleans Metal Trades Council as the workers' bargaining agent? Higgins resoundingly replied "No" to both questions.[26]

Hellman explained that the company's intent was to follow the commission's directive and give the union thirty days to prove that it represented a majority of the workers. Because of the company's answer, at ten o'clock Saturday morning, June 2, the union called for a strike effective the following Monday.

On Sunday, June 3, McDerby and his boats invaded the shores of Lake Texoma. A crowd of 35,000 watched the action from the surrounding hills as the command boat laid a smoke screen to protect the seven LCPLs as they hit the beaches with 175 men. Accompanying the personnel carrier in the assault was the big LCM, which came full throttle through the smoke and landed a light army tank high and dry on the sand.

Overhead twelve planes protected the skies, including a B-17 that dropped a Higgins airborne lifeboat to rescue men supposedly stranded at sea. On shore demolition charges went off. Troops using flame throwers burned German pillboxes, while other soldiers armed with machine guns fired blanks at the enemy. Bazooka-carrying GIs launched grenades as they attempted to complete their mission: rescuing prisoners of war held in a camp atop a four-hundred-foot bluff. When the objective was overrun, Gagnon and Bradley helped raise the flag to the roaring approval of the crowd.[27]

26. Hellman to Ross, November 12, 1945, p. 7, in Truman Papers.
27. W. M. Furey, "About 35,000 Americans View Denison's 'Colossal' Bond Show," Paris, Texas, News, n.d., n.p. (Clipping in scrapbook, McDerby Collection).

After completion of the first mock invasion, McDerby prepared on June 4 to head downriver for his next destination. Higgins meanwhile headed back to New Orleans. He was greeted with the reality that the local union leaders of the Metal Trades Council, not content with the commission's directive and upset over not being recognized as the workers' official bargaining agent, had called its members out on strike. The same day, the WLB sent a telegram to the local union leaders informing them that the strike was a violation of labor's no-strike pledge and the national policy of no strikes for the duration of the war.

The national media focused on the labor dispute because of the plant's war-related production and Higgins' controversial veterans clause. Business columnist Fred Perkins for the Scripps-Howard newspapers reported that the "Administration and Congress must decide which comes first in the post-war job hunt—service in armed forces or membership in a labor union." He noted that "Mr. Higgins, colorful and aggressive, has been regarded for years as a friend of labor." The Hearst newspapers carried an article claiming that "to expedite production . . . the company began employing returning veterans 'without forcing them to join any union.' A union leader arrogantly described this as 'magnanimously giving them the right to work without becoming members of the unions.' . . . This muddled problem of justice had better be solved quickly. It is not going to do Congress or bureaucrats or labor bosses any good to have several million service men coming home from overseas and bitterly asking themselves: WHAT HAVE WE BEEN FIGHTING FOR?"[28]

Once the work stoppage was under way the Conciliation Service certified the case to the Shipbuilding Commission, a move that Higgins had requested in mid-April. On June 5, John P. Frey, international president of the AFL Metal Trades Union, urged the five thousand striking workers to return to their jobs. The local union leadership ignored Frey's plea. The following day the local leaders also voted to defy the WLB's directive.

On June 8, the WLB issued its second back-to-work order. If the workers refused, the board could turn the matter over to Truman. The president could call for the army and navy to take over the three striking

28. "Here's What They Say About Higgins," a monthly summary of National Press-Radio Coverage of Higgins News, prepared by Public Relations Department for Information of Company Executives, 4–5, in Dawn Higgins Murphy Collection.

plants, City Park, Industrial Canal, and Bayou St. John. Once under government control, they would remain so either until a new agreement was
reached or the war ended.

By June 11, approximately eleven hundred workers loyal to Higgins
had crossed the picket lines. The WLB appealed to the remaining thirty-
nine hundred striking AFL members, promising that if they reported to
work there was a good chance that the Shipbuilding Commission's May
30 directive would be overturned. The following day, June 12, the union
membership voted to call off the strike. As the strikers returned to their
jobs, New Orleans police had to be called in to help the company guards.
Fights broke out in the shipyards between those who returned early and
those who had stayed out. Threats and intimidation were rampant.[29] The
labor force was divided, and Higgins desperately needed a common de-
nominator to pull them together. He saw the "Mighty Seventh" war-loan
drive as the perfect healing device.

McDerby had been working his way downriver from Denison to Arthur City, Texas, then to Fulton, Arkansas, next to Shreveport, Louisiana,
followed by Alexandria, Baton Rouge, and culminating with the final
show scheduled for June 17 in New Orleans. The extravaganza was an
opportunity for workers at Higgins to unite and proudly show the public
the contribution they had made toward winning the war.

Before the hometown crowd of thirty thousand, twenty landing craft
debarked 136 Pacific war veterans dry-footed on Pontchartrain Beach.
PT boats laid down a smoke screen for the amphibious forces, and, as in
Denison, a B-17 dropped an airborne lifeboat to survivors at sea. In this
case, in the small boat on the lake was a sailor, accompanied by Jean
Sprague and her four-month-old daughter, Susan. Ted had insisted that
his wife accompany the sailor so she would have a better view of the
show. He failed to mention that their small skiff was the target for the
B-17's drop. As Jean watched the bomber, she suddenly saw the lifeboat
released and falling toward her. She stood up, ready to grab Susan and
jump. The sailor, panicking because he thought she would overturn the
boat, screamed for her to sit down. The lifeboat hit the water fifteen to
twenty feet from the skiff.

Higgins and McDerby were not as lucky as Jean. As they stood watching the show, several of the planted explosive charges on the beach were

29. Hellman to Ross, November 12, 1945, pp. 8–11, in Truman Papers.

detonated. One charge, filled with sulfur, had accidentally been mixed in with the dummy explosives and planted by the military. When it detonated, hot sulfur was thrown in the direction of Higgins and McDerby, catching Higgins' suit on fire. Mac quickly beat out the flames before his boss was injured. Mac, however, was left with permanent scars on his shoulder and arm, and two hundred other people were slightly injured. In spite of the accident, the show was a tremendous success, and bonds worth over $310,000 were sold to the enthusiastic crowd.[30]

Even though his labor problems continued, Higgins remained optimistic about the future. He opened an office in New York as a step in his conversion from wartime to peacetime manufacturing. The new office was established to sell the company's soon-to-be-produced pleasure craft to the northeastern market. The models included everything from 12-foot rowboats to 90-foot houseboats. At the top of the line were several high-powered racing boats and luxury yachts.[31]

As Higgins' New York office was beginning its operation, the WLB in Washington held its hearing concerning the Shipbuilding Commission's earlier ruling. The board released its decision on July 6. Concurring with the commission's findings, the WLB ruled that Higgins Industries had the legal right to cancel its contract with the AFL as of January 1, 1945. It then informed Higgins that he had to continue abiding by the contract even though his company had the right to cancel it. The WLB urged both parties to "proceed promptly with negotiations looking toward the consummation of a new agreement." Higgins considered the latter part of the ruling an absurd, "senseless decision."[32]

As a result of the WLB's pronouncement, on July 12, C. E. Alexander, Jr., chairman of the Joint Metal Trades and Building Trades Council, wrote to Hellman hoping to arrange a meeting so negotiations could begin on a new agreement. That same day Higgins wrote to Louisiana congressman F. Edward Hebert stating, "The War Labor Board, like a mountain,—heaved, struggled, shook, and, the other day came out a mouse—a dirty, sick mouse at that." Higgins argued that the men in his

30. Richard A. McDerby, interview, August 30, 1992; Ted and Jean Sprague, interviews, August 2, 1992; "30,000 at Tokyo Beachhead Buy $310,667 in War Bonds" (Clipping in scrapbook, McDerby Collection).

31. "Higgins Opens Office Here," New York *Times,* April 26, 1945, p. 27; "Higgins Optimistic on Post-War Tasks," New York *Times,* July 25, 1945, p. 24.

32. Hellman to Ross, November 12, 1945, p. 11, in Truman Papers.

plants were being denied the right to give evidence as to who they wanted to be their bargaining agent. He complained that he was forced to continue cooperating with people who had been creating disruption and adding to his company's production costs. These same people, according to Higgins, had defied the War Labor Board and called an unauthorized strike in protest of the board's decision.[33]

Higgins agreed to abide by the ruling and reopen negotiations with the AFL, but only if his workers chose the union in a plantwide election. Herbert Thatcher, the AFL's attorney, expressed a "definite exception" to Higgins' raising the issue of representation because no other union had ever attempted to represent Higgins' employees. Higgins' attorney responded that the AFL had never been voted in by a majority of the company's present workers. He pointed out that when the original 1940 contract was consummated, the company consisted of only the small St. Charles Avenue plant and fewer than three hundred workers. The company now had seven locations and over twenty thousand employees. In the end, both parties agreed to abide by the WLB's ruling and reopen negotiations on July 18.[34]

On the eighteenth, before the scheduled meeting with the AFL, Higgins received a letter from W. T. Crist, Gulf regional director of the Industrial Union of Marine and Shipbuilding Workers of America, CIO. Crist claimed that his union represented "a substantial number" of Higgins employees, and he requested that the company not enter negotiations with the AFL until the question of representation was decided by the National Labor Relations Board (NLRB).[35]

Higgins now had three separate labor problems. First was the cancellation of the 1940 agreement between the company and the New Orleans Metal Trades Council of the AFL. Second was the issue of whether returning veterans had to join a union as a prerequisite to being hired. Now the CIO was claiming to represent his workers.

Higgins continued his negotiations with the AFL because the CIO claimed only a "substantial number," not a majority, of the workers. Given the choice, Higgins would have preferred the CIO. The AFL was a

33. *Ibid.;* Andrew Higgins to Honorable Edward Abear (Hebert), July 12, 1945, in Hebert Papers.

34. "Higgins for Contract If AFL Wins Election," New York *Times,* June 26, 1945, p. 34.

35. Hellman to Ross, November 12, 1945, p. 13, in Truman Papers.

horizontal union, consisting of several different crafts. Each craft had its own local and its own individual leadership. Members of a specific craft union could work only in their specified trade. The CIO, in contrast, was a vertical union with one set of leaders at the top. Also, a CIO member in a shipyard was listed as a shipbuilder and could be asked by management to perform any job in the yard that he was physically capable of doing. There were no craft boundaries separating the various tasks, a factor that was very appealing to Higgins.

At the July 18 meeting Hellman and the AFL agreed to exchange proposals for a new contract on July 20. As this was being accomplished, Higgins had an opportunity to state his case directly to the nation. He was invited to participate in "America's Town Meeting," sponsored by the *Reader's Digest* in cooperation with the American Broadcasting Company. The topic for the coast-to-coast broadcast was "Should War Veterans Have Job Preferences?" Besides Higgins, other guests included Major General Lewis B. Hershey, director of the Selective Service, John Green, president of the Industrial Union of Marine and Shipbuilding Workers of America, and Dennis Wiegand, executive secretary of the American Veterans Committee.

During the broadcast, Higgins suggested that the temporary transition from wartime to peacetime production might create a "few headaches but that in brief time we will all be so busy supplying worldwide consumer demands and needs and services that our question will remain academic." He agreed that the question of jobs for veterans as written in the Selective Service Law was vague and was subject to various interpretations. But he could not understand how "any group should wish to do less than their 'overall' best for the sons and brothers and sweethearts of us all. We owe them our ever lasting love and love knows no limit of gratitude and sacrifice. As for myself, I am one of the many who will within my full powers do everything to give jobs to our heroes." [36]

Hershey expressed the opinion that the granting of preference was "an effort to restore equality of job opportunity to those who have lost it because of their service in the armed forces. Paradoxical as it may seem," he stated, "preference for veterans is given to make equality for veterans possible." The opposing view was taken by Green and Wiegand. Green

---

36. Andrew Jackson Higgins, July 26, 1945, "Should War Veterans Have Job Preferences?" (Speech in McGuire Collection).

argued that through collective bargaining agreements labor had gone far-
ther than Congress in guaranteeing seniority to those who served in the
military. He was not in favor of the "super-seniority" being proposed for
veterans, which would disregard the seniority of present agreements, de-
stroy collective bargaining, and "provide a field day for anti-labor employers." Both Green and Wiegand took the stance that full employment
guaranteeing jobs for all workers, including returning veterans, was the
only logical approach. Wiegand declared that the proponents of job preference for veterans were actually offering "the jobs of other people" and
"our father's job."[37]

Higgins followed up on his speech by sending a memorandum to his
key executives dated July 30. He stated, "For various reasons, or maybe
I have a hunch, I believe the war will be over by the middle of September." He informed his staff that despite statements to the contrary, he
believed that the army and navy and other government procurement officers would cancel all contracts when Japan surrendered.[38]

To prepare for that moment, Higgins wanted all who received his
memo to formulate their ideas and then have a discussion to help determine future company procedures and policies. He also posed the question, "If the Government blows the whistle, should we blow the whistle?"
He responded: "My answer to this is 'No', and I doubt if I could be
argued out of this decision. If the Government blows a whistle and everybody blows a whistle, the country will go into a tailspin."

Higgins wanted to keep as many people as possible working. He did,
nonetheless, instruct his staff to "sift out the chaff from the wheat." He
reminded them that they would all have to be Solomons and remember
the law of "'survival of the fittest,' with a remembrance, appreciation and
consideration of the weak."

He hoped his company would set an example that others would follow. He was optimistic that despite his problems with the unions, the
leadership of the AFL would find some way of harmonizing its craft
unions to make them workable in the shipbuilding industry. He felt they
would have to do so if they were to survive. But he was not certain how
union demands could be satisfied and at the same time provide jobs for

37. "Hershey Upholds Jobs for Soldiers," New York Times, July 27, 1945, p. 16.
38. "Statement of Mr. Andrew Jackson Higgins," Dealers' and Salesmen's Bulletin,
December 1, 1945, p. 47. Quotations in the following six paragraphs are from this source.

veterans, especially when many veterans were prejudiced against the unions and refused to join them.

He warned his staff that everyone, including himself, had to be very careful as individuals and as management not to overdo "sympathy—if sympathy can be overdone—when thinking of veterans, or talking, or planning for veterans." He did not believe that the veterans should be pampered, nor should they be encouraged to set themselves up as a select group. The country already had too many special-interest groups. But, he did believe that veterans who had seen combat, and especially those who had been permanently disabled, "by God, should have a preference and they are worthy of pampering, at least for a period after the war ends—an equal length of time as to what they served."

He pointed out that there was a danger in trying to provide jobs for veterans because the company might be accused of catering to the veterans, which he did not think it should do. "It would tend to set up a class or a group antagonistic to another class. In other words, we don't want to be any party to pitting veterans against unions." If the unions "had any sense they would take the play away from us and all other industry, and go all out to give returning veterans, combat or otherwise, but particularly wounded or damaged veterans, preference over their own people."

Higgins summarized his feelings: "What I am trying to express is that I think that unusual attention should be given to the problem of the returning veteran to provide him with a job, even if it is a burden on industry. Let him get set; provide work for him until he determines where he is best adapted to be placed, or find work for his future, and do this without using him or setting him apart as a preferred person, or using him as a club against any other group, unions or otherwise. Hell, the poor boys are entitled to this. But, in our thinking and planning, let's not encourage setting up a group of veterans against a group of unions, or a group of farmers, or a group of anything else."

As Higgins' staff considered their boss's often contradictory memo, negotiations were continuing between the company and the AFL in hopes of reaching a new agreement. The parties were trying to find common ground concerning the six remaining points of difference when, on August 1, Higgins received a letter from the CIO. The CIO now insisted that it represented a majority of the company's employees and that if

Higgins continued his negotiations with the AFL, he would be in violation of the Wagner Act and interfering with his employees' right of self-determination.[39]

The same day that Higgins received the letter from the CIO, he also received an interoffice memo informing him of the final details concerning his scheduled August 10 trip to the Pacific theater. The navy had invited Higgins; W. E. Blewett, Jr., production manager for Newport News Shipbuilding and Dry Dock; McDonald, head of Hazelton Electronics; and Fred Lack, vice-president of Western Electric Company, to be its guests on a sixteen-day trip with stops at Pearl Harbor, Kwajalein, Guam, Saipan, Iwo Jima, and, tentatively, Okinawa and Ulithi.[40]

On August 4, as Higgins prepared for his trip, Hellman wrote to the AFL. He explained that Higgins Industries wished to terminate the present negotiations until the NLRB, through an election, determined which union, if any, was the proper bargaining agent for its employees. The same day he also wrote to the WLB explaining that negotiations with the AFL had been broken off so as not to be in violation of the regulations and procedures established by the NLRB. He requested an immediate response from the WLB as to its members' thoughts on his proposed course of action.[41]

Two days later, the atomic bomb was dropped on the city of Hiroshima. The result was massive devastation in which most of the city's buildings were leveled by the blast or destroyed by fire. Eighty to two hundred thousand persons were killed, depending on whether American or Japanese figures are cited.

Higgins, on business in Chicago when the bomb was dropped, told the press on the night of August 6 that the work his employees had performed on the bomb was "vile, dirty and dangerous." He described those involved as "heroes and heroines." Admitting that the work was top secret he stated, "Even my sons and I didn't know exactly what it was all about. Our right hand couldn't know what our left hand was doing."[42]

Even after the incredible destruction at Hiroshima, the Japanese mili-

---

39. Hellman to Ross, November 12, 1945, p. 14, in Truman Papers.

40. Dave McGuire to Andrew Higgins, August 1, 1945, in McGuire Collection.

41. Hellman to Ross, November 12, 1945, p. 14, in Truman Papers.

42. "Atomic Bomb Parts Made at Higgins' Micheaud Plant," New Orleans *Times-Picayune*, August 7, 1945, p. 7.

tary remained unyielding. Three days later, on August 9, Russia declared war on Japan. The same day, the U.S. Air Force dropped a second atomic bomb, this time over Nagasaki.

On August 12, as the Japanese discussed surrendering, Higgins was at Pearl Harbor beginning his tour of the Pacific theater. In New Orleans, the *Times-Picayune New Orleans States* Sunday edition carried a story officially crediting the Higgins carbon division as being a part of the Manhattan Project.[43]

At the Higgins plants most of the talk centered on the end of the war and the Manhattan Project. Hellman's thoughts meanwhile were focused on the response he had received from the WLB. The board desired that the parties resume their collective bargaining negotiations. To help facilitate the negotiations, the WLB was sending Judge William Knous as its special representative to assist in reducing the points in the dispute and to report to the board any issues that remained unresolved.

On August 14, as Knous prepared to go to New Orleans, Hellman received a telegram informing him that the CIO had filed a petition with the NLRB for representation of employees at Higgins Industries. The CIO requested that all negotiations between Higgins Industries and any other union be suspended until the NLRB settled the question of representation.[44]

As Hellman dealt with the labor problems and Higgins visited the boys in the Pacific, Morris Gottesman and Andrew Higgins, Jr., issued an announcement that the government had canceled twelve of the company's contracts valued at $20 million. Included in the cancellation were orders for LCVPs, PT boats, LCMs, steel barges, torpedo tubes, solar stills, and a variety of spare parts. Higgins Plastics, however, was to continue production of the airborne lifeboat and carbon parts for the Manhattan Project.

Gottesman and Andrew, Jr., also explained that the company's postwar production would be divided into four principal divisions. The first division was to consist of pleasure craft, which were to be mass produced using the same techniques developed for manufacturing landing craft and PT boats. The second division was to encompass commercial vessels

43. "Orleanians, from Youths to Grandmothers, Help Build Atom Bombs," New Orleans *Times-Picayune/States*, August 12, 1945, Sec. 2, p. 4.
44. Hellman to Ross, November 12, 1945, p. 16, in Truman Papers.

ranging from barges and tugs to shallow-draft freighters similar to FS
ships. It would also include a variety of other marine equipment used by
the oil industry. The third division was to be made up of building materials, including the new Higgins concrete product known as Cement-O-
Cell, and the fourth was to include all miscellaneous plastic products,
water distillation units, and marine hardware.

The Higgins helicopter, once touted as a major part of the company's
postwar plans, was not among the items listed. The aircraft had crashed
during one of its test flights, resulting in the cancellation of the project.
In 1924, a test pilot had been killed in one of the planes Higgins had
built. He was not prepared to chance another pilot losing his life.

Gottesman and Andrew, Jr., admitted in their statement that the loss
of the government contracts would result in the laying off of approximately 3,500 workers. The company had employed as many as 15,000
workers in the City Park and Industrial Canal plants during its peak in
1944. The two plants combined now employed slightly over 5,000 workers. As contracts were completed and production slowed, the work force
had been reduced. Andrew, Jr., predicted that most of the layoffs would
be temporary. He suggested that when the government's restrictions were
lifted on such items as steel, postwar production would begin and those
laid off would be recalled.[45]

Higgins Engine Company had also been reducing its payroll. The
company originally had been created to serve as an emergency supplier
of marine engines in case northern plants were sabotaged. By early 1945,
just as the plant was starting production, the government decided that
Detroit was not threatened and could manufacture all of the motors required. Higgins' contract was continuously reduced until it called for
only one hundred engines to be produced. Once this order was completed, the plant directed its attention to machining carbon parts to supplement Michaud's production. Immediately after the surrender of Japan,
the Defense Plant Corporation removed all of the machinery that it had
furnished, thus ending the company's operation.

As the engine company was going out of existence, Gottesman announced that as of August 24, Higgins Industries had over $24 million

45. "Plants Speed into Postwar Work; $25,000,000 in Orders Announced," *Higgins Worker,* August 24, 1945, pp. 1–3; "Background of Dispute," *Dealers' and Salesmen's Bulletin,* December 1, 1945, p. 5.

in postwar orders. A large portion of this was a contract to build 212 62-foot steel boats for the Netherlands East Indies government. The remainder of the orders were for a variety of commercial and pleasure craft.[46]

To Higgins, the future looked bright. He viewed South America as a vast area where his craft could be used to establish water routes and open up the Amazon. He also had plans for establishing the "Higgins Transportation System," which was intended to serve the more developed areas of the world. He predicted that it would revolutionize water and highway shipping. One of the economic principles involved in the transportation system was to minimize equipment expense by separating the semitrailer body from the chassis and power unit. This, according to Higgins, would reduce equipment costs and turnaround time for both the trucking and shipping lines, thus increasing profits. Today his premise is referred to as containerized freight.[47]

Higgins predicted that before long the company's employment would rise to near wartime levels. Before a smooth transition to postwar production was possible, however, the labor dispute had to be settled. The conflict was growing more volatile every day. The NLRB was insisting that an election be held to determine the employees' proper bargaining agent. The WLB was demanding that Higgins disregard the NLRB's directives and negotiate a new contract with the AFL. To complicate matters, both unions claimed to represent a majority of the workers.

Higgins was caught in the middle of a power struggle between two government agencies and two unions, a position he felt left him with but one option. It was so drastic that once instituted, the AFL demanded a congressional investigation, declaring that if Washington failed to act, the union would paralyze the city of New Orleans. The New York *Times*, like many other newspapers, considered Higgins' action so extreme that on November 3 it gave it front-page coverage.

46. Graham Haddock, interview, January 8, 1993.
47. *Higgins Container System of Transportation* (New Orleans, 1945), 18–19.

12

THE TRANSITION BEGINS

The war between the Allied and Axis powers was over, but the battle involving Higgins Industries, the War Labor Board, the National Labor Relations Board, and the unions was escalating. In November, 1944, Higgins had requested that the national AFL leadership meet with him and take steps to eliminate the jurisdictional disputes among the local AFL craft unions. The union's national leadership failed to seize the opportunity, and an industrialist who had often been praised by the union in poems and in the press was now an enemy of the AFL.

The New Orleans Metal Trades Council had angered Higgins considerably when it refused the time-and-a half overtime scale offered by the Maritime Commission for work on the C-1-M-AV-1 vessel. Higgins had requested that work continue on the ship while he and the union jointly tried to convince the commission that the job was repair work requiring double-time wages, not new construction, which paid the lesser scale. Higgins even agreed to pay the difference retroactively should the commission reverse its earlier ruling. Instead of joining with Higgins, the local union leadership designated the vessel a hot ship, off-limits to its members. As a consequence, the Maritime Commission canceled its contract with Higgins Industries, causing the company to lose as many as fifty other ships requiring the same work.

Higgins retaliated by canceling his 1940 closed shop agreement with the AFL. He then requested that the War Labor Board allow him to hire veterans without requiring them to join a union. The New Orleans Metal Trade Council then demanded that its 1940 closed shop agreement be renewed. When Higgins refused, the union called its members out on strike. To complicate matters, the CIO then claimed to represent a majority of Higgins' workers and demanded that an election be held to determine the employees' true bargaining agent.

To confuse the issue further, the AFL was seeking help from the War Labor Board to solve the controversy, and the CIO was requesting that the National Labor Relations Board settle the dispute. It was a complex entanglement involving two unions, two government regulatory agencies, the rights of returning veterans, and a hot-tempered industrialist who believed that the local AFL leadership was costing local workers their jobs and destroying everything that he had built.

To help solve the complicated situation, the WLB assigned Judge William Knous to mediate the dispute. Knous arrived in New Orleans and on August 16, 1945, held his first meeting with the company and the unions. During the discussions, Higgins' labor representative, Stuart Hellman, asked Knous for assurances that the company would not be found guilty of unfair labor practices should it continue to negotiate with the AFL despite the CIO's petition.

John LeBus, regional director of the NLRB, later informed Hellman that if Higgins continued to negotiate with the AFL he did so at his "own peril." Two days later, on August 18, Lloyd Garrison, vice-chairman of the WLB, countered with a telegram saying that the WLB's "Directive Order" remained "in full force and effect." He requested that Higgins and the AFL immediately meet with Judge Knous and make an earnest effort to arrive at a contract or at least to narrow the issues. Higgins was caught in the middle of a power struggle between a wartime regulatory board and a peacetime regulatory agency. It was a no-win situation.[1]

The following day, August 19, the affair became even more confused. The NLRB notified the company that the CIO had formally filed a petition for certification of representation at the Higgins plants. Disregarding this new information, on August 21, the WLB in a show of force, notified the company that it must still meet with Knous. Higgins complied, and the meeting took place as scheduled. At the conclusion of the discussions, the company and the local AFL leaders remained in disagreement over five issues. The WLB ordered Higgins Industries and the AFL to meet in Washington on October 20 to attempt to resolve their differences and consummate a new contract. The company, as ordered by the WLB, continued to recognize the AFL despite the CIO's petition.

In mid-August, while Hellman handled the labor situation, Higgins toured the Pacific as a guest of the navy. When he returned home at the

1. Hellman to Ross, November 12, 1945, pp. 16–17, in Truman Papers.

end of the month, he was faced with the continuing labor problems. In the midst of the frustrating times he did find a few bright spots. Shortly after he arrived home, he received a letter from six survivors of a downed B-29. The airmen were on Guam when Higgins visited the island, and they had wanted to thank him personally for the "ingenious" airborne lifeboat that his company had designed and built. Unfortunately, they were unable to make contact before his departure.[2]

The letter explained that on May 29, while participating in a raid on the urban district of Yokohama, their bomber was hit by heavy enemy flak. Engines three and four were knocked out, and both bomb bay doors were ripped open. The two remaining engines and the high altitude at which the plane was traveling allowed it to escape.

As the aircraft headed away from its target, the radioman made contact with a B-17. Unbeknownst to him, it was carrying a Higgins airborne lifeboat. When the damaged B-29 headed out to sea, it started losing altitude. One hundred and fifty miles from Yokohama the plane transmitted its last coordinates and the pilot prepared for an emergency landing. Weakened by the missing bomb bay doors and the damage from the flak, the aircraft broke into three pieces as it put down on the water. During the few minutes that the plane remained afloat, the crew managed to salvage a five-man and a one-man life raft.

The small raft deflated almost immediately. The crew knew that with only one raft they could not all survive. Suddenly overhead a B-17 appeared. It circled, then dropped a large black object suspended by three parachutes. The airmen had heard about the Higgins airborne lifeboat, but as one survivor said, "It seemed incomprehensible that it should be there right when we needed it."

When the object landed on the water, the men swam toward it. Aboard, they found dry clothes, blankets, rain gear, jackets, and safety lines. They had barely settled in when a heavy squall started pounding the boat. That night at approximately 9:00 P.M., the rough seas overturned the 27-foot craft. The men were thrown out, but each had been holding one of the boat's safety lines. They pulled themselves back and crawled aboard. The writer noted: "Although we were thrown out many more times that night no one had any fear of losing that boat. As long as

2. "First B-29 Crew Rescued by Airborne Boat Tells Story," *Higgins Worker*, September 21, 1945, pp. 1–2. The following six paragraphs are from this source.

we had a hold on our rope we knew that there was a boat that couldn't be sunk on the other end."

At 6:30 the following evening, after the crew had endured eighteen hours of stormy conditions, a submarine surfaced and rescued them. Its commander, not wanting the Higgins boat to fall into enemy hands, ordered his men to sink her. They fired round after round into the boat, but she wouldn't go under. It was not until they shot the gas tanks and caused the boat to burn that it was rendered useless.

The survivors wrote: "All of us have agreed many times that without that Higgins boat none of us would be alive today. . . . For those of us who went back to Japan again it was relieving to know that if ever shot down again your boat would make survival at sea a less fearful ordeal." Higgins proudly had the letter printed in the *Higgins Worker* and filed the original with letters from other crews that had been saved by his boats.

Higgins was also extremely proud of the service record of his youngest son, Roland. Roland, as a lieutenant in the U.S. Engineers Amphibian Corps, had been in charge of a "jungle shipyard" in the South Pacific, where tank lighters built and cut up at the Industrial Canal were reassembled. He had served well but had spent the last several months of the war recuperating in a hospital from a tropical disease. On August 27, 1945, he was released from the service and returned to New Orleans to work with his father.[3]

As Roland was returning to the company, Captain McDerby was leaving. After the Japanese surrender, the Higgins Boat Operators School was disbanded. Mac had trained more than thirty thousand men in the operation of landing craft, and his instruction undoubtedly had saved thousands of lives. Recognizing the importance of his work, the Army Air Rescue Service had once tried to lure him away from Higgins by offering him the rank of captain. Higgins had talked him out of it, arguing that as a civilian and a commercially licensed captain he could order majors and colonels around during the course, but as a military captain his effectiveness would be limited.

This time, Higgins could not persuade him to stay. Mac still liked

3. "Roland Higgins," *Dealers' and Salesmen's Bulletin,* December 1, 1945, p. 30; Military Record and Report of Separation Certificate of Service for Roland C. Higgins, in Skip Higgins Collection.

working for Higgins, but he liked Catherine Conaster far more. Catherine worked for the U.S. Corps of Engineers in Denison, Texas, and McDerby had met her in April when he was in town making arrangements for the "Mighty Seventh" war loan drive. The mayor of Denison, Bill Marisco, thought his guest should spend at least one evening seeing the town and arranged a blind date for Mac. The date was Catherine.

Four months later, Mac moved to Denison. He opened a marine supply store, and in October he and Catherine were married. Higgins hated to lose a man who had been such an integral part of the company for eleven years, but he understood.[4]

In September, as the company worked toward solving its union problems, it also moved forward with its postwar plans. On September 17, Higgins announced that J. Gordon Lippincott and Company of New York had won first place in the Higgins Industries national design competition. The contest was sponsored to gain outside participation in the styling of the company's postwar products. The most sensational of the winning designs was Lippincott's PT junior cruiser. It was an adaptation of the famed Higgins PT boat, which was to be marketed in over a dozen models of various sizes.

Another of Lippincott's designs put the finishing touches on Higgins' proposed amphibious pop-up camp trailer that was soon to go into production. It was a revolutionary trailer that could be towed behind a car, but when the desired location was reached, its inflatable pontoons would be filled with air, the collapsible bow put in place, the tent-top sides attached, and in a matter of minutes the trailer was ready to roll into the water. The unit was equipped with an outboard motor, table, chairs, and air mattresses to sleep four. It was advertised as a "lodge in the mountains, a cabin by the lake, a seaside cottage and now it's a cabin cruiser and houseboat deluxe." The brochure claimed: "Endless are its uses and delights; fish from it, live on it, cruise and explore in it, live on the water as long as you like. Doubles the enjoyment of owning a car; Triples the fun of owning a trailer."[5]

Higgins also had a version of his amphibious trailer for commercial use. It was designed so several could be hooked together to form a float-

---

4. Richard A. McDerby, interviews, August 30, 1992, and January 27, 1993.
5. Higgins Sales Brochure, in Strahan Personal Collection.

ing bridge for crossing rivers in undeveloped territories. Others were devised for a variety of military purposes.

In discussing the prize-winning selection from Lippincott and Company, Higgins declared: "From now on we are catering to the American woman. She is the purchasing agent whose business we are going after. The way to sell boats to the American public is to provide style and interiors appealing to American Women." He insisted, of course, that the hulls must be strong and seaworthy. But the interiors had to be as "comfortable and as pleasant as her home." To keep the prices within the range of the average American Higgins was designing his boats for assembly-line production. According to Higgins, that meant big sales, and big sales meant more jobs for veterans. "That's why we are going after this in a big way." Lippincott, discussing his company's selection, explained: "Mr. Higgins has no end of designing genius and engineering skill on his own staff. But he saw the wisdom of calling upon the knowledge of industrial designers who understand what the American consumer wants, and how to achieve it by mass production methods that will result in an appealing price."[6]

Higgins took time to write to several military personnel with whom he had developed close friendships during the war. One such letter, dated September 28, was sent to General Holland Smith. Higgins wrote: "Well the job is done! As I turn with some perplexities to the peace time job, I want to pause to acknowledge the admiration and the reverence I, in common with all Americans, hold for our wonderful Marine Corps, which is so well personified in you, Sir. It was an inspiration for me to have met you before the war started and to have followed your illustrious career and the victories you secured; for me personally and my organization, we too tried to emulate you and the Marines on the home front." Higgins mentioned that while in the Pacific he had been a guest of Admiral Nimitz and the admiral had accepted an invitation to visit New Orleans. Higgins suggested that New Orleans would be proud to honor Nimitz and the navy should the admiral's schedule allow him to come. Then he proposed: "Without a knowledge of your duties and your plans, I am inquiring as to the possibility of you and a selected group of your fellow officers, selecting a date sufficient in advance when arrangements could be made for the people of the South, and Louisiana and New Or-

6. Russell Birdwell to Newspaper Editors, September 17, 1945, in McGuire Collection.

leans, could pay you suitable honors, and through you to the Marine Corps."[7]

On the same September afternoon Higgins also answered a letter he had received from Commodore Vernon F. Grant, USN. Grant had wanted Higgins to invest in a postwar business he was starting. For some reason, it set Higgins off on a long tirade in which he summed up all his frustrations. He wrote: "First, I want to thank you for the compliment in thinking that I have some dough. To make you feel a little bit better that the guys who stayed at home did not wax fat and rich, I will break down and tell you a few things. Every goddam one of my developments, patented or not, I turned over to the Government. I sat by and saw them emasculate, bitch up, malform, frig up and frig down a lot of my designs, so that they could make the claim and try to get the credit for the development themselves. Now, this does not apply to any one particular branch of Government. They all did it."[8]

He stressed: "I gave the Government the right to have any one else reproduce my designs, with the agreement that they could only do this as long as the capacities of my own plants were engaged to their full production; further provided that our plants could produce our own design competitively to what someone else could produce it. There has been many a time when our plants were out of orders and many other people throughout the country, particularly in the East and North, with more orders than they could fill for equipment of my design, not built at our high standards, and at prices as much as 50% more than what we could produce them for."

He told Grant that the government had the Defense Plant Corporation provide funds so other manufacturers throughout the country could build plants to produce his company's designs. "Whereas," he declared, "we provided all our own plants without the Government putting a damn cent in it, with the single exception of the big aircraft plant at Michaud, which was built with OPM, that is, other peoples' money,—the taxpayers' money—the DPC. However, it was bigger than Willow Run, which cost $200,000,000, and it took thirty months to build. Ours cost $26,000,000 and was built in five and a half months."

7. Andrew Higgins to General Holland Smith, September 28, 1945, *ibid.*
8. Andrew Higgins to Commodore Vernon F. Grant, USN, September 29, 1945, *ibid.*. Quotations in the following paragraphs are from this source.

Higgins claimed that he never charged a fee for his involvement in Michaud even though he had "devoted a lot of time, heartaches and disappointments" and had gotten "rednecked" over all the frustrations. He insisted that he had invested over a quarter of a million dollars in the plant for which the government refused to reimburse him and that he had produced products in the facility that no one else could build.

He declared that when others were getting a fee of 7 percent, he refused to accept over 3 percent. Now, he informed Grant, "The war is ended. We have some gigantic plants built at our own risk and expense, and have a tremendous lot of concrete and steel buildings, and fine tools, and no working capital." He insisted that he made only 1 3/8 percent on his products, even though everything he built was at least 25 percent cheaper than items made by any other builder, including those building his equipment in government-furnished plants.

Assessing his present condition, Higgins wrote:

> Now, I have a pot to piss in, and a lot of windows to throw it out of, but my job is to get into some financial legerdemain to get operating capital, so that I can give employment, by God, preferably to veterans, and they wont have to join a goddam union to get a job, if I am able to employ them, but, more important, able to pay them!
>
> I could keep on, but I am not going to disgust such a grand fellow as you, for about the worst thing I could visualize would be to know that you are going to break down and cry.
>
> Seriously speaking, I don't need any sympathy, for some way or another we will keep our nose above water. We can't do everything we would like to do. We will have to cut our operations to what we can work with, that is, trim our sails to the wind.
>
> It would help a lot if there be some relief to where a concern could keep a portion of their profits to use as working capital, thus to permit them to expand. We are living in hope of not dying in despair.

Higgins closed by saying that Grant's idea was a good one, but "it takes a rich son-of-a-bitch to foster" such a project. Instead, he recommended that Grant consider using the new Higgins building product, Cement-O-Cell concrete blocks, to construct motels and fishing camps. These could be built near where he lived in Pensacola and rented out to tourists or to fishing parties. For the fishing camps he also suggested that Grant purchase several "wonderful Higgins boats."

Another note written by Higgins on September 28 was an interoffice memo to Dave McGuire. He had sent McGuire a copy of a sheet of paper that he had signed on the night of August 16, while on Guam. He had okayed the message on the page in two different places, initialed it twice, and signed it three different ways. On the paper Higgins had scrawled, "I invite the following honorable persons to be my guests at the Mardi Gras Festival 1947 in celebration of the end of the war between the Japanese and the U.S. Marines."[9]

Higgins had been reminded of his offer in a letter from Colonel Victor H. Krulak, the same marine who, as a lieutenant in 1937, had witnessed the Japanese using ramped landing craft in the invasion of the Yangtze River. Krulak had visited Higgins occasionally in New Orleans and was well liked and highly thought of by the shipbuilder. He wanted to remind his friend of invitations that might have been extended under less than sober circumstances.

Higgins' memo to McGuire stated: "From this [his scribbled invitation] you will see I am committed to the entertaining as my guests a bunch of Major Generals, Brigadier Generals and what have you—eight of them,—and everyone of them swears and bedams they are coming here for Mardi Gras 1947. I recommend that you have this blown up and send on around to everybody that should remember this and anticipate this and be prepared."[10]

Following the cessation of hostilities, the St. Charles Avenue plant had been closed. The retail sales division had been sold to Higgins' brother Frank P. Higgins. Frank and his two sons, Ed and Jack, formed a new company, Higgins Marine Sales Corporation, and moved to the newly renovated west side of the City Park plant. In payment for the retail branch and its inventory, Frank relinquished to Higgins Industries all of his stock in that company. Sharing the City Park plant and operating out of the east side was the newly formed appliance division of Higgins Industries.

Though the City Park plant was no longer involved in boat production, both Michaud and the Industrial Canal were. Michaud was actively building airborne lifeboats and parts for the atomic bomb and preparing

9. Andrew Higgins, August 16, 1945 (Note, handwritten, while in Guam, in Skip Higgins Collection).
10. Andrew Higgins to Dave McGuire, September 28, 1945, in McGuire Collection.

to mass produce pleasure craft. The Industrial Canal plant was concentrating on commercial craft such as workboats, barges, fishing vessels, the 212 ships ordered by the Netherlands East Indies, and large luxury yachts.

Also at the end of the war, the Higgins Boat Operators and Marine Engine Maintenance School under George Rappleyea and Captain Richard McDerby had closed. Rappleyea remained with the company as assistant to the president; McDerby headed to Denison, Texas, in hopes of marrying Catherine. Huet continued as head of the Engineering Department; Ted Sprague was placed in charge of designing and production of the company's postwar pleasure craft; and Haddock served as the project engineer and designer for the Netherlands East Indies boats.

Gottesman continued as secretary-treasurer, and Higgins' four sons remained heavily involved in the company. Frank retained his position as vice-president in charge of Higgins Plastics and the lumber operations at Michaud. Andrew, Jr., carried on in his role as vice-president and general manager, helping his father with the daily administrative duties. Ed continued as superintendent of the Industrial Canal plant, and Roland was appointed to head the new building materials and Cement-O-Cell division.

With the war over and the government contracts gone, the company was hoping to capitalize on the famous Higgins name and its worldwide reputation for quality and dependability. It had built 20,094 boats for the armed forces, worked on the atomic bomb, manufactured wing panels for C-46s, designed and produced the airborne lifeboat, built 100 FS ships for the army in record time, and designed the standardized U.S. LCP, LCPL, LCVP, and LCM and one of the two major types of PT boats that the navy used. Higgins had trained more than thirty thousand men in the handling of landing craft, designed a new marine engine, pioneered the sectionalizing of landing craft to be shipped overseas for reassembly, repaired trucks and jeeps to be redeployed in combat, designed the rocket-carrying landing craft support boats, conceived a portable saltwater desalinization still, built marine radios, campaigned heavily for Franklin Roosevelt, and was one of the first, if not the first, person to come out publicly for Truman as vice-president. Higgins was extremely proud of what his company had accomplished during the war, but the war was over and he was ready to focus his attention on the postwar markets. But before he could be competitive, he still had to solve his labor problems.

13

"GIVE ME LIBERTY"

In 1935 leaders of the American Federation of Labor created the Committee for Industrial Organization. The purpose of the new committee was to organize union membership recruiting drives in the mass-production industries. To enlarge its membership, the CIO tried to attract unskilled as well as skilled workers. The AFL leaders, upset over this infringement, suspended the CIO in 1936. By 1938 the CIO's leaders had formed their own labor federation, the Congress of Industrial Organizations, in direct competition with the AFL.

This competition had been somewhat reduced because of the outbreak of World War II. Management and labor had agreed to a wartime program of no lockouts or strikes and a peaceful settlement of any conflict that might arise. To assist in the process, in 1942 the government organized the National War Labor Board. Its primary purpose was to resolve disputes that could not be solved through normal methods.

The no-strike agreement was not always adhered to. By late 1944, work stoppages by labor were becoming more frequent as demands for increased wages rose and workers sought assurances that returning veterans would not take their jobs. By the end of the war, much of the overtime that workers were accustomed to had disappeared. Take-home pay was being reduced, but prices were remaining stable or even increasing slightly. Workers across the nation wanted wage increases, and they turned to the union leaders to secure them. The AFL and CIO were now battling each other over which one represented the disgruntled workers.

By late 1945 there were widespread work stoppages, and large segments of the population were beginning to believe that the powers of the unions were infringing upon the rights of individuals. It was an explosive situation encompassing the entire nation and drawing the attention of radio, newspapers, and Congress. It was a controversy that most corporate leaders wanted to avoid. Higgins, who was never afraid to voice his opinion, was about to thrust himself into the center of the conflict.

As Higgins tried to transform his company into a peacetime producer, much of his attention had to be focused on his union-related problems, which were becoming increasingly complex. On October 17, three days before the company's scheduled meeting in Washington with the War Labor Board and the AFL, Higgins received a notice from the National Labor Relations Board. It informed him that a hearing would be held on November 1, 1945, concerning the CIO's petition to determine representation status in his plants.[1]

Higgins informed the WLB during the October 20 meeting that the CIO now claimed to represent a majority of his three thousand workers. He announced that under these circumstances he no longer considered his company bound by the WLB's directive, which had extended his contract with the AFL. After making his point, he stood up and, to the astonishment of those in the room, he walked out, declaring that his employees' bargaining agent was undetermined. When Higgins refused to return to the meeting, his attorneys again stated his position and then they too withdrew.[2]

According to Hellman, the company believed that it would be an unfair labor practice for an employer to favor one labor union over another. Earlier the WLB had upheld the company's right to cancel the contract with the AFL as of January 1, 1945. Higgins felt that under the circumstances, if he continued to bargain solely with the AFL, he would be violating the Wagner Act. He further believed that the WLB, as a temporary wartime agency, no longer had the authority or the jurisdiction to order the company to take an action contrary to the National Labor Relations Act.

Higgins declared that his company would not negotiate with either the AFL or the CIO until an election was held to determine which union truly represented his employees. Carrying this decision a step further, on October 22, 1945, he issued orders that union representatives of the New Orleans Metal Trades Council would no longer be allowed on the plant's

---

1. Hellman to Ross, November 12, 1945, p. 18, in Truman Papers.
2. "Higgins Defies WLB as AFL, CIO Disagree," New York *Times*, October 21, 1945, p. 36.

grounds. Other AFL affiliates, such as the New Orleans Building and Construction Trades Council, which were not involved in the dispute, were allowed admittance to the yards.[3]

On October 26, John LeBus, regional director of the NLRB, held an informal meeting with the company, the AFL, and the CIO. At the meeting the AFL refused to consent to an election. Three days later, on October 29, the MTC, angry because Higgins had decided not to renew its AFL contract, called a strike just as it had done almost five months earlier, on June 2. Picket lines were set up at the Industrial Canal, Bayou St. John, and City Park plants. The St. Charles Avenue plant was not targeted because it had shut down operations when the retail operations moved to the City Park facility. Michaud was not affected because it was part of Higgins Plastics, not Higgins Industries.

As the striking workers picketed the City Park plant, Jack Higgins tried to convince them that the retail company was no longer part of Higgins Industries. The strikers countered: "It's just a different body in the same pair of pants." While the pickets walked in front of the three plants, approximately two thousand employees failed to report to work. They claimed that they had been "locked out by the company's declaration of an open shop."[4]

Higgins told reporters that he had received no notice of the strike. He declared: "The time has come for the newspapers and the public to make statements on what they think of labor's conduct." He added, "I think I'll go fishing," a reference to a threat used by the workers when they had walked out in June.[5]

Two days after the strike began, on October 31, the WLB passed a resolution directing the Shipbuilding Commission to report to the board on the issues in the dispute between Higgins and the AFL. Copies of the report were sent to both parties for their comments. Following their responses, the board proposed to hold a public hearing and then issue a directive settling the dispute as it saw "appropriate." The board also declared, "Be It Resolved Further: That the company's objection to the jurisdiction of the National War Labor Board is without merit."[6]

As a result of the WLB's resolution, on November 1, Higgins released

3. Hellman to Ross, November 12, 1945, p. 19, in Truman Papers.
4. Jack Higgins, interview, August 12, 1992.
5. "2,000 at Higgins Quit Jobs," New York *Times,* October 30, 1945, p. 12.
6. Hellman to Ross, November 12, 1945, p. 20, in Truman Papers.

a statement to his employees and the press titled "Give Me Liberty." He also had his message published as an advertisement in the New York *Times,* Washington *Post,* Los Angeles *Times,* Detroit *Free Press,* Chicago *Tribune,* San Francisco *Examiner,* St. Louis *Post-Dispatch,* Kansas City *Star-Times,* Dallas *News,* Houston *Chronicle,* and several other major publications throughout the nation. Senator John Overton of Louisiana considered the statement of such national importance that he had the essay incorporated in the *Congressional Record.* The message and the reactions that followed drew national attention and resulted in Higgins receiving thousands of letters of support. Expressing his candid thoughts, he explained to the world his personal view of the labor-management problem that was affecting not only his plants but the entire nation. Because of the statement's significance, it is reprinted here in its entirety.

Give Me Liberty!

This present and last strike called by the self-styled "elected" bargaining agents of the multitudinous crafts accepted for affiliation with the American Federation of Labor, has degenerated into violence, intimidation and sabotage. No matter what name has been applied to it— "Lockout," "Shutdown," "Stoppage," or "Fishing Expedition"—this is the last strike at Higgins Industries, Inc.

The dream I had of educating these people to co-operate and produce an example, a yardstick that would prove that Management and Labor could get along together, degenerated into a nightmare.

On every occasion when speaking to labor groups I counselled moderation, clear thinking and wise leadership to make the peace obtained at such high costs worthwhile. I preached the same theories on many occasions before employer groups.

I have fought the good battle for labor. I will continue to stand for the rights of labor. I believe in organized labor and collective bargaining, but I do not believe in and will not support any isolated pressure group that is abusing organized labor and its membership.

I consider the Wagner Act oppressive in its operation, and in the long run it will do labor and American industry a disservice. Under that law, or its interpretation, an employer is powerless to effectively plead his own case. He is denied his constitutional right of free speech. He can be accused of any outrageous thing, or deed, or intent, by any labor representative, and if he dares to defend himself to the public, or to his own employees, he is in danger of being found guilty of unfair labor practice!

The men who have been with this company have on many occasions been ordered to cease work, arbitrarily, by some steward or by some business agent, completely ignoring the bargaining contracts and agreements, or the orderly process of settling disputes provided therein.

We had resigned ourselves to work out difficulties and possibly overcome them by conciliation and the process of law, however inadequate and unjust; but within the last several days, the stream of reports and visible evidences of assault on those men coming to work, threats and intimidations to their families, threats against their lives, plus acts of sabotage, has caused this Management to come to an extreme decision that we hope will be so sacrificial and so soundly taken, that it will shock the lawmakers and those who have been abusing power; we have decided for these reasons and for the protection of the lives of our employees to call this terrible condition to the attention of the country by shutting down our manufacturing operations despite golden opportunities.

We have approximately $40,000,000 of orders on hand. If we were free of this threat, if we could be clear in our planning, we could take on more work to provide more jobs. It is a certainty that we could have provided more jobs, at equal or higher pay, than we did in our spectacular accomplishments during the war. Such an operation required cooperation of LABOR AND MANAGEMENT alike, but Labor was found unable to meet this responsibility.

These alleged labor leaders have shown a callous disregard of the interests of their members and of the industries they were serving. They never recognized the fact that by helping improve the position of the Company, or any other company they had dealings with, they would be assisting in creating works, better works, in providing better jobs at better pay.

Men that collect, handle and are custodians of immense amounts of money derived from dues and fees should be worthy of a bond!! Does the rank and file know what disposition is being made of the immense amounts so collected?

These self-styled or self-elected bargaining agents have been misleading their membership. This strike was unquestionably called for their own self-perpetuation, and the workers are their scapegoats.

These business agents of the local crafts who have gained the support of the Presidents of their International Unions have influenced these responsible and serious men against this Company. In face of the fact that I, the President of this Company, overlooking all of the difficulties I was suffering from a local condition, gave support to organized labor, subscribing as I have always done to the rights and dignity of labor, and hoping that I could add sound, workable ideas to the principles of democracy.

Contrary to these pigmy men damaging organized labor, I am still the friend of labor and of organized labor, but from now on I will support organized labor only provided labor itself does the sensible thing—to demand and elect that they be made responsible under the law, as is any other organization, and as I wrote President Truman in my letter of October 15th past: "All officers and agents of the unions should be accountable for all initiation fees, dues, fines and collections, and such officers or agents should be commercially bonded."

Organized labor unions must be made responsible under law for their agreements and their contractual obligations, the same as any other commercial organization.

We have just finished an awful war. If the poor devils that got by without being killed cannot take a job without paying a tribute for it, then it is a futile victory.

Now, this Company is a prosperous and a going concern with vast operations possible for it at the time of this decision. Its operation would have called for the employment of a great number of men vital for the prosperity of the community, this State, and this section of the Country. But, under the conditions imposed on us the ambition to take chances to take on work to create jobs has been lost to us.

To the Stockholders and Management of this Company, the chief incentive was to create good works, to provide jobs, and make a contribution to the welfare of this Country. To do so we must meet payrolls, we have been in a competitive position; we realize we cannot do so when dealing with pigmy-minded vicious men.

So, spectacularly, we are going to act as the guinea pig, and call it "quits" rather than work under these impossible conditions. These grave decisions were arrived at when we had evidence that the power, unconstitutional or not, of various Government agencies were combining and being directed in association with these local groups, fallaciously supported by their International Presidents to coerce us into impossible working contracts.

Last year the War Labor Board said we had a justifiable, full and proper right to cancel the contract with the A. F. L. crafts; ridiculously at the same time another branch of that Board said that we must continue an association with those same people under the same conditions of the contract they said we had the right to cancel.

We submitted to indignities and arbitrary contradictions because we were manufacturing vital things needed for the winning of the war. When the war ended, we believe we very properly questioned the constitutional right of this wartime board to continue its domination over us.

Here recently, we have been put in an absolutely untenable position where another group of organized labor has contended they represent a majority of our workers and have been granted hearings by an organization set up under the Wagner Labor Act. But in the face of this the War Labor Board notified me yesterday that I was in contempt or in default, and would be shortly required to go to Washington again to debate clauses of a contract that the same War Labor Board said were properly cancelled—this edict coming at a time when loyal workers are being assaulted or threatened with assault or worse; the placards carried by hired goons in front of my plant, brazenly denouncing and vilifying me, damning the Company, threatening that they were going to ruin the Company, and vocally broadcasting a boycott of the Company!

After due deliberation, we came to the decision that we would free ourselves of this oppression. We cut the tentacles of the octopus, and like the Massachusetts Colonials that threw the tea overboard from the ships, by this act we will evidence our protest against bondage. The men at our plants, like the Colonies, had no representation. They were denied the right of voting who would be their collective bargaining agents.

Five years ago a few people forced a union contract on me. The local power hounds, aided and abetted by Government departments, have held our workers in bondage and forced them to pay, not taxes, but tribute—and to whom?

Now, I don't intend to emulate Patrick Henry, or go as far as he did. He said, "Give me Liberty or Give me Death." We say for ourselves and our workers, "Give us Liberty and Life," and the right of any man to take any job that if offered and he is qualified to take without tribute to anyone.

—ANDREW JACKSON HIGGINS, President[7]

7. "Give Me Liberty!" *Dealers' and Salesmen's Bulletin*, December 1, 1945, p. 1.

Higgins read a shorter version of the same message over the Industrial Canal plant's public address system. He informed the five hundred employees who had defied the union and crossed the picket lines that he had decided to terminate the company's manufacturing activities. He praised them for their loyalty and courage, then sadly requested that they seek employment elsewhere. In closing, he offered to render whatever assistance the workers felt would be helpful and promised to see that each of them received four weeks' severance pay.[8] His feeling for those who had stood by him was not that of an employer toward an employee. It was more paternalistic. Many had started working for the company in the early days at the old St. Charles Avenue plant and had an unwavering loyalty to "the boss." Higgins, in turn, felt as if they were members of his family and treated them as such.

Those who had joined the company in more recent years and who had chosen the union's side received no sympathy from Higgins. He saw them as naïve and being misled by the local union leaders. And he blamed them for his having to close his plants. With anger in his voice, he summed up his feelings when he told his loyal crew: "It takes a pretty dirty bird to shit in his own nest."[9]

The following day, November 2, 1945, a statement on the front page of the *Higgins Worker* claimed that there was no dispute between Higgins Industries, Inc., and any labor organization. The only dispute, according to the *Worker*, was between the unions themselves.[10]

Front-page coverage the same day in the local paper, the *Times Picayune*, read "Closed to Stay, Asserts Higgins." The article explained that on Thursday, November 1, after four days of work stoppage, Higgins announced that his plants were "closed for keeps." All production on the pop-up camp trailers, pleasure boats, and new building materials was to be halted. All contract work was to be sublet, and his three plants were to be sold. Higgins Plastics, still producing airborne lifeboats and parts for the atomic bomb, as a separate company, was not affected by the strike or the closings.

Jack Rawls, vice-president of the New Orleans Metal Trades Council,

8. Andrew Higgins to "The Production Workers of Higgins Industries, Inc. Who Have Been Loyal and Refused to Accept Intimidation," November 1, 1945, pp. 1–3, in McGuire Collection.
9. Richard A. McDerby, interview, August 30, 1992.
10. "A Statement," *Higgins Worker*, November 2, 1945, p. 1.

speaking to the press, claimed that the stories of violence and intimidation were baseless. He insisted that his union did not employ goon squads nor did it try to intimidate those reporting to work. He claimed that the plants' closings were a "red herring across the trail" and that Higgins was not truly shutting down. Rawls said he based his claims on the fact that Higgins that very day was advertising for new workers.[11]

In a November 3 article published in the New York *Times*, Higgins said that he was farming out his contractual work to some East and West Coast plants. "Then," he stated, "I'm going to crusade. I'm going to crusade to see that men who want to work can get it without paying tribute to anyone." When asked about the AFL, Higgins said: "The only way I'll sit down with them is for them to show me they have enough money to buy the plants. They think they are such great business people, I'll sell them these plants. Of course, they couldn't use the name Higgins. Otherwise, I don't want anything to do with these local labor men, so called leaders and business managers." Higgins further declared that he was presently gathering affidavits from the nonstriking workers who had been threatened by the pickets. Referring to those who had supposedly intimidated his loyal employees, he said, "I'll prosecute them until hell freezes over." Despite the fact that Higgins had closed his plants and announced his intention to sell his buildings, the NLRB resumed its hearing. The agency was still trying to decide whether to grant the CIO's request for an election to determine its representation status. When Higgins heard of the meeting, he stated, "They're all meeting about something that doesn't exist—their jobs."[12]

The AFL, angry over Higgins' action, demanded that Congress investigate the closing of the three plants. William L. Donnels, AFL publicity chairman, threatened that should Congress fail to act, then 75,000 to 100,000 AFL members in the New Orleans area would be told to stay away from their jobs for twenty-four hours. Donnels declared that the union's previous requests for a congressional investigation had been ignored, but "this time we want, and mean to get action. We fought him [Higgins] all through the war. Now he is trying to make a goat out of us and we refuse to be made the goat." On November 4, Higgins notified

11. "Closed to Stay, Asserts Higgins," New Orleans *Times-Picayune*, November 2, 1945, p. 1; "Higgins Proposes to Close 3 Plants," New York *Times*, November 2, 1945, p. 8.
12. "Higgins, Defiant, Will Sell Plants," New York *Times*, November 3, 1945, p. 1.

over four hundred boat dealers throughout the nation that he had been forced to close but that they would receive their Higgins pleasure boats, "regardless of where they may be built." The same day, the WLB informed the company that its request that war veterans be exempt from having to join a union despite a closed shop agreement was denied. Also denied was the company's request that no employee at the time of the signing of an agreement be denied union membership for past activities while "in the employ of the Employer." The rejection of this item meant that those employees who had returned to work when ordered to do so by the WLB could now be disciplined by the union for following the board's order. Higgins was furious. He had promised the workers who had returned that they would be protected in any future agreement, and he fully intended to keep his word. In addition, the WLB refused to take any action to stop jurisdictional disputes between the various craft unions—the root of the problem between Higgins and the AFL. Gottesman, pointing out to the press that the plants were now closed, labeled the WLB's decisions as "moot." [13]

The following day the New York *Times* published a story saying that two leaders of AFL craft unions were requesting a congressional investigation into both management and labor practices in New Orleans. The leaders felt that a joint committee of House and Senate members should conduct the investigation. But they should include as part of their commission representatives from the National Association of Manufacturers, veterans organizations, and religious groups. The two leaders believed that the probe should examine cases of wartime sabotage, slowdowns, the financial standing of the local unions and their officers, salaries of officers, police and criminal records of all labor leaders, and the spiritual and moral being of all union members, or "anything Mr. Higgins may want investigated." In addition, the leaders requested that the committee investigate the financial structure of Higgins Industries from 1940 to the present and all of its expenditures. They further recommended that it review Higgins' personal income taxes and also explore the accusation that he maintained a department to write to servicemen all over the world inviting them to seek employment at his plants. Upon hearing about their proposal, Higgins commented that it "would be fine. I'm for it." [14]

13. "Higgins Shutdown Put Up to Congress," New York *Times,* November 4, 1945, p. 14.

14. "Itemize, Inquiry Asked on Higgins," New York *Times,* November 5, 1945, p. 32.

Editorials and feature stories were published in papers across the nation concerning the labor problems at Higgins' plants. They focused on the struggle between the AFL and the CIO, the contradictory orders from the NLRB and WLB, and Higgins' drastic decision to close his plants. An editorialist writing in the Grand Rapids *Herald* stated: "Higgins showed the way which many another big employer of labor must eventually adopt. If they are pestered with Governmental regulations and with jurisdictional strikes in which the employer is not interested or in any way a party, there is but one method apparently of making the Congress and the Government generally and the Labor Unions awaken. That one method is close down the plants and tell the employees to get jobs where they can, if they can."[15]

The editor of the New York *Daily Mirror* wrote: "We don't know at this distance who is most to blame, Andrew Jackson Higgins, the plants' owner, or the unioneers he says bedeviled him into his drastic action. . . . Higgins may be a hothead on the one hand. On the other, he seems to have had enough provocation to try a saint's patience."[16]

Arthur Krock, in a story titled "Higgins' Closing a Worry," in the November 7 issue of the New York *Times,* stated that if Higgins' example should prove contagious, the "economic and social problems of the Administration will be more burdensome than ever before." Reconversion to peacetime production would receive a devastating setback, and the domestic situation in the nation would be greatly affected. Such an action, he suggested, might ultimately lead to a general struggle with the public and law on one side and organized labor on the other. A confrontation of this nature, Krock predicted, would be costly to the nation in many ways and might lead to an "upheaval against the Administration at all polls next year." The reporter suggested that because of the far-reaching consequences of his actions, Higgins was being pressured by Washington to reopen his plants.[17]

The first public sign of that pressure was a smear campaign levied against Higgins over the radio and in the newspapers insinuating that tax problems were the true reason for his plants' closing. One of the earliest

15. Grand Rapids *Herald,* n.d., n.p. (Typed copy from 1945, in Strahan Personal Collection).

16. New York *Daily Mirror,* November 5, 1945, n.p. (Typed copy, *ibid.*).

17. Arthur Krock, "Higgins Closing a Worry," New York *Times,* November 7, 1945, p. 8.

articles to bring up the tax angle was Drew Pearson's nationally syndicated column, "The Washington-Merry-Go-Round." Pearson suggested
that Higgins' closing had caused a "lot of smiles among insiders." He
questioned whether this had "any connection with a very stormy, but
secret night just one year ago when Higgins was Chairman of the Business Men's Committee to re-elect Franklin D. Roosevelt." According to
Pearson, shortly before Higgins was to introduce Roosevelt at the president's rally in Philadelphia, the shipbuilder received "word" that Henry
Morgenthau had sent tax collectors to his New Orleans plants and demanded several million dollars in back Social Security taxes.[18]

Pearson claimed that Higgins was so furious that he threatened to
announce his support for Governor Dewey. To assure that this did not
happen, Howard Hunter, formerly of New Orleans and a close friend of
Harry Hopkins, was assigned to sit with Higgins all evening. Finally,
according to Pearson, Hunter got the shipbuilder calmed down and Higgins sat on stage with Roosevelt in Philadelphia the following day, introducing him to a crowd of thousands.

Pearson's article also suggested that Higgins had hired Truman's old
friend Hugh Fulton as his lawyer, resulting in a sweetheart deal that allowed him to pay his back taxes on the installment plan. In addition, the
columnist alleged that there was still a lot of money to be paid and that
some insiders were wondering if Higgins' threat to close his plants had
anything to do with trying to avoid paying the taxes.

It was an absurd accusation. Higgins had always taken great pride in
the fact that years earlier, even after he had declared bankruptcy, he re-
paid all of his creditors. He had stolen bronze shafting from a Texas oil
field company to finish the first tank lighters and once had held over
$500,000 of Finland's money, but according to Andrew, Jr., his father
made certain that both were fully reimbursed. Higgins also refused to
accept cost-plus contracts and had once negotiated a contract with the
government in which he would receive less payment, not more. He had
paid all the expenses of the Higgins Boat Operators and Marine Engine
Maintenance School out of his own pocket. For him to try to avoid taxes
now would have been totally out of character.

Krock contacted Higgins to discuss whether Washington was applying

18. Drew Pearson, November 7, 1945 (Clipping from unknown paper, in Strahan Personal Collection).

pressure to get him to reopen his plants. He also wanted to question the shipbuilder about the recent smear campaign against him. In speaking to the reporter, Higgins described the pressures as "terrible" and "powerful" and coming from "many people up there." He insisted that he would not yield even though some of his friends who were elected officials were now opposing his actions and advising him to reopen his plants. He said the smear tactics would have no effect on his plans. He "scoffed" at the articles crediting tax problems for his closing and continued to insist that the real issues facing not only his company but all American businessmen were veterans' rights, freedom for employees to choose their labor representative, and jurisdictional disputes between local unions. Krock told his readers, "In Government and labor circles here there are predictions that Mr. Higgins will 'find some way to save his face or get his pound of flesh and then reopen.'" He then reported that the shipbuilder's statements on the telephone did not suggest that he was going to back down.[19]

Antilabor sentiment was growing across the United States. The number of strikes had not increased drastically after victory, but the number of men involved in the strikes had risen, as had the length of time each man was out. Between V-E and V-J day a reported 2 million manpower days a month were lost in the United States because workers were idle. In September, 1945, the number of days lost had increased to 4.3 million; by October it had risen to nearly 9 million. In November alone, 180,000 workers in General Motors plants went on strike. Strikes by other huge CIO unions followed the United Auto Workers' lead. By February, 1946, the total days lost per month due to strikes and walkouts had exploded to 23 million as union leaders pushed for increased wages.

The labor problem was complicated further because the government had not properly prepared for postwar reconversion. It had assumed that after V-E day in May, 1945, a year would pass before the war in Asia would be won. With the sudden surrender of Japan, there was little time to convert from wartime to peacetime production. The War and Navy departments drastically added to the problem by almost immediately canceling one hundred thousand contracts estimated to be worth over $20 billion. Nationally unemployment rapidly rose to over 3 million.[20]

19. Krock, "Higgins Closing a Worry," 8.
20. Joseph G. Rayback, *A History of American Labor* (New York, 1959), 378–96.

Those who had lost their jobs and returning veterans looking for work had little sympathy for the union members who chose to go out on strike.

Those affected as a result of the overwhelming reconversion problems facing the nation looked for someone they could believe in and trust, someone with a commonsense approach to the problem. In Higgins they saw an industrial leader who wanted to keep his plants producing, hire veterans, and pay a fair wage but whose actions were being thwarted by unions and government. They saw him as a man who was publicly saying what they thought.

As Higgins continued with the liquidation of his company, letters of support poured in from people across the nation who had read his "Give Me Liberty" statement. From Pennsylvania, Ivan Baker wrote, "If you intend to resist gangster unionism and fight it to a finish, I will close my business and help you. I am an old shop man and know a great deal about labor both good and bad, as I have worked in various parts of the U.S."[21]

Frank Brownlow of Abingdon, Virginia, wrote, "Washington the father of our country—Lincoln the savior—and Higgins the man who has started the way to preserve the AMERICAN WAY OF LIFE." From San Diego, California, came a letter stating: "Thank God for men who have the real old American intestinal fortitude that you have. Good luck, Shipmate." A bank president in Lake Geneva, Wisconsin, sent his advice: "Stand by your guns. It is only a question of right or wrong and you are right."

Three other letters typified the support Higgins received from across the nation. They were from R. L. Bradshaw, Jr., of Gulfport, Mississippi, Mrs. Walter P. Koempel of Old Greenwich, Connecticut, and Robert H. Williams of Denver, Colorado. Bradshaw wrote: "This is just to congratulate you on having 'guts' enough to stick up for the rights and privileges that we fought for on the battlefields of the world. I am an exserviceman of officer grade. I returned to the States from the ETO about six weeks ago. The labor-management situation was then, and is now, something to bring both anger and despair to the minds of the returning soldiers. Last night I sat down to write a letter of application to you for a job. I heard a radio news flash that told of your decision. This morning,

21. Quotations in this and the following four paragraphs are from Collection of letters (1945), in Strahan Personal Collection.

I discarded the letter of application and sat down to express my sincere thanks and appreciation to an industrialist of your spirit."

Mrs. Koempel's letter read: "May I, a Gold Star mother, who does not wish to trade on that fact, congratulate you from the bottom of my heart? As a family, since the war's end, we have been hurt almost as much by the disgusting labor situation and the governmental wish-wash, as by the grim telegram we received one evening."

Robert Williams told Higgins that "there are a hundred million Americans crying for this kind of legislation. But we have no leader. That is the biggest job opening for the right man I know of. It will not be filled by one of our present political leaders, I am afraid, because those men don't want to lose their votes. The job will have to be filled by somebody who doesn't care about votes. Then he, fighting for principles, will suddenly find himself hailed by many millions of voters. I am writing on my own, to urge that you fill that job."

On November 8, as the letters of support poured in, Higgins prepared to liquidate. The mayor of New Orleans, Robert S. Maestri, urged the industrialist to reconsider and reopen his three plants. Simultaneously, the AFL requested that Truman call on Congress to investigate the closings.[22]

The following day, the company released a statement to the press saying that its board of directors had unanimously voted to place the company in voluntary liquidation out of court and had appointed Higgins and Gottesman as co-liquidators. The liquidation was to become effective immediately.[23]

The union's first reaction came from William L. Donnels, the AFL's publicity chairman: "I think Higgins is still playing to the galleries. He has the idea of striking a mortal blow at labor and making himself a martyr and hero overnight. But it is not working out that way. I think he planned all along to liquidate Higgins Industries." A reporter asked Higgins, "Does this mean that Andrew Higgins is through in New Orleans?" Higgins responded: "You asked me if Andrew Higgins is through in New Orleans. Andrew Higgins is not through. Period."[24]

22. "Mayor Appeals to Higgins," New York *Times,* November 8, 1945, p. 11.

23. "Statement for Release to the Press and Public," November 9, 1945 (Typescript in McGuire Collection).

24. "Vote to Liquidate Higgins Company," New York *Times,* November 10, 1945, p. 26.

Raymond Moley, an Associated Press syndicated columnist, shared Higgins' assessment. Moley claimed that "to any one who knows Andrew Jackson Higgins, the news of his determination to close up shop is no surprise. Mr. Higgins is a man of impulse, of something close to imaginative genius, of boundless energy and ambition. To close the books on ambition is no hardship for such a personality. His vivid genius can open a dozen others. Heaven knows what will come next, but something will." Moley contended that the impasse with the AFL was not only the end of Higgins' "manufacturing project" but "probably of a political one as well." The columnist said that Higgins' friends in 1942 and 1943 were talking about his being a "natural" for a national political office. If he could have been convinced to run, he would have been a candidate born in the North but whose career was in the South. He was a Democrat with an Irish name. He had a "gift for gab" and was a friend of FDR. He had a large family, "color, vitality, a vigorous eloquence, and ideas by the boatload." At the time, he also had the wholehearted support of the AFL. Now, according to Moley, any such political ideas would be damaged by the loss of the union's backing. It was a problem that did not concern Higgins. He had never desired to be a part of the Washington bureaucracy. Moley wanted to make one point before ending his article. He warned others who might try to emulate Higgins not to do so: "This is a moment for more and still more efforts for a mutual understanding and for an increase in the production of the things this country needs."[25]

As Moley was urging restraint, Higgins was writing to J. H. Kurth, Jr., an old acquaintance from the lumber business. He was trying to find a copy of a small booklet that he had written in 1912, when he was with the "goddam Prussian, Bavarian, Germanic firm of Phil I. Adam." The guidebook included information on kiln drying and the proper air drying of lumber. Higgins needed information that he had forgotten over the years. In his letter he mentioned: "It looks like I have started something that will have a profound corrective and sobering effect on the United States. Many of the big leaders of industry have phoned and written me that my action has given their directors a new backbone. It was a tough decision to make; to close down a flourishing industry, but goddam it, it

25. Raymond Moley, "The Unpredictable Boatman," Washington *Star*, November 15, 1945, n.p. (Typescript in McGuire Collection).

would not have been flourishing long and they certainly could not have picked a better time for me to have to make such a decision. It will be costly to us, but it will pay dividends to America. Three months ago, or before that during the war, I could not have done it, and three months from now I would be so deep in post-war work that we could not have done it."[26]

At least eight cities in the nation tried to lure the industrialist to relocate in their communities. Higgins received a telegram signed by Nebraska's governor and the mayor of Omaha offering superb plant facilities and an honest and fair labor market.[27] Florida's attorney general, Tom Watson, wanted Higgins to move the company to his state. He personally visited the industrialist and tried to persuade him to accept his offer.

Watson said his attempt at enticing the shipbuilding company to relocate was the "first step" in enforcing Florida's new constitutional amendment, which prohibited denial of a person's right to work because of membership or nonmembership in a labor union. Higgins divulged to the press that Watson had come to see him and had offered interesting inducements to relocate his company in a Florida city. Higgins told the reporters: "It was rather disturbing to learn there is a new association or organization raising a considerable fund to be used to advertise New Orleans outside the state to bring new industries here to New Orleans. But there doesn't seem to be any great concern or effort being made to solve conditions that may cause New Orleans to lose its largest industry."[28]

Although other cities tried to lure Higgins to relocate in their communities, the company proceeded with its liquidation. Then, unexpectedly, on November 29, Higgins partially reopened his Industrial Canal plant. That morning thirty workers, including six veterans, crossed the picket lines. Other workers loyal to Higgins trickled in throughout the day. The AFL, attempting to stop the crack in its ranks, increased the number of pickets to approximately thirty. Union members questioned those entering the plant, but no violence was reported. Higgins announced that he planned to boost the number of workmen by about two

26. Andrew Higgins to J. H. Kurth, Jr., November 19, 1945, *ibid.*
27. "Omaha Seeks Higgins Plant," New York *Times*, November 11, 1945, p. 35.
28. "Florida Beckons, Higgins Reveals," New Orleans *Times-Picayune*, November 17, 1945, p. 1.

hundred per day so that he could fulfill his present commitments. No figure was announced as to exactly how many people he planned to rehire.[29]

The following day, November 30, Higgins addressed the nation on the American Broadcasting Company's radio program "Headline Edition." He told the audience: "There is an enemy in our country threatening greater damage to this Democracy than our exterior enemies could ever do. Thousands are on strike. Industry is strangled—But The Congress, motivated politically, investigates 'Pearl Harbor.' "[30]

He informed the listeners that there were about 14 million labor union members in the nation. Many of those, he claimed, joined because of closed shop provisions that required workers to belong to a craft union if they wished to be employed. There were, he explained, "another 125 million Americans who were not members of any 'pressure group', craft-union, manufacturers' association, bankers' association, or what-have-you."

"Democracy," Higgins declared, "means the rule of the majority, requiring laws for the benefit of the majority. The time has come for this great inarticulate group to convince their representatives in Congress that the National Labor Relations Act, called the Wagner Act, has failed for its noble purpose."

Higgins believed that the people needed to convince Congress to repeal or amend the present labor laws so that the nation could go back to work. He argued, as he had previously, that unions should be subject to the same laws as business and that the unions' financial matters should be subject to the same scrutiny by government as those of any business. He further claimed that unions should be subject to antitrust laws and that employers should have their right of free speech restored, which he suggested had been taken away by the Wagner Act.

Higgins proposed that union members be given the right of secret ballot each year to determine their bargaining agent. Then he told the audience that the "Closed Shop" was un-American and that "no American, able, or desiring work, should be forced to PAY TRIBUTE TO ANYONE to

29. "Higgins Reopens One of His Boat Plants to Workers Crossing AFL Picket Lines," New York *Times*, November 30, 1945, p. 15.
30. "Let Pearl Harbor Wait, Mr. Congressman," *Dealers' and Salesmen's Bulletin*, December 1, 1945, p. 11. The following four paragraphs are from this source.

get a job." He ended his fifteen-minute speech by saying, "Oh, yes, and our service veterans are returning—returning to what? Strife? Strikes? Turmoil and Possible Chaos?" To eliminate this, he demanded that "the country should call on Congress TO WAKE UP and ENACT A FREE ENTER-PRISE LAW, giving ALL the right to work, and giving Management and Labor EQUALITY." Only then, he suggested, could "America survive happily."

The following day, December 1, journalist Gladstone Williams, a friend of Higgins' for several years, interviewed congressmen and senators on Capitol Hill. He reported that the reaction ran "from red hot in support" of Higgins to a "passive though favorable interest." [31]

Senator Allen Ellender of Louisiana told Williams that "if industry had more men with guts like Higgins we would be able to solve the present labor crisis without too much difficulty." Representative Paul H. Maloney of New Orleans suggested that Higgins' situation had "given rise to the necessity of congress passing legislation making arbitration of labor disputes mandatory, just as contestants go to court to settle some legal dispute." Maloney felt that a few more examples across the nation would result in action being taken.

Williams also wanted Higgins to know that the labor group that had traveled to Washington demanding a congressional investigation into the plant closings did not "get to first base." The journalist claimed that Ellender refused to consider their request and that they were "stupid to even propose such a thing." Senator John Overton of Louisiana, Williams added, told them that he was not interested in listening if that was all they had to talk about. Williams declared that for such an investigation to get anywhere, it had to have the support of the Louisiana delegation. And according to his survey, "the agitators were p——d on at every turn. So the investigation idea was a fizzle from the start."

He also told Higgins that Senator Walter F. George of Georgia thought that his actions had given "a little backbone" to the management representatives participating in the National Labor-Management Conference that had been going on in Washington. The senator had told Williams that he was especially impressed with Higgins' tactic of having his

31. Gladstone Williams to Andrew J. Higgins, December 1, 1945, in McGuire Collection. Quotations in the following four paragraphs are from this source.

"Give Me Liberty" statement published as an advertisement in the Washington *Post* on the opening day of the labor-management conference. Truman had called the conference to find a way to resolve conflicts between management and labor without either party resorting to lockouts or strikes.

"The truth of it," Williams stated, "is that a lot of senators and congressmen would like to pick up your theme and echo it on the floors of congress. But you can understand how, being politicians all of them are dependent on votes for election, they are somewhat restrained."

The journalist believed that the president was watching the developments closely but probably would not take a definite position until the situation clarified itself further. Williams stressed that the consensus on Capitol Hill was that if there was "any chance of licking that crowd by holding a new election, that would seem to be the best course."

Higgins, deciding that Washington might need a little push, published a pamphlet on December 19, titled *Equal Justice for All,* in which he accused Congress and the administration of experimenting and groping for a labor policy that would be mutually agreeable to both organized labor and management. He argued that "it is high time we stop fiddling. The situation cries out for the elimination of bad laws and the substitution of good laws which will give equal rights to management and labor." Admitting that it was easy to focus on the negative, Higgins stated, "I do not wish to criticize without offering a solution." His answer was a bill that he proposed called "The Free Enterprise Act," which would amend various sections of the Wagner Act. Higgins hoped that these amendments would put management and labor on an equal basis. He felt it would encourage both sides to try to settle controversies without interruption of production or the obstruction of the free flow of commerce. He had offered his suggestions. Now it was up to Congress to decide whether to implement them.[32]

On December 13, Higgins made another spectacular move. He presented the appliance division of Higgins Industries, worth approximately $100,000, to its three top executives, L. V. Busenlener, J. O. Crary, and William H. Bramblett. In a letter to the three men Higgins praised them for their energy and enthusiasm and for having devised the well-defined plan for the organization of the appliance division. Through their efforts,

32. Andrew J. Higgins, *Equal Justice for All,* December 19, 1945, pp. 3–4, *ibid.*

the division had been formed and manufacturers and suppliers aligned, all within a period of a few months.

Higgins explained his gift: "The executions of the Unions have no effect on the strictly merchandising set-up of our business, and we not caring to involve your activities, and feeling that it is no great prejudice to the stockholders of Higgins Industries, Incorporated, have chosen to again set the example where Management appreciates loyalty and efficiency by making you three gentlemen a present of that 'going' section of our business, the Appliance Division. We foresee and wish for you the success which you richly deserve." Crary, Busenlener, and Bramblett, in a statement to the press, said that they were "completely overwhelmed."[33]

As the new owners of the appliance division settled in and changed its name to Industries Sales Corporation, the AFL was wondering what Higgins' next move might be. Meanwhile, in Washington the NLRB was considering the CIO's petition concerning worker representation at the Higgins plants.

Finally, on December 29, 1945, the NLRB issued its ruling. The board directed that an election by secret ballot be conducted to determine the proper bargaining agent for the workers of Higgins Industries. The election should take place not later than sixty days from the date of the ruling and was to be held under the direction of the NLRB's regional director for the Fifth Region. All employees presently working at Higgins, on strike, on vacation, laid off, absent because of illness, and in the armed forces but who presented themselves at the polls would be allowed to vote. Former employees who had quit or were dismissed for just cause would not be allowed to cast a ballot.[34]

In response to the ruling, on January 6, Higgins announced: "We want to operate our business in a liberal democratic way and with sane people. The national labor relations board has at long last ordered a bargaining agent election to be held within 60 days. This election will determine who will represent our workers. The workers can choose for themselves finally in a democratic way whether they want the AFL or the CIO, or no union to represent them. The recent action of the national labor relations board

33. $100,000 Higgins Unit Given to 3 Employees," New York *Times*, December 13, 1945, p. 17; "Appliance Division Becomes Industries Sales Corporation," *Dealers' and Salesmen's Bulletin*, December 1, 1945, p. 42.

34. *Decisions and Orders of the NLRB, December 28, 1945–February 27, 1946*, Vol. 65 (Washington, D.C., 1946), 55.

gives us incentive and encouragement to create new work and to give more employment."[35]

Higgins continued with the liquidation of Higgins Industries, but he was once again enthusiastic about the future. It was a new year with new challenges. He looked forward eagerly to leaving the problems of the past behind.

35. "Higgins Planning to Open Plants," New Orleans *Times-Picayune*, January 6, 1946, p. 1.

14

USEFUL THINGS FOR PEACEFUL TIMES

On November 7, 1945, journalist Arthur Krock had reported from Washington: "In Government and labor circles here there are predictions that Mr. Higgins will 'find some way to save his face or get his pound of flesh and then reopen.'"[1] Krock proved to be correct. As Higgins continued to liquidate Higgins Industries, on Monday, January 7, 1946, he announced the formation of a new company, Higgins, Incorporated. It was a move similar to one he had made years earlier when he had liquidated A. J. Higgins Lumber and Export Company and formed Higgins Lumber and Export. He now removed Higgins Industries from the union controversy and prevented his new company from being used as a pawn in the power struggle between the War Labor Board and the National Labor Relations Board.

The new corporation was to produce commercial boats, pleasure craft, and amphibious pop-up camp trailers. It would also offer its stock to the public through the investment firm of Van Alstyne, Noel and Company of New York. The $10 million Higgins, Inc., would receive from the stock issue was projected to give the company the operating capital necessary to be competitive in the postwar period.[2]

On January 29, as Van Alstyne prepared to sell the Higgins stock, the National Labor Relations Board prepared for the election to be held at the Industrial Canal plant. The vote, scheduled for the following day, would at long last decide which union, if any, would represent Higgins' employees.

1. Krock, "Higgins Closing a Worry," p. 8.
2. "Higgins to Form $12,000,000 Firm," New Orleans *Times-Picayune,* January 8, 1946, p. 1.

315

Before the election, three priests, Vincent J. O'Connell, C. C. Chapman, and J. A. Drolet, showed up outside the plant's gate with a loudspeaker system, which they used to urge the workers to cast pro-union ballots. That same evening the priests published an advertisement in the New Orleans *Item*, "A Message to Higgins Workers." Their ad, appearing under the name of the "Committee for Social Action of the Archdiocese of New Orleans," stated: "We do not pass judgment here on the dispute between the company and the AFL unions. But we do say: VOTE FOR A UNION."

Immediately after declaring that they were not passing judgment, they stated that Higgins' workers would be foolish to believe that as individuals they could adequately protect their rights when dealing with a powerful corporation. The priests professed that Higgins, Inc., was a highly organized company. Its workers needed to be organized in order to get a square deal and to get from management the respect and consideration to which they, "as free men endowed with the dignity of children of God," were entitled. It further insisted that workers who refused to join a union violated "an obligation of justice. They are like a parishioner who uses and enjoys all the services that a parish offers, yet makes no contribution to the support of the parish."

The priests saved their strongest arguments for last. Near the bottom of the ad they exclaimed that "unions elsewhere through suffering, privation and sacrifice have brought wages up to where they are." It then informed the workers: "You enjoy the results of their sacrifices, and as men with self-respect you now want to carry your fair share of the common burden, by voting FOR A UNION! This is a simple application of the Divine commandment: Thou shalt love thy neighbor."

The ad claimed that everyone presently working at Higgins was a veteran in one way or another. It encouraged those who had worked in the plants during the war and those who had served overseas to unite as one and insisted that they should not be "fooled by unscrupulous and greedy ones who would divide and enslave" them and mislead them into voting "no union." Workers' lack of organization, according to the committee, meant low wages, poor purchasing power, unemployment, and bread lines. Organization, the priests claimed, meant fair wages, fair profits, increased purchasing power, jobs for all, and national prosperity.

After seeing the advertisement, Higgins was furious. He immediately called Archbishop Joseph Rummel to bring the advertisement and a related radio broadcast to his attention. He asked Rummel if these actions had been taken with his "cognizance, consent, or approval." The archbishop professed to know nothing about it. Higgins later recalled, "I advised him that I was gratified to hear that he knew nothing of it, for it restored in me respect for the dignity of his office; that I considered the three reverends were asinine and had been made tools of by the goons of the AFL." Higgins explained to the archbishop that he had always been a friend of Catholicism, though he himself was not a Catholic. Now, however, he felt "that the 'cloth' had gone far afield in this and had made strange bedfellows." He stressed that he resented the inference that his company was unscrupulous and greedy, seeking to divide its workers, enslave them, and mislead them. He also took offense at the claim that the corporation was trying to deprive its employees of a share in the country's prosperity and to deny them a decent wage, resulting in "poor purchasing power, unemployment, and a breadline." He also took exception to the priests proclaiming that the only resource left for the workers was to join a union. Angrily, Higgins, in a typed statement, wrote, "The poor, foolish priests did not say which union would succor them!" They refrained from telling the workers "that the only thing left for them was their regimentation and enslavement by the oldest of bigotries! . . . I am wondering if the Archbishop,—the new group of Cardinals, countenance and will aid and abet this going afield of the 'cloth' into new realms. Maybe they do, as the first step to have the new Cardinals in their present number (if not in increasing numbers) take over and have Rome tell America what the hell to do!" He closed his note, "Please page Joe Stalin."[3]

On January 31, 1946, Higgins' employees cast their ballots, choosing the CIO as their bargaining agent.[4] Although forced to accept a union, Higgins found some delight in the fact that the local AFL was no longer a part of his Industrial Canal plant. Now one union leader represented all of the plant's employees instead of different leaders representing each individual craft. This he felt would finally put an end to jurisdictional disputes and wasted man-hours.

Although Higgins' labor problems appeared to be ending, he was confronted with a new problem. On February 6, 1946, the Securities and

3. Andrew Higgins, January 30, 1946 (Typed note in McGuire Collection).
4. *Decisions and Orders of the NLRB*, Vol. 73 (Washington, D.C., 1948), 543–47.

Exchange Commission (SEC) instituted proceedings to determine whether the broker-dealer registration of Van Alstyne, Noel and Company should be revoked or suspended. The SEC alleged that the investment firm had sold Higgins, Inc., stock before the company's registration statement was filed, in fact, even before the company was legally formed on January 9, 1946. If true, the SEC said, the brokerage firm had violated Section 5(A)(1) of the Securities Act of 1933.[5]

David Van Alstyne, a principal partner of the investment firm, was a New Jersey state senator and a Republican candidate for governor. The same day that he was cited for investigation by the SEC concerning the sale of Higgins stock, he announced that he was withdrawing from the gubernatorial race.[6]

During February, as the SEC probed into the questionable stock sale, Higgins announced two major projects that would soon be under way. The first was devised to give his company a large amount of press coverage and remind potential customers that Higgins boats were superior to those of the competition. He planned to send a boat 175 miles up the Neches River in Texas. The river had not been navigated from the Gulf of Mexico to the city of Diboll in over seventy-five years.

Boat travel up the Neches had been studied by the U.S. Engineers from 1935 to 1939, but the cost of building a channel was considered prohibitive. In June, 1945, McDerby's trip up the Red River to Denison for the "Mighty Seventh War Loan Drive" had made the citizens of Diboll reconsider the idea of navigating the Neches. Not long after the "Mighty Seventh," Major Chester D. Bintliff, an army transportation officer from Houston, announced in Washington plans to run a barge operation from Mobile, Alabama to Brownsville, Texas. During the interview, he informed reporters that he thought new types of boats could even make it up Texas' Trinity River.

As a result of the announcement, several members of the Angelina County Chamber of Commerce, which encompasses Diboll, again brought up the idea of establishing a water route to the Gulf. The chamber contacted Bintliff about the possibility of barge traffic up the Neches. The idea intrigued the major, and in June, 1945, he visited several leading shippers in the area. All exhibited a strong interest.

5. "SEC Charges Van Alstyne, Noel Sold Higgins, Inc. Stock Illegally," New York *Times*, February 7, 1946, p. 30.

6. "Van Alstyne Quits Race for Governor," New York *Times*, February 7, 1946, p. 18.

Bintliff then recommended to the chamber that it should make a trial run using a Higgins boat. The board immediately approved the idea and contacted Higgins. He was enthusiastic about the challenge, but his company was in the midst of a labor strike. By February, 1946, Higgins' new corporation had been formed and he was eager to showcase his boats.

Higgins called McDerby in Denison insisting that he make the historic run. McDerby resisted, explaining that his own marine service business demanded his attention. Higgins proved too persuasive, and Mac's respect and love for his old boss were too strong. Mac gave in.

Higgins sent an LCPL by truck to Port Arthur, Texas, on February 11. On February 13, in a driving rain, McDerby and his crew headed upriver. Sunday, February 17, they were greeted by two thousand people at Lufkin after having traveled 175 miles and proving that the river was navigable. It was predicted that water rates would soon be established and barge traffic would be operating as far up as the Lufkin-Diboll area.[7] The citizens along the Neches had achieved their goal, and Higgins had received favorable publicity throughout the entire trip.

Even as McDerby was working his way slowly up the Neches, on February 15, 1946, Higgins announced his second major project, plans to build a new type of housing costing as little as $5,000 for a three-bedroom home. He described the new units as "revolutionary" and claimed: "This is a gigantic thing. . . . The new building material and process will make it possible to raise a dwelling in three days. Work will be started on the project as soon as steel is available." Enthusiastically, Higgins described his proposed houses as vermin-proof, tornado-proof, earthquake-proof, fireproof, airtight, and dust-tight. "The homes," he stated, "will be there forever" and are "an architect's dream."[8]

The idea originated with Maury Diggs, an Oakland, California, architect. Diggs easily sold Higgins on the new concept as a way to solve the nation's housing shortage. Several hundred thousand returning soldiers who had either recently married or would do so in the near future were looking for homes of their own. Added to this new group of buyers were hundreds of thousands of other couples, who during the Depression

---

7. Richard A. McDerby, interview, January 27, 1993; Unidentified clipping in scrapbook, McDerby Collection.

8. "Higgins to Build Plastic Houses," New Orleans *Times-Picayune*, February 15, 1946, p. 1; "Higgins Plans House Output," n.d. (Clipping in University Relations Central Files—Andrew Jackson Higgins, Creighton University, Omaha, Nebraska).

had moved into cramped quarters with friends or relatives and now were again in the market for housing.

Higgins envisioned the building of the houses as creating new job opportunities for returning veterans and others of an ambitious nature. In conjunction with the project, he proposed establishing a school in New Orleans to provide instruction in the construction of the new units.

The houses were to be built of materials Higgins called Thermo-Namel and Thermo-Con. Thermo-Namel panels were sheets of metal covered with porcelain enamel attached to a frame made of noncarbon iron. These highly durable panels were to be used to form identical interior and exterior walls that also served as the house's form. The airspace between the panels was to be filled with Thermo-Con, a Higgins product made from ordinary Portland cement and a secret ingredient. The new material, Higgins claimed, possessed "high thermal qualities" and great strength. Because of its enamel doors, windows, walls, and ceiling the house required no painting and limited maintenance. Construction cost was projected to run approximately 20 percent less than that of a frame and plaster house.[9]

Production of the new houses was to begin gradually, with an eventual goal of five hundred a day. Panel walls and steel framing were to be produced at Michaud, and all construction would be completed on site. From start to finish a house could be ready in less than 250 man-hours.

On February 18, Higgins went to Washington for a meeting with Wilson W. Wyatt, national housing administrator. Wyatt had been instructed by Truman to build 2.7 million new low-cost homes to overcome the nation's housing shortage. It was an ambitious undertaking. Higgins was certain that Diggs's idea was one of the most inexpensive and logical ways to achieve the goal.

Others had also come up with revolutionary manufacturing techniques to capture the new market. R. G. LeTour of Peoria, Illinois, had developed an enormous machine that would turn out a two-bedroom house with an 18-x-11½-foot-living room, on site, in twenty-four hours. Kaiser, who had earlier experience in construction of private homes, planned to enter the field again in a massive way. One of his company officials projected constructing as many as 100,000 houses a year.[10]

9. "Higgins to Build Plastic Houses," 1; Unidentified clipping, February 19, 1946, in University Relations Central Files—Andrew Jackson Higgins; Unidentified clipping, February 27, 1946, *ibid.*
10. "Assembled Houses Will Cost More," New York *Times*, February 19, 1946, p. 20;

After only one day in Washington Higgins went from enthusiastic to pessimistic. He remarked to a reporter that he was ready to abandon his housing plans. Wyatt had given him no encouragement, and he thought the War Assets Corporation's fee to use Michaud was "so outlandish it was impossible to consider it." The corporation wanted 8 percent of the gross sales as rental. Higgins contended that he could have built a manufacturing facility in New Orleans' best business district on a 3 percent basis. "If these agencies are so shortsighted that they make it impossible for a man who wants to produce at his own expense, it doesn't add up," Higgins stated. He described Washington's policy as "confused lethargy" and informed the reporter that he was "going home before the lethargy hit him too." [11]

Frustrated, Higgins returned to New Orleans to focus his attention on finding a new investment firm to handle the sale of his company's stock. Van Alstyne, Noel and Company had received a ten-day suspension from the SEC. Higgins, therefore, chose to have another firm handle the public offering of his company's stock. Higgins was also working on having Higgins, Inc., acquire the remaining subsidiaries of Higgins Industries. On March 15, the Michaud companies, with their combined total of twenty-one employees, were transferred to Higgins, Inc.[12]

After finally consolidating his holdings, on March 20 Higgins filed an amendment to his registration statement with the SEC. Listed in the amendment were three new underwriters to replace Van Alstyne. The companies in the new group were Newburger and Hano, Kobbe, Gearhart and Company of New York, and Weil and Company of New Orleans. Out of an authorized issue of 2 million shares of common stock, 900,000 were to be sold for $11 per share, of which 90 cents a share was to be retained as an underwriting commission. Three hundred thousand shares were to be issued to Higgins, Inc., along with a cash settlement in consideration of the transfer of assets.

Revenue not used to buy assets and property from Higgins Industries, which was then in statutory liquidation, was to be available for general corporate use, including purchasing additional property if necessary. As-

---

Mark S. Foster, *Henry J. Kaiser: Builder in the Modern American West* (Austin, 1989), 133.

11. "'Confused Lethargy' Grips Washington, Higgins Says," New York *Times*, February 20, 1946, p. 15.

12. *Decisions and Orders of the NLRB*, Vol. 73, p. 544.

sets taken over from Higgins Industries included all work in progress, contracts, and inventories. Higgins planned to produce pleasure craft and commercial boats such as tugs, dredges, fishing vessels, ramp-type craft, and pop-up amphibious camp trailers.[13]

Newburger and Hano publicly offered the 900,000 shares of Higgins stock on March 22. Incredibly, by closing time that evening the stock had been oversubscribed and the books closed. A few days later, Higgins announced that "Higgins, Inc. has been operating since Feb. 1 and has been in production during that period. With the additional working capital supplied by the recent financing, we can now rapidly increase production on our heavy backlog of orders." The new company had orders for pleasure craft secured by deposits and protected by priority delivery certificates exceeding $20 million and contracts for commercial craft totaling over $6 million. In addition, the company had just been awarded a contract by the United Nations Relief and Rehabilitation Administration for several steel shallow-draft cargo boats similar to LCMs. It also had $21 million in dealer requests for its new camp trailers.[14]

To increase sales even more, between April 20 and 25, Higgins participated in the Higgins Motor Boat Show sponsored by Macy's and Bamberger's department stores in New York. The show, held at the Seventeenth Regent Armory at Park Avenue and Thirty-fourth Street, was the first of its kind to be held in New York since January, 1941. Displayed were Higgins runabouts, cruisers, an auxiliary sloop, and a variety of smaller craft. The showpiece of the flag-draped armory was the 28-foot Eureka. It was a smaller, refined, two-toned version of the famous Higgins LCPL used during the war. Now converted to a pleasure craft, it was appealing to former servicemen and others familiar with its outstanding reputation and war exploits. Higgins pleasure craft of 32, 42, and 55 feet were available, but they were too large to be squeezed through the armory's doors.[15]

The show, attended by over 125,000 persons, resulted in purchases of over $1,250,000 worth of Higgins boats. At the show's conclusion, Higgins predicted that "an era of great prosperity was ahead for this nation, with standards of living rising to heretofore unknown heights."[16]

13. "Higgins Nominates a New Syndicate," New York *Times,* March 21, 1946, p. 39.

14. "Higgins Discloses Big Order Backlog," New York *Times,* March 28, 1946, p. 39.

15. "Two Boat Shows Usher in New Era," New York *Times,* April 21, 1946, Sec. 5, p. 5.

16. "Higgins Sees Prosperity," New York *Times,* April 25, 1946, p. 23.

While Higgins prepared for the future, he was again confronted with labor problems. On April 17, 1946, the CIO requested that Higgins recognize it as the exclusive bargaining agent of the four hundred workers now employed at the Michaud plant. The workers, originally employees of Higgins Plastics, had not been involved in the earlier labor actions of Higgins Industries or the strike that had crippled the Industrial Canal plant. Higgins refused the CIO's request because the AFL claimed that it represented a majority of Michaud's workers. Because of his refusal, on April 29, the CIO filed a petition with the NLRB, resulting in hearings during May and June and continuing into midsummer.[17]

At about the same time, General Holland Smith prepared to retire from the Marine Corps. Higgins had sent Smith a scale model of a Higgins LCPL as a token of appreciation for the general's longtime support. Smith responded on May 6, expressing his sincere "thanks" and "deep emotion" for the "beautiful trophy." He also informed his wartime ally that "one week from today I haul down my flag and I shall 'live in a little house by the side of the road and be a friend to my fellow man'." The general continued:

> I am not unmindful of the magnificent contribution you made toward winning World War II. Indeed, in all of my forty-one years of service I have never known anyone filled with a higher sense of patriotism than you. In the various public addresses I have made over the West Coast I have never failed to pay you a deserved tribute for your part in this war.
>
> Recently the Navy Department sponsored a portrait of me in my utility suit. In the background there are Higgins boats and the model for these boats is the beautiful one you sent me.
>
> I shall live in La Jolla, California, and would be highly honored if you would come to see me should you ever come to the West Coast.
>
> Again, I thank you from the bottom of my heart for remembering me.
>
> With feelings of friendship, admiration, and affection.[18]

On June 2, Higgins left his labor problems behind and headed toward Argentina. A Higgins representative stationed there had presented General Juan Perón with an invitation, allegedly signed by Louisiana's governor Jimmie Davis, inviting him to visit the state. When the U.S. State Department objected to the invitation, the governor repudiated the letter

17. *Decisions and Orders of the NLRB,* Vol. 73, p. 545.
18. Lieutenant General Holland Smith to Andrew Higgins, May 6, 1946, in Strahan Personal Collection.

as a forgery. In response, Perón invited Higgins to Argentina. The press suggested that Perón was trying to show the American public that he liked the United States but disliked the State Department, especially Assistant Secretary of State Spruille Braden. Braden had publicly declared that Perón was a dictator and did not have the approval of his people.

Higgins, in an interview with an English-language newspaper in Buenos Aires, stated: "I, simply as an American citizen, protest that one man—Braden—can involve two great peoples in discord." He insisted that as a U.S. citizen he had been humiliated by Braden's reference to the president-elect as a dictator. Further, he stated: "I disagree with this policy, as we have seen evidence that Gen. Juan D. Perón has been elected by a majority of his people as President. In addition, Perón is idolized by the majority of the people, and the will of the majority of the people signifies true democracy. This is undoubtedly the opinion of a majority of American citizens and I feel I can voice these sentiments." Higgins was also critical of the news reporting by special correspondents and news agencies that had covered Perón's political campaign: "In recent months I have been greatly concerned at the deterioration of Argentine–United States relations—a deterioration which many people in the United States attribute to controlled reports. The American public is not, by any means, satisfied with the 'doctored' reports appearing in the American press." [19]

On June 9, as Higgins departed from Buenos Aires, George S. Messersmith, the new U.S. ambassador to Argentina, held several private meetings with Perón. Reports suggested that some progress was being made in finding a solution to the difficulties between the United States and Argentina. On June 16, when Higgins visited Miami en route back to New Orleans, he told the press: "I was extremely impressed by Perón and his sincerity. He is deeply hurt by the way his motives are misunderstood." As a parting shot, Higgins charged that Spruille Braden, during his years as ambassador to Argentina, had been more of a dictator than was Perón. "The United States has been guilty of insulting the Argentine republic and it behooves us to make amends for the affronts we have given them," Higgins told the reporters. [20]

19. "Braden Sows U.S.-Argentine Discord, Says Higgins, 'Humiliated' by Slur to Perón," New York *Times,* June 5, 1946, p. 11.

20. "Higgins Praises Perón," New York *Times,* June 17, 1946, p. 43; "Envoy Said to See Perón," New York *Times,* June 9, 1946, p. 21.

On June 8, workers at the Industrial Canal plant assembled the first of the new Thermo-Namel houses. Real estate companies, mortgage industry executives, government housing officials, and those in the building fields were invited to inspect the new dwelling. The demonstration model, containing three rooms and a bath, was constructed using attractive pastel-colored enamel panels that Higgins hoped to begin mass producing at Michaud. If successful, he estimated that he would soon be employing as many as eleven thousand new workers.[21]

While Higgins prepared to mass produce the new houses, the Industrial Canal plant and Michaud continued with the production of pleasure boats and commercial craft. Additionally, Higgins announced development of a new craft, the Swamp Skipper. This amphibian craft was designed by Higgins' "imagineer," John Poche, for use by oil companies and public service organizations in the swampy lowlands of the South. The marsh buggy was capable of pulling a sleigh loaded with one and a half tons of equipment through all manner of adverse conditions.

During the war, when Higgins came up with one of his wild ideas, he often called on Poche to draw a design for the contraption. Poche was an artist and an inventor but not a formally trained engineer. Higgins contended that since Poche had never been told by some professor that something was impossible to do and he didn't know that it couldn't be done, he would often come up with a workable idea. The Swamp Skipper was just such an example, born from a prototype developed during the war.

Another project, completed during July, 1946, was Higgins' new 256-foot ship the *Angele Higgins*. She was the first of a proposed twenty ships in the new Higgins Las Americas Line. The *Angele* was to continue a sailing heritage established by clippers and brigantines that had sailed for Higgins years before. He intended that she and several more like her would eventually sail up the Amazon, the Orinoco, even the Yangtze in China, delivering general cargo and returning with mahogany and other raw materials.

Presently, the *Angele* was to serve as the first ship in the steamship service tying the Gulf Coast to Central and South America. As a specially designed shallow-draft cargo ship, she could enter the small harbors inaccessible to commercial cargo vessels. Higgins could practically write

21. "Higgins Displays New-Type House," New Orleans *Times-Picayune*, June 8, 1946, p. 17.

his own shipping rates because no other craft could go where the *Angele* could sail. The steamship service, according to Graham Haddock, was Higgins' longtime dream.

When profitable lightweight cargo was unavailable, the *Angele* would often haul a load of rice from Lake Charles, Louisiana, to Central America. Sale of the cargo generally covered expenses. Profits were made by bringing unprocessed lumber back to New Orleans for use in the sawmill and veneer facilities at Michaud. According to Higgins, the materials would be used to produce "useful things for peaceful times."[22]

To Higgins, the future looked bright. He had just executed an agreement with the CIO to represent his employees in both the Michaud and Industrial Canal plants.[23] Then, suddenly and unexpectedly, he was dealt a devastating blow by the Department of Justice, a blow that he felt unjustly destroyed everything he had worked for. Local and national newspapers on August 6, 1946, reported that Higgins was the target of a federal investigation concerning alleged wartime fraud. The stories claimed that the federal district attorney of southern Louisiana had impaneled a grand jury to explore the charges.

J. Frank Cunningham, special attorney of the Department of Justice, took an oath of office on August 7 and revealed that he would probe the wartime activities of Higgins Industries based on information received by the Justice Department. Others included in the investigation were Morris Gottesman and Milton P. Chatry, past executives of Higgins Industries; Frank O. Higgins, Higgins' son; and Higgins Plastics, as well as any other individuals, companies, corporations, or firms that might now be unknown to the Justice Department but connected with Higgins. In a sworn statement, Cunningham accused Higgins and the others of "making and causing to be made and presented for payment and approval false claims against the United States Government, knowing such claims to be false, fictitious and fraudulent."[24]

Higgins adamantly denied any knowledge of illegal actions. Later that afternoon he told the press: "These obviously are trumped-up charges. I know some of our people have gone down to answer some questions, but all of this can be cleared up. I don't see what right anyone has to make

22. Caption, *Higgins Worker,* July 5, 1946, p. 5; Graham Haddock, interview, January 8, 1993.

23. *Decisions and Orders of the NLRB,* Case 15-CA-27, Vol. 90, May 31–August 29, 1950 (Washington, D.C., 1950), 189.

24. "Higgins Is Accused of Wartime Fraud," New York *Times,* August 7, 1946, p. 19.

such charges until they are confirmed. Right now they're just a lot of barroom gossip and can be cleared up. But the publicity from the bare accusation is enough to eat the heart out of a man who has worked so hard during the war. I guess there are more enemies than Japs and Germans."[25]

Several hours later, Higgins issued a formal written statement in which he claimed that he was "surprised and amazed that accusations against" himself and members of his "organization should be made prior to complete investigation. To my knowledge," he stated, "the action and conduct of Higgins Industries and its affiliate companies have been subjected to the strictest scrutiny of all branches of the Government services, both during and after the war. This was done with our fullest cooperation. No irregularities have been brought to our attention. I am confident that none exist."[26]

In a letter to Cunningham, U.S. Attorney General Tom C. Clark alleged that Higgins and his associates had "concealed and covered up by trick, scheme or device, material facts." The attorney general also accused Higgins and the others of intentionally making false bills, receipts, vouchers, rolls, accounts, claims, certificates, and affidavits. Higgins became even more infuriated when he could not find anyone in government to explain the exact charges that had been levied against him. To find out, he had to call the United Press office and ask that Clark's letter be read to him over the phone. After listening to the accusations and excerpts from the attorney general's letter, an angry Higgins responded, "Some one is going to pay for this."[27]

The following day, after the story had been published nationwide, the Justice Department released a statement. It declared that authorization for one of its war fraud lawyers to appear before a New Orleans grand jury in the Higgins investigation must not "be construed as a charge of criminal misconduct, but merely a form used since the passage of the statute many years ago requiring the authorization of the Attorney General before an appearance may be made by a Department of Justice attorney." Following established grand jury policy, the department refused to discuss any evidence that might be presented.[28]

In August, 1946, sixty-five auditors from the army air force began

25. Ibid.
26. Ibid.
27. Ibid.
28. "Charging of Crime to Higgins Denied," New York *Times,* August 8, 1946, p. 13.

investigating the accounts of Higgins Aircraft, while the Federal Bureau of Investigation began its search into the records of Higgins, Inc. Trying to maintain normal operations, Higgins moved forward with his plans for Thermo-Namel homes. Housing expediter Wilson W. Wyatt of the National Housing Administration (NHA) revealed on October 13 that the NHA had already concluded guaranteed-market contracts with other manufacturers for approximately 29,400 prefabricated homes of various designs to be built by the end of 1947. Of importance to New Orleans was Wyatt's announcement that negotiations were under way for a government-guaranteed contract calling for Higgins to produce materials to construct 10,000 Thermo-Namel houses for veterans. Higgins was to supply the wall panels, ceilings, bathroom floor tiles, window frames and sash, gutters, and a variety of small incidentals. Other companies would furnish the doors, roofs, flooring, trim, electrical work, and cabinets.

Higgins estimated that his portion of the package would cost approximately $2,400 per house, making the proposed contract worth $24 million. The house, when completed, excluding the land, kitchen range, refrigerator, window screens, and blinds, would be priced at $7,150.00.[29] All were to be constructed during 1947.

Hoping to receive the money to finance his housing project, Higgins applied for an $11 million Reconstruction Finance Corporation (RFC) loan. His application was rejected, just as four others recommended by the National Housing Administration had been rejected the week before. Truman wanted the houses built, the NHA had approved the construction, yet the RFC for some unknown reason refused to supply the funds.

Disgusted, on November 7, Higgins told reporters: "I'm not surprised. I never expected anything from Washington. This delay with the Government has just lost us a year and a half of fooling around." He announced that the houses would be built even without federal assistance but failed to mention how he was going to fund the project.[30]

In December, 1946, the company lost one of its key figures, Morris Gottesman. On December 5, Gottesman submitted his letter of resignation to the board of directors of Higgins, Inc., informing the board that because of medical reasons he could no longer fulfill his duties as

29. "Higgins to Make Housing 'Panels,'" New York *Times*, October 16, 1946, p. 48.
30. "RFC Bars Loan to Higgins," New York *Times*, November 8, 1946, p. 8.

secretary-treasurer. In the latter part of 1943 he had been afflicted with a liver ailment that required him to be hospitalized twice in the beginning of 1944. His doctors had advised him that his condition could be cured only through rest. In his letter he explained, "I could not follow the physicians' recommendations on account of the War work in which I was engaged then and have carried on my work irrespective of the consequences to my health." He said that in the last three months a condition similar to the one that had affected him in 1943 had begun developing. This time, to follow his doctors' advice, he stated, "I herewith tender my resignation as Secretary-Treasurer and Director of the company, effective immediately."[31]

Gottesman's health was one important reason for his resignation, but those close to the situation suggest that there were other considerations that brought about his action. Gottesman wanted to approach the postwar markets in a slower, more deliberate fashion than did Higgins. According to Haddock, Gottesman wanted to be cautious, producing one model of pleasure craft, expanding production and models as the market dictated. Gottesman also wanted to eliminate Michaud, viewing it as a "white elephant." He recommended pulling all production back into the Industrial Canal plant.

Higgins, however, wanted to mass produce a full line of pleasure craft. His theory was that the company should keep production up, cost down, stock his distributors across the nation to the maximum, and thereby increase the number of jobs the plant could offer. He was intent on keeping his wartime promise of supplying employment for as many people as he possibly could. He also wanted to retain Michaud for building his housing products, camp trailers, and pleasure craft.

Haddock views Gottesman's leaving as the beginning of the company's downfall. Ted Sprague suggests that "you can look at it two ways, he [Gottesman] left and that caused the decline, or he left because of the decline—seeing that the decline was coming." Jack Higgins contends that Gottesman wanted to get out while the company still had enough money to purchase his stock. Whatever the true reason, Gottesman, the man who had overseen the financial aspects of Higgins' boat-building enterprise since the mid-1930s and the days of the Boat Services Company,

31. Morris Gottesman to Board of Directors, Higgins, Inc., December 5, 1946, in Strahan Personal Collection.

was no longer a part of the management team. Michael Macheca, Gottesman's assistant for several months, took over his duties.[32]

Gottesman had left the company, but he was still a target of Cunningham's ongoing investigation. As the investigation continued, Higgins went to Washington in early January to try to recover $1,730,000 that he claimed the War Department still owed him from war-related contracts. While there, he again became infuriated over the accusations of wartime fraud and decided to defend his and his company's actions.

On January 10, 1947, sitting in his room at the Statler Hotel, Higgins dictated a twenty-page document. He claimed that his statement was being given in response to the great negative publicity that had gone out worldwide over the news wires. False stories, he charged, had been printed because an attorney for the U.S. Attorney General's Office had filed a letter of authority to act in the federal court of Louisiana.[33]

It was normal that those in the defense industry who held billions of dollars in government contracts would be investigated and their performances monitored. The Truman Committee had been set up to help curb abuse. In Higgins' case, however, the attorney's letter was unusual in that it went beyond simply authorizing an investigation. The letter discussed the penalties under federal law assigned to various possible misdemeanors, crimes, and so on that an individual or a corporation could commit in time of war.

Incensed, Higgins maintained that the manner in which the letter was constructed made it appear that he and the others named were guilty of all of the acts mentioned. This, he claimed, was a "very damaging and a cruel blow to the pride of all the officers and department heads of the various Higgins activities."

Higgins argued that Higgins, Inc., was a new corporation, not a successor of Higgins Industries. He insisted that the adverse publicity because of the investigation had done great damage to the new corporation's reputation and thus had affected his company's sales and his employees' morale.

He claimed that during the last eighteen months from ten to sixty government auditors had been going over the records of his various com-

32. Ted Sprague, interview, August 2, 1992; Graham Haddock, interview, June 26, 1975.
33. Statler Hotel Statement, 19–20. The following paragraphs are from this source.

panies. During this period, the time of his auditing and accounting staffs had been almost completely taken up answering questions and providing material for the auditors. According to Higgins, the investigation was not only destroying the past reputation of Higgins Industries and its subsidiaries, but it was also damaging his new corporation. He reported that the key personnel of Higgins, Inc., were having to devote a majority of their time to answering inquiries from investigators. The accounting department had been so involved in preparing responses that it had been impossible for it to prepare a statement of the operation of Higgins, Inc., from its inception in January, 1946, through August 5, 1946.

Higgins considered the cost in dollars of the employees' time taken up in answering Cunningham's questions to be "an unfair burden" on his new company as it tried to establish its operations. He admitted that some of the wartime expenditures made during "the hasty tempo of the defense program could perhaps take on a different light in the calm scrutiny of peacetime 'quarterbacking.'" In his defense, however, he cited several cases in which large losses had been sustained. He felt that these proved that he and his companies were not greedy or attempting to defraud the government but instead were "inspired by patriotism." As an example, he mentioned his early bids on the 81-foot torpedo boats, which he knew were so low that his company would have to absorb a large loss. He also recalled PT 72, a 78-foot boat, which cost him $180,000 to build and which he sold to the navy for $117,000. He also mentioned the original tank lighter produced by his company in sixty-one hours and the additional forty-nine that had to be delivered as soon as possible. The length of these boats had increased from 45 feet to 50 feet by the time the last boat was delivered, and each succeeding boat had improved characteristics over the previous one. All of the boats, Higgins claimed, were delivered at his original "off-the-cuff price."

Another topic Higgins discussed was the expansion of the City Park plant. "Certainly, the same people who took the chance of extending the City Park Plant over a graveyard didn't change overnight to a group motivated by greed." He said he was aware of how desperate the military was for landing craft, and he argued that he knowingly and willingly expanded the plant to increase production, fully realizing his legal exposure.

Also mentioned in the statement were the costs that Higgins had personally absorbed during the building of Michaud, from the time it was proposed to build Liberty ships through to the present. He suggested that his opposition to cost-plus contracts and his reducing his profit from 6 percent to 3 percent on aircraft production should show that he was not motivated by greed. The fact that his plants, except Michaud, were built out of his company's own finances should prove that he was not trying to defraud the government.

Other projects listed in his defense were the production of the Higgins torpedo tube, which was a superior tube produced at a fraction of the cost that the navy had previously been paying. About the airborne lifeboat, Higgins said, "I have never received any thanks for this contribution, nor has the company been reimbursed for their development expenditures." The Manhattan Project was another instance for which Higgins claimed not to have been fully reimbursed. He wrote: "There has been vast publicity and credit given to many and our name has been conspicuously unmentioned. Not only that, but despite our losses, caused by changes, cancellations and stop-orders, the very negotiations for the recovery of some $200,000 due on this project has been frozen, and all payments suspended by some mysterious edict or order."

During the preceding seven-year period, Higgins completed over $400 million worth of business for the government. At the same time, he estimated that his company had trained more than thirty thousand men in amphibious operations and the care and maintenance of landing craft at no cost to the government. An additional four thousand men were trained in celestial navigation. He stated, "I don't know how many squadrons of PT boats were commissioned and went away from our plant to war; but I personally entertained at my home every member of the amphibious schools, and all the PT squadrons, both officers and men, and I gave the privates or the gobs the same kind of liquor I gave the officers—and I drank some of it myself."

"Republics they say are ungrateful. Certainly this *war contractor* has good reason to confirm this," declared Higgins. He ended his statement by saying, "The mistakes of the military leaders are excused or forgotten no matter how costly in terms of wealth, material or human lives; but the people that create or build to make victory possible and after victory exert their every effort to maintain the economy of our country are 'war profiteers' to be subjected to suspicion, to be investigated, to be harassed—their business destroyed—yes—and their character and honor smirched! WHAT PRICE OR CREDIT PATRIOTISM."

Higgins sent a copy of his statement to Louisiana's senator John H. Overton, who sent it to President Truman. Truman replied: "I think Mr. Higgins must have sent this statement to everyone of his acquaintances. I have had at least a half dozen of them and I am trying my best to get the matter straightened out."[34]

On February 7, 1947, United States Attorney Herbert W. Christenberry announced that the federal grand jury investigation into Higgins and his companies had ended and that the grand jury had "concluded there is no basis for criminal prosecution." Informed of the decision, Higgins responded: "The fact that the grand jury has found no basis for criminal prosecution in its investigation of Higgins, Industries, Inc. was not a surprise. The result is most pleasing."[35]

Now, seventeen months after the end of the war, Higgins hoped his company could finally devote its attention to being competitive in the postwar markets. Nature was not going to allow that to happen.

34. Harry Truman to John H. Overton, January 29, 1947, in Truman Papers, Official File No. 633.

35. "Higgins Is Cleared on War Contracts," New York *Times*, February 8, 1947, p. 14.

15

DEMISE AND REBIRTH

On February 11, 1947, just four days after being exonerated of wartime fraud, Higgins received notification that the Reconstruction Finance Corporation had reconsidered its decision and approved his loan. The RFC made available $9 million for construction of Thermo-Namel houses.[1] A little over ninety days later, Higgins announced that he had abandoned his negotiations with the government agency because the company had been unable to come to satisfactory terms for leasing Michaud. Higgins explained, "The loan wouldn't have done us any good without a place to put our machinery."[2]

A second and just as critical problem was that Higgins could not get steel to manufacture the Thermo-Namel panels. The country was in the midst of a massive steel shortage. The same grade of steel used to produce the enamel houses was also used to manufacture refrigerators, washing machines, automobile bodies, and several other consumer products. Large manufacturers such as General Electric, Westinghouse, Ford, and Chevrolet had a higher priority rating for the metal, which was distributed by the manufacturers on an allocation system based on prewar usage. Before the war Higgins purchased approximately three to four hundred tons of steel a year. During the war his usage exceeded that in a single day.

The American public was starving for consumer products. Few had been manufactured since 1941, and now the tremendous demand was devouring all available steel. The little steel that Higgins could buy was

---

1. "Higgins Gets RFC Loan," New York *Times*, February 11, 1947, p. 48.
2. "Higgins Plans Homes Without RFC Loan," New York *Times*, May 18, 1947, Sec. 8, p. 1.

dedicated to marine projects. Higgins realized that without steel his housing project was doomed so he gave up the Thermo-Namel idea and began designing a house constructed primarily of Thermo-Con.[3]

Meanwhile, his boat production lines were operating in high gear mass producing pleasure craft. He hoped that as citizens began to cash in their war bonds some of the money would be spent on his company's 17-foot Deluxe Utility pleasure boat, its 19-foot Deluxe Runabout, his cabin cruisers, or his unique amphibious camp trailers.

During the same period, the Industrial Canal plant was working on a 168-foot seagoing yacht, 108-foot steel refrigerated shrimping vessel, 50-foot steel tug, several smaller vessels, barges, and an LST that Higgins bought and was converting into a commercial ship to join the *Angele Higgins* in his Las Americas Line. Ironically, the ship was christened the *Andrew Jackson Higgins*.[4]

Within five months, the company would undergo dramatic changes. On July 23, 1947, the contract that had been negotiated the previous summer between Higgins and the CIO expired. The maintenance and production employees of Higgins, represented by the CIO, demanded that an across-the-board twelve cents an hour pay raise be included in any new contract. Higgins claimed that it would be economically disastrous for him to raise the wages of common laborers that much. He offered to implement the desired increase at the Industrial Canal plant and to make wage adjustments at Michaud, where non–shipbuilding activities were taking place. In response, the union called its 2,086 members out on strike on July 24. Five days later, Higgins notified the CIO that the walkout was in violation of their agreement and therefore the union had "forfeited any rights it might have had to represent the employees." Contract negotiations were suspended. On July 31, the union, realizing that Higgins was not going to reverse his decision, called for its members to return to work unconditionally.

Two days later, on August 2, the union contacted Higgins by letter. It claimed that it was still the official certified bargaining agent for Higgins, Inc.'s employees, and it requested a resumption of negotiations. Higgins refused. Eventually, he rehired all those who had gone on strike except

3. Graham Haddock, interview, January 8, 1993.
4. "Pleasure Boat Production Lines Now in High Gear," *Higgins Worker*, April, 1947, p. 1; Higgins Production Ledger, 8–9, in Strahan Personal Collection.

approximately 150 of the strike leaders. Not rehired were all union officers, executive board members, and stewards, whom Higgins considered
responsible for causing and continuing the walkout. Many of the executive officers, including Local 73 president John W. Weightman and local
secretary Harold Caillouet, had to seek employment in other cities.

Because of the unsuccessful job action and the loss of the local officers,
the parent organization, the Industrial Union of Marine and Shipbuilding
Workers of America, appointed Arthur Leary, its national representative
in the New Orleans area, to take control of Local 73. Leary made several
attempts to persuade Higgins to negotiate. Each time, Higgins reiterated
his statement that the union had forfeited its representative status by initiating the strike, thereby violating the terms of their agreement. The
union filed a complaint with the NLRB.[5]

On August 29 the Port of New Orleans purchased the Michaud facility from the government as surplus property for $10 million. Higgins
simultaneously bought the plywood and veneer plant located near Michaud for $800,000. He also negotiated a contract with Michaud's new
owners that included his present floor space, plus an additional four hundred thousand square feet for his housing project.[6]

Higgins and his staff were optimistic. They were making arrangements
to set up their Thermo-Con venture at Michaud when a hurricane moved
into the Gulf of Mexico. On September 18, the New Orleans *Times Picayune* reported that the fierce storm was heading across the Gulf following a track that would strike Louisiana's coast sometime Friday, September 19. By Thursday evening, September 18, wind gusts up to fifty-five
miles an hour were recorded in New Orleans.

The city was on full alert, taking all necessary emergency precautions,
including the opening of storm shelters. As many as 3,000 persons filled
the Municipal Auditorium in the city, many of them French-speaking
trappers, fishermen, and truck farmers who had evacuated the flooded
bayou settlements south of New Orleans. Between 3,000 and 4,000 residents of Ourtown had been evacuated and brought to shelters. Forty
schools in the metropolitan area had been converted to rescue facilities
and housed upward of 20,000 people. The St. Bernard Parish courthouse,

5. *Decisions and Orders of the NLRB*, Case 15-CA-27, May 31, 1950–August 29,
1950, Vol. 90 (Washington, D.C., 1951), 189–191.
6. "Michaud Ship Plant Sold," New York *Times*, August 29, 1947, p. 35.

in nearby St. Bernard Parish, housed as many as 2,500 evacuees. As residents made final preparations for the storm, the hurricane, which covered an area of approximately five hundred miles and had sustained winds of eighty to one hundred miles an hour, moved closer to the city.[7]

The fierce winds struck New Orleans before dawn. The eye, or center, passed over the city at approximately 9:30 A.M. Shortly after noon, the gusts diminished as the storm headed inland, leaving behind a path of destruction and at least twelve dead in the lowlands on the eastern edge of town. Considerable flooding occurred along the lakefront and the Gentilly area bordering Lake Pontchartrain as towering waves crashed over the sea wall, stranding persons in their homes. Trucks and emergency vehicles manned by city employees, soldiers, and volunteers were virtually useless because of high water. Higgins' shallow-draft boats were called in to aid in the rescue attempt. Residents were evacuated and taken to shelters throughout the city.[8]

Later that afternoon Ted Sprague, then serving as director of development of pleasure craft, accompanied by Roland Higgins, went by boat to Michaud to survey the damage. Production of pleasure craft had been under way, and the plant contained hundreds of boats. Michaud had suffered severe damage. When they arrived, they found seven feet of water in the plant, floating logs, and twenty-eight black plant workers from Mississippi clinging to the rafters. The workers, not aware of the severity or closeness of the hurricane, had shown up for work and gotten trapped by the storm. It was impossible to transport all of the men to safety in the small boat. Sprague and Roland tied a long piece of hose to the boat, had the men hang on, then pulled them to higher ground.

The wind's impact combined with the surge of floodwaters had forced open the plant's doors on the upstream side. The doors at the opposite end of the plant, where aircraft were intended to go out, had held. Sprague recalled, "We had everything from alligators, to snakes, to raccoons and rabbits inside the plant. They shot a shark at the main gate."[9]

When the waters receded, the cleanup began. Approximately $3 mil-

7. "City Expected to Feel Hurricane in Full Force by Mid Morning," New Orleans *Times-Picayune*, September 19, 1947, pp. 1–2; "Toll of Hurricane Surprisingly Low," New Orleans *Times-Picayune*, September 20, 1947, p. 1.

8. "Toll of Hurricane Surprisingly Low," p. 1; "Twelve Dead in Floods in Swampland Area," New Orleans *States*, September 22, 1947, p. 1.

9. Ted Sprague, interview, August 2, 1993.

lion worth of damage had been done to the twenty-one buildings that made up Michaud. Boats had been thrust against one another, flooded, and partially destroyed. The main plant was filled with debris, mud, and logs. Machinery had been covered with saltwater. Haddock remembered that "as the water went down, all the boats, hundreds of them tried to get out of one door. They just floated over there with the water and it was just a jumble of boats. They got wet and stayed wet in that building and they started sprouting mushrooms."[10]

Sprague recalled: "That was a real savage blow to be starting out with a whole new line of boats and have a hurricane come along and wipe out so much of our files and where we were. They were just floating upside down. It was a damn mess. There was nothing lost beyond repair. But there was an awful lot to be done to get it that way. There was the saw-mill, the veneer mill, the toilet seat and wood flooring mill, and all the boat production in the main building, the offices in the main building, the offices out where we were. Just everything was a mess." After the cleanup, work at Michaud started over again. According to Haddock, the most severe blow was that the hurricane took the last money Higgins had. He had put all his capital into pleasure boat production, camp trailers, materials, labor, and new production lines for wooden toilet seats and oak block flooring. Because the damage was caused by flooding, it was not covered by the company's insurance. "From that moment on," Haddock said, "they were in the hands of the banks." Instead of paying dividends, stockholders' money was now going to pay interest on loans.[11]

Besides the hurricane, Higgins faced other problems. The U.S. government was placing thousands of surplus army and navy boats on the market. Those in need of tugs and barges could buy them as military surplus. Aircraft rescue boats and PT boats were being purchased and converted to workboats, fishing boats, and yachts. Haddock recalled, "The commercial boat building end just fizzled out. You couldn't get any work." Adding to the company's problems, Frank Higgins had convinced his father to use a substitute wood in making marine plywood. The South American lumber looked similar to mahogany, but unfortunately it did not have the same characteristics. True mahogany was used on the outer

10. Graham Haddock, interview, June 26, 1975.
11. Ted Sprague, interview, August 2, 1993; Graham Haddock, interview, June 26, 1975; Untitled article, New Orleans *States,* August 22, 1947, n.p. (Clipping in Strahan Personal Collection).

layers with the inferior substitute wood sandwiched on the inside. The result was that plywood used in making hundreds of pleasure craft rotted from the inside out. At his own expense, Higgins brought the boats back to his plant and had them rebuilt using a better grade of marine plywood. It was a massive undertaking that drained money that was desperately needed as working capital. The use of an inferior wood was uncharacteristic of Higgins, a man who had built his reputation on his knowledge and use of fine lumber. It seems to have been a mistake caused by something as simple as a father desperately wanting to show faith in a son. That Higgins was warned about the wood by Ralph Casselman, technical director for Higgins Plastics, yet decided to ignore Casselman's advice, lends credibility to that theory. In any case, exactly who was responsible and why is of less importance than that it was a costly mistake at a time when the company was fighting for its very existence.[12]

Merchant shipbuilding throughout the nation had declined 50 percent during 1947. In January, 1948, H. Gerrish Smith, president of the Shipbuilders Council of America, stated, "Unless new orders are placed shortly, practically all seagoing merchant shipbuilding in the country will be ended by the middle of 1948." Conversion and repair work were keeping many yards going, but Smith stated: "This type of work does not provide for the maintenance of the technical staffs necessary for ship design and construction. The Industry cannot count long on the present employment in the repair yards, for the reason that the reconversion program, like ship construction activity, will run out in a matter of months."[13]

Despite the flooded markets of early 1948, Higgins was actively seeking commercial work. At the same time, he continued mass producing pleasure craft at Michaud. Production focused on several new inboard models, the 19-foot Deluxe Runabout, a 23-foot convertible Sports Speedster, a 26-foot cabin cruiser, and a variety of smaller outboard craft. His new line of boats was exhibited at the 1948 New York Boat Show, where his 17-foot Sport Speedster utility was perhaps the most popular model.

During the same period, the Industrial Canal plant produced a 256-

12. Jack Higgins, interview, August 12, 1992; Graham Haddock, interview, January 8, 1993; Ralph Casselman, interview, December 5, 1992; Ted Sprague, interview, January 24 and 30, 1993.

13. H. Gerrish Smith, "Rough Road Ahead," *Work Boat*, January, 1948, p. 21.

foot sister ship to the *Angele Higgins,* named the *Haus Bris,* for a foreign concern, two 54-foot ferry barges, an 80-foot ferry barge, several dredges, a 120-foot general purpose barge, two 56-foot ramp-type Eurekas, six Swamp Skippers, and approximately twenty additional commercial craft, many of which were oil field service boats.[14] Higgins was finding work because of his salesmanship and reputation, but he was having difficulty buying steel. Andrew, Jr., told a reporter: "We're getting some, but not nearly enough. Just give us plenty of steel, and with the wide needs for marine construction, we'll keep this plant busy and our workers well paid and happy!"[15]

During March, 1948, the FHA gave lenders approval to begin accepting applications for Higgins Thermo-Con houses. Meanwhile, Higgins had two units under construction in New Orleans being built by his first franchisee, the McLaney Construction Company. Higgins, Inc., intended to manufacture the laminated wood forms into which the Thermo-Con was poured and also manufacture the equipment for mixing and pumping the material. Higgins Resources, Inc., a newly formed company, was to serve as engineers, sell franchises, and service the equipment. Higgins hoped that within a few months his new business would be booming.[16]

Instead, by the fall of 1948 Higgins, Inc.'s future looked bleak. Haddock saw it as the company's lowest point. "They were out of money," he said. "The 10 million [from the sale of stock] was gone." It had been used in the building of the *Angele Higgins,* mass producing pleasure craft and camp trailers, producing wooden toilet seats and wood flooring, restoring the pleasure boats built with the inferior wood, daily operating expenses, the enormous costs of recovering from the hurricane, and buying out Gottesman.

Also damaging was the fact that the large pool of consumer money that had been available when the "E" bonds were cashed in at the end of the war had dried up. The company had overproduced and Michaud was filled with pleasure craft and camp trailers for which there were no buyers. The bottom had also fallen out of the commercial and retail markets.

14. Higgins Industries Production Ledger, 10–11, in Strahan Personal Collection.

15. "World Markets Ready for Marine Equipment," *Work Boat,* June, 1948, p. 36.

16. "Loans on Higgins House Approved," New Orleans *Times-Picayune,* March 20, 1948, p. 1.

Crews had to be laid off. As the company's economic situation worsened, acres at Michaud were covered with pleasure boats bearing yellow ribbons that read "pledged to the Whitney Bank." The boats had been seized as security on loans.

By the fall of 1948, the company was pulling out of Michaud, reducing overhead, and moving everything into the Industrial Canal plant. It was a move that Gottesman had recommended to Higgins two years before. Higgins was also suing the Reynolds Metal Company for $1,336,006. He alleged that Reynolds had sold him 3 million pounds of defective metal, part of which was used to manufacture two thousand camp trailers that, according to Higgins, were unsalable. The remainder of the unused metal supposedly had been sold at a loss. Reynolds denied supplying inferior aluminum and claimed that Higgins, Inc., had failed to file a complaint in the sixty-day period covered by the warranty.[17]

Higgins was down, but he refused to give up. During October, 1948, he contracted to build a 95'6" yacht for John Jacobs of Florida. Jacobs visited the plant over Thanksgiving and saw that the keel had been laid and production started. The contract called for a March 15 completion date.

Shortly after work began on the yacht, Higgins, Inc., ran out of operating capital. The company's credit was so bad by now that it was on a C.O.D. basis with every supplier. A company that had once employed over twenty thousand workers and had hundreds of millions of dollars worth of contracts was by Christmas, 1948, down to seventy-five workers and unable to raise enough money to finish a single boat.

Jacobs showed up over the Christmas holidays to view the progress and saw that the yacht still looked just as it had at Thanksgiving. He was furious. He walked up to a young man in the yard standing near the boat and asked, "Who the hell are you?" The man replied that he was David Levy, an employee of Equitable Equipment Company. Jacobs inquired, "Well, what the hell are you doing here?" Levy explained that Equitable was considering buying the plant and he and Haddock were making a full inventory of equipment and materials. Jacobs responded, "I hope somebody buys it and runs it right because it is the worst run plant I ever saw." While the conversation took place, Higgins and Huet were standing nearby. Jacobs talked loudly enough to make certain that they heard

17. "Higgins Ordered to Provide Data," New Orleans *Times-Picayune*, September 23, 1948, p. 11.

every word. As Jacobs continued spouting off, Higgins was getting madder and madder. Finally, Levy recalled, Higgins couldn't stand it anymore and as he angrily turned to walk off, he tripped over a large piece of wood blocking, falling flat on his face. Higgins got up and kicked the block. Levy said, "It sounded like he broke every bone in his foot and the last I saw he was limping off and cursing the whole time." [18]

Haddock, who was standing with Levy, recalled Jacobs saying: "I know why you haven't done any more work on the boat. I deal around Wall Street and I know you don't have any money." Jacobs declared that the contract was canceled, but Andrew, Jr., informed him that, according to the terms, they had until March 15 to complete the yacht. Andrew, Jr., had Haddock, who had designed the boat, come up with a schedule to finish the yacht on time. Haddock recalled: "So I studied it and saw how many man-hours were left and everything else. There were two things. If we worked every day, including weekends, from the Christmas holidays to March 15, we could finish the boat. But I also needed a $25,000 fund that would be for that boat only—to buy materials, pay the labor and everything else so that nothing would affect the production of that one boat." [19]

Higgins contacted Jacobs and, using the best of his salesmanship, convinced him to return to the plant. After listening to the plan, Jacobs agreed to let Higgins finish the boat, with the stipulation that a friend of his would come from Florida to monitor the progress. Jacobs even offered to send with him the $25,000 needed to complete the job. His main concern was that he had invited some of his best friends to help him sail the boat back to Florida, and he wanted to be positive that the boat would be completed by the March 15 deadline. Haddock remembered him saying, "That boat had better be ready because if you embarrass me in front of my friends and that boat isn't ready to sail, the Supreme Court of the United States won't make the contract stick." Jacobs returned on March 10, 1949, five days early. The yacht was finished except for minor paint touch-ups and installation of a few small decorative pieces. Dock trials had been run on the boat, but it still had not undergone sea trials. The day Jacobs arrived, he stocked the boat with the supplies for its future voyage. The following day, she was put through a quick run down

18. David Levy, interview, September 20, 1975.
19. Graham Haddock, interview, January 8, 1993.

the nearby Intercoastal Waterway. Haddock said, "When we got back from the sea trials Jacobs said, 'O.K. everybody off, I'm satisfied,' and away he went."[20]

While his crew was working on the yacht, Higgins had put all his efforts into securing two new contracts, one from the 2nd Coast Guard District of St. Louis, Missouri, for six 36-foot steel Eurekas and the second from the Socony-Vacuum Company for six 48-foot steel tunnel riverboats.[21] In a plant where 8,800 men had once feverishly worked to build a hundred 180-foot FS vessels and thousands of 50-foot LCMs, 75 people were working on two contracts totaling twelve boats and a variety of smaller repair jobs. Higgins had sworn that bats would never roost in the rafters of his plants, but they were circling ever so close.

As work progressed on the twelve boats, Higgins became involved in two other projects. First, to prove how strongly he believed in his Thermo-Con construction, he sold his home in the Garden District of New Orleans and moved into one of his small demonstration models. He then took the money from the sale of his house to begin constructing a new large Themo-Con home on Tern Street near the shores of Lake Pontchartrain.

The new house was designed with a living room, dining room, library, game room with a bar made from the stern of a landing craft, kitchen, pantry, closed-in porch, laundry room, and servants' bath downstairs. Upstairs was a large master suite and two bedrooms with an adjoining bath. Higgins had also included in the design a separate section upstairs complete with kitchen and bath. This was for his sisters Joy, Mary, and Bessie. All, like Higgins, were intelligent, independent, and successful in life.

Joy had traveled to England during World War I as part of the Gompers labor commission, had worked for the internal revenue department, and later became involved in the theater. In 1932 she had put on a religious pageant in Baltimore, importing a virtually unknown actor named Henry Fonda as one of her stars. She and Fonda had worked together years before at the Omaha Playhouse. More recently, Joy had served as head of the recreation department for Higgins Industries.

Mary had attended New York University Law School and later mar-

20. *Ibid.*
21. Higgins Industries Production Ledger, 12–13, in Strahan Personal Collection.

ried a marine officer, Hugh Matthews, who retired as a general. Bessie, who also had married, was a writer. Her two most famous books were *Out of the West* and *Rain Upon the Roof.* Joy had never married, and Mary's and Bessie's husbands were deceased. Higgins, always sentimental, wanted his family nearby.[22]

The second project that Higgins became involved with was the designing of a new 90-foot prototype LCM. He had been invited by the Bureau of Ships to submit a bid on an LCM capable of carrying a seventy-five-ton tank. By the summer of 1949 his engineers had designed a workable model. It was taken along with three bows and two sterns to the University of Michigan testing laboratory, where experiments were run to discover the best bow and stern combination. As a result of the tests, Higgins was awarded a contract and began building a prototype tank lighter.

The contracts from the Coast Guard and Socony-Vacuum had kept the company alive, but by December, 1949, the money had been used to cover operating expenses and the company was again financially busted. Haddock recalled that "they had a zero credit rating and everything was cash on the barrelhead."[23]

On the wall in Higgins' office hung a framed motto that bore his signature. It read: "I don't wait for opportunity to knock. I send out a welcoming committee to drag the old harlot in."[24] In this instance, he did exactly that. Fighting for his company's life, Higgins secured a contract to convert four LSTs into ships for carrying coal and iron ore. Then he convinced the Brazilian government that his yard was the most qualified to build four 136-foot passenger ferries and two 144-foot truck ferries for it. Once the contracts were secured, he turned the financial responsibilities over to Mike Macheca, who had replaced Morris Gottesman as treasurer. Higgins then put his efforts into procuring more work.

Haddock said Macheca called all the superintendents and foremen together and said: "Look, you all know we have got a 'Z' credit rating. The plan is we are going to build these ships on other people's money. We are not going to buy on price, we are going to buy on terms. If somebody offers you something that cost more, but they will give you ninety days instead of thirty days, take the ninety days. If you can get it on

22. Dawn Higgins Murphy, interview, February 6, 1993.
23. Graham Haddock, interview, January 8, 1993.
24. *Bill Cunningham Visits Higgins* (New Orleans, n.d.), in Strahan Personal Collection.

consignment that's so much the better." Higgins had negotiated both contracts so he would receive 10 percent down. With this up-front money he purchased the four surplus LSTs. That took all of the down payments. Macheca, however, needed working capital. The contract with Brazil called for another 10 percent to be paid when the keels for the ferries were laid. Higgins had his men go out in the yard and set six sets of keel blocks and keels so the company could get another cash advance on the contract. Macheca did not borrow a penny in the building of the ten ships. He used the progress payments from the ships to purchase supplies, transferring funds from one job to the other so he would constantly have capital coming in. The last of the ten vessels was delivered in May, 1950, a month before the start of the Korean War. With the profits, Higgins paid off all his back debts and miraculously had his company approximately $100,000 in the black.[25]

On June 8, 1950, twenty-two days before U.S. troops were authorized to help the South Koreans, the NLRB finally issued its decision on the 1947 Higgins labor dispute. The board ruled that the CIO had violated its agreement by walking out when Higgins refused its request for a twelve-cent an hour pay raise. It also found that Higgins was within his rights not to bargain with the CIO while its members were out on strike. Once the workers returned, however, the NLRB concluded that Higgins was again obligated to negotiate. Its decision demanded that Higgins cease and desist from refusing to bargain with Local 73 of the CIO. It also insisted that he not engage in "any acts" that would interfere with the union's efforts to negotiate for or represent the employees in his plant and that, "upon request, [he] bargain with said union; post notice."[26]

As Higgins began to negotiate a new labor agreement with the CIO, his company was finishing the 90-foot LCM(8H). H designated that it was a Higgins boat. In the summer of 1950 the LCM(8H) was completed and delivered to Norfolk, Virginia, where it competed against two bureau-designed LCM8s. The bureau's LCM(8V) had a "vee" hull, while its LCM(8W) had a "cathedral" or "W" hull configuration. The trials seemed like a flashback from the past. Haddock remembered that during

---

25. Graham Haddock, interview, January 8, 1993.
26. *Decisions of the NLRB, Labor Relations Reference Manual, "Higgins, Inc.,"* Vol. 26, May 1, 1950–October 31, 1950 (Washington, D.C., 1950).

the competition held at Virginia Beach water poured over the bows of both bureau boats. He proudly recalled: "The Higgins boat as usual ran through and up on the beach. It helped salvage the other two boats." The bureau's LCMs had broached and were stranded in the shallow water. After the competition, Haddock said, "the Bureau put the plans in a pigeon hole somewhere" and no contracts were let.[27]

Higgins, meanwhile, was working on getting other military business. During mid-August, 1950, he had demonstrated to high-ranking officials of the army, navy, and air force how to use his quick-drying Thermo-Con cement to construct airstrips that could be used by light planes in five to six hours. James Wise, general engineer for Headquarters, USAF, told reporters that he was very much interested in Thermo-Con for possible use in runway construction for light aircraft or even heavy bombers. Further research, he said, must be done before considering the material for strips for heavy bombers. "But I feel sure, without further study, that an air strip constructed from this cement can be used for lighter planes." Naval architect Charles Roach of the marine branch of the transportation, development, and experiment station commented, "We are very much interested in all of this—the Transportation Corps is responsible for supplies in supporting operations—anything which can be built in a hurry is of utmost importance." Others watching with interest were Brigadier General Frank Besson, assistant chief of transportation, U.S. Army; Lieutenant Colonel Robert C. Hanes, an army research and development expert; Captain W. E. Daniel of the Marine Corps Aviation Technical School at Quantico; and at least twenty other military representatives from the various services.[28]

As the military investigated the use of Thermo-Con, the Army Corps of Engineers on November 5, 1950, breathed new life into the company. It awarded Higgins a $2 million contract to build 194 27-foot specially designed bridge erection boats. The boats had been designed by the Corps of Engineers Research and Development Laboratories at Fort Belvoir, Virginia, and were described as powerful and portable.

Higgins, Inc., had been chosen by the corps because of its reputation for tackling the unusual. Higgins readily accepted the challenge and had

27. Graham Haddock, interview, January 8, 1993.
28. "Higgins to Show Quickie Airstrip," New Orleans *Times-Picayune*, August 13, 1950, p. 16; "Service Officers Watch New Type of Air Strip Material," New Orleans *Times-Picayune*, August 15, 1950, p. 3.

his staff begin working out the details for constructing the lightweight aluminum boats. They devised ingenious new methods for cutting, forming, and applying the expensive metal to jigs that saved both time and material. In a feature story, accompanied by a full front-cover photograph, the trade magazine *Maritime Reporter* examined the building of the unique sectionalized boats. It described Higgins' production line "as a model of modern, efficient production." The contract moved Higgins, Inc., closer toward financial stability.[29]

Higgins simultaneously was moving his company into new fields. Based on his experience with wood and Thermo-Con, he began experimenting with a new product known as the Higgins Polar Panel. It was a combination of hardwood and foamed plastic that created an amazingly strong, light, and versatile building panel. The company described it as "ideal for construction ranging all the way from housing to defense projects—from the arctic to the tropics."[30]

By late 1950, Higgins had convinced the air force to try his new panels. In January, 1951, Ted Sprague began production of six experimental alert shelters for housing fighter aircraft up to and including the F-89. The shelters had to be light enough to be flown into the Arctic by cargo aircraft and easy for unskilled labor to assemble in a minimum amount of time. They also had to be capable of housing the airplane and its crew.

This proved to be Sprague's last project at Higgins. In July, 1951, he asked for a leave of absence so he could go home to Pennsylvania. Sprague recalled: "I think he [Higgins] knew that I wasn't coming back. My daughter was seven years old. There is something about where you are raised that makes you want to go back." During one of his last meetings with Higgins, Sprague recalled his boss telling him: "You've reached great heights. You may not have a Mr. Higgins to get you to do that again." Sprague admits: "It's true. He got out of me everything that I could possibly do. I've done a lot of things since then, but they weren't the sort of things where a guy says here take this project. Not telling you how to do it, just go in and do it. Talk about a million dollars today, it's peanuts. It's nothing, nobody even thinks about it. But in those days if you had a million to spend and it was your decision to get anything you

29. "Powerful and Portable," *Maritime Reporter*, May 15, 1952, pp. 11–15, in Dawn Higgins Murphy Collection.
30. *The Higgins Polar Panel* (New Orleans, 1950), 1, in Strahan Personal Collection.

wanted for this project, well that's a lot of leeway. That's showing a lot of confidence in somebody. I think he knew I wasn't coming back. He gave me a watch and some shares in the Hibernia National Bank."[31]

In late summer, shortly after Sprague left, Higgins was awarded a contract by the Bureau of Ships to build fourteen 65-foot cargo and passenger vessels. Another thirty-two boats were later added to the contract, bringing the total to forty-six. On November 9, 1951, the navy announced the awarding of contracts to seven private yards to produce a total of thirty 165-foot wooden minesweepers. Higgins received a contract for ten of the boats, increasing his government contracts to a total of $30 million.[32] After a long, hard fight, Higgins had his company on the way back.

Hurricanes had been his nemesis. They had destroyed his Alabama timber tract, sunk the *Edith*, and flooded Michaud. But wars had been his savior, and Korea was no different. When the military demanded immediate production, it unhesitatingly turned to Higgins. Suddenly, he had contracts to build 10 minesweepers and 21 100-foot tugboats, and his contract for 194 bridge erection boats had been increased to 900 craft. Additionally, his company was building well-drilling platforms for the Gulf, survey barges, and a variety of metal fabricated parts for the oil industry. Employment rose to approximately thirty-five hundred.

Higgins had guided his company through the toughest of times. He had refused to accept defeat, and his dogged determination and the Korean War had brought his company back to the forefront of American shipbuilding. Unfortunately, Higgins was not able to take it to even greater heights, for on August 1, 1952, at the age of sixty-five, he died of a stomach ailment. He had entered Hotel Dieu hospital in New Orleans earlier in the week for a periodic checkup when complications occurred. Higgins was a diabetic and suffered from bleeding ulcers. At the time of his death, his company had commercial and military contracts totaling more than $61 million dollars.[33]

The production genius who never knew the meaning of "can't," the strong-willed ardent foe of the Washington bureaucracy, the outspoken opponent of cost-plus contracts, had passed away at what for him seemed

31. Ted Sprague, interview, August 2, 1992.
32. "Gets Minesweeper Contract," New York *Times,* November 12, 1951, p. 33.
33. "Industrialist Noted as War Shipbuilder," New Orleans *States,* August 1, 1952, p. 1.

an early age. Bill Cunningham, syndicated columnist and friend of Higgins for many years, theorized that "maybe he simply pined away because, with the cessation of hostilities, he had no more Admirals to chew on."[34]

Robert C. Ruark, another well-known columnist of the period, wrote of Higgins: "He was a tough old boy and an all-male man and there aren't too many of his like left. I hope there's bourbon where he's stationed, and boats or something for his restless brain and heavy hands to build."[35]

Years later, retired Lieutenant General Victor H. Krulak, in his memoirs, captured Higgins' true character, describing him as "the Marines' kind of man."[36]

34. Unidentified clipping in Dawn Higgins Murphy Collection.

35. Robert C. Ruark, "A Fabulous Old Boy, Andrew J. Was" (Clipping in University Relations Central Files—Andrew Jackson Higgins, Creighton University, Omaha, Nebraska).

36. Krulak, First to Fight, 88.

16

KOREA AND BEYOND

In mid-1952 the nation was deeply involved in the Korean War. The navy was in need of a new LCM capable of carrying the modern seventy-five-ton tank. The Bureau of Ships went to its files and pulled out the plans that it felt could most successfully fulfill the requirements. Incredibly, the bureau chose its LCM8-V, one of the two lighters that Higgins' 90-foot LCM8 had had to rescue in the 1950 trials. It was a new military conflict but an old bureaucratic war.

The bureau sent its drawings to Palmer and Baker, civil engineers and naval architects in Mobile, Alabama, requesting that plans and specifications be prepared. Higgins, Inc., was the successful bidder on 322 of the approximately 500 LCM8s. By the spring of 1953, the company was ready to begin production.

By virtue of its contract, Higgins was made the lead yard. By the time the first tank lighter was completed in the summer of 1953, another twenty were rapidly moving down the production line. The initial LCM8 was taken from plant, down the Industrial Canal, and into Lake Pontchartrain for its preliminary trials. The boat started out slowly and gradually built up speed. Suddenly, as it was almost at full throttle, water started pouring over the bow ramp, flooding the cargo well. When the coxswain reversed engines, water forced under the stern, combined with the weight of the flooded cargo well, caused the LCM8 to dive nose down to the bottom of the shallow lake. She came to a sudden stop, and the stern kicked out of the water with the propellers rising above the surface.

The LCM8, equipped with flotation compartments, was buoyant. She quickly came to rest on the surface, her freeing ports draining most of the water. Those on board considered the occurrence to be a freak; there was not a chance in a million that it would happen again. The same set of circumstances was reconstructed, and when the water started pouring over the bow the coxswain chopped the throttle. According to Haddock, the wave caught up under the stern and pushed the bow down again. Test after test yielded identical results.

Andrew Higgins, Jr., Haddock, and the others involved could not believe the lighter's dismal failure. The navy's trial board, there to witness the test, refused to accept the boat. Haddock said: "It was a nine-million-dollar contract. It was lucrative for us and we didn't want to lose it." [1]

Andrew Higgins, Jr., who had taken his father's place as head of the company, got together with Huet and Haddock and went over the plans of the Higgins 90-foot prototype LCM8 built in 1950. The Higgins lighter had a workable bow and ramp and the same cross-section amidship as the bureau's LCM8. Higgins, Jr., directed that before the next boat came off the production line, its bow was to be cut off and replaced with a Higgins-designed bow and ramp.

While the crew made the modifications, the navy inspector in the yard saw what was occurring and reported the action to headquarters. The bureau sent a second examiner to New Orleans. The new investigator inspected the craft and took a copy of Higgins' modified plans back to Washington.

The bureau, which still had many of the same navy and civilian personnel that had been there during World War II, came up with its own design changes that looked very similar to those drawn by Huet and Haddock. It was a new military action, there was a new bureau chief, Higgins, Sr., was gone, and this time, according to Haddock, some of the old bureau personnel desperately wanted a victory.

The next boat off the line incorporated the bureau's changes. It, along with the original LCM8 and the lighter with the new Higgins bow and ramp, were transported to Gulfport, Mississippi, where trials were to be held at Ship Island. The original boat was unable to keep up with the modified lighters even in the calm ship channel. It was immediately disqualified.

The remaining two boats were tested for two days making landings on the island and running sea trials in the Gulf. On the run back to Gulfport, after the final tests, the navy's trial board made the most diplomatic of all choices. It decided to recommend producing the LCM8

---

1. Graham Haddock, interview, January 8, 1993.

with the bureau's hull and Higgins' bow and ramp. There would be no Congressional investigation, no prolonged hearings, no major conflicts. The most proficient of the three craft had been chosen and controversy avoided. The bureau could lay partial claim to the design, and Higgins, Inc., retained its lucrative contract.[2]

Higgins, Inc., was kept busy building the 322 tank lighters and the 10 minesweepers for several years. The last of the minesweepers was completed in 1955. Also during this period, Higgins, Inc., continued doing repair work and building new commercial craft, oil field platforms, supply boats for the oil industry, and pleasure craft. It had also put $2 million of its profits into expanding the north side of the shipyard so that it could build a three-hundred-foot derrick barge for Brown and Root Company. It hoped that other large contracts for oil field equipment would soon follow.

Despite its expansion, however, in the late 1950s the yard was too large to compete against the smaller yards yet too small to bid competitively against the larger companies. The yard was also greatly affected by the steel strike of 1957. It was caught unprepared with a low inventory of steel. Once steel production began again, the company gambled and purchased $2 million worth of the metal to assure that it would never again be hampered by a similar situation.

Higgins, Inc., now had steel but lacked business. Because of the state and federal governments' dispute over where the federal boundary began in the Gulf of Mexico, there was a reduction in oil-field-related business. Also, in Venezuela, where the company was having a good deal of success, a change in leaders occurred and orders from the foreign government had come to a halt.[3]

The Higgins family and Higgins, Inc., had speculated in several new ventures that for a variety of reasons had proven unsuccessful. By 1959 Higgins, Inc., was again in financial trouble. It was forced to sell out to New York Ship to pay its outstanding debts to the Whitney National Bank. New York Ship later sold to Equitable, which within a few years sold to Equity Industries. Equity in turn sold to Trinity Marine. Trinity presently operates the Industrial Canal plant and recently was building a 112-foot modern version of a PT boat designated PCF (patrol craft, fast) for the Ecuadorian and Philippine governments.

2. *Ibid.*
3. Jack Higgins, interview, August 12, 1992.

Today, where the St. Charles Avenue plant once stood is a restaurant. Where the City Park plant was located is the New Orleans Municipal Training Center for police and firemen and an extension of Delgado College. Martin Marietta is presently producing the main fuel tanks for the space shuttles at Michaud.

Not far from Michaud, Textron Marine Systems is continuing New Orleans' landing craft legacy. It is currently manufacturing the landing craft air cushion—the most revolutionary development in amphibious warfare since Higgins' men added the ramp to the Eureka. The extraordinary 87-foot (on cushion) LCAC travels at speeds of forty knots and can land assault troops and equipment on 70 percent of the world's beaches.

Angele, "the barefoot Contessa," as Higgins lovingly referred to his wife, is deceased, as are all four of their sons. Daughters Andrée and Dawn are still living. Andrée Higgins Stefferud and her husband, David, live in Madisonville across Lake Pontchartrain from New Orleans. Dawn Higgins Murphy and her husband, Bob, live in Jackson, Mississippi.

Jack Higgins and his brother Ed operated Higgins Marine Sales at the City Park location until 1970. The business was forced to change locations when the lease on the grounds expired. The company continued operating at a new location for another five years. Jack still lives in New Orleans and enjoys spending his retirement fishing the marshes of south Louisiana. Ed is deceased.

Graham Haddock worked at the Industrial Canal plant until he retired in 1982. He remains active and serves as a special consultant in ship design. Ted Sprague and Jean are living happily in Pennsylvania. Sprague remains busy operating a yacht club that he had helped his father start in the 1930s before his adventuresome nature brought him south.

Richard McDerby returned to New Orleans from Denison, Texas, after Catherine's death. He is retired but serves as floor manager for the annual New Orleans Boat Show. In June, 1992, I had the honor of making several beach landings in one of the hybrid LCM8s with Mac and Chief Warrant Officer Alex J. Pearson of the U.S. Coast Guard. The landings on Lake Pontchartrain were part of a program sponsored by the University of New Orleans commemorating the forty-eighth anniversary of D-Day. Mac, at eighty-two, in the words of Andrew Higgins, can still "put the damn boat on the beach."

The Higgins name is no longer a factor in boat building. Few persons not old enough to remember World War II are aware of the contributions made by the dynamic, innovative industrialist. There are no statues or plaques in New Orleans to alert locals or tourists that Higgins or his plants ever existed. Because of his brashness, strong personality, outspokenness, and midwestern birthplace, Higgins was never accepted by the city's Old South society. Even worse, he was an outsider, who, during the war, was nationally viewed as New Orleans' most prominent citizen, a situation that infuriated the socially elite but pleased Higgins and thousands of his blue-collar supporters.

Though not willing to accept Higgins in their social circles, many prominent New Orleanians were willing to purchase stock in his company when it went public in 1946. Those who had invested in Higgins, Inc., became more anti-Higgins when the value of the stock declined. They now associated his name with a bad investment instead of the Higgins PT boats, LCMs, LCVPs, and production miracles of World War II.

Others who had not been investors had also long awaited the demise of the Higgins name. In building his industrial complex, Higgins had hired thousands of employees, many of whom left lesser-paying jobs to work in his wartime plants. His higher wages had forced other businesses in the area to increase their pay scale or shut their doors. Businessmen forced to accept reduced profits were not about to honor Higgins, even after his death.

U.S. naval historians, writing at the end of the war, only briefly mention Higgins. To give credit to Higgins' accomplishments, they would have to recognize the Bureau of Ships' failures. It was easier to avoid controversy and highlight the navy's heroes and successes.

In contrast, the marines' Lieutenant General Holland Smith, Lieutenant General Victor H. Krulak, and Lieutenant Colonel Kenneth J. Clifford in their memoirs and writings have tried to provide Higgins the recognition that they feel he justly deserves. Higgins single-handedly fought the navy bureaucracy to assure that the amphibious forces were equipped with the safest, best-designed landing craft possible. The U.S. Marine Corps never lost sight of Higgins' valiant efforts.

As time passes and others objectively study Higgins and his company's design and development of the LCP, LCPL, LCVP, LCM, PT boat, and airborne lifeboat, his participation in the Manhattan Project, his design and construction of the first successful LCM in sixty-one hours, the

20,094 boats that his company built for the Allies during the war, his innovative Higgins Boat Operators and Marine Engine Maintenance School, his fight against the Bureau of Ships, his exposure of the black market in steel, and his crusade against labor racketeers in the airplane production industry, he will undoubtedly be awarded a more prominent place in the history of World War II.

Scholars are just discovering Higgins, but every soldier who hit the beach at Guadalcanal, in North Africa, Sicily, Normandy, Leyte, Iwo Jima, Okinawa, or on any of the hundreds of lesser-known islands during World War II recognizes his name and understands the importance of his accomplishments. Their successful assaults were testimony to Higgins' imaginative genius and the quality of products that his company produced.

BIBLIOGRAPHY

PUBLISHED WORKS

Books

Barbey, Vice Admiral Daniel E., USN (Ret.). *MacArthur's Amphibious Navy: Seventh Amphibious Force Operations, 1943–1945*. Annapolis, 1969.

Bill Cunningham Visits Higgins. New Orleans, n.d. In Strahan Personal Collection.

Bulkley, Captain Robert J., USNR (Ret.). *At Close Quarters: PT Boats in the United States Navy*. Washington, D.C., 1962.

Burns, James MacGregor. *Roosevelt: The Soldier of Freedom, 1940–1945*. New York, 1970.

Chandler, Alfred D., Jr., and Stephen E. Ambrose, eds. *The War Years*. Baltimore, 1970. Vol. I of *The Papers of Dwight David Eisenhower*.

Charles, Ronald W. *Troopships of World War II*. Washington, D.C., 1947.

Clifford, Lieutenant Colonel Kenneth J., USMCR. *Progress and Purpose: A Developmental History of the U.S. Marine Corps, 1900–1970*. Washington, D.C., 1973.

Dyer, Vice Admiral George Carrol, USN (Ret.). *The Amphibians Came to Conquer: The Story of Admiral Richmond Kelly Turner*. Washington, D.C., 1969.

Eisenhower, Dwight D. *Crusade in Europe*. New York, 1948.

Foster, Mark S. *Henry J. Kaiser: Builder in the Modern American West*. Austin, 1989.

Frank, Benis M., and Henry I. Shaw, Jr. *Victory and Occupation*. Washington, D.C., 1968. Vol. V of *History of U.S. Marine Corps Operations in World War II*.

Garand, George, and Truman R. Stronbridge. *Western Pacific Operations*. Washington, D.C., 1971. Vol. IV of *History of U.S. Marine Corps Operations in World War II*.

Ginger, Ray. *Six Days or Forever? Tennessee v. John Thomas Scopes.* Boston, 1958.

Hall, H. Duncan. *North American Supply.* London, 1955. Part of History of the Second World War: United Kingdom Civil Series.

Hall, H. Duncan, and C. C. Wrigley. *Studies of Overseas Supply.* London, 1956. Part of History of the Second World War: United Kingdom Civil Series.

Harrison, Gordon A. *Cross Channel Attack.* Washington, D.C., 1951. Vol. I of *United States Army in World War II: The European Theater of Operations.*

Higgins Container System of Transportation. New Orleans, 1945. In Strahan Personal Collection.

Higgins Engineers Report on Venezuela. New Orleans, n.d. In Strahan Personal Collection.

The Higgins Polar Panel. New Orleans, 1950. In Strahan Personal Collection.

King, Ernest J., and Walter Muir Whitehall. *Fleet Admiral King: A Naval Record.* New York, 1952.

Krulak, Lieutenant General Victor H., USMC (Ret.). *First to Fight: An Inside View of the U.S. Marine Corps.* Annapolis, 1984.

Landstrom, Bjorn. *The Ship: An Illustrated History.* Garden City, N.Y., 1961.

Lane, Fredrick C. *Ships for Victory: A History of Shipbuilding Under the U.S. Maritime Commission in World War II.* Baltimore, 1951.

McCullough, David. *Truman.* New York, 1992.

Miller, Francis Trevelyan. *History of World War II.* Philadelphia, 1945.

Pierce, Lieutenant Colonel Phillip N., USMC, and Lieutenant Colonel Frank O. Hough, USMCR. *The Compact History of the United States Marine Corps.* New York, 1960.

Polenberg, Richard. *War and Society: The United States, 1941–1945.* Philadelphia, 1972.

Potter, E. B., and Chester W. Nimitz, eds. *Sea Power: A Naval History.* Englewoods Cliffs, N.J., 1960.

Rappleyea, George W. *Operators Manual: 36' "Eureka" Landing Motor Boats.* New Orleans, 1943. In Strahan Personal Collection.

Rayback, Joseph G. *A History of American Labor.* New York, 1959.

Riddle, Donald H. *The Truman Committee: A Study in Congressional Responsibility.* New Brunswick, N.J., 1964.

Roskill, Captain S. W., D.S.C., R.N. *The Offensive.* London, 1960. Vol. III of *The War at Sea, 1939—1945.*

Ryan, Cornelius. *The Longest Day.* 1959; rpr. New York, 1967.

Smith, General Holland M., USMC (Ret). *Coral and Brass.* New York, 1949.

Sward, Keith. *The Legend of Henry Ford.* New York, 1972.

City Guides and Directories

1920 telephone directory. Cumberland Telephone and Telegraph Company, South Central Bell, New Orleans.

Soard's New Orleans City Directory. New Orleans, 1904—33.

Magazine Articles

"A. J. Higgins Visits Omaha." *Eureka News Bulletin,* II (March, 1943), 1–4.

"All Higgins Hiring Now Assembled Under One Roof." *Eureka News Bulletin,* II (December, 1943), 1–2.

"America's Editorial Opinions on the Higgins Cancellation." *Eureka News Bulletin,* I (August–September, 1942), 23, 25, 28.

"Amphibian Carrier Boats Are Planned for Jungles of South America." *Eureka News Bulletin,* I (June, 1942), 1, 6.

"Andrew Jackson Higgins Honored." *Eureka News Bulletin,* II (June, 1943), 1, 5, 6.

"Another Great War Plant." *Eureka News Bulletin,* I (March, 1942), 30.

"Appliance Division Becomes Industries Sales Corporation." *Dealers' and Salesmen's Bulletin,* December 1, 1945, p. 42.

"Army and Navy 'E'." *Eureka News Bulletin,* I (August–September, 1942), 1, 50.

"Aviation Armament Plant Brought to Our City by Higgins." *Eureka News Bulletin,* I (March, 1942), 1–2.

"Background of Dispute." *Dealers' and Salesmen's Bulletin,* December 1, 1945, p. 4.

"Bellanca, Famous Aircraft Designer, Joins Higgins." *Eureka News Bulletin,* II (February, 1943), 1, 4, 5.

"Boat Racing on the Mississippi." *Eureka News Bulletin,* II (April, 1943), 62.

"The Boss." *Fortune,* July, 1943, pp. 101–103, 210, 212, 214, 216.

"British Author Lauds Higgins as Outstanding Industrialist." *Eureka News Bulletin,* III (January–March, 1944), 71–72.

Burck, Gilbert. "Mr. Higgins and His Wonderful Boats." *Life,* August 16, 1943, pp. 100–102, 105–106, 108, 110–12.

"Business Will Not Fade When War Ends." *Eureka News Bulletin,* I (February, 1942), 3, 24.

"City Park Plant." *Eureka News Bulletin,* I (February, 1942), 19.

Edson, Peter. "Contract Row Makes Higgins Older, Wiser, More Disgusted." *Eureka News Bulletin,* I (August–September, 1942), 22.

Eureka News Bulletin, I (October, 1942), 51, caption.

———, I (November, 1942), 5, caption.

————, I (December, 1942), 11, caption.

————, II (November, 1943), 7, caption.

————, III (January–March, 1944), 118, caption.

————, III (January–March, 1944), 137, caption.

"Eurekas and Crocodiles Tops, Says Wounded Gob." *Eureka News Bulletin*, II (January, 1943), 18.

"Famous Automobile Manufacturer Joins Higgins-Tucker." *Eureka News Bulletin*, II (June, 1943), 2, 3.

"First of Hundreds of Higgins Army Cargo Ships Launched." *Eureka News Bulletin*, II (August, 1943), 1.

"First Time in History That a Complete Welding Course Has Been Published in an Industrial House Organ." *Eureka News Bulletin*, II (February, 1943), 61–80.

"Give Me Liberty!" *Dealers' and Salesmen's Bulletin*, December 1, 1945, p. 1.

"Higgins Accepts Contract for Cargo Planes." *Eureka News Bulletin*, I (November, 1942), 1, 5.

"Higgins Boat Operators School." *Eureka News Bulletin*, I (January, 1942), 15.

"Higgins Boat School Under New Set Up." *Eureka News Bulletin*, I (August–September, 1942), 2, 6, 7.

"Higgins Industries Five Years Ago." *Eureka News Bulletin*, II (April, 1943), 44, 45–48.

"Higgins Industries Gets Green Light on the Building of 1200 Cargo Planes." *Eureka News Bulletin*, II (February, 1943), 1, 2.

"Higgins Industries Now Firm of the Hour." *Eureka News Bulletin*, I (March, 1942), 1, 4.

"Higgins Output Leading Nation, Senator Reveals." *Eureka News Bulletin*, II (September, 1943), 1–3.

"Higgins Reveals Plans for Cheap Helicopter, All-Wing Cargo Plane." *Eureka News Bulletin*, II (March, 1943), 15.

"Higgins Speeds Work on Tank Lighters with New Water Production Line." *Eureka News Bulletin*, II (June, 1943), 58–59.

"Higgins the Boatbuilder Begins Training of Women." *Eureka News Bulletin*, I (November, 1942), 23.

"How It All Started." *Eureka News Bulletin*, I (January, 1942), 1–3, 8, 14.

"Job Vacancies to Be Filled by Employees' Women Relatives." *Eureka News Bulletin*, II (May, 1943), 3.

"A 'Knock-Down' Cruise." *Airlines*, May, 1944, pp. 34, 55.

"Landing Boats Represent 92% of U.S. Navy." *Eureka News Bulletin*, II (October, 1943), 1, 4.

"Large Crowd Attends Higgins Aircraft Plant Dedication." *Eureka News Bulletin*, II (November, 1943), 1–3.

"Let Pearl Harbor Wait, Mr. Congressman." *Dealers' and Salesmen's Bulletin,* December 1, 1945, p. 11.

McGuire, Jack B. "Andrew Higgins Plays Presidential Politics." *Journal of the Louisiana Historical Association,* XV (Summer, 1974), 273–84.

"Men of Higgins Build a Navy." *Eureka News Bulletin,* I (August–September, 1942), 13, 16, 53, 56, 58.

"New Higgins Plant on the Industrial Canal." *Eureka News Bulletin,* I (January, 1942), 5.

"News from Industrial Canal Plant." *Eureka News Bulletin,* I (October, 1942), 47.

"A Newspaper Is Born." *Eureka News Bulletin,* I (January, 1942), 4.

Oakes, David S. "Boat Builder to the United Nations." *Central Manufacturing District Magazine,* XXVIII (March, 1944), 9–20.

"Orleans Pays Real Tribute to Heroes of Ships." *Eureka News Bulletin,* I (May, 1942), 1, 3.

"A Pledge." *Eureka News Bulletin,* II (May, 1943), inside front cover.

"Powerful and Portable." *Maritime Reporter,* May 15, 1952, pp. 11, 13, 15. In Dawn Higgins Murphy Collection.

"Presentation Ceremony of Army-Navy 'E' to Men of Higgins." *Eureka News Bulletin,* I (October, 1942), 1–4, 13, 16, 36, 45, 51, 53.

"President Roosevelt Pays Special Visit to Higgins; City Park Plant Only N.O. Stop." *Eureka News Bulletin,* I (November, 1942), 4.

"Roland Higgins." *Dealers' and Salesmen's Bulletin,* December 1, 1945, p. 30.

"Roland Higgins Off to War; Quits Job for Service." *Eureka News Bulletin,* II (January, 1943), 5.

"The Saga of Higgins—A Musical, Dramatized Tableau." *Eureka News Bulletin,* I (May, 1942), 1–2, 4–5, 14, 28, 43.

"Saturday Evening Post Features Higgins." *Eureka News Bulletin,* I (July, 1942), 9, 12, 16, 18–19, 22–23.

"Ship Tycoon Higgins, the Ford of Dixie?" *Peoples World,* March 19, 1945, n.p. Typed copy in David R. McGuire Papers, Tulane University Library, New Orleans.

Smith, H. Gerrish. "Rough Road Ahead." *Work Boat,* January, 1948, p. 21.

"A Speedy Production Line Assured at Higgins-Tucker." *Eureka News Bulletin,* II (June, 1943), 3, 4.

"Statement of Mr. Andrew Jackson Higgins." *Dealers' and Salesmen's Bulletin,* December 1, 1945, p. 47.

"The Story of the Sea Scamp." *Eureka News Bulletin,* III (January-March, 1944), 76–77.

"To Train Thousands." *Eureka News Bulletin,* II (October, 1943), 7.

"Truman Committee Member Praises Higgins Workers." *Eureka News Bulletin,* II (September, 1943), 1, 3–4.

"Truman Committee of Congress Pays Tribute to the 'Men of Higgins.'" *Eureka News Bulletin,* II (April, 1943), 1, 2.

"Two Years Ago—When the School Was Young." *Eureka News Bulletin,* II (July, 1943), 41.

"Washington Comments on Hitler's Editorial About Higgins Activities in South America." *Eureka News Bulletin,* II (October, 1943), 39.

"What About Higgins in Aviation?" *Eureka News Bulletin,* II (January, 1943), 1–3, 5.

"Who's Afraid of the Big Bad Wolf? Who's Afraid of the Men of Higgins? No One Less Than Adolf Hitler Himself!" *Eureka News Bulletin,* II (August, 1943), 2.

"World Markets Ready for Marine Equipment." *Work Boat,* June, 1948, pp. 28, 29, 36.

"WPB Double-Talk on Steel Violations." *PM,* August 18, 1942, p. 11.

"X Ray Boat Comes Home." *Eureka News Bulletin,* II (December, 1943), 12, caption.

Eureka News Bulletin can be found in the Dawn Higgins Murphy Collection, Jackson, Mississippi.

Central Manufacturing District Magazine can be found in Strahan Personal Collection.

Newspaper Articles

"A. J. Higgins Dies of Brief Illness." New Orleans *Times-Picayune,* August 2, 1952, p. 25.

"A. J. Higgins Tells Programs for Veterans." *Higgins Worker,* June 23, 1944, p. 1.

"Andy Higgins Dies: Built Boats in War." New York *Times,* August 2, 1952, p. 15.

"Assembled Houses Will Cost More." New York *Times,* February 19, 1946, p. 20.

"Atomic Bomb Parts Made at Higgins' Micheaud Plant." New Orleans *Times-Picayune,* August 7, 1945, p. 7.

"Braden Sows U.S.—Argentine Discord, Says Higgins, 'Humiliated' by Slur to Perón." New York *Times,* June 5, 1946, p. 11.

"Brownell Claims Ohio and Michigan." New York *Times,* October 21, 1944, p. 9.

Burgess, Glenn. "Chamber of Commerce Manager Outlines Efforts Leading to Higgins Boat Trip." Clipping in scrapbook, Richard McDerby Collection, Metairie, Louisiana.

"Charging of Crime to Higgins Denied." New York *Times,* August 8, 1946, p. 13.

"City Expected to Feel Hurricane in Full Force by Mid Morning." New Orleans *Times-Picayune,* September 19, 1947, pp. 1–2.

"Closed to Stay, Asserts Higgins." New Orleans *Times-Picayune,* November 2, 1945, p. 1.

"'Confused Lethargy' Grips Washington, Higgins Says." New York *Times,* February 20, 1946, p. 15.

Cunningham, Bill. "Higgins Famous as Brass-Blaster." Clipping in Dawn Higgins Murphy Collection, Jackson, Mississippi.

"Dedication Program, Higgins City Park Plant." New Orleans *Item,* August 23, 1941, p. 22.

"Envoy Said to See Perón." New York *Times,* June 9, 1946, p. 21.

"First B-29 Crew Rescued by Airborne Boat Tells Story." *Higgins Worker,* September 21, 1945, pp. 1–2.

"Florida Beckons, Higgins Reveals." New Orleans *Times-Picayune,* November 17, 1945, p. 1.

Furey, W. M. "About 35,000 Americans View Denison's 'Colossal' Bond Show." Paris (Texas) *News.* N.d. Clipping in scrapbook, Richard McDerby Collection, Metairie, Louisiana.

"Gets Minesweeper Contract." New York *Times,* November 12, 1951, p. 33.

"Hershey Upholds Jobs for Soldiers." New York *Times,* July 27, 1945, p. 16.

"Higgins, Defiant, Will Sell Plants." New York *Times,* November 3, 1945, p. 1.

"Higgins Defies WLB as AFL, CIO Disagree." New York *Times,* October 21, 1945, p. 36.

"Higgins Discloses Big Order Backlog." New York *Times,* March 28, 1946, p. 39.

"Higgins Displays New-Type House." New Orleans *Times-Picayune,* June 8, 1946, p. 17.

"Higgins for Contract If AFL Wins Election." New York *Times,* June 26, 1945, p. 34.

"Higgins Gets RFC Loan." New York *Times,* February 11, 1947, p. 48.

"Higgins Has Housing Plan." February 19, 1946. Clipping in University Relations Central Files—Andrew Jackson Higgins, Creighton University, Omaha, Nebraska.

"Higgins Is Accused of Wartime Fraud." New York *Times,* August 7, 1946, p. 19.

"Higgins Is Cleared on War Contracts." New York *Times,* February 8, 1947, p. 14.

"Higgins Nominates a New Syndicate." New York *Times,* March 21, 1946, p. 39.

"Higgins Opens Office Here." New York *Times,* April 26, 1945, p. 27.

"Higgins Optimistic on Post-War Tasks." New York *Times,* July 25, 1945, p. 24.

"Higgins Ordered to Provide Data." New Orleans *Times-Picayune*, September 23, 1948, p. 11.

"Higgins Outlines Big Plane Program." New York *Times*, November 7, 1942, p. 9.

"Higgins Planning to Open Plants." New Orleans *Times-Picayune*, January 6, 1946, p. 1.

"Higgins Plans Homes Without RFC Loan." New York *Times*, May 18, 1947, Sec. 8, p. 1.

"Higgins Plans House Output." February 27, 1946. Clipping in University Relations Central Files—Andrew Jackson Higgins, Creighton University, Omaha, Nebraska.

"Higgins Praises Congress." New York *Times*, July 29, 1942, p. 11.

"Higgins Praises Perón." New York *Times*, June 17, 1946, p. 43.

"Higgins Proposes to Close 3 Plants." New York *Times*, November 2, 1945, p. 8.

"Higgins Reopens One of His Boat Plants to Workers Crossing AFL Picket Lines." New York *Times*, November 30, 1945, p. 15.

"Higgins Resigns as Finn Consul Here; Tells Why." New Orleans *Times-Picayune*, November 29, 1941, pp. 1, 4.

"Higgins Sees Prosperity." New York *Times*, April 25, 1946, p. 23.

"Higgins Staff Is Made Up of Craftsmen." N.d. Clipping in Skip Higgins Collection, Port Allen, Louisiana.

"Higgins Shutdown Put Up to Congress." New York *Times*, November 4, 1945, p. 1.

"Higgins to Build Plastic Houses." New Orleans *Times-Picayune*, February 15, 1946, p. 1.

"Higgins to Form $12,000,000 Firm." New Orleans *Times-Picayune*, January 8, 1946, p. 1.

"Higgins to Make Housing 'Panels.'" New York *Times*, October 16, 1946, p. 48.

"Higgins to Show Quickie Airstrip." New Orleans *Times-Picayune*, August 13, 1950, p. 16.

"Higgins' War-Time Success in Boat Business Recalled." New Orleans *Times-Picayune*, February 10, 1963, Sec. 2, p. 17.

"Industrialist Noted as War Shipbuilder." New Orleans *States*, August 1, 1952, p. 1.

"Itemize, Inquiry Asked on Higgins." New York *Times*, November 5, 1945, p. 32.

Krock, Arthur. "Higgins Closing a Worry." New York *Times*, November 7, 1945, p. 8.

"Little Red Schoolhouse Opens Monday for Ourtown Children." *Higgins Worker*, October 13, 1944, p. 6.

"Loans on Higgins House Approved." New Orleans *Times-Picayune*, March 20, 1948, p. 1.

"Mail Delivery Is Established in Our Town." *Higgins Worker*, July 28, 1944, p. 1.

"Mayor Appeals to Higgins." New York *Times*, November 8, 1945, p. 11.

"Michaud Ship Plant Sold." New York *Times*, August 29, 1947, p. 35.

Moley, Raymond. "The Unpredictable Boatman." Washington, D.C., *Star*, November 15, 1945. Typescript in David R. McGuire Collection, Tulane University Library, New Orleans, Louisiana.

"Navy Officials Pay Tribute to Higgins Ind." *Higgins Worker*, July 28, 1944, pp. 1, 8.

"Nelson Considers Utilizing Higgins." New York *Times*, October 15, 1942, p. 14.

"New Higgins Plant Dedicated." New York *Times*, October 25, 1943, p. 8.

"Omaha Seeks Higgins Plant." New York *Times*, November 11, 1945, p. 35.

"$100,000 Higgins Unit Given to 3 Employees." New York *Times*, December 13, 1945, p. 17.

"Orders Increase in Superbombers." New York *Times*, August 11, 1944, p. 6.

"Orleanians, from Youths to Grandmothers, Help Build Atom Bombs." New Orleans *Times-Picayune/States*, August 12, 1945, Sec. 2, p. 4.

"Ourtown Brownies to Be Invested." *Higgins Worker*, July 28, 1944, p. 1.

"OWI Wants Picture of James Murray." *Higgins Worker*, October 13, 1944, p. 5.

Pearson, Drew. November 7, 1945, n.p. Untitled clipping in Strahan Personal Collection.

———. "The Washington Merry-Go-Round." Washington *Post*, September 21, 1942, Sec. 2, p. 5.

"Plants Speed into Postwar Work; $25,000,000 in Orders Announced." *Higgins Worker*, August 24, 1945, pp. 1, 3.

"Pleasure Boat Production Lines Now in High Gear." *Higgins Worker*, April, 1947, p. 1.

"Pledge Higgins AF of L Cash Aid." New York *Mirror*, July 24, 1942, p. 42. In Dawn Higgins Murphy Collection, Jackson, Mississippi.

"RFC Bars Loan to Higgins." New York *Times*, November 8, 1946, p. 8.

"Roosevelt Praises Higgins Achievements." *Higgins Worker*, July 28, 1944, p. 1.

Ruark, Robert C. "A Fabulous Old Boy, Andrew J. Was." N.d. Clipping in University Relations Central Files—Andrew J. Higgins, Creighton University, Omaha, Nebraska.

"SEC Charges Van Alstyne, Noel Sold Higgins, Inc. Stock Illegally." New York *Times*, February 7, 1946, p. 30.

"Secure the Future with Roosevelt and Truman." *Higgins Worker*, October 13, 1944, pp. 4–5. Transcript of radio broadcast.

"Service Officers Watch New Type of Air Strip Material." New Orleans *Times-Picayune*, August 15, 1950, p. 3.

"Shipbuilding Here." New Orleans *States*, September 27, 1940, p. 6.

"A Ship Is a Thing of Beauty." *Higgins Worker*, July 5, 1946, p. 5. Caption under photograph.

"Ship Steel Sales on 'Black Market' Bared at Inquiry." New York *Times*, August 5, 1942, p. 1.

"Shipyard Closing Protested in South." New York *Times*, July 19, 1942, p. 1.

"A Statement." *Higgins Worker*, November 2, 1945, p. 1.

"Statement Tells Trap Rumor Is Unfounded." *Higgins Worker*, October 13, 1944, p. 1.

"Sunken 'Jinx Ship' Recalls Last Launching." New Orleans *Item-Tribune*. N.d. Clipping in Skip Higgins Collection, Port Allen, Louisiana.

"30,000 at Tokyo Beachhead Buy $310,667 in War Bonds." N.d. Clipping in scrapbook, Richard McDerby Collection, Metairie, Louisiana.

"Those Higginses There Was a Family." Omaha *World-Herald*, n.d., Sec. C, p. 4. Clipping in University Relations Central Files—Andrew Jackson Higgins, Creighton University, Omaha, Nebraska.

"Thousands See Ship Launched at Canal Plant." *Higgins Worker*, July 28, 1944, p. 1.

"Toll of Hurricane Surprisingly Low." New Orleans *Times-Picayune*, September 20, 1947, p. 1.

"Truman Guest of A. J. Higgins at Aircraft." *Higgins Worker*, October 13, 1944, p. 1.

"Twelve Dead in Floods in Swampland Area." New Orleans *States*, September 22, 1947, p. 1.

"Two Boat Shows Usher in New Era." New York *Times*, April 21, 1946, Sec. 5, p. 5.

"2,000 at Higgins Quit Jobs." New York *Times*, October 30, 1945, p. 12.

Untitled articles:

Daily Mirror, November 5, 1945, n.p. Typed copy in Strahan Personal Collection.

Grand Rapids *Herald*, 1945, n.p. Typed copy in Strahan Personal Collection.

New Orleans *Item-Tribune*, April 14, 1940, n.p. Clipping in Dawn Higgins Murphy Collection, Jackson, Mississippi.

New Orleans *States*, August 22, 1947, n.p. Clipping in Strahan Personal Collection.

New York *Tribune Herald*, August 3, 1942, n.p. Clipping in Dawn Higgins Murphy Collection, Jackson, Mississippi.

"Van Alstyne Quits Race for Governor." New York *Times,* February 7, 1946, p. 18.
"Vote to Liquidate Higgins Company." New York *Times,* November 10, 1945, p. 26.
"We the People." Cleveland *Plain Dealer,* May 10, 1944, n.p. Clipping in David R. McGuire Collection, Collection No. 271, Manuscripts Department, Howard-Tilton Memorial Library, Tulane University.
"Younger Men Take Ship Bureau Posts." New York *Times,* October 18, 1942, Sec. 5, p. 10.

Public Documents

Decisions and Orders of the National Labor Relations Board: December 28, 1945–February 27, 1946. Vol. 65. Washington, D.C., 1946, pp. 50–55.
———. *1948.* Vol. 73. Washington, D.C., 1948, pp. 543–47.
———. *May 31, 1950—August 29, 1950.* Vol. 90. Case 15-CA-27. Washington, D.C., 1951, pp. 184–201.
———. *Labor Relations Reference Manual.* "Higgins, Inc." *May 1—October 31, 1950.* Vol. 26. Washington, D.C., 1950, pp. 1181–82.
House Documents. 77th Cong., 2nd sess., No. 2652. Interim Report. *Investigation of Cancellation of Higgins Contract.*
House Documents. 77th Cong., 2nd sess., No. 281. *Higgins Contracts.*
National Defense Committee. "Higgins Experimental Landing Boat: Report of Tests." *USS Arkansas.* Washington, D.C., June 7, 1938. Record Group 46, Box 182, OP-5, Navy Department Matters Ships, Shipbuilding and Related Matters.
National Defense Committee. H. L. Rosenthal, *Higgins Industries, Inc., New Orleans, Louisiana.* Washington, D.C., August 8, 1942. OP4, Box 96, Minor Investigations—Companies and Other Organizations: Higgins Industries to W. R. Holt & Associates.
Senate Documents. 78th Cong., 2nd sess., No. 71, Report 10, Part 15. *Investigation of the National Defense Program.*
Senate Documents. Record Group 46, SEN 79A-F30, OP5, Box 185. *Report on Landing Boat Program of the Navy Department.*
United States Eastern District Court of Louisiana, New Orleans Division, Debtor's Petition, Civil Case No. 3174, Andrew Higgins Bankruptcy. 1926.

FILMS

Ideas for United Nations. Higgins Industries, Inc., n.d. (ca. 1945). Gayle Higgins Jones Collection, New Orleans.

UNPUBLISHED WORKS

Manuscript Collections

Andrews, Mark. Chief of Procurement. Papers. Harry S. Truman Library, Independence, Missouri.

Hebert, F. Edward. Papers. Manuscripts Department, Howard-Tilton Memorial Library, Tulane University.

Higgins, Skip. Collection. Port Allen, Louisiana.

History and Museums Divisions, United States Marine Corps, Envelope 22, PC 382: General Holland M. Smith. Washington, D.C.

McDerby, Richard A. Collection. Metairie, Louisiana.

McGuire, David R. Collection. Collection No. 271, Manuscripts Department, Howard-Tilton Memorial Library, Tulane University.

Murphy, Dawn Higgins. Collection. Jackson, Mississippi.

Strahan, Jerry. Personal Collection. Kenner, Louisiana.

Truman, Harry S. Papers. File 633, Harry S. Truman Library, Independence, Missouri.

University Relations Central Files—Andrew Jackson Higgins, Creighton University, Omaha, Nebraska.

INTERVIEWS WITH AUTHOR

Ambrose, Stephen E. February 4, 1993.

Casselman, Ralph. December 5, 1992.

Flautt, Robert A. June 25, 1975.

Haddock, Graham. June 26, July 23, September 13, November 9, 10, 1975, March 12, 1976, September 24, 1991, July 25, March 25, 1992, January 8, 1993.

Hall, Leroy. June 23, 1975.

Higgins, Andrew J., Jr. April 20, 1973, March 29, 1975.

Higgins, Jack. August 12, 1992.

Horil, Fred. November 12, 1992.

Levy, David. September 20, 1975.

McDerby, Richard A. April 11, August 30, 1992, January 27, 1993.

Morrison, Congressman Jimmy. September 21, 1991.

Murphy, Dawn Higgins. November 14, 1992, February 6, 1993.

Poche, John. October 28, 1975.

Searles, Robert. August 16, 1992.

Sprague, Jean. August 2, 1992.

Sprague, Ted. August 2, August 4, 1992, January 24, January 30, 1993.

Stefferud, Andrée Higgins. October 16, 1992.

INDEX

ing plants, subsidiary companies, and types of boats

Higgins Lumber and Export Company, 14–15, 17, 50, 315

Higgins Marine Sales Corporation, 291, 353

Higgins Motor Boat Show, 322

Higgins Plastics Corporation, 194, 259, 280, 292, 300, 323, 326, 339

Higgins Transportation System, 282

Higgins-Tucker Engine Company, 172–73, 178, 184, 197–98, 203

"Higgins Victory March," 143, 144

Higgins Worker (company newspaper), 193, 196, 229–30, 234–35, 286, 300

Hinckley, R. M., 58

Hirt, Al, 143

Hitler, Adolf, 3, 64, 157, 166, 167, 177, 203

Hockensmith, George, 195

Hopkins, Harry, 232, 304

Horcasitas, Mrs. Andres, 228

Horil, Fred, 133–34

Houghton, Col. J. H., 164

Houma plant, 128, 133–34

Housing, 222–25, 319–21, 325, 328, 334–36, 340, 343

Howard, Adm., 75, 82

Huet, George, 15, 16, 19–21, 41, 51, 60, 74, 94, 103, 104, 292, 341, 351

Hughes, Howard, 158

Hunter, Howard, 304

Hurricanes, 9, 12, 336–38, 348

Huse, Comdr. Jack, 68

Hussey, Capt. T. A., 96

Hutchinson, Owen R., 184

Hydroplane steps, 204–206

Ickes, Harold, 237–38, 239

Industrial Canal plant: plans for, 93–94; boat production at, 98, 162, 164–65, 173–75, 182, 198, 199, 217–18, 258, 263; dedication of, 140–43; expansion of, 155, 164; Higgins' knowledge of, 184; training at, 189–90, 203; Higgins'

memos on, 194–96; employee housing project near, 222–24; production records set by, 230; Higgins' speech to, 234; strike at, 273, 295; employees of, 281; postwar production at, 291, 292, 325, 335, 339–40; superintendent of, 292; closing of, due to labor difficulties, 300; partial reopening of, after closing due to labor problems, 309–10; election for bargaining agent in, 315–17; CIO as bargaining agent for, 317, 326; Thermo-Namel house production at, 325; current operation of, 352

Industries Building, 194, 203

Industries Sales Corporation, 313

Jackson, Samuel, 225

Jacobs, John, 341–43

Jacobs, Adm. Randall, 90

Jamieson, Comdr. Red, 90

Johnston, D. V., 13

Johnston (D. V.) Company, 12, 13–14

Jones, Claude A., 75, 82, 86, 93, 107, 146, 172

Jones, John Paul, 8

Jones, Sam, 103, 141–42, 145, 190

Jouett, Col. John H., 147–48, 158, 160, 212–14, 218

Justice Department investigation, 326–28, 330–33

Kaiser, Henry J., 158, 165, 166, 217, 239–40, 320

Kalman, Andrew, 218

Kearnes, Comdr., 161

Kennedy, Edward, 267

Kern, Comdr. J. W. (Bill), 82, 86

Kilgore, Harley M., 183–84

King, Adm. Ernest J., 55, 89, 92, 149, 168, 169

Knous, William, 280, 284

Knox, Frank, 67, 134–35, 139, 145–46, 149, 216

Koempel, Mrs. Walter P., 306, 307

Koonce, Henry T., 33

izing of, for shipping, 180, 203. *See also* LCMs
Tedesco, Nick, 257–58
Textron Marine Systems, 353
Thatcher, Herbert, 275
Thermo-Con, 320, 335, 336, 340, 343, 346
Thermo-Namel houses, 320, 325, 328, 334–35
Tirado, A. Ortiz, 228
Todd-Johnson Shipyard, 199
Towboats, 59–60
Training: at Higgins Boat Operators and Marine Engine Maintenance School, 90–91, 128–33, 163–64, 286, 292, 304, 332, 355; by navy, 129, 179; of women for shipyard employment, 149–51; for workers at Industrial Canal plant, 189–90, 203; of disabled veterans, 222
Trinity Marine, 352
Trudeau, Col. A. G., 161
Truman, Harry: as vice-presidential candidate, 3, 220–22, 225–26, 229, 232, 234, 237, 292; as originator and chairman of Special Committee to Investigate the National Defense Program, 66–67; and tank lighter controversy, 104–105, 134–35, 139, 145–46, 149, 222; visit to Higgins Industries plants, 183; and labor racketeering, 222; campaigning of, 234, 237; election as vice-president, 238–39, 240; and Higgins on Cochrane, 265–66; and Roosevelt's death, 266–67; and German surrender in World War II, 267; and Higgins' suggestions on battlefield policy, 267–69; as president, 267–69, 272–73, 298, 307, 320, 333; strike-breaking power of, 272–73; Higgins' correspondence to, on labor unions, 298; and AFL's request for congressional investigation of Higgins Industries' plant closings, 307; and postwar housing, 320; on Higgins' defense

during Justice Department investigation, 333
Truman Committee: and Higgins' accomplishments, 3; creation of, 66–67, 330; and tank lighter controversy, 67, 78–80, 84, 86, 107, 128, 134–35, 148, 149, 213; corporate leaders' testimony before, 165–66; and labor racketeering, 210–12, 214, 222
Tucker, Preston, 102, 173, 178, 197–98
Tunnel boats, 11, 16

Unions. *See* Labor unions
United Auto Workers, 225, 305
United Nations Relief and Rehabilitation Administration, 322
USS *George F. Elliott*, 132
USS *McCawley*, 55
USS *Memphis*, 82

Van Alstyne, David, 318
Van Alstyne, Noel and Company, 315, 318, 321
Van Keuren, Rear Adm. A. H., 53, 146
Vandenberg, Arthur, 267
Vaughan, Col. Harry, 266–69
Veterans, employment of, 222, 276–78, 290, 302, 306
Vickery, Adm. Howard L., 99, 100, 108
Von Rundstedt, Gerd, 261

Wage Stabilization Unit, 211
Wagner Act, 279, 296–97, 299, 310, 312
Wallace, Henry, 221, 225, 226
War Labor Board (WLB), 213, 214, 258, 261, 267, 272–75, 279–80, 282–84, 293–95, 299, 302, 303, 315
War Manpower Commission, 210, 213, 223
War Production Board (WPB), 136, 137, 145, 168, 169, 170, 212, 213, 230
Watkins, Col. Duval, 198, 199
Watson, Tom, 309
Watt, Capt. N. Morgan, Jr., 266

Weathers, Edward A., 132–33
Weightman, John W., 336
Weinmann, R. J., 103
Welin Davit and Boat Corporation, 32, 34, 38–41, 44, 46
Wheeler, Capt. William J., 26–27, 33
White (J. G.) Engineering, 138
Whitt and Chambers, Ltd., 44, 45
Wiegand, Dennis, 276–77
Wiley, Adm. Henry A., 142
Wiley, Sen. Alexander, 182
Williams, Gladstone, 167, 235, 311–12
Williams, Robert H., 306, 307
Williams, Roger, 165
Willkie, Wendell, 217, 233
Willow Run, 190, 191, 225, 289
Wilson, Charles E., 169, 212, 213
Winchell, Walter, 192
Wise, James, 346
WLB. See War Labor Board (WLB)
Women, 149–51, 238, 288
Wonderboats, 22–23, 26
World War I, 10, 12, 39, 41, 73, 83, 84, 96, 156, 223, 343

World War II: outbreak of, 25, 42; lack of interest in landing craft early in, 39–40; British navy's destruction of part of French fleet, 45–46; and Hitler's invasion of Poland, 64; Pearl Harbor attack, 94; Higgins on, 156–57, 261, 267–69; battle over London, 171; D-Day, 220; Battle of the Bulge, 261; Germany's surrender, 267; Higgins on chemical warfare in, 267–68; atomic bombs dropped on Japan, 279–80; Japan's surrender, 281, 305
WPB. See War Production Board (WPB)
Wyatt, Wilson W., 320, 328

Yachts, 21, 341–43
Young, Dave, 19, 130–31
Young, Robert, 269

Zetzmann, William, 104
Zorn, Maj. Harvey, 129